PRODUCT INNOVATION & ENTREPRENEURSHIP

AUTHOR

Vigneswaran Chidambaram
Assistant Professor (Selection Grade),
Department of Production Engineering,
PSG College of Technology,
Coimbatore

REVIEWER

Dr. Mir Irfan Ul Haq
Assistant Professor,
School of Mechanical Engineering,
Shri Mata Vaishno Devi University, Katra,
Jammu and Kashmir

All India Council for Technical Education
Nelson Mandela Marg, Vasant Kunj,
New Delhi, India

Dear Readers,

To prevent the piracy, this book is secured with HIGH SECURITY HOLOGRAM on the front title cover. In case you don't find the hologram on the front cover title, please write us to at contact@khannabooks.com or whatsapp us at +91-99109 09320 and avail special gift voucher for yourself.

Specimen of Hologram on front Cover title:

Moreover, there is a SPECIAL DISCOUNT COUPON for you with EVERY HOLOGRAM.

How to avail this SPECIAL DISCOUNT:

Step 1: Scratch the hologram

Step 2: Under the scratch area, your "coupon code" is available

Step 3: Logon to www.khannabooks.com

Step 4: Use your "coupon code" in the shopping cart and get your copy at a special discount

Step 5: Enjoy your reading!

ISBN: 978-93-5538-375-4

Book Code: UG490EN

Product Innovation & Entrepreneurship

by Vigneswaran Chidambaram

First Edition: 2026

Originally Published by:
All India Council for Technical Education, Ministry of Education, GOI

Exclusively Published & Distributed by:
Khanna Book Publishing Co. (P) Ltd.
4C/4344, Ansari Road, Daryaganj,
New Delhi (INDIA)

Visit us at: **www.khannabooks.com**
Write us at: **contact@khannabooks.com**

To view complete list of books, Please scan the QR Code:

Printed in Bharat.

प्रो. टी. जी. सीताराम
अध्यक्ष
Prof. T. G. Sitharam
Chairman

अखिल भारतीय तकनीकी शिक्षा परिषद्
(भारत सरकार का एक सांविधिक निकाय)
(शिक्षा मंत्रालय, भारत सरकार)
नेल्सन मंडेला मार्ग, वसंत कुंज, नई दिल्ली–110070
दूरभाष : 011–26131498
ई–मेल : chairman@aicte-india.org

ALL INDIA COUNCIL FOR TECHNICAL EDUCATION
(A STATUTORY BODY OF THE GOVT. OF INDIA)
(Ministry of Education, Govt. of India)
Nelson Mandela Marg, Vasant Kunj, New Delhi-110070
Phone : 011-26131498
E-mail : chairman@aicte-india.org

FOREWORD

Engineers are the backbone of any modern society. They are the ones responsible for the marvels as well as the improved quality of life across the world. Engineers have driven humanity towards greater heights in a more evolved and unprecedented manner.

The All India Council for Technical Education (AICTE), have spared no efforts towards the strengthening of the technical education in the country. AICTE is always committed towards promoting quality Technical Education to make India a modern developed nation emphasizing on the overall welfare of mankind.

An array of initiatives has been taken by AICTE in last decade which have been accelerated now by the National Education Policy (NEP) 2020. The implementation of NEP under the visionary leadership of Hon'ble Prime Minister of India envisages the provision for education in regional languages to all, thereby ensuring that every graduate becomes competent enough and is in a position to contribute towards the national growth and development through innovation & entrepreneurship.

One of the spheres where AICTE had been relentlessly working since past couple of years is providing high quality original technical contents at Under Graduate & Diploma level prepared and translated by eminent educators in various Indian languages to its aspirants. For students pursuing 2nd year of their Engineering education, AICTE has identified 87 books, which shall be translated into 12 Indian languages - Hindi, Tamil, Gujarati, Odia, Bengali, Kannada, Urdu, Punjabi, Telugu, Marathi, Assamese & Malayalam. In addition to the English medium, books in different Indian Languages are going to support the students to understand the concepts in their respective mother tongue.

On behalf of AICTE, I express sincere gratitude to all distinguished authors, reviewers and translators from the renowned institutions of high repute for their admirable contribution in a record span of time.

AICTE is confident that these outcomes based original contents shall help aspirants to master the subject with comprehension and greater ease.

T. G. Sitharam

(Prof. T. G. Sitharam)

ACKNOWLEDGEMENT

The authors are grateful to the authorities of AICTE, particularly Prof. T. G. Sitharam, Chairman; Dr. Abhay Jere, Vice-Chairman; Prof. Rajiv Kumar, Member-Secretary, Dr. Ramesh Unnikrishnan, Advisor-II and Dr. Sunil Luthra, Director, Training and Learning or their planning to publish the books on ***Product Innovation & Entrepreneurship.***

I sincerely acknowledge the valuable contributions of the reviewer of the book Dr. Mir Irfan Ul Haq, Assistant Professor, School of Mechanical Engineering, Shri Mata Vaishno Devi University, Katra; Dr. K.Prakasan, Principal, PSG College of Technology, Coimbatore; Dr. M. Senthilkumar, Professor and Head, Dept. of Production Engineering, PSG College of Technology, Coimbatore; Dr. G. Madhan Mohan, Professor, Dept. of Production Engineering, PSG College of Technology, Coimbatore; Dr. R. Mohanraj, Assistant professor, Dept. of Production Engineering, PSG College of Technology, Coimbatore; and Dr. Brajesh Kumar Kanchan, former Assistant professor, Dept. of Production Engineering, PSG College of Technology, Coimbatore. I am also thankful to my wife G Srimathi; my son V Rudhrahari & V Sairudhvik, as without their support, this work would not have come to realisation.

I would also like to acknowledge the reference books that have been instrumental in the preparation of this book: "Technology Entrepreneurship" by Bill Aulet; "Innovation and Entrepreneurship" by Peter F. Drucker; "Innovision" by Chelat Bhuvanachandran; "Technology Ventures: From Ideas to Enterprise" by Byers, Dorf, and Nelson; "The Startup Owner's Manual" by Steve Blank; "Entrepreneurship - A South Asian Perspective" by T.V. Rao. Additionally, I extend my gratitude to my students, over the years, who have made significant contributions that have enriched my experience and expertise in this subject. I am immensely grateful for their valuable input for making this book students' friendly and giving a better shape in an artistic manner.

This book is an outcome of various suggestions of AICTE members, experts and authors who shared their opinion and thought to further develop the engineering education in our country. Acknowledgements are due to the contributors and different workers in this field whose published books, review articles, papers, photographs, footnotes, references and other valuable information enriched us at the time of writing the book.

Vigneswaran Chidambaram

PREFACE

Welcome to the world of Product Innovation & Entrepreneurship! This book serves as your comprehensive guide to understanding the principles, concepts, and applications of innovation and entrepreneurship in the realm of product development. Whether you are a student embarking on a journey of learning or a professional seeking to delve deeper into the world of entrepreneurship, this book is designed to equip you with the knowledge and skills necessary to thrive in this dynamic field.

Product innovation and entrepreneurship have transformed industries, economies, and societies, shaping the way we live, work, and interact with the world around us. From ground-breaking technological advancements to innovative business models, product innovation and entrepreneurship drive progress and prosperity in today's rapidly evolving landscape.

In this book, we will explore the intricacies of product innovation and entrepreneurship, examining the processes, strategies, and mind-sets that drive successful ventures. We will delve into the principles of design thinking, creativity, and problem-solving, exploring how entrepreneurs identify opportunities, develop innovative solutions, and bring them to market.

Throughout the chapters, we will adopt a hands-on approach to learning, providing practical examples, case studies, and exercises to reinforce key concepts and foster critical thinking. We will examine the various stages of the innovation process, from ideation and prototyping to commercialization and scaling, offering insights and strategies for navigating each stage successfully.

As you progress through this book, we encourage you to engage actively with the material, reflect on your own experiences, and explore how you can apply the principles and strategies discussed to your own entrepreneurial journey. Innovation and entrepreneurship are not just academic concepts but practical skills that can be honed and cultivated over time.

We would like to express our gratitude to the researchers, educators, and entrepreneurs who have contributed to the field of product innovation and entrepreneurship. Their insights, experiences, and contributions have enriched our understanding of this dynamic field and inspired countless individuals to pursue their entrepreneurial dreams.

We hope that this book will serve as a valuable resource for aspiring entrepreneurs, innovators, and changemakers, empowering you to unleash your creativity, drive innovation, and make a meaningful impact in the world of product development and entrepreneurship.

May your journey through the pages of this book be filled with discovery, insight, and inspiration. Happy exploring and may your learning journey in Product Innovation & Entrepreneurship be as enriching as it is rewarding!

Vigneswaran Chidambaram

OUTCOME BASED EDUCATION

For the implementation of an outcome based education the first requirement is to develop an outcome based curriculum and incorporate an outcome based assessment in the education system. By going through outcome based assessments evaluators will be able to evaluate whether the students have achieved the outlined standard, specific and measurable outcomes. With the proper incorporation of outcome based education there will be a definite commitment to achieve a minimum standard for all learners without giving up at any level. At the end of the programme running with the aid of outcome based education, a student will be able to arrive at the following outcomes:

PO1. Engineering knowledge: Apply the knowledge of mathematics, science, engineering fundamentals, and an engineering specialization to the solution of complex engineering problems.

PO2. Problem analysis: Identify, formulate, review research literature, and analyze complex engineering problems reaching substantiated conclusions using first principles of mathematics, natural sciences, and engineering sciences.

PO3. Design / development of solutions: Design solutions for complex engineering problems and design system components or processes that meet the specified needs with appropriate consideration for the public health and safety, and the cultural, societal, and environmental considerations.

PO4. Conduct investigations of complex problems: Use research-based knowledge and research methods including design of experiments, analysis and interpretation of data, and synthesis of the information to provide valid conclusions.

PO5. Modern tool usage: Create, select, and apply appropriate techniques, resources, and modern engineering and IT tools including prediction and modelling to complex engineering activities with an understanding of the limitations.

PO6. The engineer and society: Apply reasoning informed by the contextual knowledge to assess societal, health, safety, legal and cultural issues and the consequent responsibilities relevant to the professional engineering practice.

PO7. Environment and sustainability: Understand the impact of the professional engineering solutions in societal and environmental contexts, and demonstrate the knowledge of, and need for sustainable development.

PO8. Ethics: Apply ethical principles and commit to professional ethics and responsibilities and norms of the engineering practice.

PO9. Individual and team work: Function effectively as an individual, and as a member or leader in diverse teams, and in multidisciplinary settings.

PO10. Communication: Communicate effectively on complex engineering activities with the engineering community and with society at large, such as, being able to comprehend and write effective reports and design documentation, make effective presentations, and give and receive clear instructions.

PO11. Project management and finance: Demonstrate knowledge and understanding of the engineering and management principles and apply these to one's own work, as a member and leader in a team, to manage projects and in multidisciplinary environments.

PO12. Life-long learning: Recognize the need for, and have the preparation and ability to engage in independent and life-long learning in the broadest context of technological change.

COURSE OUTCOMES

After completion of the course the students will be able to:

CO-1: understanding of the principles of entrepreneurship, including the role of entrepreneurship in economic development, entrepreneurial mindset, motivation, and competencies.

CO-2: Developing proficiency in product innovation, including opportunity scanning, market surveying, need identification, and problem definition.

CO-3: Enhance their problem-solving abilities by analysing various marketing and finance skills market segments size them, develop customer personas and value propositions for venture creation.

CO-4: developing business models and business canvases, building start-up teams and partnerships, understanding the start-up ecosystem and stakeholders, and navigating technology business incubators and parks.

CO-5: Applying the concepts learned throughout the course to real-world scenarios by identifying market needs, develop innovative solutions, create comprehensive business plans, and devise go-to-market strategies

Course Outcomes	Expected Mapping with Programme Outcomes (1- Weak Correlation; 2- Medium correlation; 3- Strong Correlation)											
	PO-1	PO-2	PO-3	PO-4	PO-5	PO-6	PO-7	PO-8	PO-9	PO-10	PO-11	PO-12
CO-1	3	2	2	2	1	-	-	-	-	-	-	-
CO-2	3	1	3	1	2	-	-	-	-	-	-	-
CO-3	3	3	2	1	1	-	-	-	-	-	-	-
CO-4	3	2	3	2	2	-	-	-	-	-	-	-
CO-5	3	3	2	2	2	-	-	-	-	-	-	-
CO-6	3	3	3	1	2	-	-	-	-	-	-	-

GUIDELINES FOR TEACHERS

To implement Outcome Based Education (OBE) knowledge level and skill set of the students should be enhanced. Teachers should take a major responsibility for the proper implementation of OBE. Some of the responsibilities (not limited to) for the teachers in OBE system may be as follows:

- Within reasonable constraint, they should manoeuvre time to the best advantage of all students.
- They should assess the students only upon certain defined criterion without considering any other potential ineligibility to discriminate them.
- They should try to grow the learning abilities of the students to a certain level before they leave the institute.
- They should try to ensure that all the students are equipped with the quality knowledge as well as competence after they finish their education.
- They should always encourage the students to develop their ultimate performance capabilities.
- They should facilitate and encourage group work and team work to consolidate newer approach.
- They should follow Blooms taxonomy in every part of the assessment.

Bloom's Taxonomy

Level	Teacher should Check	Student should be able to	Possible Mode of Assessment
Create	Students ability to create	Design or Create	Mini project
Evaluate	Students ability to justify	Argue or Defend	Assignment
Analyse	Students ability to distinguish	Differentiate or Distinguish	Project/Lab Methodology
Apply	Students ability to use information	Operate or Demonstrate	Technical Presentation/ Demonstration
Understand	Students ability to explain the ideas	Explain or Classify	Presentation/Seminar
Remember	Students ability to recall (or remember)	Define or Recall	Quiz

GUIDELINES FOR STUDENTS

Students should take equal responsibility for implementing the OBE. Some of the responsibilities (not limited to) for the students in OBE system are as follows:

- Students should be well aware of each UO before the start of a unit in each and every course.
- Students should be well aware of each CO before the start of the course.
- Students should be well aware of each PO before the start of the programme.
- Students should think critically and reasonably with proper reflection and action.
- Learning of the students should be connected and integrated with practical and real life consequences.
- Students should be well aware of their competency at every level of OBE.

ABBREVIATIONS AND SYMBOLS

List of Abbreviations

Abbreviations	Full form	Abbreviations	Full form
AGVs	Automated guided vehicles	MRR	Monthly Recurring Revenue
AR	Augmented reality	MVP	Minimum Viable Product
ARR	Annual Recurring Revenue	MVPs	Minimum viable products
BMC	Business Model Canvas	NPD	New Product Development
BOM	Bill of Materials	PDCA	Plan Do Check Act
CAC	Customer Acquisition Cost	PLM	Product Lifecycle Management
CCC	Cash Conversion Cycle	PPC	Pay-Per-Click
CCPA	California Consumer Privacy Act	PR	Public Relations
CLV	Customer Lifetime Value	R&D	Research and development
CMMs	Coordinate measuring machines	ROI	Return on Investment
CNC	Computer Numerical Control	SAM	Serviceable Addressable Market
COGS	Cost of goods sold	SASB	Sustainability Accounting Standards Board
CSR	Corporate Social Responsibility	SEO	Search Engine Optimization
DAU	Daily Active Users	SERPs	Search Engine Results Pages

Abbreviations	Full form	Abbreviations	Full form
DEI	Diversity, equity, and inclusion	SMEs	Small and medium enterprises
DFA	Design for Assembly	SOM	Serviceable Obtainable Market
DFM	Design for Manufacturing	SOPs	Standard operating procedures
DTC	Direct-to-consumer	SPC	Statistical Process Control
EBIT	Earnings before interest and taxes	SRI	Socially responsible investing
EIN	Employer Identification Number	SROI	Social Return on Investment
ERP	Enterprise Resource Planning	TAM	- Total Addressable Market
ESG	Environmental, social, and governance	TBIs	Technology Business Incubators
GDPR	General Data Protection Regulation	TCO	Total Cost of Ownership
GRI	Global Reporting Initiative	TQM	Total Quality Management
GTM	Go-To-Market	TRL	Technology Readiness Level
IoT	Internet of Things	UCD	User-centered design
IP	Intellectual property	UGC	User-Generated Content
IPO	Initial Public Offering	USCIS	U.S. Citizenship and Immigration Services
IRS	Internal Revenue Service	USP	Unique Selling Proposition
JIT	Just-in-Time	UVP	Unique value proposition

Abbreviations	Full form	Abbreviations	Full form
KPIs	Key Performance Indicators	VC	Venture Capitalist
LLC	Limited liability company	VR	Virtual reality
MAU	Monthly Active Users	WIPO	World Intellectual Property Organization

List of Symbols

Symbol	Symbol Name in Maths	Symbols Meaning	Example
|	vertical line	&	ampersand
+	plus		

LIST OF FIGURES

Title of Figure	*Page No.*
Unit 1 Fundamentals of Entrepreneurship	
Fig. 1.1: Components of Entrepreneurial Competency Framework	*4*
Fig. 1.2: Characteristic steps of Agile and lean product development	*5*
Fig. 1.3: Components of product reach to the market Needs	*25*
Fig. 1.4: Iterative design loop of various stages	*26*
Fig. 1.5: Functions versus manufacturability – a sample plot	*33*
Fig. 1.6: Various Stages in Team Dynamics	*44*
Unit 2 Product Innovation	
Fig. 2.1: Supply chain management workflow	*85*
Fig. 2.2: Optimized Manufacturing and Assembly Workflow – an example	*87*
Fig. 2.3: Essential Factors of Quality Assurance Framework	*91*
Fig. 2.4: Stages of Intellectual Property Life Cycle Management	*96*
Unit 3 Marketing and Finance	
Fig. 3-1: Features of sustainable business models	*107*
Fig. 3-2: An Example of Market Segmentation Techniques	*108*
Fig. 3-3: Components of a customer persona	*115*
Fig. 3.4: Value Proposition Canvas	*121*
Fig. 3.5: Key Elements of a Go-to-Market Strategy	*122*
Fig. 3.6: Comparisons of Distribution Channels	*124*
Fig. 3.7: Digital marketing funnel	*126*
Fig. 3.8: Perspective of the Funding Lifecycle	*135*
Fig. 3.9: Funding Requirements at Different Stages	*136*
Fig. 3.10: Scale-Up Financial Planning Roadmap	*138*
Fig. 3.11: Pros and Cons of Different Funding Sources	*156*
Fig. 3.12: Scaling Strategies and Corresponding Financing Options	*159*

Title of Figure	*Page No.*

Unit 4 Venture Creation

Fig. 4.1: Key Components of a Business Model *171*
Fig. 4.2: Stakeholder Engagement Strategies *177*
Fig. 4.3: Team Roles and Responsibilities *189*
Fig. 4.4: Mapping the Start-up Ecosystem *198*
Fig. 4.5: Advantages of Technology Incubators *206*
Fig. 4.6: Components of Incubator Program Lifecycle *209*
Fig. 4.7: Elements of a Compelling Business Proposal *216*
Fig. 4.8: Legal Considerations for Start-up Incorporation *224*
Fig. 4.9: Start-up Incorporation Workflow *228*
Fig. 4.10: Components of Social Impact Assessment *240*

Unit 5 Course Project

Fig. 5.1: Visualizing the Course Project Journey *253*
Fig. 5.2: Market Need Identification *256*
Fig. 5.3: Components of a Business Plan *270*
Fig. 5.4: Project Presentations Overall Evaluation Criteria *284*
Fig. 5.5: Overview of a Business Model Canvas *287*
Fig. 5.6: Reflective Questions for Project Evaluation *291*
Fig. 5.7: Continuous Learning and Improvement *294*

Contents

Foreword *iii*
Acknowledgement *v*
Preface *vi*
Outcome Based Education *viii*
Course Outcomes *x*
Guidelines for Teachers *xi*
Guidelines for Students *xiii*
Abbreviations and Symbols *xiv*
List of Figures *xvii*

Unit-1: Fundamentals of Entrepreneurship 1

1.1 Introduction to Entrepreneurship.... 3
1.2 Definition and Evolution 5
1.3 Role of Entrepreneurship in Economic Development 6
1.3.1. Catalyses Creation.... 7
1.3.2. Innovation and Technological Advancement:.... 7
1.3.3. Economic Diversification.... 8
1.3.4. Wealth Creation and Redistribution 9
1.3.5. Global Competitiveness 9
1.3.6. Continuous Renewal and Adaptation 10
1.4 Significance in Technological Advancements 10
1.4.1. Innovative Solutions to Unmet Needs 10
1.4.2. Tech Start-ups and Disruptive Technologies.... 11
1.4.3. Ecosystems for Innovation 11
1.4.4. Global Connectivity and Market Expansion 11

1.4.5. Job Creation in Technology-Driven Sectors 12
1.4.6. Efficiency and Sustainability 12
1.4.7. Technological Literacy and Empowerment 12
1.4.8. Continuous Learning and Adaptation 13
1.5. Entrepreneurial Mind-set, Motivation, and Competencies 13
1.5.1. Developing an Entrepreneurial Mind-set - Adaptability and Resilience 13
1.5.2. Innovative Thinking 14
1.5.3. Visionary Perspective 14
1.5.4. Resourcefulness and Initiative 14
1.5.5. Continuous Learning and Curiosity 15
1.5.6. Customer-Centric Focus 15
1.6 Motivations for Entrepreneurship 16
1.6.1. Passion and Personal Fulfilment 16
1.6.2. Autonomy and Independence 16
1.6.3. Financial Opportunities 17
1.6.4. Innovation and Problem-Solving 17
1.6.5. Legacy and Impact 18
1.6.6. Flexibility and Work-Life Balance 18
1.6.7. Learning and Growth 19
1.6.8. Contributing to Community 19
1.7 Key Competencies for Successful Entrepreneurs 19
1.7.1. Visionary Leadership 20
1.7.2. Effective Communication 20
1.7.3. Strategic Decision-Making 20
1.7.4. Innovative Thinking 20
1.7.5. Adaptability and Resilience 21
1.7.6. Networking and Relationship Building 21

1.7.7. Financial Literacy 21
1.7.8. Team Building and Management 21
1.7.9. Customer-Centric Focus 22
1.7.10. Negotiation and Persuasion 22
1.7.11. Time Management 22
1.8. Market Dynamics and Technology Influence - Market Pull vs. Technology Push Factors 23
1.8.1 Understanding Market Pull Factors 23
1.8.2. Unleashing Technology Push Factors 24
1.8.3. Striking a Balance 25
1.9 Identifying Market Needs through Research 26
1.9.1. Market Segmentation 26
1.9.2 Crafting Compelling Value Propositions 27
1.9.3 Aligning Solutions with Customer Goals 27
1.9.4. Marketing (Go-to-Market) Strategy 27
1.9.5. Distribution Channels and Sales Network 28
1.9.6. Assessing Technology Readiness Levels 28
1.9.7. Understanding Technology Readiness Levels 28
1.9.8. Technology Development Phases 29
1.9.9. Strategic Considerations: 29
1.9.10. Regulatory Compliance 29
1.10. New Product Development Lifecycle - Phases of Product Development 30
1.10.1. Ideation and Conceptualization 30
1.10.2. Feasibility Assessment (Concept Development) 31
1.10.3. Design and Prototyping 31
1.10.4. Iterative Testing and Iteration 31
1.10.5. Manufacturing and Assembly Planning 31
1.10.6. Product Testing and Quality Assurance 33

1.10.7. Market Introduction and Launch 33
1.10.8. Post-Launch Evaluation and Feedback 34
1.10.9. Scaling and Market Expansion 34
1.10.10. Product Lifecycle Management 34
1.11. Agile and Lean Approaches in Product Development 35
1.11.1 Agile Methodology 35
1.11.2 Key Principles of Agile 35
1.11.3 Implementation in Entrepreneurship 35
1.12. Prototyping and Iterative Design 35
1.12.1. Prototyping 36
1.12.2. Key Benefits of Prototyping 36
1.12.3. Iterative Design 36
1.12.4. Key Components of Iterative Design 36
1.12.5. Implementation in Entrepreneurship 37
1.13. Validating Problem-Solution Fit 37
1.13.1. Understanding the Problem Landscape: 37
1.13.2. Creating Innovative Solutions: 38
1.13.3. Testing and Validating Problem-Solution Fit: 38
1.14. Commercialization Pathways 39
1.14.1. Exploring Routes to Commercialization 39
1.14.2. Licensing and Partnership Strategies 40
1.14.3. Intellectual Property Considerations 40
1.15. Crafting a Business Vision and Leadership 41
1.15.1. Defining the Business Vision 41
1.15.2. Leadership Styles in Entrepreneurship 42
1.15.3. Nurturing Visionary Leadership 45
1.16. Building and Managing Effective Teams - Importance of Team Composition 45

1.16.1. Strategies for Team Management 46

1.16.2. Collaborative Decision Making 46

Unit summary 47

Tutorial questions for practice 47

Review Questions........ 49

References for Suggested Reading 51

Unit-2: Product Innovation 52

2.1. Opportunity Scanning and Market Survey........ 54

2.1.1 Introduction to Opportunity Scanning........ 54

2.1.2 Techniques for Market Survey 55

2.1.3 Identifying Unmet Needs and Problem Definition........ 57

2.2. Creative Design Thinking for Concept Generation........ 59

2.2.1 Fundamentals of Design Thinking 59

2.2.2 Ideation and Conceptualization 60

2.2.3 Integrating User-Centred Design 62

2.3. Detailed Design and Prototyping 64

2.3.1 Transition from Concept to Detailed Design........ 64

2.3.2 Prototyping Techniques and Tools........ 65

2.3.3 Iterative Design and Feedback........ 66

2.4. Functionality and Manufacturability........ 68

2.4.1 Balancing Functionality and User Experience 68

2.4.2 Design for Manufacturability 69

2.4.3 Materials Selection and Process Optimization 71

2.5. Bill of Materials and Components Supply Chain........ 73

2.5.1 Creating a Comprehensive Bill of Materials (BOM) 73

2.5.2 Strategic Components Sourcing........ 75

2.5.3 Supply Chain Management in Product Innovation 77

2.6. Manufacturing and Assembly Plan 79
2.6.1 Choosing the Right Manufacturing Processes 79
2.6.2 Assembly Line Planning and Optimization 82
2.6.3 Cost-effective Manufacturing Strategies 84
2.7. Product Testing and Quality Assurance 88
2.7.1 Importance of Rigorous Product Testing 88
2.7.2 Establishing Quality Assurance Protocols 90
2.7.3 Continuous Improvement in Product Quality 93
2.8. Intellectual Property Rights Management 94
2.8.1 Understanding Intellectual Property (IP) 94
2.8.2 Types of IP Protection (Patents, Trademarks, etc.) 97
2.8.3 Creating and Implementing an IP Strategy 98
Unit summary 99
Tutorial questions for practice: 100
Review Questions 100
References for Suggested Reading 103
Unit-3: Marketing and Finance 104
3.1 Market Segmentation and Market Sizing 107
3.1.1 Understanding Market Segmentation 108
3.1.2 Techniques for Effective Market Sizing 110
3.1.3 Market Trends Analysis 112
3.2. Customer Persona and Value Proposition 115
3 2.1 Creating Customer Personas 115
3.2.2 Crafting a Compelling Value Proposition 118
3.2.3 Aligning Value Proposition with Customer Needs 119
3.3. Marketing (Go-to-Market) Strategy 121

3.3.1 Components of a Go-to-Market Strategy 122
3.3.2 Digital Marketing Techniques 125
3.3.3 Building Brand Awareness and Loyalty 127
3.4. Distribution Channels and Sales Network 128
3.4.1 Exploring Different Distribution Channels 128
3.4.2 Developing an Effective Sales Network 129
3.4.3 Channel Management and Optimization 131
3.5 Funding Lifecycle 134
3.5.1 Aligning Funding with Milestones 136
3.5.2 Capital Structure Considerations 137
3.6. Source of Funding for Start-up Ventures 138
3.6.1 Bootstrapping and Self-financing 139
3.6.2 Angel Investors and Venture Capital 141
3.6.3 Crowd funding and Alternative Funding Models 143
3.7. Financial Projections and Accounting 145
3.7.1 Building Realistic Financial Projections 146
3.7.2 Key Financial Metrics for Start-ups 148
3.7.3 Best Practices in Start-up Accounting 150
3.8 Start-up to Scale-up Financing 153
3.8.1 Transitioning from Start-up to Scale Up 153
3.8.2 Series Funding and Scaling Strategies 156
3.8.3 Managing Finances in the Growth Phase 159
Unit summary **161**
Tutorial questions for practice: **162**
Review Questions **163**
References for Suggested Reading **166**

Unit-4: Venture Creation **167**

4.1. Sustainable Business Options and Pathways 170
4.1.1 Exploring Sustainable Business Models 171
4.1.2 Aligning with Environmental and Social Responsibility 174
4.1.3 Pathways to Sustainable Venture Creation 178
4.2. Business Model and Business Canvas 180
4.2.1 Components of a Business Model 180
4.2.2 Business Canvas: A Visual Framework 183
4.2.3 Iterative Development of Business Models 185
4.3. Start-up Team and Business Partners 188
4.3.1 Building a Dynamic Start-up Team 188
4.3.2 Roles and Responsibilities of Team Members 190
4.3.3 Collaborating with Business Partners for Success 194
4.4. Start-up Ecosystem and Stakeholders 196
4.4.1 Understanding the Start-up Ecosystem 197
4.4.2 Identifying and Engaging with Stakeholders 200
4.4.3 Navigating Ecosystem Challenges 201
4.5. Technology Business Incubators and Parks 204
4.5.2 Benefits of Incubator Programs 207
4.5.3 Choosing the Right Incubation Environment 211
4.6. Proposal Pitching and Agreements 214
4.6.1 Crafting a Compelling Business Proposal 214
4.6.2 Effective Pitching Techniques 217
4.6.3 Negotiating and Drafting Agreements 220
4.7. Start-up Company Incorporation 222
4.7.1 Legal Aspects of Start-up Incorporation 222

4.7.2 Choosing the Right Business Structure 226
4.7.3 Compliance and Registration Processes 229
4.8. Social Impact and Responsibility 232
4.8.1 Integrating Social Impact into Business 232
4.8.2 Corporate Social Responsibility (CSR) 235
4.8.3 Measuring and Communicating Social Impact 238
Unit summary 241
Tutorial questions for practice 242
Review questions 243
References for Suggested Reading 247

Unit-5: Course Project 248

5.1. Introduction to the Course Project 250
5.1.1 Overview of the Course Project 250
5.1.2 Importance of Integrating Theory into Practice 251
5.1.3 Project Milestones and Deliverables 255
5.2. Need Identification 257
5.2.1 Techniques for Conducting Market Research 258
5.2.2 Identifying Unmet Needs and Pain Points 261
5.2.3 Defining the Scope of the Project 262
5.3. Innovative Solution Development 264
5.3.1 Applying Creative Design Thinking Principles 264
5.3.2 Prototyping and Iterative Design Process 265
5.3.3 Evaluating Feasibility and Viability 267
5.4. Business Plan Formulation 269
5.4.1 Components of a Comprehensive Business Plan 269
5.4.2 Financial Projections and Funding Requirements 272
5.4.3 Aligning the Business Plan with Project Goals 274

5.5. Go-to-Market Strategy ... 276
5.5.1 Crafting a Targeted Go-to-Market Plan ... 276
5.5.2 Marketing and Distribution Channels ... 277
5.5.3 Integrating Feedback for Strategy Optimization ... 277
5.6. Project Presentation and Evaluation ... 279
5.6.1 Effective Proposal Pitching Techniques ... 279
5.6.2 Addressing Questions and Concerns ... 282
5.6.3 Peer and Instructor Evaluation Criteria ... 283
5.7. Project Implementation ... 288
5.7.1 Transitioning from Planning to Execution ... 288
5.7.2 Overcoming Implementation Challenges ... 290
5.7.3 Monitoring and Adjusting the Project Plan ... 292
5.8. Reflection and Learning ... 295
5.8.1 Individual and Team Reflections ... 295
5.8.2 Learning from Successes and Setbacks ... 297
5.8.3 Extracting Lessons for Future Entrepreneurial Endeavours ... 298
Unit summary ... 302
Tutorial questions for practice ... 303
Review questions ... 304
References for Suggested Reading: ... 307
Course outcome attainment table ... 308
Index ... 308

UNIT 1 Fundamentals of Entrepreneurship

UNIT SPECIFICS

This unit explores into the foundational aspects of entrepreneurship, exploring critical elements that contribute to economic development. The content is structured to provide a comprehensive understanding of entrepreneurial principles and their role in shaping economies. The unit covers the following key aspects:

1. **Entrepreneurial Fundamentals and Economic Impact**
   - Exploration of the fundamental concepts of entrepreneurship.
   - Examination of the crucial role played by entrepreneurship in fostering economic development.
2. **Entrepreneurial Mind-set, Motivation, and Competencies**
   - Analysis of the mind-set and motivation that drive successful entrepreneurs.
   - Identification and development of critical competencies essential for entrepreneurial success.
3. **New Product Development Lifecycle**
   - In-depth study of the new product development lifecycle, from ideation to market launch.
   - Examination of critical stages, challenges, and strategies for successful product development.
4. **Market Pull and Technology Push Factors**
   - Understanding the dynamics between market demands and technological advancements.

5. **Commercialization Pathways and Product-Market Fit Validation**

    - Evaluation of different pathways for commercializing innovative products.
    - Methods for validating and ensuring a strong product-market fit for entrepreneurial ventures.

6. **Business Vision and Leadership:**

    - Discussion on the significance of a clear business vision in entrepreneurship.
    - Examination of effective leadership traits and strategies in entrepreneurial ventures.

7. **Team Composition and Management**

    - Exploration of the composition of successful entrepreneurial teams.
    - Strategies for effective team management and collaboration.

RATIONALE

This unit is designed to provide students with a robust foundation in entrepreneurship, emphasizing its pivotal role in driving economic development. Students will gain valuable insights into the entrepreneurial journey by delving into successful entrepreneurs' mind-sets, motivations, and competencies. Exploring market dynamics, technology trends, and product development will equip students with practical knowledge applicable to real-world scenarios. Additionally, the unit focuses on leadership and team dynamics, essential elements for navigating the challenges of entrepreneurial ventures.

PRE-REQUISITES

A basic understanding of business concepts and economic principles

UNIT OUTCOMES

Upon completion of this unit, students should be able to:

U1-O1: Demonstrate a comprehensive understanding of entrepreneurship and its impact on economic development.

U1-O2: Analyse and apply the critical components of an entrepreneurial mind-set, motivation, and competencies.

U1-O3: Evaluate the impact between market demands and technological advancements in entrepreneurial decision-making.

U1-O4: Navigate the new product development lifecycle, from ideation to market launch.

U1-O5: Strategically assess commercialization pathways, ensuring a strong product-market fit for entrepreneurial ventures.

Unit-1 Outcomes	Expected Mapping with Programme Outcomes *(1- Weak Correlation; 2- Medium correlation; 3- Strong Correlation)*				
	CO-1	CO -2	CO -3	CO -4	CO -5
U1-O1	3	2	2	2	1
U1-O2	3	1	1	2	2
U1-O3	3	2	2	1	1
U1-O4	3	3	3	2	2
U1-O5	3	3	2	1	1

1.1 Introduction to Entrepreneurship

Welcome to the exciting world of entrepreneurship, a realm where innovation sparks, ideas flourish, and visionary leaders pave the way for transformative change. As we embark on this educational journey, this sets the stage for a captivating exploration into the dynamic and ever-evolving landscape of entrepreneurial ventures.

This journey extends beyond theories and definitions; it dives deep into the core elements that fuel entrepreneurial success. The book explores the entrepreneurial mind-set, examining how individuals cultivate a unique way of thinking that thrives on innovation, risk-taking, and a relentless pursuit of excellence. The exploration extends to motivations and competencies, recognizing that successful entrepreneurs embody a blend of passion, resilience, and a diverse skill set. Figure 1.1 sketches the essential components of Entrepreneurial Competency Frameworks, offering a comprehensive understanding of essential entrepreneurial skills and attributes.

As we navigate through the introductory segments, the spotlight shines on entrepreneurship's pivotal role in economic development. Beyond individual aspirations, the following discussion explores how entrepreneurial initiatives catalyse societal progress, fostering employment and financial stability and cultivating vibrant communities. The narrative unfolds, highlighting how visionary leaders use entrepreneurship to drive positive change on a grand scale.

At its essence, entrepreneurship is more than a mere endeavour—it is a mind-set, a force that propels individuals to challenge the status quo and shape the future. In the introductory chapters, we unravel the multifaceted dimensions of entrepreneurship, delving into its historical roots and tracing its evolution through the annals of time. From its inception as a concept to its present-day manifestations, we illuminate the tapestry that forms the foundation of entrepreneurial thinking.

The entrepreneurial journey would only be complete with an understanding of the impact between market dynamics and technological influences. We unravel the forces that shape entrepreneurial landscapes, exploring the delicate equilibrium between market pull and technology push. In doing so, we equip ourselves to navigate the ever-evolving terrain where entrepreneurship meets innovative advancements.

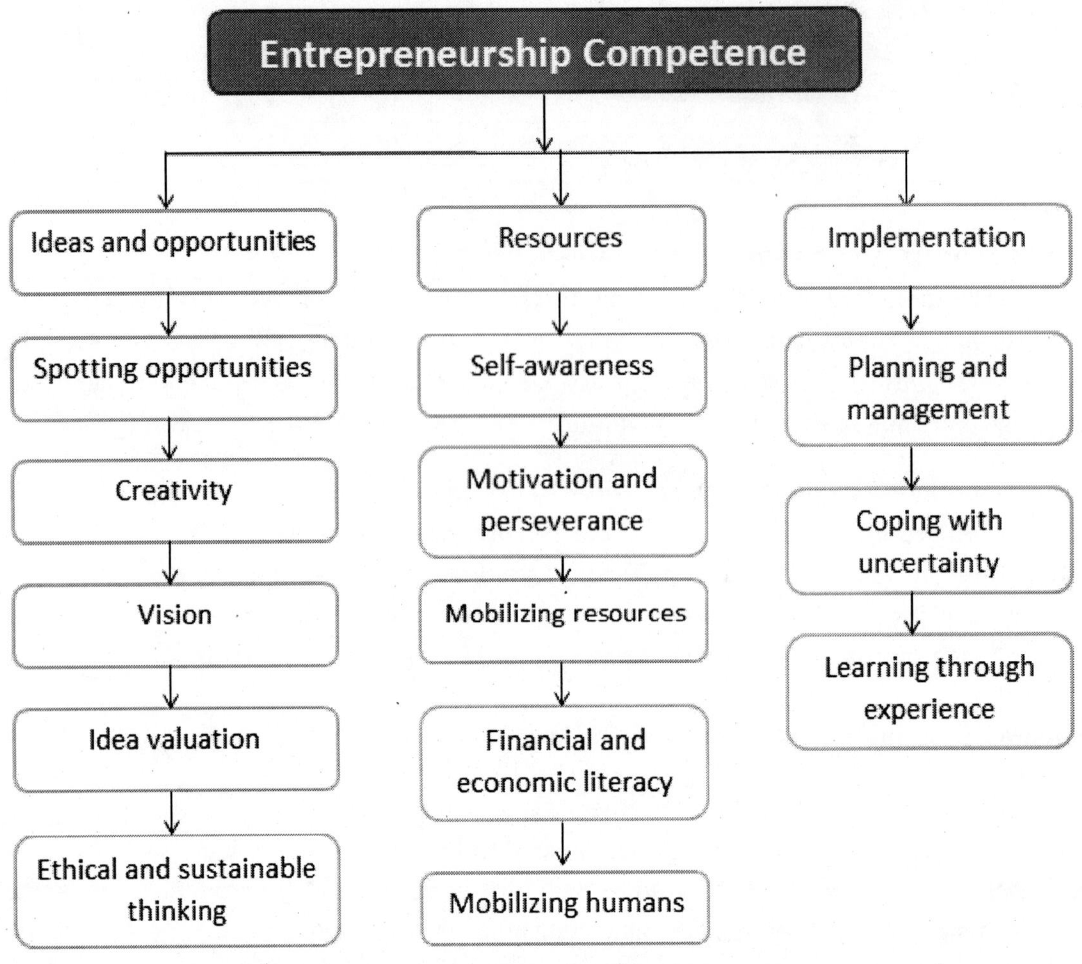

Figure 1.1 Components of Entrepreneurial Competency Framework

At the heart of entrepreneurial endeavours is bringing ground-breaking ideas to life. We explore the development lifecycle, charting the course from idea conception through agile and lean approaches to prototyping. This serves as a compass, guiding us through the practical aspects of transforming conceptual innovation into tangible products that resonate with the market. Figure 1.2 illustrates the characteristic steps of Agile and Lean Product Development, offering a visual depiction of product development embraced by these methodologies. This diagram highlights the involvement in Agile and Lean Product Development, emphasizing rapid iteration, customer feedback integration, and continuous improvement throughout the product development lifecycle.

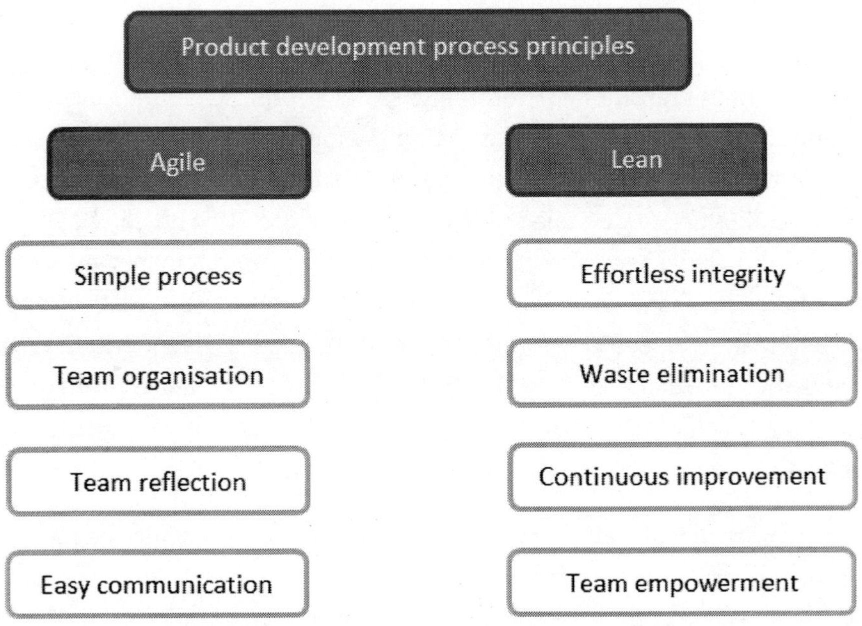

Figure 1.2 characteristic steps of Agile and lean product development

As a reader, you immerse yourself expect not only to gain theoretical insights but also to get a practical understanding that transcends the pages. Prepare to be inspired, challenged, and empowered as we traverse the captivating landscape where entrepreneurial spirit converges with real-world impact. Once again, welcome to a journey that transcends boundaries and sparks the creativity and ambition that define the true essence of entrepreneurship.

1.2 Definition and Evolution

Entrepreneurship is a multifaceted concept encapsulating the dynamic processes, activities, and mind-set associated with showing opportunities, taking calculated risks, and creating value. At its core, an entrepreneur is an individual who conceptualizes and materializes innovative ideas, products, or services, often with a keen eye for addressing unmet needs in the market. Entrepreneurship extends beyond mere business ventures; it embodies a proactive and innovative approach to problem-solving, using creativity, resilience, and strategic thinking.

Entrepreneurs, the driving forces behind entrepreneurship, are characterized by their ability to navigate uncertainty, adapt to change, and envision possibilities where others may see challenges. They often exhibit a unique mind-set, combining a passion for innovation with a willingness to embrace risk to pursue growth and success.

The evolution of entrepreneurship is deeply intertwined with societal, economic, and technological shifts. Historically, entrepreneurship has manifested in various forms, from early traders and merchants to industrialists and, more recently, tech innovators. The concept has evolved as economies transitioned from agricultural to industrial and, eventually, to knowledge-based societies. Entrepreneurship was often synonymous with small-scale trade and local businesses in the initial stages. With the industrial revolution, entrepreneurs emerged as industrialists, establishing large-scale enterprises. In the late 20th and early 21st centuries, the rise of technology and the digital age ushered in a new era of entrepreneurship characterized by start-ups, innovation ecosystems, and global interconnectedness. Nowadays, entrepreneurship transcends traditional boundaries, encompassing diverse sectors such as technology, social enterprise, and creative industries. It is marked by a spirit of optimistic influence, where entrepreneurs use technological advancements, global connectivity, and a collaborative ethos to create ventures that redefine industries and contribute to economic development.

The evolution of entrepreneurship reflects a continual adaptation to changing circumstances, emerging opportunities, and evolving societal needs. It is a dynamic and resilient force that remains central to economic development, job creation, and the continuous renewal of industries and economies. As we navigate the intricate tapestry of entrepreneurial evolution, it becomes clear that the essence of entrepreneurship lies not only in its historical roots but also in its ability to shape the future through innovation and visionary leadership.

1.3 Role of Entrepreneurship in Economic Development

Entrepreneurship is a foundation in economic development and is pivotal in fostering innovation, job creation, and overall economic prosperity. Beyond creating, the entrepreneurial spirit infuses dynamism into economies, propelling them towards growth and sustainable development. Here, we explore into how entrepreneurs contribute to and catalyse economic advancement.

1.3.1. Catalyses Creation

Entrepreneurs establish small and medium enterprises (SMEs) by driving economic growth and employment opportunities. These enterprises, known for their flexibility and responsiveness to market demands, are vital contributors to job creation, especially at the grassroots level. By starting small and gradually expanding their operations, entrepreneurs generate employment opportunities that have a tangible effect on local communities and economies. Moreover, entrepreneurial ventures often lead to innovative start-ups that introduce ground-breaking solutions and disrupt traditional industries. These start-ups, fuelled by the entrepreneurial spirit, not only generally generate direct employment and growth of ancillary industries and services. As they scale and penetrate new markets, innovative start-ups stimulate demand for complementary products and services, nurturing the added jobs of ordinary sectors.

The entrepreneurial ecosystem, including SMEs and innovative start-ups, is a dynamic job creation and economic development engine. By nurturing entrepreneurship and developing an environment conducive to innovation, economies can harness the full potential of small-scale enterprises and start-ups to drive sustainable growth and prosperity.

1.3.2. Innovation and Technological Advancement:

Entrepreneurs are catalysts for change, driven by their innate innovative spirit to address unmet needs and solve pressing challenges. This relentless pursuit of innovation propels technological advancements, spurring progress and development across various industries. By introducing novel solutions and disrupting traditional models, entrepreneurs contribute to the evolution of industries, driving forward momentum and shaping the future landscape of economies. In particular, the rise of technology-driven entrepreneurship has resulted in transformative changes, revolutionizing how products and services are developed, delivered, and consumed. The impact of tech entrepreneurship extends beyond individual ventures, influencing entire industries and ecosystems. By creating innovative technologies and digital solutions, tech entrepreneurs enhance global competitiveness, positioning economies at the forefront of innovation and driving justifiable growth in the digital age.

For example, Emerging technologies such as artificial intelligence (AI), block chain, the Internet of Things (IoT), and 5G connectivity are at the forefront of this technological revolution. AI, for instance, enables businesses to optimize operations, predict market trends, and deliver personalized customer experiences. Block chain technology offers unprecedented levels of security and transparency, particularly in financial transactions and supply chain management. IoT connects devices and systems, facilitating real-time data exchange and operational efficiency. Meanwhile, 5G connectivity promises faster, more reliable internet access, unlocking new possibilities in remote work, telemedicine, and smart cities. The integration of these technologies is redefining traditional business models. Subscription-based services, platform-based ecosystems, and data-driven decision-making are becoming the standard. Companies are leveraging cloud computing to scale-up operations seamlessly and adopting cyber security measures to protect sensitive information. These technological shifts enable businesses to be more agile, responsive, and customer-centric, fostering a culture of continuous innovation. Technological advancements are significantly enhancing efficiency and productivity across various sectors. In manufacturing, automation and robotics streamline production processes, reduce errors, and lower costs. In healthcare, telemedicine, wearable devices, and health informatics improve patient outcomes and accessibility to care. In agriculture, precision farming techniques utilize data analytics and drones to optimize crop yields and resource management.

Each of these examples highlights how technology-driven innovation is not only transforming industries but also addressing global challenges such as sustainability, health, and food security. Looking forward, the potential for further technological innovation remains vast. Quantum computing, biotechnology, and renewable energy technologies are among the fields poised to make ground-breaking contributions. However, these advancements also bring challenges, including ethical considerations, cyber security threats, and the need for continuous up skilling of the workforce. It is crucial for policymakers, industry leaders, and educational institutions to collaborate in an environment that supports sustainable technological growth while mitigating associated risks.

1.3.3. Economic Diversification

Entrepreneurship acts as a catalyst for economic diversification, encouraging the growth of various industries. By promoting the growth of various sectors, entrepreneurship helps reduce dependence on a single industry, thereby enhancing the resilience of economies to economic fluctuations and shocks. This diversification strategy mitigates risks and creates a more stable foundation for sustained growth and development.

Furthermore, the entrepreneurial spirit extends beyond traditional sectors to encompass cultural and creative industries. These industries, including arts, media, and entertainment, thrive on innovation, creativity, and entrepreneurial endeavours. By supporting cultural and creative entrepreneurship, societies reap economic benefits and experience enrichment in their cultural landscape. These industries contribute to the cultural heritage, generating economic growth and creating employment opportunities, promoting a vibrant and dynamic society.

1.3.4. Wealth Creation and Redistribution

Successful entrepreneurs play a pivotal role in wealth accumulation, generating prosperity for themselves, their employees, and stakeholders. Through their ventures, entrepreneurs create avenues for economic growth by generating employment opportunities, stimulating demand for goods and services, and fostering innovation. This kind of wealth creation catalyses broader economic development, driving productivity gains by enhancing overall prosperity within communities and nations.

In addition to their economic contributions, entrepreneurs often extend their impact to address pressing societal challenges through philanthropy and social entrepreneurship initiatives. By using their resources, networks, and innovative approaches, entrepreneurs engage in activities to improve communities' well-being and promote social welfare. Through charitable donations, community development projects, or initiatives tackling environmental sustainability, their social impact complements economic growth, creating a more inclusive and sustainable society. This dual focus on wealth creation and social responsibility underscores entrepreneurs' multifaceted role as economic and social progress drivers.

1.3.5. Global Competitiveness

Entrepreneurial ventures, especially those with an international perspective, are critical in driving global markets and bolstering a country's competitiveness on the world stage. By expanding into international markets, these ventures create export opportunities, establish global supply chains, and elevate the presence of nations in the interconnected global economy. Through their innovative products, services, and business models, entrepreneurial ventures contribute to shaping and influencing global trends, thereby enhancing the global competitiveness of their home countries.

Supportive entrepreneurial ecosystems, characterized by diverse stakeholders such as incubators, accelerators, venture capital firms, and reputed universities, play an essential part in nurturing the growth of start-ups and innovation. These ecosystems offer vital tools, mentorship, and financial options, allowing entrepreneurs to turn their ideas into profitable enterprises. By initiating collaboration, knowledge sharing, and networking among entrepreneurs and industry experts, these ecosystems contribute to developing a vibrant entrepreneurial landscape. They enhance a nation's global standing in innovation and business by fostering the growth of high-potential start-ups and enabling them to compete effectively globally.

1.3.6. Continuous Renewal and Adaptation

Entrepreneurs must be able to adapt to shifting market conditions and technical landscapes. This adaptability ensures economies remain dynamic and responsive to evolving challenges and opportunities. By embracing innovation and adjusting their strategies in response to shifting trends, entrepreneurs play a crucial role in driving economic growth and maintaining competitiveness in an ever-changing global landscape. Additionally, the constant renewal nurtured by entrepreneurship contributes significantly to economic resilience. By introducing innovative ideas, products, and business models, entrepreneurs stimulate innovation and create growth opportunities, especially in adversity. This adaptability allows nations to navigate uncertainties and recover from economic downturns more effectively, for long-term stability and prosperity.

In conclusion, the role of entrepreneurship in economic development is dynamic and transformative. It goes beyond mere business activities, flooding various aspects of society to create a ripple effect that promotes innovation, inclusivity, and sustained progress. As we explore the relationship between entrepreneurship and economic development, it becomes clear that supporting entrepreneurial activities is essential for economic growth and societal progress.

1.4 Significance in Technological Advancements

In the landscape of economic development, entrepreneurship and technological advancements are intertwined forces propelling societies toward innovation, efficiency, and global competitiveness. Entrepreneurship's significance in technological progress goes beyond business ventures; it is a driving force that shapes industries, disrupts traditional models, and catalyses transformative change. Let us explore the profound impact of entrepreneurship on technological advancements.

1.4.1. Innovative Solutions to Unmet Needs

Entrepreneurs should have an exceptional knack for spotting opportunities, curiosity to push boundaries where others might see challenges, and a keen ability to find market gaps and envision novel solutions to address unmet needs. Curiosity leads to a drive for innovation powered by an in-depth understanding of customer behavior and market dynamics. By recognizing emerging trends and foreseeing potential disruptions, entrepreneurs proactively build goods and services that adapt to evolving demands, driving market growth and competitiveness. Moreover, entrepreneurial ventures often disrupt existing markets by introducing ground-breaking technologies and innovative business models. These disruptive innovations challenge traditional norms and practices, forcing established players to adapt or risk becoming obsolete. Through technology and change, entrepreneurs create new growth opportunities and inspire industry-wide transformation, shaping the future of commerce and society at large.

1.4.2. Tech Start-ups and Disruptive Technologies

Entrepreneurial ventures, particularly start-ups, represent the vanguard of technological disruption in today's business landscape. These flexible and inventive companies use innovative technology such as artificial intelligence, blockchain, and the Internet of Things to drive the development of new goods and services. By embracing these advanced technologies, start-ups can address emerging market needs and capitalize on evolving consumer preferences, driving the frontier of innovation. Moreover, the competitive environment cultivated by start-ups catalyses the acceleration of innovation across industries. Fuelled by a spirit of entrepreneurship and a hunger for market disruption, these agile entities continually push boundaries and challenge established norms. Through their relentless pursuit of innovation and willingness to take calculated risks, start-ups inspire traditional companies to adapt and evolve, fostering a culture of innovation that helps the entire business ecosystem.

1.4.3. Ecosystems for Innovation

Within entrepreneurial ecosystems, incubators, reputed universities, and accelerators play pivotal roles in cultivating technological innovation. These dynamic environments serve as incubation hubs, providing Start-ups with essential resources, mentorship, and funding to refine their innovative ideas and transform them into market-ready solutions. By offering access to experienced mentors, industry experts, and venture capitalists, these incubators and accelerators help entrepreneurs negotiate the complexity of the business landscape and accelerate their growth trajectories.

Moreover, entrepreneurial networks within these ecosystems ease collaboration and knowledge exchange among diverse stakeholders. By fostering an environment where entrepreneurs, investors, researchers, and industry professionals converge, these networks encourage the cross-pollination of ideas and expertise. Through collaborative initiatives, such as co-working spaces, networking events, and industry-specific workshops, entrepreneurial ecosystems create fertile grounds for cultivating innovative solutions to pressing societal challenges. Technological advancements are propelled through these collaborative efforts and knowledge exchanges, driving sustained economic growth and societal progress.

1.4.4. Global Connectivity and Market Expansion

The emergence of technology-focused entrepreneurial ventures has reshaped the global business landscape, transcending traditional geographical constraints. In today's interconnected world, these ventures use the power of technology to penetrate global markets, giving their innovative solutions far beyond their local origins. Through digital platforms, online marketplaces, and cross-border collaborations, technology-driven entrepreneurs navigate the complexities of the global economy, adopting interconnectedness and interdependence among nations.

Furthermore, technology-driven entrepreneurship fuels market expansion on a significant scale. These ventures can rapidly expand their reach and impact locally and globally by harnessing the scalability inherent in digital technologies. Technology-driven entrepreneurs seize opportunities to tap into new markets through strategic partnerships, digital marketing strategies, and e-commerce platforms, driving economic growth and creating value across diverse geographical regions. This expansion increases the competitiveness of individual ventures. It also helps to maintain the global economy's dynamic and resilience.

1.4.5. Job Creation in Technology-Driven Sectors

Entrepreneurship benefits the national economy while promoting job growth, particularly in high-tech industries such as software development, data analytics, cyber security, and other digital fields. Moreover, the demand for skilled professionals in technology-driven industries prompts continuous skill development initiatives. Entrepreneurs and businesses invest in training programs, workshops, and educational resources to equip individuals with the technical ability to thrive in the digital age. This emphasis on skill development addresses current workforce needs and prepares individuals for the evolving demands of the technology-driven economy, ensuring a competitive edge in the job market.

1.4.6. Efficiency and Sustainability

Entrepreneurial endeavours harness technology to drive operational efficiency, streamline processes, and minimize costs. By using innovative solutions, entrepreneurs optimize resource utilization and workflow management, leading to heightened productivity and competitiveness in the market. Moreover, entrepreneurs are pivotal in developing technological solutions that address sustainability challenges. Through research and innovation, these entrepreneurs pioneer eco-friendly technologies, renewable energy solutions, and sustainable practices. These efforts not only lessen environmental impact but also promote social responsibility. These sustainability-focused innovations align with ethical business practices and contribute to long-term environmental stewardship and societal well-being.

1.4.7. Technological Literacy and Empowerment

Entrepreneurial ventures are pivotal in democratizing technology, dismantling barriers, and extending access to advanced solutions to a broader audience. Through the creation of user-friendly applications and platforms, entrepreneurs enable individuals to leverage the advantages of technology, irrespective of their technical proficiency or background. This inclusivity in technology-driven solutions adopts inclusion and empowers individuals to engage in the digital economy. Through online entrepreneurship, remote work opportunities, and access to educational resources, individuals can use technology to create economic opportunities and enhance their livelihoods. The democratization of technology catalysed by entrepreneurial ventures contributes to more significant societal equity and economic prosperity.

1.4.8. Continuous Learning and Adaptation

Flexibility in technology entrepreneurship is paramount, as ventures in this domain embrace a perpetual learning and adaptation culture. This agility is crucial in an era where technology evolves rapidly; ensuring businesses stay relevant and resilient in the face of change.

In summary, the significance of entrepreneurship in technological advancements is transformative. It not only shapes the trajectory of industries but also influences how societies operate, connect, and innovate. As we navigate the intricate relationship between entrepreneurship and technology, it becomes clear that creating an environment supportive of entrepreneurial endeavours is instrumental in driving continuous technological progress and societal advancement.

1.5. Entrepreneurial Mind-set, Motivation, and Competencies

In entrepreneurship, the entrepreneurial mind-set, motivation, and abilities merge to build an integrated structure in which creativity, resilience, and strategic insight are deeply interconnected. The following discussion explores how entrepreneurs develop crucial mind-sets, draw motivation from internal sources, and hone competencies that set them apart. It also examines the fundamental elements and approaches for fostering an entrepreneurial mind-set. Explore the foundational elements defining the entrepreneurial spirit, gaining insights into the mind-set, motivations, and competencies propelling individuals toward transformative ventures.

In the entrepreneurship landscape, the mind-set cultivated by individuals plays a pivotal role in navigating challenges, seizing opportunities, and driving innovation. Developing an entrepreneurial mind-set is not merely about starting a business; it is a transformative approach to problem-solving, risk-taking, and continuous learning.

1.5.1. Developing an Entrepreneurial Mind-set - Adaptability and Resilience

Entrepreneurs thrive in dynamic environments by embracing change as a constant. The entrepreneurial mind-set recognizes that change presents opportunities for innovation and growth. By remaining adaptable and resilient, entrepreneurs can navigate shifting circumstances and capitalize on emerging trends, driving forward momentum in their ventures. Central to the entrepreneurial mind-set is the willingness to take calculated risks. Rather than running away from uncertainty, entrepreneurs approach risk-taking as an inherent part of the journey toward success. By carefully assessing risks, making informed decisions, and learning from successes and failures, entrepreneurs can position themselves to seize opportunities and achieve their goals. This proactive approach to risk management enables entrepreneurs to push boundaries, explore new horizons, and realize their full potential.

1.5.2. Innovative Thinking

Entrepreneurs approach challenges with a creative lens, unleashing their creativity to find innovative solutions to unmet needs. Entrepreneurs can uncover new opportunities and disrupt existing markets by thinking outside traditional boundaries and being open to unconventional ideas. This creative approach is essential for staying ahead in dynamic and competitive business environments. Central to the entrepreneurial mind-set is a proactive problem-solving orientation. By adopting a problem-solving mind-set, entrepreneurs tackle obstacles head-on, seeking creative solutions and turning setbacks into stepping stones toward success. This problem-solving orientation is crucial in overcoming hurdles, navigating uncertainties, and achieving entrepreneurial goals.

1.5.3. Visionary Perspective

Entrepreneurs exhibit a forward-thinking mind-set with a visionary perspective that predicts future trends and envisions long-term goals. This forward-looking approach guides strategic decision-making, allowing entrepreneurs to adapt to changing landscapes and capitalize on emerging opportunities proactively. By embracing innovation and predicting market shifts, entrepreneurs maintain a competitive edge, driving the evolution of their ventures and industries. Moreover, the entrepreneurial mind-set is deeply rooted in a powerful sense of purpose and mission-driven ambition. Beyond mere profit-making, entrepreneurs desire to create meaningful impact and contribute to societal development. Whether solving severe social concerns or promoting environmental sustainability, entrepreneurs use their passion and drive to make a difference in the world. This mission-driven philosophy inspires innovation and develops a sense of fulfilment and purpose in entrepreneurial endeavours.

1.5.4. Resourcefulness and Initiative

Resource optimization is a hallmark of the entrepreneurial mind-set, where entrepreneurs excel in maximizing available assets and finding innovative solutions to overcome constraints. Particularly crucial in the initial stages of venture development, this resourcefulness enables entrepreneurs to achieve more with limited resources, setting the groundwork for long-term growth and success. Furthermore, the entrepreneurial mind-set is marked by a proactive approach to seizing opportunities and driving progress. Entrepreneurs prove initiative by taking charge of projects and initiatives, actively seeking new possibilities, and pursuing innovative solutions.

1.5.5. Continuous Learning and Curiosity

Lifelong learning is a foundational principle for entrepreneurs, reflecting their dedication to continual personal and professional development. This commitment involves actively seeking opportunities to expand knowledge and skills and remaining adaptable in evolving industries and market landscapes. By embracing a mind-set of perpetual learning, entrepreneurs position themselves to navigate complexities and seize emerging opportunities effectively. Curiosity fuels the entrepreneurial journey, igniting a passion for exploration and discovery. Entrepreneurs approach challenges with an inquisitive mind-set, driven to understand underlying dynamics and uncover innovative solutions. This curiosity drives creativity and cultivates a sense of openness to innovative ideas and possibilities. By nurturing this innate curiosity, entrepreneurs cultivate a mind-set that thrives on exploration, enabling them to uncover untapped opportunities and drive meaningful change.

Furthermore, resource optimization is a critical tenet of the entrepreneurial mind-set, reflecting the ability to maximize available resources and find inventive solutions to constraints. Entrepreneurs demonstrate resourcefulness by using existing assets creatively and seeking unconventional problem-solving approaches. This proactive approach to resource management enables entrepreneurs to overcome obstacles and capitalize on opportunities, even in challenging environments.

1.5.6. Customer-Centric Focus

In addition to prioritizing a customer-centric mind-set, entrepreneurs emphasize empathy and understanding towards their target audience. Through a deep understanding of their customers' needs and pain points, entrepreneurs can customize their products, services, and marketing strategies to address these concerns effectively. This empathetic approach creates stronger connections with customers and enhances overall business decision-making by ensuring alignment with customer preferences and expectations. Moreover, entrepreneurs recognize the importance of iterative improvement in refining their offerings and meeting evolving market demands. They actively seek customer feedback, viewing it as a valuable source of insight for identifying areas of improvement and innovation. Entrepreneurs engage in iterative cycles of feedback and adjustments, constantly refining their products and services to meet the needs of their target audience more effectively. This commitment to iterative improvement develops a culture of innovation and responsiveness within entrepreneurial ventures, driving sustained growth and success.

In developing an entrepreneurial mind-set, individuals embark on a transformative journey transcending traditional boundary. It is a mind-set that embraces challenges as opportunities, values innovation, and remains resilient despite uncertainties. As we negotiate the complexities of creating an entrepreneurial mind-set, remember that it is a never-ending process that moulds businesses and individuals who begin on the exciting path of entrepreneurship.

1.6 Motivations for Entrepreneurship

Unveiling the motivations that propel individuals into entrepreneurship reveals a diverse tapestry of aspirations, ranging from personal fulfilment to societal impact. Understanding these drivers provides insights into the varied paths that lead individuals to embark on entrepreneurial journeys. The following discussion explores into the multifaceted motivations that fuel the entrepreneurial spirit.

1.6.1. Passion and Personal Fulfilment

Driven by a profound passion for their ideas or a particular industry, many entrepreneurs embark on their entrepreneurial endeavours with the fervent pursuit of personal fulfilment and the realization of long-held dreams. For these individuals, entrepreneurship is not merely a means to an end but a deeply ingrained passion that fuels their creative energies and propels them forward in their journey toward success.

Furthermore, entrepreneurs are motivated by the aspiration to align their work with their passions, effectively transforming what they love into a vocation. By integrating their interests and aspirations into their entrepreneurial pursuits, these individuals derive intrinsic satisfaction from their work, finding fulfilment in the pursuit of their passions. This alignment between passion and profession is a powerful motivator, inspiring entrepreneurs to overcome obstacles, persevere through challenges, and achieve their goals.

1.6.2. Autonomy and Independence

Pursuing autonomy and independence is a compelling driver for entrepreneurship, reflecting a fundamental desire for control over one's professional endeavours. Entrepreneurs are motivated by the prospect of charting their paths, free from the confines of traditional employment structures. This quest for autonomy extends beyond mere control over work and decisions; it encompasses the freedom to shape the direction and trajectory of their ventures according to their vision and values. By venturing into entrepreneurship, individuals seize the opportunity to break free from conventional hierarchies and establish their domains of influence. Moreover, entrepreneurship offers a platform for individuals to exercise their creativity and innovation, unencumbered by bureaucratic constraints or organizational red tape. The entrepreneurial journey empowers individuals to unleash their entrepreneurial spirit, enabling them to explore uncharted territories, experiment with novel ideas, and pursue unconventional solutions to complex problems. This creative autonomy promotes a sense of empowerment and ownership, fuelling the drive to pursue entrepreneurial endeavours with passion and determination.

Furthermore, autonomy in entrepreneurship goes hand in hand with the opportunity for self-expression and self-fulfilment. By taking control of their professional destinies, entrepreneurs can align their work with their values, passions, and personal aspirations. This alignment enhances job satisfaction and the pursuit of meaningful work that resonates with their core beliefs. Autonomy and independence in entrepreneurship represent more than a career choice; they embody a profound quest for personal freedom, self-determination, and fulfilment in pursuing one's entrepreneurial dreams.

1.6.3. Financial Opportunities

Wealth creation is a central pillar motivating entrepreneurial pursuits, with entrepreneurs viewing their ventures as potent avenues for income generation and long-term prosperity. Recognizing the inherent correlation between risk and reward in entrepreneurial endeavours fuels this opportunity. Entrepreneurs should be willing to undertake calculated risks, understanding that navigating uncertainties is often a prerequisite for realizing financial success. This dynamic relationship between risk-taking and the potential for substantial rewards underscores the inherent entrepreneurial mind-set, where the pursuit of wealth creation is a powerful impetus driving innovation and economic growth.

1.6.4. Innovation and Problem-Solving

Entrepreneurs are often driven by a compelling urge to tackle real-world challenges with innovative solutions, aiming to make a tangible difference in society. The opportunity to address pressing issues and improve lives through creative problem-solving is a powerful motivator, propelling entrepreneurs to pursue ventures with a positive social impact. This focus on solving real-world problems underscores the intrinsic connection between entrepreneurship and societal advancement, as entrepreneurs use their ingenuity to address pressing needs and contribute to positive change.

Also, entrepreneurs are often drawn to disrupting established industries or introducing transformative innovations that challenge the status quo. The allure of reshaping markets, revolutionizing existing practices, and pioneering new paradigms inspires entrepreneurs to push boundaries and pursue ventures with disruptive potential. By daring to challenge entrenched norms and conventional wisdom, entrepreneurs embrace the role of catalysts for change, driving innovation and progress across industries. This relentless pursuit of disruption underscores entrepreneurship's dynamic and transformative nature as entrepreneurs strive to create lasting impact through bold ideas and visionary leadership.

1.6.5. Legacy and Impact

Entrepreneurs are driven by a powerful desire to leave a legacy, encouraged by the idea of founding a firm or creating items that will outlast their own lives. The opportunity to leave a mark on the world through innovative solutions, influential businesses, or impactful initiatives becomes a compelling force that propels entrepreneurs to pursue their visions with unwavering dedication. This highlights the importance of entrepreneurship in achieving a long-term impact and meaningful contributions to society.

Moreover, entrepreneurship is a powerful platform for individuals to effect positive social change and address pressing societal issues. Driven by a sense of responsibility and a commitment to making a difference, some entrepreneurs channel their energies towards initiatives that aim to improve the well-being of communities, advance social causes, or tackle systemic challenges. By using their entrepreneurial skills and resources to create social impact, these individuals exemplify the transformative potential of entrepreneurship as a force for positive change. Their efforts not only benefit society at large but also inspire others to use entrepreneurship to drive meaningful societal progress.

1.6.6. Flexibility and Work-Life Balance

Entrepreneurs are often drawn to flexible work arrangements and a better work-life balance, seeing entrepreneurship as a pathway to crafting personalized work structures that align with their lifestyle preferences. The autonomy to set their schedules and prioritize personal commitments alongside professional responsibilities drives their decision to embark on entrepreneurial ventures. Although building a business demands considerable time and effort, entrepreneurs are willing to invest in their ventures, knowing that the flexibility offered by entrepreneurship offers greater freedom and control over their daily routines and overall life satisfaction. This pursuit of flexibility and work-life balance underscores the appeal of entrepreneurship to achieve personal fulfilment and autonomy in both professional and personal spheres.

1.6.7. Learning and Growth

Entrepreneurs are driven by a relentless pursuit of learning and growth, viewing the entrepreneurial journey as an ongoing educational experience. They are driven by the potential to learn new skills, broaden their knowledge base, and receive valuable experiences that will benefit their personal and professional development. This commitment to continuous learning enables entrepreneurs to adapt and evolve to changing market dynamics and emerging challenges. Moreover, they embrace adaptability and agility as essential traits for navigating the uncertainties of entrepreneurship, recognizing that each obstacle presents an opportunity for learning and refinement. This emphasis on learning and growth underscores the resilience and determination inherent in the entrepreneurial mind-set as individuals strive to expand their capabilities and drive success in their ventures.

1.6.8. Contributing to Community

Entrepreneurs are driven by more than just personal success; they want to make a substantial difference in the communities where they work. This commitment goes beyond financial gains and encompasses initiatives that enhance the social fabric and support local causes. One significant way entrepreneurs contribute to their communities is through job creation. Recognizing the importance of economic development, entrepreneurs strive to generate employment opportunities within their localities. By hiring locally and investing in workforce development, entrepreneurs play a crucial role in bolstering local economies, reducing unemployment rates, and creating a sense of stability and growth. Moreover, job creation provides individuals with livelihoods and stimulates economic activity, helping businesses and communities.

Understanding the diverse motivations for entrepreneurship will provide a nuanced perspective on the drivers that lead individuals to embark on this challenging yet rewarding journey. Whether fuelled by personal passion, the pursuit of financial success, or a commitment to social impact, these motivations collectively shape the entrepreneurial landscape and contribute to the vibrancy of innovative ventures.

1.7 Key Competencies for Successful Entrepreneurs

Successful entrepreneurs have unique abilities and competencies that allow them to negotiate the complexities of the business environment. These key competencies extend beyond technical knowledge, encompassing diverse abilities contributing to visionary leadership, innovation, and sustained success. The following discussion illuminates the crucial competencies for entrepreneurs to succeed in the current dynamic and competitive environment.

1.7.1. Visionary Leadership

Visionary leadership is a cornerstone of successful entrepreneurship, characterized by the ability to articulate a strategic vision that inspires others. Entrepreneurs possess a keen understanding of their ventures' long-term goals and objectives, enabling them to chart a course for success amidst uncertainty and complexity. Moreover, adaptive leadership skills are vital for navigating the ever-changing business landscape. Entrepreneurs demonstrate agility and resilience, making informed decisions and adjusting strategies to emerging challenges and opportunities. This adaptive approach ensures that ventures stay agile and responsive to evolving market dynamics, driving sustained growth and success.

1.7.2. Effective Communication

Effective communication is a foundational skill for entrepreneurs, encompassing clear articulation and active listening. Entrepreneurs must adeptly convey their ideas, strategies, and vision to diverse stakeholders, understanding and alignment. Clear and articulate communication enables entrepreneurs to inspire confidence and rally support for their ventures. Additionally, active listening plays a crucial role in entrepreneurship, as successful entrepreneurs value input from others and seek to understand diverse perspectives. Entrepreneurs gain valuable insights that inform decision-making and drive innovation by actively listening to team members, customers, and stakeholders. This combination of effective communication and active listening empowers entrepreneurs to build strong relationships, foster collaboration, and navigate challenges effectively.

1.7.3. Strategic Decision-Making

Strategic decision-making lies at the core of entrepreneurial success, requiring a blend of analytical ability and risk management insight. Entrepreneurs adeptly analyse data and market trends to inform their choices, employing analytical thinking to decipher complex scenarios. Furthermore, they embrace calculated risk-taking, evaluating potential rewards against inherent uncertainties. Entrepreneurs mitigate adverse outcomes by implementing robust risk management strategies while capitalizing on lucrative opportunities. This dynamic approach to decision-making enables entrepreneurs to navigate the ever-changing business landscape with confidence and foresight, positioning their ventures for sustained growth and success.

1.7.4. Innovative Thinking

Innovative thinking is the hallmark of entrepreneurial success, characterized by creative problem-solving and a penchant for embracing technological advancements. Entrepreneurs adeptly navigate challenges by exploring inventive solutions that resonate with market needs, developing a culture of continuous innovation within their ventures. Moreover, they demonstrate a keen willingness to adopt and integrate innovative technologies, recognizing their transformative potential in enhancing operational efficiency and maintaining competitiveness. By harnessing the power of innovation, entrepreneurs propel their ventures forward, positioning themselves at the forefront of industry evolution and driving sustainable growth in dynamic market landscapes.

1.7.5. Adaptability and Resilience

Adaptability and resilience are integral traits of successful entrepreneurs, allowing them to thrive amidst constant change and uncertainty in the business landscape. Entrepreneurs embrace change as an inherent aspect of business evolution, demonstrating a proactive approach to navigating dynamic environments. Moreover, they exhibit resilience in the face of setbacks, viewing challenges as opportunities for growth rather than impediments to progress. By learning from setbacks and leveraging failures as valuable learning experiences, resilient entrepreneurs continually refine their strategies and enhance their capabilities, ensuring they remain agile and resilient in pursuing their entrepreneurial goals.

1.7.6. Networking and Relationship Building

Networking and relationship building are pivotal for entrepreneurial success, facilitating growth and opportunity. Entrepreneurs strategically connect with mentors, peers, and industry experts to gain insights and collaboration prospects. Stakeholder engagement, involving investors, customers, and partners, builds trust and loyalty, which is vital for sustained growth. Authentic connections based on mutual respect and transparency empowers entrepreneurs to navigate challenges effectively. Entrepreneurs cultivate a supportive ecosystem that champions their ventures by prioritizing meaningful relationships. In the dynamic business landscape, networking and relationship building are indispensable tools for unlocking opportunities, driving innovation, and ensuring long-term success.

1.7.7. Financial Literacy

Financial literacy is a foundation of entrepreneurial success, requiring entrepreneurs to understand financial principles and practices deeply. This expertise empowers them to manage budgets, forecast revenues, and make informed decisions that drive their ventures' financial health and growth. By mastering financial literacy, entrepreneurs can effectively allocate resources, strategically balance budgets, and maximize the impact of available funds. This ability to optimize resource allocation enables entrepreneurs to allocate funds to areas that generate the highest return on investment, thereby fuelling the growth and sustainability of their ventures.

1.7.8. Team Building and Management

Entrepreneurs recognize that effective team building, and management are essential for the success of their ventures. They strategically assemble teams comprising individuals with diverse skills, experiences, and perspectives, promoting creativity and innovation. By promoting a collaborative work environment, entrepreneurs harness the collective intelligence of their teams to tackle challenges and seize opportunities. Additionally, successful entrepreneurs demonstrate strong leadership capabilities, guiding their teams with vision and purpose. They delegate tasks efficiently, empowering team members to take ownership of their responsibilities and contribute to achieving organizational goals. Through effective team building and management practices, entrepreneurs cultivate high-performing teams that drive sustained growth and success.

1.7.9. Customer-Centric Focus

Entrepreneurs with a customer-centric focus prioritize understanding and meeting the needs of their target audience. They invest time and effort in comprehending market dynamics, consumer preferences, and pain points to inform product development and service enhancements. By actively soliciting and incorporating customer feedback, entrepreneurs ensure that their offerings resonate with their audience, leading to increased satisfaction and loyalty. Moreover, successful entrepreneurs go beyond transactional interactions to build meaningful, long-term customer relationships. By nurturing these relationships and delivering exceptional experiences, entrepreneurs cultivate brand loyalty and advocacy, driving sustained business growth and success.

1.7.10. Negotiation and Persuasion

Entrepreneurs frequently navigate negotiations with stakeholders, partners, and investors, where the ability to negotiate effectively is paramount. Proficiency in negotiation allows entrepreneurs to broker mutually beneficial agreements and secure favourable outcomes for all parties involved. Moreover, successful entrepreneurs go beyond mere negotiation; they excel in persuasive communication, adeptly articulating their vision to instil confidence and garner support from diverse stakeholders. Through persuasive communication, entrepreneurs effectively convey their ideas, inspire trust, and rally support, paving the way for realizing their entrepreneurial goals.

1.7.11. Time Management

Time management is a critical skill for entrepreneurs navigating the fast-paced business environments. Effective entrepreneurs prioritize tasks meticulously, ensuring their activities align with strategic goals. Entrepreneurs can efficiently allocate their time and resources by identifying and prioritizing crucial activities, maximizing productivity, and achieving desired outcomes within tight deadlines. Moreover, mastering time management enhances efficiency and productivity in entrepreneurial endeavours. Entrepreneurs who effectively manage their time can streamline workflows, eliminate unnecessary tasks, and focus their energy on activities that yield the highest returns. This optimized approach accelerates progress toward business objectives and cultivates a culture of productivity within the entrepreneurial ecosystem, driving sustained growth and success.

In cultivating these key competencies, entrepreneurs enhance their capabilities and fortify the foundation of their ventures. Each competency contributes to the holistic skill set required to lead, innovate, and succeed in the ever-evolving entrepreneurship landscape.

1.8. Market Dynamics and Technology Influence - Market Pull vs. Technology Push Factors

In the dynamic landscape of entrepreneurship, the symbiotic relationship between market dynamics and technological influence shapes the contours of innovation and business evolution. Entrepreneurs create their ideals on a canvas of market dynamics, which capture the fluctuation of customer wants, competition, and economic trends. Concurrently, technology acts as the transformative brush, adding new dimensions to the entrepreneurial landscape. The following discussion explores into the intricate relationship between market forces and technological advancements. It explores how savvy entrepreneurs navigate these realms to identify opportunities, address challenges, and strategically position their ventures for success. As we untangle the complexity of market dynamics and technological influence, we begin on a journey in which foresight, flexibility, and a thorough awareness of the changing terrain serve as guidelines for pursuing entrepreneurial endeavours.

In product innovation and entrepreneurship, the relationship between market pull and technology push factors defines the trajectory of ventures. Market pull represents the gravitational force exerted by consumer needs and demands, drawing entrepreneurs toward solutions that resonate with the market. Conversely, technology push emanates from the innovation engine, propelling entrepreneurs to create novel solutions and disrupt existing paradigms. The following discussion navigates the nuanced relationship between market dynamics and technological advancements, dissecting the forces that drive entrepreneurs to either respond to market needs or proactively shape the market through technological innovation.

1.8.1 Understanding Market Pull Factors

Understanding market pull factors is crucial for entrepreneurs venturing into product innovation and entrepreneurship. Market pull is intricately linked to comprehending consumer needs and demands. Entrepreneurs who wish to identify market pull meticulously analyse trends, preferences, and pain points within their target audience. This consumer-centric approach forms the foundation for product development, ensuring that solutions address the genuine needs of the market. Market research and validation play pivotal roles in responding to market pull. Entrepreneurs undertake comprehensive market research to validate assumptions and gather insights into market dynamics. This phase involves various methods such as surveys, focus groups, and data analysis to decipher consumer behaviour and preferences. Market validation serves as the litmus test for the viability and acceptance of a product or service, providing valuable feedback for refining the offering. Agility in response to market changes is imperative in addressing market pull effectively. Successful entrepreneurs remain vigilant to shifts in consumer behaviour and swiftly adapt their strategies accordingly. The ability to pivot and adjust to evolving market dynamics ensures that ventures stay responsive and aligned with the ever-changing demands of the target audience. By staying attuned to market pull factors and maintaining agility, entrepreneurs can position their ventures for success in dynamic and competitive markets.

1.8.2. Unleashing Technology Push Factors

Unleashing technology push factors are essential for entrepreneurs navigating the landscape of product innovation and entrepreneurship. These factors stem from innovation and technological advancements, driving entrepreneurs to create novel solutions by leveraging innovative technologies. This proactive approach places them at the forefront of industry trends and positions their ventures as pioneers in their respective fields. Entrepreneurs embracing technology push prioritize investment in robust research and development initiatives. This involves exploring emerging technologies, experimenting with prototypes, and pushing the boundaries of what is currently feasible. The overarching goal is to not only meet existing market needs but also to shape the market by introducing disruptive innovations that have the potential to redefine industries. A critical aspect of addressing technology push involves creating solutions ahead of market awareness. Entrepreneurs in this realm anticipate future needs and trends, introducing products or services that may not yet have a defined market but possess the potential to revolutionize industries. This forward-thinking approach not only demonstrates foresight but also positions ventures as industry leaders, driving market evolution and setting new standards of excellence.

As depicted in Figure 1.3, effective product development requires a comprehensive approach that encompasses market research, customer feedback, and refinement of the value proposition. This visual representation highlights the critical elements necessary for ensuring a product's alignment with market requirements and customer demands. By integrating technology push factors with market pull considerations, entrepreneurs can develop innovative solutions that resonate with consumers and drive sustainable growth in dynamic and competitive markets.

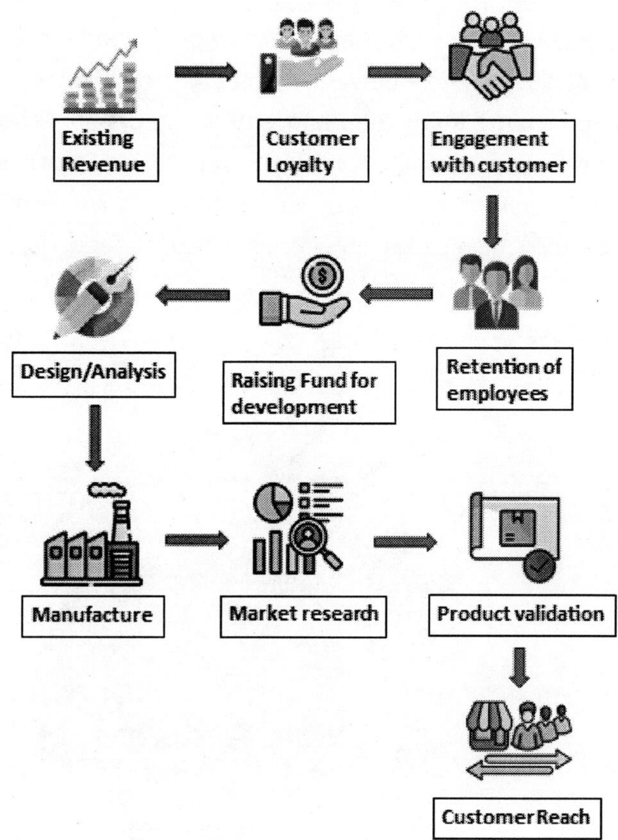

Figure 1.3 Components of product reach to the market Needs.

1.8.3. Striking a Balance

Striking a balance between market pull and technology push is paramount for successful entrepreneurs navigating the landscape of product innovation and entrepreneurship. Integrated innovation lies at the core of this balance, where consumer insights are interrelated with technological capabilities to create solutions that not only address current needs but also anticipate future requirements. The journey from market pulls to technology push and vice versa is iterative in nature. Entrepreneurs engage in continuous feedback loops with the market, gathering insights, iterating on their solutions, and refining their strategies accordingly. This cyclical process ensures that ventures remain dynamic, adaptive, and well-positioned in the ever-evolving entrepreneurial landscape.

As we explore into the dynamic relationship between market demand and technological innovation, it becomes evident that successful entrepreneurs navigate these forces with strategic skill. Whether responding to existing market demands or pioneering technological advancements, the ability to discern, adapt, and innovate defines the resilience and success of ventures in the competitive arena of product innovation and entrepreneurship. Figure 1.4 illustrates the iterative design loops encompassing various stages of the design process. This visual representation elucidates the iterative nature of design, demonstrating how each stage informs and influences subsequent iterations. By highlighting the importance of feedback, refinement, and iteration, it underscores the essential role of continuous improvement in achieving optimal design outcomes and driving innovation forward.

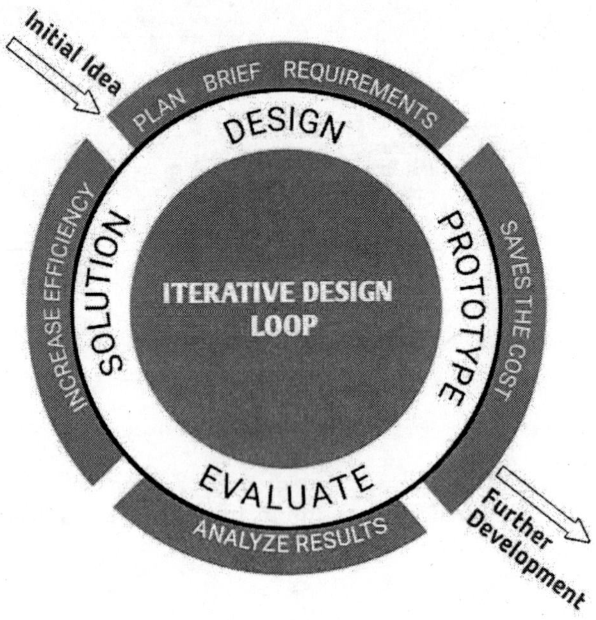

Figure 1.4 Iterative design loop of various stages

1.9 Identifying Market Needs through Research

In the complex entrepreneurship landscape, identifying market needs through research is the compass guiding the entrepreneurial journey. Successful ventures are founded on a profound understanding of consumer demands, preferences, and pain points. The following discussion illuminates the significance of meticulous market research as the cornerstone of product innovation and business strategy.

1.9.1. Market Segmentation

Market segmentation involves categorizing potential buyers based on demographics, geography, behaviour, or psychographic factors to better understand and market to them. Defining target audiences is the cornerstone of effective market research for entrepreneurs. It involves segmenting the target audience based on demographics, psychographics, and behavioural patterns. By understanding the diverse needs within these segments, entrepreneurs can tailor product development and marketing strategies to resonate with specific consumer groups. Persona development is a crucial step in understanding the target audience on a deeper level. Entrepreneurs create detailed customer personas that embody the characteristics of their target audience. These personas humanize the consumer base, providing valuable insights into their motivations, challenges, and aspirations, which in turn inform product development and marketing efforts.

Further, market sizing plays a vital role in assessing the potential of the target market. Entrepreneurs utilize quantitative methods such as surveys, interviews, and data analysis to determine the overall size and growth potential of the market. This information is instrumental in making decisions regarding the scalability of the venture and devising effective market penetration strategies. Trend analysis complements market sizing by providing insights into industry trends and consumer behaviour. Entrepreneurs closely scrutinize emerging patterns and shifts in consumer preferences to stay ahead of the curve. By staying abreast of trends, ventures can adapt their offerings to align with evolving market dynamics, ensuring relevance and competitiveness in the marketplace.

1.9.2 Crafting Compelling Value Propositions

Armed with insights from market segmentation and sizing, entrepreneurs craft compelling value propositions. These propositions articulate the unique value their products or services bring to specific customer segments. A well-defined value proposition resonates with the identified market needs.

1.9.3 Aligning Solutions with Customer Goals

Successful entrepreneurs align their solutions with customer goals. By understanding what motivates their target audience, ventures ensure that their offerings address essential needs and aspirations. This alignment enhances the perceived value of the product or service.

1.9.4. Marketing (Go-to-Market) Strategy

Tailored marketing approaches are essential outcomes of comprehensive market research. Entrepreneurs utilize insights gathered from their research to develop customized marketing strategies that resonate with their target audience. This involves identifying the most effective channels, crafting compelling messages, and planning promotional activities that align with the preferences and behaviours of their audience. By tailoring their marketing efforts, entrepreneurs can maximize the impact of their campaigns and increase the likelihood of engaging and converting potential customers. Further, competitor analysis is another critical component of effective market research. By understanding their competitors, entrepreneurs gain valuable insights into the strengths, weaknesses, opportunities, and threats present in the market landscape. Through thorough competitor analyses, entrepreneurs can identify areas for differentiation, refine their strategies, and capitalize on market gaps. This allows them to position their offerings more effectively and stand out in crowded markets, enhancing their competitive advantage and driving business success.

1.9.5. Distribution Channels and Sales Network

Optimizing distribution channels is a crucial aspect of market research for entrepreneurs. By leveraging insights gained from their research, entrepreneurs can make informed decisions about the most efficient and cost-effective ways to deliver their products or services to consumers. This optimization ensures that ventures reach their target audience strategically, maximizing the effectiveness of their distribution efforts and enhancing their market reach. Building a robust sales network is another key outcome of market research. Entrepreneurs use their research findings to identify potential partners, distributors, and sales channels that align with their target market and business objectives. By establishing strong relationships with these stakeholders, entrepreneurs can enhance the accessibility of their products or services to the intended customers, driving sales and revenue growth. Identifying market needs through comprehensive research is not a one-time endeavour but a continuous process. Successful entrepreneurs understand the iterative nature of market research and recognize that consumer preferences and market dynamics evolve over time. By committing to on-going research and staying attuned to changing trends and preferences, entrepreneurs can remain agile, responsive, and poised to meet the ever-changing needs of their target audience. This on-going commitment ensures that ventures remain competitive and adaptable in dynamic and competitive markets.

1.9.6. Assessing Technology Readiness Levels

In the intricate journey of product innovation and entrepreneurship, evaluating the Technology Readiness Level (TRL) becomes a pivotal step in ensuring the successful development and deployment of innovative solutions. TRL is a systematic metric used to assess the maturity and viability of technologies, guiding entrepreneurs in understanding the readiness of their innovations for market integration. The following discussion explores the significance of assessing TRL and the strategic considerations entrepreneurs must undertake in this critical phase of technological advancement.

1.9.7. Understanding Technology Readiness Levels

Technology Readiness Levels (TRL), ranging from 1 to 9, serve as a systematic framework for evaluating the maturity of a technology. At Level 1, the technology is at its nascent stage, representing basic principles, while Level 9 indicates full commercialization. Entrepreneurs leverage this framework to assess the readiness of their technologies across various stages of development. Each TRL level corresponds to specific milestones in the technology's evolution, from concept formulation (TRL 1-3) to full-scale deployment and commercialization (TRL 8-9). This structured approach enables entrepreneurs to track progress, identify key developmental milestones, and make informed strategic decisions throughout the technology's lifecycle.

1.9.8. Technology Development Phases

In the initial stages of conceptualization (TRL 1-3), entrepreneurs focus on formulating the basic principles of their technology. As feasibility studies progress and initial experiments validate concepts, the technology advances to TRL 2 and 3. At this point, entrepreneurs define the scope and potential applications of the innovation. Moving into the mid-range TRL levels (TRL 4-6), entrepreneurs shift their focus to development and validation. Prototypes are developed, tested, and iterated upon (TRL 4-5), leading to a pre-commercial prototype or demonstration in a relevant environment (TRL 6). Rigorous testing ensures the technology's functionality and performance. In the final stages, entrepreneurs progress to TRL 7, where the technology undergoes a full demonstration in an operational environment. This stage serves as a precursor to commercialization (TRL 8-9), where the technology is fully integrated into the market, addressing end-user needs and realizing its commercial potential.

1.9.9. Strategic Considerations:

Assessing Technology Readiness Levels (TRL) plays a crucial role in resource allocation and risk mitigation strategies for entrepreneurs. By evaluating the current TRL of their technology, entrepreneurs can allocate resources effectively, striking a balance between further development needs and associated risks. This strategic approach optimizes resource utilization and reduces uncertainties, fostering efficient progress toward commercialization. Moreover, aligning the technology's TRL with market demands is essential. Entrepreneurs must consider both market readiness and technological readiness, ensuring that the innovation addresses current needs and can be seamlessly integrated into the market at the opportune moment. Additionally, leveraging TRL assessments enables entrepreneurs to identify collaboration opportunities and attract funding. Investors and partners often assess the maturity of technologies before engagement, and a transparent understanding of TRL enhances credibility and initiates collaboration, facilitating the advancement of innovative solutions toward commercial success.

1.9.10. Regulatory Compliance

Regulatory compliance stands as a crucial aspect of technology commercialization, and entrepreneurs rely on assessing Technology Readiness Levels (TRL) to gauge their technology's preparedness to meet regulatory requirements. This proactive approach ensures a smoother transition through regulatory processes, facilitating the path to market entry. The iterative nature of TRL assessment is integral to this process, constituting a continuous evaluation rather than a one-time activity. Entrepreneurs continuously assess the TRL of their technologies as they progress through development phases, recognizing the dynamic nature of technological advancements and market demands. Moreover, entrepreneurs perceive TRL assessments as learning opportunities, particularly when faced with setbacks or failures at specific TRL stages. Such occurrences provide valuable insights and lessons learned which inform future iterations and contribute to enhancing the overall innovation process. By viewing TRL assessments through this lens, entrepreneurs leverage failures as stepping stones to progress, fostering resilience and adaptability in the face of challenges.

The systematic evaluation of Technology Readiness Levels serves as a strategic compass for entrepreneurs navigating the complexities of product innovation. This structured framework empowers them to make informed decisions, allocate resources judiciously, and align technological advancements with market demands effectively. As the entrepreneurial journey unfolds, the iterative assessment of TRL becomes an invaluable guide, propelling innovations toward successful commercialization and meaningful market impact.

1.10. New Product Development Lifecycle - Phases of Product Development

In the dynamic landscape of entrepreneurship, navigating the New Product Development (NPD) lifecycle is a critical undertaking. The NPD process is the blueprint for transforming innovative ideas into tangible, market-ready products. The following discussion explores the distinct phases of the product development lifecycle, providing entrepreneurs with a structured roadmap to shepherd their creations from conception to commercialization.

1.10.1. Ideation and Conceptualization

Entrepreneurs start their journey with ideation, where they produce fresh and creative ideas to meet the needs of the market. This phase involves a few key steps. First off, they gather in brainstorming sessions to throw around lots of different ideas, working together to generate as many possibilities as they can. Then, they use a method called creative design thinking, which helps them think creatively and produce innovative solutions. Another important part is checking out what is happening in the market right now through market trend analysis. This helps them spot any gaps or opportunities they could fill with their idea. But there are challenges too, like making sure their idea is not just a copy of something that is already out there and making sure it is something people want. To tackle these challenges, they use tools like mind mapping and SWOT analysis to refine their ideas and make sure they are on the right track.

1.10.2. Feasibility Assessment (Concept Development)

Once entrepreneurs have brainstormed and produce some promising ideas, they move on to the feasibility assessment phase to see if those ideas are achievable. In this phase: First, they refine their concepts, narrowing down their options to the ones that seem most likely to succeed. Then, they do some initial market surveys to get a sense of whether people might be interested in what they are offering. Further, they check out the technical side of things to see if the technology they need is available and practical. But there are challenges here too, like figuring out exactly how much demand there will be for their product and dealing with any technical problems that might pop up. To tackle these challenges, they often run pilot studies and get advice from experts in the field.

1.10.3. Design and Prototyping

Once entrepreneurs have confirmed that their concept is feasible, they move on to the design and prototyping phase. Next the engineers and designers team up to produce detailed plans for how the product will work and what it will look like. Then, they start building the first versions of the product, known as prototypes. As they build and test these prototypes, they keep making improvements based on the feedback they get. But there are some challenges they face, like making sure the product looks good, works well, and can be made efficiently. To help speed things along, they might use rapid prototyping technologies like 3D printing, which can make the process quicker and easier.

1.10.4. Iterative Testing and Iteration

After creating prototypes, the entrepreneurs dive into iterative testing and iteration. They put the prototypes through serious testing to make sure they work well, last long, and provide a pleasant experience for users. This testing phase involves doing lots of different tests to find any problems and fix them. They also gather feedback from people who might use the product and **analyse** what they say. Based on this feedback, they make any necessary changes to improve the product. But there are challenges here too, like making sure they stick to their testing schedule and getting feedback from enough people. To keep everything organized, they make sure to document all the changes they make and keep track of how the product improves over time.

1.10.5. Manufacturing and Assembly Planning

Upon finalizing the design, entrepreneurs explore into manufacturing and assembly planning. This phase involves selecting suppliers, establishing manufacturing processes, and optimizing the supply chain. Entrepreneurs ensure that the production processes align with quality standards and cost-effectiveness. The importance of integrating ease of assembly, cost management, operational efficiency, and material availability in manufacturing and assembly planning is symbolized in Figure 1.5. The figure evaluates several factors critical to manufacturing and assembly planning, including customer satisfaction, ergonomic factor, ease of use, and converting time, with respect to ease of assembly, cost, operations, and material availability. From the data, it is evident that ease of assembly consistently scores high across all categories, indicating that simplifying assembly processes can positively impact customer satisfaction (score of 8), ergonomics (score of 8), ease of use (score of 8), and converting time (score of 7). This highlights the importance of designing products with straightforward assembly procedures to enhance overall performance and user experience.

Cost is also a significant factor, particularly in customer satisfaction and ergonomic considerations, both scoring 8. This suggests that managing production costs effectively without compromising quality is crucial for maintaining high customer satisfaction and ergonomic standards. Operational factors vary in their impact, with notable scores in customer satisfaction (7), ergonomic factor (7), ease of use (6), and converting time (6). This variability indicates that while operational efficiency is important, there may be other contributing elements that influence these areas. Material availability shows a strong influence on customer satisfaction (score of 7) and converting time (score of 7), emphasizing the necessity of a reliable supply chain and the availability of materials to ensure smooth manufacturing and timely product delivery.

By focusing on these factors, manufacturers can optimize production processes, enhance product quality, and ensure important levels of customer satisfaction and ergonomic performance.

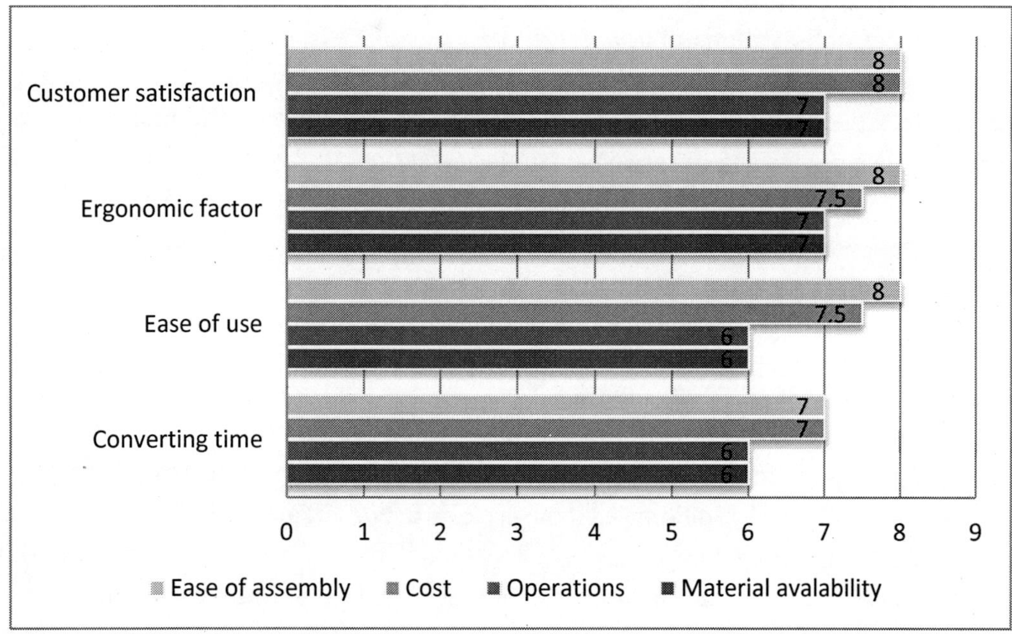

Figure 1.5 Functions versus manufacturability – a sample plot

1.10.6. Product Testing and Quality Assurance

Before a product hits the market, it goes through thorough testing to make sure it meets all the specifications and quality standards. They do final tests to check if the product does what it is supposed to do and performs well. They also put in place protocols to make sure the quality stays consistent and work on minimizing any defects that might pop up. But there are challenges like keeping up with strict testing standards and managing the costs of production. To help with this, they might use automated testing systems, which can make things quicker and more accurate.

1.10.7. Market Introduction and Launch

The final stage of the New Product Development (NPD) cycle is the introduction and launch of the product to the market. Entrepreneurs develop and carry out strategic marketing campaigns to build excitement around the product. They also make sure that distribution channels are all set up and ready for the product's launch. Additionally, they reach out to early adopters to get their feedback and engage with them. However, there are some challenges they face, like effectively communicating the value of the product and handling the coordination of the supply chain. To overcome these challenges, they might use social media and digital marketing to maximize the impact of the launch.

1.10.8. Post-Launch Evaluation and Feedback

Following the product launch, the New Product Development it enters the post-launch evaluation and feedback phase. Entrepreneurs keep an eye on how the market responds to the product by tracking sales and observing customer reactions. They also continue gathering feedback from users, analysing it to find areas for improvement. Additionally, they assess how the product performs in real-world situations to ensure it meets expectations. However, there are challenges in accurately interpreting feedback and addressing issues promptly. To tackle this, entrepreneurs should have a strong customer support system in place can boost post-launch success.

1.10.9. Scaling and Market Expansion

As the product gains momentum, entrepreneurs shift their focus towards scaling production and expanding market reach. They work on refining manufacturing processes to handle the growing demand more efficiently. Additionally, they explore new markets and sales channels to reach a broader audience. Ensuring compliance with local regulations in these new markets is also crucial. However, challenges arise in maintaining product quality during scaling and managing the complexities of global logistics. To overcome these challenges, strategic partnerships and collaborations can help facilitate smoother market expansion.

1.10.10. Product Lifecycle Management

Beyond the initial launch, entrepreneurs are involved in product lifecycle management, which involves several key aspects: First, they consistently monitor how the product is performing in the market. They then focus on implementing updates and improvements based on feedback from customers and advancements in technology. Additionally, they make strategic decisions regarding the product's lifecycle, such as diversifying the product range, enhancing existing products, or retiring out-dated ones. However, challenges arise in anticipating market changes and adapting accordingly. Employing data analytics can provide valuable insights to facilitate effective lifecycle management.

Embracing the phases of the New Product Development lifecycle equips entrepreneurs with a structured approach to innovation. From the spark of an idea to market saturation, the NPD process empowers entrepreneurs to navigate challenges, seize opportunities, and bring transformative products to the forefront of the market. As a dynamic and iterative framework, the NPD lifecycle serves as a guiding compass, ensuring that each phase contributes to the success and longevity of entrepreneurial ventures.

1.11. Agile and Lean Approaches in Product Development

In the fast-paced product development landscape, embracing Agile and Lean methodologies becomes imperative for entrepreneurial ventures aiming to stay responsive, adaptive, and customer-centric. This heading explores into the significance of Agile and Lean approaches in product development, elucidating how these frameworks empower entrepreneurs to navigate uncertainties and efficiently deliver innovative solutions.

1.11.1 Agile Methodology

Agile methodology is a dynamic and iterative approach to product development, emphasizing collaboration, adaptability, and customer feedback. Entrepreneurs adopting agile break down the development process into small, manageable increments called sprints. These iterative cycles allow for continuous refinement, rapid adaptation to changing requirements, and prompt delivery of valuable features.

1.11.2 Key Principles of Agile

Customer collaboration is at the heart of our development process, ensuring that our product evolves coordinated with the changing needs and expectations of our customers. Through iterative progress, we continuously refine and enhance our offerings based on feedback and the dynamic nature of the market. Our cross-functional teams work closely together, fostering a shared understanding of our goals and facilitating efficient problem-solving. Adaptability is ingrained in our approach, allowing us to embrace change fluidly. Agile teams pivot as needed, adjusting priorities and strategies in response to emerging insights and challenges, ensuring our continued success in a rapidly evolving landscape.

1.11.3 Implementation in Entrepreneurship

In entrepreneurship, implementing the Scrum framework is a widespread practice, leveraging its principles to foster agility and efficiency. Scrum breaks down development into manageable, time-boxed sprints, usually spanning two to four weeks, during which teams strive to deliver a potentially shippable product increment. Complementing this framework are daily stand-up meetings, serving as checkpoints for teams to synchronize, review progress, and address any obstacles hindering development. These daily interactions promote rapid issue resolution, maintaining the momentum crucial for entrepreneurial success.

1.12. Prototyping and Iterative Design

Prototyping and iterative design are integral to product development, allowing entrepreneurs to refine concepts, enhance functionality, and validate assumptions before full-scale production. The following discussion explores the importance of prototyping and iterative design in nurturing innovation and minimizing risks.

1.12.1. Prototyping

Prototyping involves creating scaled-down versions or models of the product to visualize design concepts and test functionality. Entrepreneurs leverage prototypes to gather user feedback, validate design decisions, and identify potential improvements. Prototyping is a tangible representation that bridges the gap between conceptualization and the final product.

1.12.2. Key Benefits of Prototyping

User feedback is integral to our development process, facilitated by early prototypes that undergo rigorous testing. These prototypes serve as valuable tools for understanding user preferences, expectations, and potential challenges, allowing us to tailor our product accordingly. Additionally, prototyping enables effective risk mitigation by identifying design flaws and functional issues early on, thereby minimizing risks and avoiding costly modifications in later stages of development. Through iterative refinement, we continuously enhance our prototypes based on feedback, ensuring that the final product closely aligns with user needs and expectations, enhancing its market viability and user satisfaction.

1.12.3. Iterative Design

Iterative design involves a cyclical process of refinement based on continuous testing, evaluation, and user feedback. Entrepreneurs iterate on design elements, features, and functionalities, gradually enhancing the product with each cycle. This iterative approach promotes continuous improvement and responsiveness to changing market dynamics.

1.12.4. Key Components of Iterative Design

User-centric principles are essential in product development, with user-centred design as a foundational approach. This methodology places paramount importance on understanding and addressing user needs and experiences throughout the design process. By prioritizing user feedback and iteratively refining designs based on user input, developers ensure that the final product resonates with its intended audience. Complementing user-centred design, usability testing is crucial in validating design decisions and uncovering potential usability issues. Through regular testing sessions with representative users, developers gain valuable insights into how users interact with the product, enabling them to make informed adjustments and improvements. Fostering cross-functional collaboration among designers, engineers, and end-users enhances the development process. By integrating diverse perspectives and expertise from different domains, teams can devise more comprehensive and innovative solutions that effectively address user needs and preferences.

This collaborative approach fosters creativity and ensures the final product meets user expectations and achieves its intended objectives.

1.12.5. Implementation in Entrepreneurship

In entrepreneurship, implementation strategies focus on agility and user-centricity, facilitated by rapid prototyping and continuous user feedback loops. Entrepreneurs harness rapid prototyping tools to swiftly create and test prototypes, accelerating the development cycle. These tools streamline the prototyping process, enabling rapid iterations and adjustments based on user feedback. Establishing efficient feedback loops with target users is paramount, ensuring that each iteration incorporates valuable insights and aligns the product closely with market needs. By embracing these strategies, entrepreneurs can iterate quickly, validate assumptions, and deliver products that resonate with their target audience, fostering innovation and competitive advantage in dynamic markets.

In the dynamic realm of entrepreneurship, Agile and Lean methodologies, coupled with prototyping and iterative design, form a potent combination. By embracing these approaches, entrepreneurs infuse agility, adaptability, and user-centricity into their product development processes, enhancing the likelihood of delivering successful and market-aligned innovations.

1.13. Validating Problem-Solution Fit

In the entrepreneurship journey, validating the problem-solution fit is a pivotal phase where entrepreneurs ensure that their innovative solutions precisely address identified market needs. The following discussion explores the systematic process of understanding the problem landscape, creating innovative solutions, and rigorously testing to validate the problem-solution fit.

1.13.1. Understanding the Problem Landscape:

Entrepreneurs begin by thoroughly understanding the problem landscape in the journey towards creating impactful solutions. This entails a multi-faceted approach that starts with defining the problem statement.

Through extensive market research, direct engagement with potential users, and a comprehensive analysis of existing solutions, entrepreneurs aim to identify the target market's pain points, challenges, and unmet needs. Moreover, entrepreneurs recognize the importance of user empathy and persona development. By stepping into end-user's shoes and creating detailed personas, they gain profound insights into their target audience's motivations, behaviours, and pain points. This empathetic approach ensures a nuanced understanding of the problem from the user's perspective, guiding solution development effectively. Additionally, competitor analysis plays a crucial role in shaping the entrepreneurial journey. By assessing existing solutions in the market, entrepreneurs gain valuable insights into competitor offerings, strengths, and weaknesses. This analysis helps identify gaps in addressing user needs and paves the way for differentiation and innovation in their solutions. Overall, a thorough understanding of the problem landscape sets the foundation for entrepreneurs to create impactful and sustainable solutions that resonate with the needs of their target market.

1.13.2. Creating Innovative Solutions:

In the pursuit of creating innovative solutions, entrepreneurs embark on a journey fuelled by creativity and problem-solving. Beginning with ideation and creative design thinking, entrepreneurs leverage their profound understanding of the problem landscape to generate many ideas to address identified challenges. Through creative design thinking sessions, they encourage out-of-the-box thinking, nurturing innovation and novel approaches tailored to meet market needs effectively. Transitioning from ideation to tangible solutions involves prototyping and iterative design. Entrepreneurs embrace prototyping to transform abstract ideas into visual representations that can be tested and refined. The iterative design process enables continuous refinement based on user feedback, ensuring the solution evolves to align closely with user expectations and needs. Moreover, the successful integration of technological elements is crucial for the feasibility and effectiveness of the proposed solution. Entrepreneurs meticulously evaluate technical aspects, including scalability, resource requirements, and technological readiness. This assessment ensures that the solution is innovative, technically viable, and capable of addressing market needs efficiently and sustainably. Creating innovative solutions involves a dynamic interaction between creative ideation, iterative design, and thoughtful technological integration, guided by a deep understanding of user needs and market dynamics. By embracing this comprehensive approach, entrepreneurs can develop solutions that drive meaningful impact and value in the ever-evolving business landscape.

1.13.3. Testing and Validating Problem-Solution Fit:

Validating the problem-solution fit is a pivotal stage in the entrepreneurial journey, requiring rigorous testing and assessment to ensure alignment between the solution and the identified problem. Entrepreneurs employ various strategies to validate this fit effectively. Firstly, user testing and feedback serve as the cornerstone of validation efforts. Entrepreneurs gather invaluable insights into its usability, functionality, and overall satisfaction by exposing the solution to a targeted user group. This iterative testing approach enables continuous refinement based on real-world user experiences, ensuring the solution resonates with its intended audience. Moreover, entrepreneurs establish Key Performance Indicators (KPIs) that are aligned with the problem-solution fit to measure success quantitatively. Metrics such as user engagement, conversion rates, and user satisfaction scores provide tangible benchmarks for evaluating the solution's effectiveness. A pilot launch in a controlled environment also facilitates market validation, allowing entrepreneurs to assess the solution's performance under real-world conditions. This phase is a crucial opportunity to validate assumptions, gather additional insights, and make final adjustments before a full-scale launch. Entrepreneurs embrace an iterative refinement approach throughout the validation process, continually iterating based on user feedback and performance metrics. This adaptive mind-set ensures that the solution remains responsive to evolving market dynamics and user needs, positioning the venture for sustained success.

To validate the problem-solution fit, entrepreneurs navigate a dynamic process that harmonizes a profound understanding of the problem landscape by creating innovative solutions. Rigorous testing, user feedback loops, and iterative refinement converge to ensure that the final solution addresses market needs and does so with precision and effectiveness. The successful validation of the problem-solution fit positions entrepreneurs for the subsequent stages of commercialization and business planning.

1.14. Commercialization Pathways

Embarking on the commercialization journey marks a critical juncture for entrepreneurs transitioning from validating their innovative solutions to bringing them to market. The following discussion outlines the strategic considerations and pathways entrepreneurs navigate during commercialization.

1.14.1. Exploring Routes to Commercialization

Entrepreneurs embark on a strategic journey to effectively bring their innovations to market by exploring routes to commercialization. This journey begins with a comprehensive evaluation of various market entry strategies tailored to suit the unique nature of their innovation and the specific characteristics of their target market. Among the array of strategies available, entrepreneurs commonly consider options such as direct sales, wherein products or services are sold directly to end-users, or utilizing distribution channels, which involve leveraging intermediaries like retailers or distributors to reach a broader audience. Additionally, entrepreneurs may explore the possibility of licensing agreements, granting other entities the rights to use or sell their innovation in exchange for royalties or fees. A crucial aspect of this exploration process involves assessing the market readiness for their innovation. This entails thoroughly analysing consumer demand, the competitive landscape, and regulatory considerations. By carefully evaluating market readiness, entrepreneurs gain valuable insights into whether the market conditions are conducive to their innovation's success. These assessments allow entrepreneurs to make informed decisions and adapt their commercialization strategies accordingly.

Furthermore, entrepreneurs recognize the dynamic nature of markets and the need for agility in their approach to commercialization. As market dynamics evolve, entrepreneurs remain flexible, adjusting their strategies in response to changing conditions. This adaptability may manifest in various forms, including flexible pricing models, shifts in distribution channels, or alterations to marketing approaches. By staying attuned to market shifts and proactively adapting their strategies, entrepreneurs ensure that their commercialization efforts remain responsive and aligned with market demands.

1.14.2. Licensing and Partnership Strategies

Entrepreneurs often explore licensing agreements as a strategic avenue for commercialization. This approach involves granting the rights to use, produce, or sells the innovation to another entity, leveraging their existing capabilities and resources. By entering into licensing agreements, entrepreneurs can expedite the route to market and tap into their partners' established networks and expertise. Collaborative partnerships are instrumental in commercialization, enabling entrepreneurs to access resources and expertise beyond their capabilities. Entrepreneurs pursue strategic alliances with various entities to enhance their commercialization efforts, including industry partners, distribution partners, and strategic investors.

Collaborating with companies operating in related industries allows entrepreneurs to leverage complementary strengths and resources. These partnerships facilitate the exchange of knowledge and resources, accelerating the commercialization process and enhancing the innovation's market potential. Forming partnerships with entities possessing established distribution networks enables entrepreneurs to reach target markets and customers effectively. By leveraging the distribution capabilities of partners, entrepreneurs can expand their market reach and streamline the distribution process. Entrepreneurs seek strategic investors who provide funding and bring industry expertise and valuable networking opportunities. Strategic investors can be pivotal in accelerating commercialization efforts and enhancing the innovation's market positioning. Strategic alliance is the key for penetrating target markets efficiently. Entrepreneurs strategically align with partners whose capabilities complement their own, enhancing the overall value proposition. These alliances may be joint ventures, co-marketing agreements, or collaborative development initiatives to maximize market impact and competitiveness.

1.14.3. Intellectual Property Considerations

As entrepreneurs progress through the commercialization phase, safeguarding intellectual property (IP) becomes a pivotal concern. This encompasses a range of measures to preserve innovative concepts and maintain a competitive edge. Initially, entrepreneurs pursue patent protection to safeguard novel inventions, preventing unauthorized usage or replication.

Concurrently, they prioritize trademark protection to establish distinct brand identities, recognition, and differentiation in the market. Furthermore, copyright measures are essential for safeguarding creative works, from software code to literary and artistic creations. Additionally, entrepreneurs uphold trade secrets, ensuring the confidentiality of proprietary processes within their organizations. Moreover, they explore avenues for IP licensing and monetization, leveraging agreements to permit others to utilize their innovations for licensing fees, thus generating revenue streams and broadening market outreach. Lastly, in instances of IP infringement, entrepreneurs may resort to litigation to strategically uphold their rights, ensuring that their innovations remain competitive in the market landscape.

By navigating the multifaceted commercialization landscape, entrepreneurs position their innovations for market success. Whether through direct sales, licensing agreements, strategic partnerships, or robust intellectual property protection, the commercialization phase is a strategic dance that demands foresight, adaptability, and a keen understanding of the market ecosystem. Successful commercialization sets the stage for sustained growth, market leadership, and the realization of the entrepreneurial vision.

1.15. Crafting a Business Vision and Leadership

As entrepreneurs transition from the ideation and commercialization phases, crafting a compelling business vision and effective leadership becomes integral to steering the venture toward sustained success. The following discussion explores the strategic aspects of defining a business vision, the various leadership styles in entrepreneurship, and the nurturing of visionary leadership within the organizational framework.

1.15.1. Defining the Business Vision

Defining the business vision serves as the foundation of the entire entrepreneurial journey. The vision acts as a guiding North Star, providing a clear and inspirational destination for the organization to strive towards. Entrepreneurs articulate a compelling vision that encapsulates the long-term aspirations, values, and impact the venture seeks to achieve, laying the groundwork for its future endeavours. A well-crafted vision is deeply rooted in the entrepreneur's and the organization's core values. It aligns with the principles that define the venture's identity and resonates with stakeholders, including team members, investors, and customers. This alignment fosters a shared sense of purpose and commitment, uniting all stakeholders behind a common goal. Moreover, a dynamic business vision acknowledges the ever-evolving nature of the business landscape. Entrepreneurs craft visions that are adaptable to changing market dynamics, technological advancements, and societal shifts. By embracing adaptability and a future-oriented mind-set, entrepreneurs can anticipate challenges and opportunities, positioning the venture for resilience and sustained growth in an increasingly competitive environment.

1.15.2. Leadership Styles in Entrepreneurship

Transformational Leadership: Entrepreneurs often adopt transformational leadership styles that inspire and motivate teams toward innovation and excellence. Entrepreneurs often embody transformational leadership styles that catalyse team innovation and excellence. Several vital attributes characterize these leadership approaches. Firstly, visionary thinking is paramount, as leaders articulate a compelling vision that energizes and aligns team members toward common goals. Empowerment is another essential element, as leaders encourage team members to take ownership and initiative, promoting a sense of autonomy and accountability. Emotional intelligence is vital in transformational leadership, as leaders understand and manage emotions to cultivate positive team dynamics and foster collaboration. Servant leadership principles are embraced, prioritizing the team's and stakeholders' needs above personal interests.

Active listening and empathy are fundamental traits as leaders engage with team members and demonstrate empathy toward their concerns and perspectives. Supporting personal growth is also prioritized, with leaders encouraging individual development and well-being. Collaboration is encouraged within the team, creating an inclusive work environment where diverse perspectives are valued. In dynamic entrepreneurial environments, adaptive leadership is essential, with leaders exhibiting flexibility in their strategies and approaches to navigate changing circumstances effectively. Entrepreneurs also exhibit a learning orientation, embracing a continuous learning mind-set and encouraging experimentation and innovation. Finally, resilience is a guarantee of transformational leadership, as leaders navigate uncertainties with determination and inspire the same resilience in their teams, driving them toward success despite challenges. Figure 1.6 illustrates the progression of team dynamics across various stages of entrepreneurship, including Ideation, Concept & Screening, Business Development, Launch Preparation, and Scaling. Each stage represents a crucial phase in the entrepreneurial journey, marked by distinct team dynamics and interactions aimed at advancing the venture toward success.

At the Ideation stage, team dynamics are characterized by creativity, brainstorming, and idea generation. Members collaborate closely to explore innovative solutions to identified problems, promoting a supportive and open-minded environment conducive to idea generation. In the Concept & Screening stage, team dynamics shift towards critically analysing and evaluating proposed ideas. Discussions focus on feasibility, market potential, and alignment with the venture's goals. Decision-making becomes more structured, with team members engaging in thorough assessments to determine the viability of concepts. In the Business Development phase, team dynamics emphasize strategic planning, networking, and resource acquisition. Collaboration extends beyond the core team to include partners, investors, and advisors. Clear roles and responsibilities are defined, and communication channels are established to facilitate effective coordination and progress tracking. As the venture progresses to the Launch Preparation stage, team dynamics become more action-oriented and goal-driven. There is a heightened sense of urgency as the team works towards finalizing product/service offerings, marketing strategies, and operational plans. Close collaboration and efficient task execution are essential to meet deadlines and ensure a successful launch.

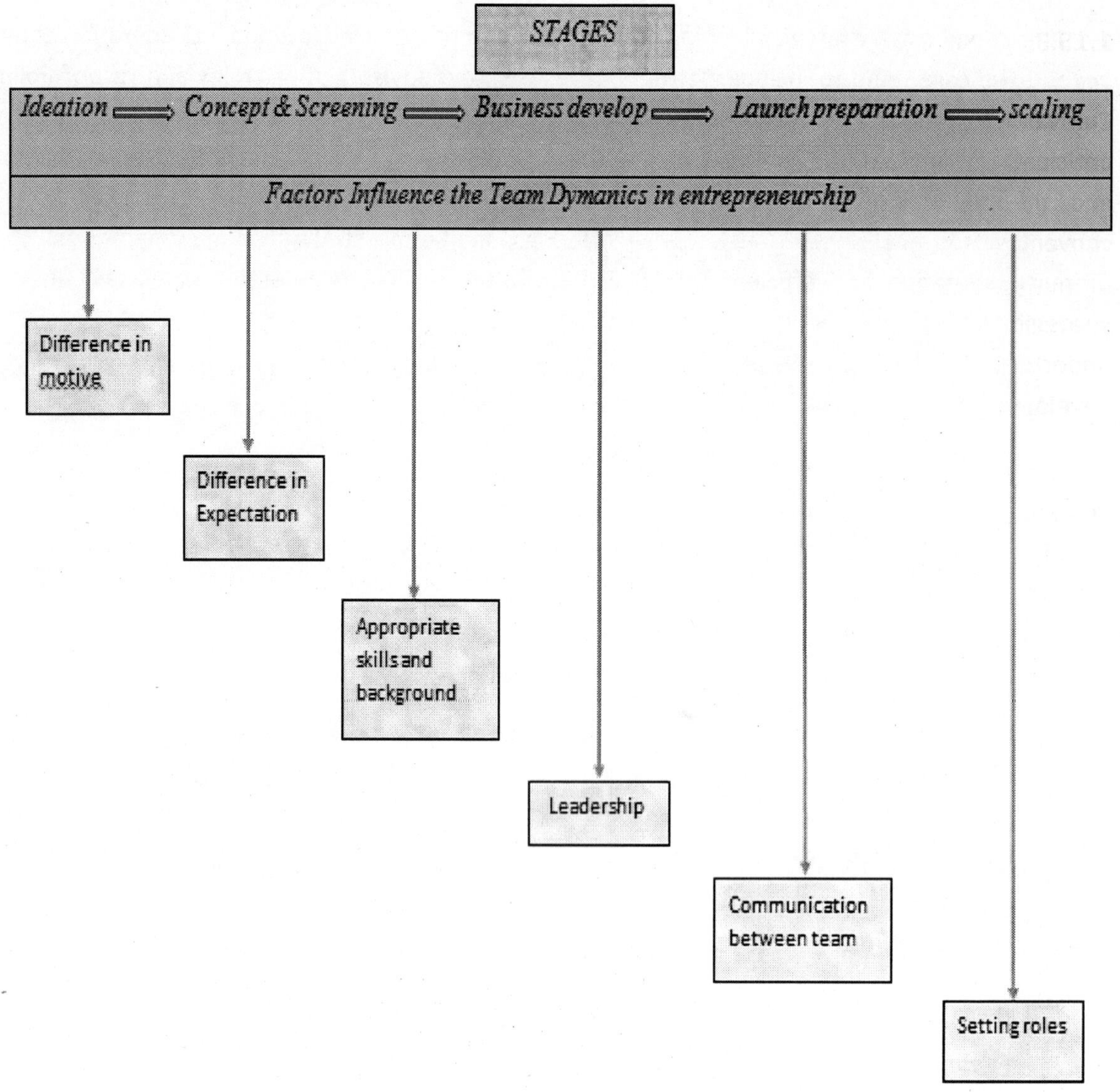

Figure 1.6 Various Stages in Team Dynamics

In the Scaling stage, team dynamics evolve to accommodate growth and expansion. The focus shifts towards scalability, efficiency, and managing increased complexity. Team members may need to adapt to new roles, processes, and challenges as the venture reaches new milestones and targets. Several factors influence team dynamics in entrepreneurship, including leadership style, team composition, communication channels, organizational culture, and external factors such as market conditions and competition. Effective leadership, clear communication, mutual trust, and a shared vision are essential for positive team dynamics and driving entrepreneurial success.

1.15.3. Nurturing Visionary Leadership

Nurturing visionary leadership is integral to the success of any entrepreneurial venture. Cultivating a visionary mind-set involves fostering creativity, forward-thinking, and the ability to anticipate future trends. Entrepreneurs create an environment that encourages ideation, curiosity, and the exploration of innovative solutions, empowering team members to think beyond conventional boundaries. Investing in leadership development programs is another essential aspect of nurturing visionary leadership. These programs focus on honing leadership skills, fostering strategic thinking, and instilling a deep commitment to the organization's vision. By providing opportunities for continuous learning and growth, entrepreneurs enable their team members to develop the capabilities needed to lead effectively and drive the realization of the business vision.

Establishing mentorship and coaching programs further enhances the development of visionary leaders within the organization. Seasoned entrepreneurs or industry experts can offer valuable guidance, insights, and feedback, nurturing the growth and development of aspiring leaders. Through mentorship and coaching, emerging leaders gain invaluable perspectives and support, accelerating their professional growth and leadership potential. Encouraging a culture of risk-taking and innovation is also crucial for nurturing visionary leadership. Entrepreneurs create environments where calculated risks are embraced as opportunities for growth, and where creativity is valued as a catalyst for achieving the business vision. By fostering a culture that encourages experimentation, entrepreneurship, and innovation, entrepreneurs empower their team members to push boundaries, explore new possibilities, and drive meaningful change within the organization. In the culmination of crafting a business vision and leadership, entrepreneurs shape not only the direction of their ventures but also the organizational culture and impact on the broader business ecosystem. A convincing vision and effective leadership propel the organization toward its goals, raise a resilient and innovative culture, and set the stage for long-term success in the entrepreneurial landscape.

1.16. Building and Managing Effective Teams - Importance of Team Composition

The success of an entrepreneurial venture hinges on the ability to build and manage effective teams. The following discussion explores into the strategic aspects of team composition, team management strategies, and the importance of collaborative decision-making in substituting a dynamic and high-performing organizational culture.

Effective team composition is paramount for entrepreneurial success, with entrepreneurs meticulously aligning the skills and expertise of team members with their respective roles within the organization. This strategic alignment ensures that each team member's strengths are leveraged to drive organizational objectives forward. Moreover, entrepreneurs recognize the transformative power of diversity within teams. By embracing diversity in perspectives, backgrounds, and experiences, teams become fertile grounds for innovation. Diverse teams bring unique insights to the table, enabling them to tackle challenges with creativity and resilience. Additionally, cohesive teams nurture a culture of collaboration and unity. Entrepreneurs prioritize building cohesive teams where members share common goals and values, adopting an environment where collaboration flourishes. Through effective team composition, entrepreneurs create dynamic and high-performing teams poised for success in today's competitive landscape.

1.16.1. Strategies for Team Management

In the effective team management, clear communication and setting expectations are foundational. Entrepreneurs ensure that team members share a mutual understanding of goals, responsibilities, and performance expectations. They establish regular communication channels to foster openness and transparency within the team. Empowering team members and granting them autonomy within their roles is another key aspect. Entrepreneurs trust their teams to make decisions and take initiative, fostering a sense of ownership and accountability among team members. This approach creates an environment where individual contributions are valued, and team members feel empowered to contribute their best work. Acknowledging and recognizing individual and team achievements are integral to team management. Entrepreneurs implement feedback mechanisms to provide constructive input, celebrate successes, and identify areas for improvement. A culture of continuous feedback promotes personal and collective growth within the team, fostering a positive and supportive work environment.

1.16.2. Collaborative Decision Making

Collaborative decision-making is integral to entrepreneurial success, driven by inclusive processes that harness the diverse perspectives of team members. Entrepreneurs understand the significance of inclusivity, recognizing that decisions are enriched when various viewpoints are considered. They raise brainstorming and ideation sessions to facilitate this, allowing team members to share insights and contribute ideas. These collaborative sessions serve as breeding grounds for innovation, often yielding creative solutions to complex challenges. Moreover, entrepreneurs prioritize consensus building, striving to reach agreement among team members through open dialogue and negotiation. Consensus-based decisions cultivate a sense of shared ownership and commitment within the team. Furthermore, entrepreneurs empower team members by delegating decision-making authority, allowing individuals to make informed decisions within their areas of expertise. This delegation not only distributes decision-making responsibility but also develops a culture of trust and empowerment within the organization. Through collaborative decision-making processes, entrepreneurs leverage the collective intelligence of their teams to drive informed and effective decision-making, positioning their ventures for success in dynamic environments.

Entrepreneurs are pivotal in building and managing effective teams to create a collaborative, dynamic, and resilient organizational culture. Strategic team composition, effective management strategies, and collaborative decision-making contribute to the venture's success by harnessing the team members' collective capabilities and potential.

Unit summary

This unit focuses on the foundational principles of entrepreneurship and its crucial role in economic development. Students will explore the entrepreneurial mind-set, motivation, and competencies, gaining insights into market dynamics and technology trends. The unit covers the entire new product development lifecycle, emphasizing commercialization strategies and product-market fit validation. Business vision, leadership, and effective team composition are highlighted, equipping students with a comprehensive understanding of entrepreneurial success factors. The unit aims to raise a comprehensive approach to entrepreneurship, preparing students to navigate the challenges of innovation, business leadership, and market dynamics in pursuing economic growth and development.

Tutorial questions for practice

Task 1: Analysing Entrepreneurial Mind-set and Competencies

Provide students with case studies or real-life examples of successful entrepreneurs. Ask students to analyse the mind-set, motivation, and competencies demonstrated by these entrepreneurs in their ventures. Encourage students to identify key traits such as risk-taking, resilience, creativity, and problem-solving skills.

Objective: Enable students to understand the importance of entrepreneurial mind-set and competencies in driving business success. Facilitate critical thinking and reflection on the qualities necessary for entrepreneurial endeavours.

Task 2: Market Pull vs. Technology Push Analysis

Divide students into groups and assign each group a scenario representing either market pull or technology push factors driving innovation. Ask students to research and analyse the implications of their assigned factor on product development and commercialization. Discuss how entrepreneurs can leverage market pull or technology push to create successful ventures.

Objective: Develop students' understanding of the factors influencing innovation and product development. Enhance their ability to recognize and respond to market opportunities and technological advancements.

Task 3: New Product Development Lifecycle Simulation

Present students with a hypothetical product development scenario and guide them through the new product development lifecycle stages, including ideation, concept development, prototyping, testing, and commercialization. Assign roles within each group to simulate each stage's decision-making process and challenges.

Objective: Provide students with hands-on experience navigating the new product development lifecycle—Foster teamwork, critical thinking, and problem-solving skills essential for entrepreneurial ventures.

Task 4: Technology Readiness Levels (TRL) Assessment

Introduce students to the Technology Readiness Levels (TRL) concept and provide examples of products at different TRL stages. Ask students to assess the TRL of a given technology or innovation and discuss its implications for commercialization. Encourage students to consider technical feasibility, scalability, and market readiness.

Objective: Deepen students' understanding of technology readiness and its significance in commercialization. Develop their ability to evaluate and strategize the adoption of emerging technologies.

Task 5: Business Vision and Leadership Analysis

Present students with case studies of successful business leaders and entrepreneurs known for visionary leadership. Facilitate group discussions on the importance of having a clear business vision and effective leadership in driving entrepreneurial ventures forward. Encourage students to identify key leadership traits and strategies for inspiring and motivating teams.

Objective: Enable students to recognize the role of vision and leadership in entrepreneurial success. Cultivate their leadership skills and inspire them to develop their visionary business approach.

Task 6: Team Composition and Management Exercise

Task students with forming teams and assigning roles based on their strengths and expertise. Please provide them with a hypothetical business scenario and ask each team to develop a plan for team composition and management, including strategies for encouraging collaboration, communication, and conflict resolution.

Objective: Empower students to understand the importance of effective team composition and management in entrepreneurial ventures. Enhance their teamwork and leadership abilities through practical application and problem-solving.

Review Questions

1. Define entrepreneurship and its role in economic development.
2. Identify two elements of an entrepreneurial mind-set.
3. Analyse the impact of market pull and technology push factors on entrepreneurial decision-making.
4. Discuss the stages of the new product development lifecycle.
5. Evaluate the significance of technology readiness levels in developing new products.
6. Develop a hypothetical strategy for validating product-market fit, considering market dynamics.
7. Define technology readiness levels and their relevance in entrepreneurship.
8. List two competencies essential for entrepreneurial success.
9. Compare and contrast market pull and technology push factors, providing examples of each.
10. Discuss the commercialization pathways available for entrepreneurial ventures.
11. Formulate a business vision statement for a fictional entrepreneurial venture.
12. Evaluate the role of team composition and management in entrepreneurial success.
13. Define product-market fit.
14. Identify one leadership trait crucial for entrepreneurial success.
15. Explain the concept of business vision and its importance in entrepreneurship.
16. Discuss the characteristics of effective team composition in entrepreneurial ventures.
17. Analyse the relationship between energy and momentum in semiconductor physics.
18. Develop a comprehensive strategy for assessing and enhancing the mobility of carriers in semiconductors.
19. Define the term "entrepreneurial motivation."
20. Identify one factor influencing the success of a product in the market.
21. Discuss the characteristics of a successful entrepreneurial mind-set.
22. Analyse the application of E-K diagrams in semiconductor physics.
23. Formulate a hypothetical scenario highlighting the need for an entrepreneurial mind-set in a specific industry.
24. Evaluate the design considerations for resistors in semiconductor applications.

Multiple Choice Questions (MCQs)

1. Entrepreneurship plays a significant role in economic development by:
    a) Increasing unemployment rates
    b) Decreasing innovation and creativity
    c) Stimulating job creation and economic growth
    d) Slowing down technological advancements

    Answer: c) Stimulating job creation and economic growth

2. The entrepreneurial mind-set is characterized by the following:
    a) Avoiding risks and challenges
    b) Resisting change and innovation
    c) Embracing risks and seeking opportunities
    d) Preferring stability overgrowth

    Answer: c) Embracing risks and seeking opportunities

3. Market pull factors in entrepreneurship refer to:
    e) External forces that drive innovation based on market demands
    f) Internal motivations and personal aspirations of entrepreneurs
    g) Government regulations restricting business activities
    h) Technological advancements influencing product development

    Answer: a) External forces that drive innovation based on market demands

4. The new product development lifecycle typically consists of the following stages:
    i) Ideation, prototyping, testing, and commercialization
    j) Market research, funding, and expansion
    k) Recruitment, training, and management
    l) Branding, marketing, and sales

    Answer: a) Ideation, prototyping, testing, and commercialization

5. Technology Readiness Levels (TRL) assess:
    m) The financial stability of a company
    n) The feasibility of a product idea
    o) The market demand for an innovative technology
    p) The scalability and market readiness of a technology

    Answer: d) The scalability and market readiness of a technology

Fill in the blanks:

1. Entrepreneurial __________ involves identifying and exploiting opportunities to create value and drive economic growth.
   Answer: Mind-set
2. __________ factors drive innovation by responding to market demands and consumer needs.
   Answer: Market pull
3. The __________ outlines the stages a new product goes through from concept to market launch.
   Answer: new product development lifecycle
4. Technology Readiness Levels (TRL) assess the __________ of a technology for commercialization.
   Answer: readiness
5. Effective leadership is essential for providing a clear __________ and guiding teams towards achieving business goals.
   Answer: Vision

References for Suggested Reading

1. Aulet, Bill. "Technology Entrepreneurship," 4th ed., Tata McGraw Hill, 2014.
2. Drucker, Peter F. "Innovation and Entrepreneurship," 1st ed., Harper Business, 2006.

UNIT 2 Product Innovation

UNIT SPECIFICS

This unit explores into the intricacies of product innovation, encompassing various stages of the development process. Key aspects covered include:

1. **Opportunity Scanning and Need Identification**
    - Techniques for identifying opportunities in the market.
    - Conducting market surveys to understand consumer needs and define problems that innovative products can address.
2. **Creative Design Thinking for Concept Generation**
    - Introduction to creative design thinking methodologies.
    - Techniques for generating innovative concepts and ideas for new products.
3. **Detailed Design, Prototyping, and Functionality Assessment**
    - In-depth exploration of detailed product design.
    - Prototyping methods and tools for testing and validating product functionality.
4. **Bill of Materials, Components Supply Chain, and Manufacturing Plan**
    - Understanding the creation of a Bill of Materials (BOM).
    - Supply chain considerations and the development of a manufacturing and assembly plant.
5. **Product Testing, Quality Assurance, and Intellectual Property Rights**
    - Strategies for rigorous product testing and quality assurance.
    - Overview of intellectual property rights management, protecting innovations and designs.

RATIONALE

This unit is designed to give students a comprehensive understanding of product innovation and development. By guiding students through opportunity identification, creative design thinking, and detailed design, the unit care for the skills necessary for successful product conceptualization. Emphasis is placed on the practical aspects of manufacturing, including supply chain considerations, testing, and quality assurance. Intellectual property rights management is integrated to ensure students grasp the importance of protecting innovative ideas in the competitive business landscape.

PRE-REQUISITES

A basic understanding of fundamental design principles and business concepts is preferred.

UNIT OUTCOMES

Upon completion of this unit, students should be able to:

U2-O1: Conduct effective opportunity scanning and market surveys to identify potential areas for product innovation.

U2-O2: Apply creative design thinking methodologies to generate innovative concepts for new products.

U2-O3: Develop detailed product designs, create prototypes, and assess functionality.

U2-O4: Formulate a Bill of Materials (BOM) and devise a comprehensive supply chain plan for manufacturing.

U2-O5: Implement product testing and quality assurance measures while understanding the importance of intellectual property rights management in the context of product innovation.

Unit-2 Outcomes	Expected Mapping with Programme Outcomes *(1- Weak Correlation; 2- Medium correlation; 3- Strong Correlation)*				
	CO-1	CO -2	CO -3	CO -4	CO -5
U2-O1	3	2	2	2	1
U2-O2	3	1	3	1	2
U2-O3	3	2	2	1	2
U2-O4	3	3	3	2	1
U2-O5	3	3	2	1	1

Product Innovation is a crucible where the sparks of creativity and ingenuity transform into tangible solutions that meet market needs. This unit propels aspiring entrepreneurs into the heart of the innovation process, guiding them through the intricacies of identifying opportunities, unleashing creative design thinking, and navigating the journey from conceptualization to market-ready products.

2.1. Opportunity Scanning and Market Survey

Identifying and seizing opportunities is the cornerstone of entrepreneurial success in the dynamic product innovation landscape. The following discussion illuminates the strategic process of opportunity scanning and market surveys, guiding aspiring entrepreneurs through the different terrain of understanding market needs and identifying unmet demands.

2.1.1 Introduction to Opportunity Scanning

Opportunity scanning forms the bedrock of entrepreneurial strategy, constituting a systematic approach to navigating the business landscape and identifying fertile grounds for innovation. Entrepreneurs engage in a proactive and continuous quest to identify emerging trends, identify gaps, and pinpoint potential areas ripe for exploration. This process is driven by a keen understanding of market dynamics, consumer behaviours, and industry trends, enabling entrepreneurs to detect nascent opportunities or areas where existing solutions falter. Competitive analysis is crucial, providing insights into competitors' strengths and weaknesses, thereby informing differentiation strategies.

Market surveys are pivotal in gathering valuable data from potential customers or target audiences, unveiling preferences, pain points, and expectations. Entrepreneurs meticulously design surveys, tailoring methodologies to align with research objectives and target demographics. The selection of target respondents is paramount, ensuring that the survey captures insights relevant to the innovation goals. Upon collecting survey data, entrepreneurs leverage robust analysis techniques to extract meaningful patterns and insights, facilitating informed decision-making. Integration with the innovation process is seamless, with opportunity scanning and market surveys guiding entrepreneurs in crafting solutions that directly address identified market needs and preferences. This iterative approach acknowledges the dynamic nature of markets, prompting entrepreneurs to revisit and refine their understanding of market dynamics regularly. By proactively scanning for opportunities and conducting thorough market surveys, entrepreneurs mitigate risks associated with product development. Informed decision-making, underpinned by comprehensive insights, enhances the likelihood of successful product launches and market acceptance.

2.1.2 Techniques for Market Survey

Conducting effective market surveys requires a thoughtful approach and applying various techniques to gather valuable insights. The following discussion explores into the essential techniques entrepreneurs can employ to design and execute impactful market surveys that provide different perspectives on consumer preferences, market trends, and potential areas for innovation.

2.1.2.1. Online surveys

Online surveys utilize digital platforms to administer questionnaires and collect responses from a targeted audience, offering convenience, cost-effectiveness, and real-time data collection. The advantages of online surveys are manifold: they possess a wide reach, transcending geographical constraints to engage a large and diverse audience. Moreover, their digital nature reduces printing and distribution costs associated with traditional methods, ensuring cost efficiency. Additionally, instantaneous data collection enables prompt analysis and decision-making, facilitating agile responses to emerging trends or insights. During the implementation of online survey techniques, several suggestions can enhance effectiveness. Firstly, designing user-friendly, mobile-responsive surveys enhances accessibility and encourages participation across various devices. Secondly, leveraging survey platforms with robust analytics capabilities streamlines data analysis, enabling actionable insights to be gleaned efficiently. Lastly, offering incentives such as discounts or giveaways can further incentivize participation, increasing response rates and enriching the quality of collected data.

2.1.2.2. In-Person Interviews:

In-person interviews are characterized by direct, face-to-face interactions between interviewers and respondents, offering a more intimate and personal approach to gathering information. This method goes beyond mere question-and-answer sessions, allowing interviewers to establish rapport, build trust, and delve deeper into responses. The face-to-face nature of these interviews enables interviewers to observe non-verbal cues such as body language, facial expressions, and tone of voice, providing valuable insights into respondents' attitudes, emotions, and level of engagement. This individualized touch promotes a more comfortable and open environment, facilitating candid and nuanced responses that may not be easily elicited through other forms of communication.

The advantages of in-person interviews include the generation of rich insights, as personal interactions often yield more detailed and nuanced responses, offering valuable qualitative data. Additionally, interviewers can seek immediate clarifications or additional information on the spot, enhancing data accuracy. During the implementation of this technique, several suggestions should be considered to optimize its effectiveness. First, interviewers should be trained to maintain neutral behavior and avoid influencing respondents, ensuring the authenticity of responses. Second, standardizing interview protocols can help ensure consistency across interactions, maintaining the quality and reliability of the data collected. Finally, pilot-testing questions before widespread implementation can refine the interview process, addressing any potential issues and ensuring the effectiveness of the approach.

2.1.2.3. Focus Groups:

Focus groups convene small, diverse groups of individuals guided by a moderator through structured discussions, encouraging interaction and dynamic exchanges among participants. This method supports the in-depth exploration of opinions, attitudes, and perceptions on a particular topic or product. By bringing together individuals with varied backgrounds and perspectives, focus groups offer a rich source of qualitative data, unveiling insights that may not emerge in individual interviews or surveys. The role of the moderator is pivotal in steering the conversation, encouraging participation from all members, and ensuring that key topics are thoroughly explored. Through collaborative dialogue and constructive group interaction, focus groups facilitate a deeper understanding of complex issues and provide valuable input for decision-making and strategy development.

The advantages of focus groups include the revelation of group dynamics, where interactions among participants can uncover shared perspectives, disagreements, or consensus, and the provision of qualitative depth, offering insights into attitudes, perceptions, and emotions. To implement focus groups effectively, several suggestions should be considered. Carefully selecting participants ensures diversity and representation, framing open-ended questions encourages discussion and exploration of diverse viewpoints, fostering a more comprehensive understanding of the topic. Finally, effective moderation is essential, balancing participation and maintaining group dynamics to ensure a productive and insightful session.

2.1.2.4. Telephone Surveys:

Telephone surveys entail contacting respondents via phone to collect data and insights, maintaining relevance despite the prevalence of digital communication channels. This method is particularly effective for specific demographics and regions where internet access may be limited, or individuals prefer voice communication. Conducting surveys over the phone allows researchers to directly engage with respondents, posing questions and recording responses in real-time. While it may pose challenges in reaching a broad audience and eliciting detailed responses compared to online surveys, telephone surveys offer significant advantages. Researchers can clarify questions, address concerns immediately, and maintain a distinctive touch in data collection efforts. Moreover, for segments of the population less inclined toward digital communication, such as older demographics, telephone surveys provide an accessible means of participation, ensuring broader inclusivity in research endeavours.

The advantages of telephone surveys include personalized interaction, as they offer a direct line of communication, creating a more engaging experience for respondents. Additionally, immediate responses allow for on-the-spot clarifications and adjustments to survey questions, enhancing the accuracy and relevance of the collected data. To implement telephone surveys effectively, several suggestions should be considered. Researchers must comply with regulations regarding unsolicited calls and ensure adherence to privacy guidelines to maintain ethical standards. Keeping surveys concise respects respondents' time and encourages participation, increasing response rates. Utilizing random sampling techniques helps maintain survey objectivity, ensuring that the data collected is representative of the target population.

Selecting the appropriate survey techniques depends on the nature of the research objectives, the target audience, and the available resources. Entrepreneurs may combine these techniques to triangulate data and gain a comprehensive understanding of market dynamics, laying the groundwork for informed product innovation strategies.

2.1.3 Identifying Unmet Needs and Problem Definition

Successful product innovation involves pinpointing unmet market needs and defining problems that resonate with potential consumers. Entrepreneurs thoroughly explore the market, actively searching for gaps, inefficiencies, or challenges that current products or services may not adequately address. This process involves identifying unmet needs, manifesting as unfulfilled desires, unresolved problems, or areas where existing solutions fall short of consumer expectations. In-depth observational research is integral to uncovering these unmet needs. Entrepreneurs immerse themselves in real-world scenarios, keenly observing consumer behaviours, preferences, and pain points. This hands-on approach allows them to discern subtle shades that might be overlooked in traditional survey methods. Furthermore, entrepreneurs prioritize creating feedback loops through direct customer engagement to comprehend the dynamic landscape of consumer needs. By establishing avenues for continuous dialogue via customer support channels, social media platforms, or interactive events, they facilitate on-going interactions with customers, enabling the gathering of valuable insights. This direct engagement ensures that entrepreneurs remain closely attuned to evolving consumer preferences and expectations, facilitating the development of solutions that truly resonate with their target audience.

In the quest to develop effective solutions, entrepreneurs prioritize précised problem definition once unmet needs are identified. This entails articulating the challenges, obstacles, or deficiencies that hinder consumers from achieving their desired outcomes. A well-defined problem serves as the cornerstone for crafting targeted and impactful solutions. Central to the problem definition process is a user-centric approach, which aligns with the experiences and perspectives of the target audience. Entrepreneurs immerse themselves in the user's world, empathizing with their struggles and challenges. By understanding the user's perspective, entrepreneurs can articulate problems in a manner that truly resonates with the end user, ensuring that solutions address genuine pain points. Moreover, problem definition is an iterative process that evolves through continuous feedback and refinement. Entrepreneurs actively engage in dialogue with users, incorporating their insights and perspectives to enhance the accuracy and relevance of the defined problem. This iterative approach ensures that the problem statement remains closely aligned with user realities, leading to the development of solutions that meet genuine needs effectively.

Identifying unmet needs and defining problems act as a bridge between market insights and innovative solutions. Entrepreneurs leverage this understanding to ideate and design products that directly address the identified problems, providing meaningful value to consumers. During the prototyping phase, entrepreneurs validate their problem definition through prototyping. This stage is a crucial checkpoint where entrepreneurs assess how well their prototypes align with the defined problems. By scrutinizing the prototypes about the identified challenges, entrepreneurs ensure that their solutions remain focused on resolving the specific issues identified in the market. Through this validation process, entrepreneurs can refine their prototypes to address the targeted problems better, enhancing the effectiveness of their solutions. Furthermore, market fit validation is the ultimate validation of the alignment between problem definition and product innovation. Entrepreneurs gauge the degree to which their solutions resonate with the target audience, assessing how well the product addresses the identified unmet needs. By closely monitoring market reception and feedback, entrepreneurs can determine whether their solutions effectively solve the defined problems and meet the expectations of their intended users. This validation process is essential for ensuring that the developed products or services are well-aligned with market demands and capable of delivering meaningful value to customers.

Entrepreneurs compose the work of product innovation in the elaboration between identifying unmet needs and defining problems. This process requires a keen understanding of market dynamics, commitment to empathy, continuous refinement, and a user-centric approach. By precisely defining the problems they aim to solve, entrepreneurs lay the groundwork for transformative solutions that meet the authentic needs of their target audience.

2.2. Creative Design Thinking for Concept Generation

In product innovation, creative design thinking emerges as the catalyst that transforms ideas into tangible and innovative solutions. Problem definition involves identifying and understanding the needs, challenges, and opportunities in the market or within a specific domain. This process often entails market research, customer feedback, and analysis of existing solutions to pinpoint gaps or areas for improvement. By clearly defining the problem, entrepreneurs can focus their efforts on developing solutions that effectively address customer pain points or fulfil unmet needs.

Once the problem is defined, concept generation methodologies come into play to generate innovative ideas and potential solutions. Brainstorming sessions, where team members generate a wide array of ideas through collaborative discussions, are a common approach *(also discussed in the section 1.16.2)*. Creative design thinking, which applies design principles to foster innovation, can also stimulate idea generation. Additionally, techniques like market trend analysis help entrepreneurs identify emerging trends and opportunities that can inspire new concepts. Throughout these processes, it is crucial to use structured methodologies like mind mapping and SWOT analysis to refine ideas and ensure alignment with market demands. Problem definition and concept generation lay the groundwork for the subsequent phases of product development, guiding entrepreneurs in creating solutions that resonate with their target audience and address market needs effectively.

The following discussion explores the fundamentals of design thinking, providing aspiring entrepreneurs with a structured approach to concept generation beyond traditional problem-solving methods.

2.2.1 Fundamentals of Design Thinking

Design thinking is a problem-solving approach that revolves around human-centred design principles, emphasizing empathy for end-users. Unlike traditional methods, it promotes a holistic understanding of challenges and encourages the exploration of innovative solutions through iterative processes. Empathy is at the core of design thinking, serving as its foundational element. Entrepreneurs prioritize understanding and resonating with the experiences, needs, and emotions of end-users. By immersing themselves in the user's perspective, they develop genuine connections that inform every aspect of the design process. This empathetic approach ensures solutions are effectively tailored to address real user needs.

Design thinking embraces an iterative and non-linear process, acknowledging that problem-solving rarely follows a linear path. Entrepreneurs are encouraged to iterate experiment, seek feedback, and refine their solutions continuously. This iterative nature allows for flexibility, adaptability, and the incorporation of new insights, leading to continuous improvement and innovation in the design process. Design thinking encompasses several vital stages that guide entrepreneurs through creating innovative solutions that resonate with end-users. Firstly, the Empathize stage involves conducting thorough User Research to gain insights into the target audience's needs, preferences, and challenges. This may include engaging in User Interviews to gather personal stories and emotions that provide a more profound understanding. Next, in the Define stage, entrepreneurs articulate the problem based on the insights gained from empathetic understanding. This involves creating User Personas, detailed representations of different user segments, to focus on specific needs effectively. The Ideate stage encourages Divergent Thinking, developing a wide range of creative ideas without judgment. Brainstorming Sessions with diverse teams further generate innovative concepts.

In the Prototype stage, entrepreneurs create Visual Prototypes such as sketches or mock-ups to provide tangible representations of ideas. These prototypes are then tested with end-users in the User Testing stage to gather feedback and identify areas for improvement. Entrepreneurs engage in Iterative Testing during the Test stage, continuously refining and iterating based on feedback. This involves integrating User Insights into the design process to inform further iterations. Throughout the process, Design Thinking emphasizes Human-Centred Ideation, ensuring solutions resonate with end-users' context, emotions, and aspirations. Cross-disciplinary collaboration enriches the ideation process by bringing together individuals with diverse skills and perspectives. Finally, a continuous learning mind-set is fundamental to design thinking, encouraging entrepreneurs to approach challenges with curiosity and embrace failures as opportunities for growth. This iterative and adaptive mind-set enables entrepreneurs to navigate uncertainties and refine solutions over time. By embracing the fundamentals of design thinking, entrepreneurs lay the groundwork for a dynamic and user-centric approach to concept generation. This methodological shift from problem-solving to human-centred ideation equips innovators with the tools to generate solutions that meet market needs and resonate deeply with the individuals they aim to serve.

2.2.2 Ideation and Conceptualization

Ideation and conceptualization are pivotal stages within the creative design thinking process, where the seeds of innovative solutions are sown and nurtured. The following discussion explores the techniques and principles that drive effective ideation and guide the conceptualization of ideas into tangible, market-ready concepts.

2.2.2.1 Techniques for Ideation

In the realm of ideation, entrepreneurs employ various techniques to support creativity and explore innovative solutions. Brainstorming sessions are a cornerstone, encouraging participants to unleash their creativity without inhibition. The emphasis lies on generating many ideas, creating a free flow of creative thinking. By inviting individuals from diverse backgrounds and expertise, brainstorming sessions harness the power of diverse perspectives, preventing groupthink and enriching the pool of ideas. Mind mapping offers a structured yet visually stimulating approach to ideation. Participants visually organize ideas around a central theme, exploring interconnected concepts and uncovering hidden relationships. This structured framework facilitates a more organized exploration of ideas, allowing participants to explore potential solutions deeper.

The SCAMPER technique, an acronym for Seven Idea Transformation Actions, prompts participants to explore ideas through a series of transformative actions. By encouraging individuals to Substitute, Combine, Adapt, Modify, put to another use, Eliminate, and Reverse ideas, this technique challenges the status quo and stimulates creative thinking. Role-storming introduces a unique approach to ideation by encouraging participants to adopt different personas or roles. Viewing challenges from diverse perspectives, participants engage in unconventional thinking, breaking away from their usual mind-set. This technique explores ideas outside traditional boundaries, promoting innovation and novel solutions.

2.2.2.2 Principles of Conceptualization

Conceptualization in entrepreneurial endeavours adheres to several guiding principles that ensure the development of viable and user-centric solutions. At its core, conceptualization maintains a user-centric focus, emphasizing an empathetic understanding of end-users. Entrepreneurs immerse themselves in the user's world, envisioning solutions that address their needs, preferences, and pain points. Moreover, feasibility assessment is integral to the conceptualization process. Entrepreneurs balance innovation with feasibility by evaluating technical viability, resource requirements, and alignment with organizational goals. This ensures that innovative concepts are creative but also realistic and implementable. Prototyping and visualization play a crucial role in conceptualization, enabling entrepreneurs to translate abstract concepts into tangible representations. Entrepreneurs understand how the idea will manifest by creating prototypes or visual depictions, facilitating further refinement and effective communication.

Iterative refinement characterizes the conceptualization process, driven by a continuous feedback loop. Entrepreneurs refine their concepts based on insights gathered from prototypes, user testing, and feedback loops, ensuring that the final product closely aligns with user needs and expectations. Scalability considerations are also vital during conceptualization. Entrepreneurs assess how the idea can evolve and scale as the product or solution gains traction, ensuring long-term viability and growth potential. Lastly, conceptualization seamlessly integrates with the broader design thinking process. User insights obtained during empathetic understanding inform ideation, and resulting concepts are tested and refined to ensure alignment with user needs. This seamless flow ensures conceptualization remains grounded in user-centric principles throughout the design and development journey.

Entrepreneurs embark on a journey of creative exploration, innovation, and refinement in the dynamic relationship between ideation and conceptualization. By adopting diverse ideation techniques and principles of adequate conceptualization, aspiring entrepreneurs cultivate a rich soil where ground-breaking ideas flourish, paving the way for transformative products that resonate with end-users.

2.2.3 Integrating User-Centred Design

Integrating user-centred design (UCD) is a fundamental aspect of the creative design thinking process, ensuring that products and solutions are innovative and profoundly resonate with the end-users. The following discussion explores the principles and methodologies for seamlessly integrating UCD into the ideation and conceptualization phases.

2.2.3.1 Principles of User-Centred Design:

User-centred Design (UCD) operates on several foundational principles that prioritize users' needs, preferences, and experiences throughout the design process. Firstly, UCD begins with an empathetic understanding rooted in in-depth user research. Entrepreneurs employ various methods such as interviews, surveys, and observational studies to gain comprehensive insights into user behaviours, needs, and pain points. Additionally, creating detailed user personas based on research findings helps personalize the design process, guiding decision-making by aligning solutions with specific user characteristics. Moreover, UCD operates on an iterative design process characterized by continuous feedback loops. This iterative approach allows for refinement and improvement based on real-world insights. Prototyping and testing play a crucial role in this process, as entrepreneurs create prototypes to visualize concepts and test them with real users, gaining invaluable insights for further refinement. User involvement is another fundamental aspect of UCD, with users actively participating in decision-making. Their input is sought not only during testing but also in the ideation and conceptualization phases. Collaborative decision-making and co-creation workshops facilitate this participatory approach, developing a sense of ownership among users and ensuring that the final product meets their needs effectively.

Furthermore, UCD emphasizes accessibility and inclusivity, recognizing the importance of designing for diverse user groups. Entrepreneurs consider factors such as age, gender, abilities, and cultural backgrounds to create inclusive designs that cater to a broad spectrum of users. Adhering to accessibility standards further ensures that products are usable by individuals with diverse abilities, enhancing the reach and impact of the designed solutions.

2.2.3.2 Methodologies for Integrating UCD:

User-centred Design (UCD) methodologies are pivotal in integrating user-centric principles into the design process, ensuring that solutions effectively meet user needs and preferences. Initially, user journey mapping visually represents the entire user experience, from initial engagement to post-interaction phases. This methodology helps entrepreneurs identify touch points, pain points, and opportunities for improvement, enabling them to design more intuitive and user-friendly experiences. Usability testing offers a hands-on approach to understanding user interactions by observing users interact with prototypes or the product. This real-world analysis provides invaluable insights into how users navigate, understand, and engage with the design, guiding iterative refinement based on user feedback. Contextual inquiry involves studying users in their natural environments, allowing entrepreneurs to gain a deeper understanding of the contextual factors that influence their behaviours and preferences. By observing users in real-life situations, entrepreneurs can better tailor solutions to meet their specific needs and challenges. Persona-based design centres around creating solutions tailored to specific user personas, ensuring that design decisions align with the characteristics and needs of representative user groups. This approach helps entrepreneurs prioritize features and functionalities that resonate with their target audience, enhancing overall user satisfaction.

Additionally, responsive design addresses the need for solutions to adapt seamlessly to different platforms and screen sizes. With the proliferation of devices, entrepreneurs prioritize a consistent and user-friendly experience across various platforms, ensuring accessibility and usability for all users. Integrating user-centred design into the ideation and conceptualization phases represents a commitment to creating solutions that meet user needs, delight, and engage. By infusing the design process with empathetic understanding, iterative refinement, and direct user involvement, entrepreneurs support a culture of user-centric innovation that sets the stage for developing transformative products.

2.3. Detailed Design and Prototyping

The transition from concept to detailed design is a critical phase in the product innovation journey, where ideas take on tangible form through meticulous planning and prototyping. The following discussion explores the processes of moving from conceptualization to detailed design, laying the foundation for robust prototypes. Concurrent engineering, an approach emphasizing collaboration and simultaneous activities among different departments and disciplines involved in the design and manufacturing process plays a pivotal role in this phase. Unlike traditional sequential methods, concurrent engineering promotes parallelism, allowing multiple stages of product development to occur concurrently rather than one after the other. This approach aims to streamline the product development cycle, reduce time-to-market, and improve overall product quality by identifying and addressing potential issues early in the process. By encouraging cross-functional teamwork and communication, concurrent engineering facilitates faster decision-making, enhances innovation, and promotes a more efficient use of resources throughout the product lifecycle.

2.3.1 Transition from Concept to Detailed Design

Transitioning from concept to detailed design is a crucial phase in the product development journey, marked by several key considerations and approaches. At the outset, detailed design involves the in-depth specification of the product, where entrepreneurs meticulously define every component, feature, and interaction. This phase entails a deep dive into technical aspects, addressing materials, dimensions, manufacturing processes, and technological integrations. Iterative refinement is inherent to the detailed design process, with entrepreneurs integrating feedback from earlier stages. This feedback loop, which includes insights from user testing, prototyping, and continuous evaluation, ensures that the final design aligns seamlessly with user expectations and experiences. Collaboration is paramount during detailed design; with cross-functional teams working together to ensure the comprehensiveness of the design. Effective communication of design intent is essential, achieved through visual aids, technical documentation, and interactive tools. Comprehensive technical documentation serves as a blueprint for product development, encompassing specifications for each element and articulating the rationale behind design decisions. Prototyping is integrated into the detailed design phase, serving as a validation tool to test the envisioned product's functionality, usability, and manufacturability.

Risk mitigation and optimization are also prioritized during detailed design, with entrepreneurs proactively identifying potential risks and optimizing the design for efficiency. This includes addressing issues related to manufacturability, technical feasibility, and scalability while exploring opportunities to enhance performance and reduce production costs. The transition from concept to detailed design is a strategic bridge that transforms visionary ideas into a concrete roadmap for product development. With a meticulous focus on specifications, collaboration, technical documentation, and prototyping, entrepreneurs navigate this critical phase with precision and agility. The result is a detailed design reflecting the initial concept's creative essence and a robust foundation for the subsequent stages of product innovation.

2.3.2 Prototyping Techniques and Tools

Prototyping is a crucial stage in product development, allowing entrepreneurs to test and refine their designs before moving into production. Various techniques and tools facilitate prototyping, each offering unique advantages and capabilities. One of the noticeable techniques is 3D printing, utilized for rapid prototyping. This method enables the creation of physical prototypes layer by layer, making it invaluable for visualizing complex designs and testing form and fit. Entrepreneurs can quickly iterate and modify designs based on feedback from 3D-printed prototypes, facilitating an agile design process. Another technique is CNC (Computer Numerical Control) machining, which produces high-precision prototypes by subtracting material from a solid block. This method is ideal for creating functional prototypes with accurate dimensions and supports a wide range of materials, allowing entrepreneurs to prototype components that closely mimic the properties of the final product. Injection moulding prototypes offer another valuable approach, mimicking mass production to create prototypes that closely resemble the final product's material properties and manufacturing process. This technique is particularly suitable for producing high-fidelity prototypes when materials and structural integrity are critical considerations. Paper prototyping is a low-cost method involving hand-drawn or printed representations of user interfaces and product structures. This approach is excellent for testing basic concepts and user interactions, allowing entrepreneurs to gather early feedback on design layouts and usability before investing in more advanced prototyping methods. Wire framing and mock-ups focus on the visual representation of user interfaces and product layouts. These static representations help entrepreneurs refine design aesthetics and user interactions, enabling quick iteration and stakeholder feedback before moving to more dynamic prototypes. By leveraging these various prototyping techniques, entrepreneurs can effectively develop and refine their products, ensuring they meet user needs and market demands.

Further, prototyping tools are essential for creating and refining designs before moving into production, offering various features to cater to various aspects of the design process. Each tool brings unique capabilities, enhancing the efficiency and effectiveness of prototyping efforts. Figma is a web-based design tool that facilitates collaborative prototyping. It allows teams to work simultaneously on the same project, creating interactive prototypes with transitions and animations. This collaborative environment offers a realistic preview of the final user experience, making it a valuable tool for team-based projects. Sketch is another popular tool, known for its simplicity and efficiency in creating detailed interface designs and interactive prototypes. As a vector-based design tool, it offers precision and scalability. Its extensive plugin ecosystem further enhances its capabilities, allowing entrepreneurs to extend functionality for specific prototyping needs. InVision provides robust features for creating interactive and animated prototypes. It supports collaboration through feedback and iteration features, enabling teams to refine their designs based on collective input. 'InVision' also includes user testing capabilities, allowing entrepreneurs to gather insights into user interactions and preferences, making it a comprehensive tool for both design and testing. Proto.io specializes in mobile app prototyping, offering interactive features specific to mobile design. It allows entrepreneurs to simulate app interactions and user flows, providing a realistic experience of how the app will function. Its real-time collaboration features enhance team communication and streamline the prototyping process, making it ideal for mobile-focused projects. Axure RP is a comprehensive prototyping tool suitable for complex projects with intricate user interactions. It supports the creation of dynamic and data-driven prototypes, including features such as conditional logic. This allows entrepreneurs to simulate dynamic user experiences based on various scenarios, making it an excellent choice for projects that require high fidelity and detailed interaction simulations.

The selection of prototyping techniques and tools depends on factors such as the nature of the product, project timelines, and the level of fidelity required for testing. By leveraging these tools, entrepreneurs can navigate the prototyping phase with versatility and precision, ensuring their designs are thoroughly validated before moving into full-scale production. This strategic approach helps mitigate risks, optimize resources, and align product development with user needs and market demands.

2.3.3 Iterative Design and Feedback

Iterative design and feedback form the dynamic core of the prototyping phase, providing a structured approach for refining and enhancing the detailed design based on real-world insights. The following discussion explores the principles and methodologies behind iterative design, emphasizing the significance of continuous feedback loops.

2.3.3.1 Principles of Iterative Design

Iterative design embodies a dynamic and continuous refinement process where entrepreneurs prioritize gradual enhancements to their designs. This iterative approach acknowledges that each of the iteration presents an opportunity for improvement, supporting a mind-set of continuous evolution. By implementing changes incrementally, entrepreneurs minimize the risk of disruptive alterations, ensuring that modifications are thoroughly validated before integration. The user's perspective is central to the iterative design, with entrepreneurs actively seeking feedback at every process stage. User insights are seamlessly integrated into subsequent iterations, driving adjustments that resonate with user experiences and preferences. This empathetic approach ensures that the final product aligns closely with end-user expectations, enhancing its usability and appeal. Cross-functional collaboration is pivotal in iterative design, bringing together individuals with diverse expertise to contribute to the refinement process. Designers, engineers, and user experience experts collaborate to ensure design decisions consider aesthetic and technical dimensions. Efficient communication among team members supports a shared understanding of design goals, facilitating effective problem-solving and decision-making.

Prototyping is a crucial feedback mechanism in iterative design, providing stakeholders tangible validation of the design concepts. Prototypes allow for real-world interaction with the design, enabling stakeholders to identify areas for improvement in user interactions, functionality, and aesthetics. This tangible validation informs subsequent iterations, driving iterative refinement and leading to developing a well-optimized final product.

2.3.3.2 Feedback Mechanisms

Feedback mechanisms are integral to the iterative design process, enabling entrepreneurs to gather valuable insights and refine their designs iteratively. Several feedback mechanisms play critical roles in this process, offering unique advantages and insights. User testing stands out as a foundational feedback mechanism involving the observation of real users interacting with prototypes. This method provides direct insights into usability, user satisfaction, and areas requiring adjustment. Entrepreneurs design structured testing scenarios to focus on specific design aspects, ensuring testing aligns with predefined objectives. Stakeholder workshops offer another avenue for feedback, bringing together diverse perspectives for collective ideation. Participants provide input on design elements, for a collaborative environment conducive to rapid idea generation and problem-solving. Entrepreneurs leverage this collective intelligence to address challenges and explore innovative solutions. Remote feedback platforms provide accessibility to a geographically dispersed audience, allowing entrepreneurs to gather insights from diverse perspectives. Users can provide digital annotations on specific design elements, offering detailed feedback that enhances the precision of communication.

Usability metrics and analytics offer a quantitative assessment of user interactions, providing valuable data such as click-through rates, task completion times, and error rates. Entrepreneurs leverage these insights for data-driven decision-making, using usability metrics as objective benchmarks for evaluating design performance. Feedback integration tools streamline the collection and organization of feedback from various sources. These tools centralize feedback into a single hub, ensuring systematic addressing and implementation. Additionally, they facilitate traceability and accountability by tracking the status of feedback items and assigning responsibilities for their resolution. By combining these feedback mechanisms, entrepreneurs can gather comprehensive insights and iteratively refine their designs to better meet user needs and expectations.

Iterative design and feedback intertwine to create a responsive and adaptive design process. By adhering to the principles of continuous refinement, embracing a user-centred approach, creating cross-functional collaboration, and leveraging diverse feedback mechanisms, entrepreneurs ensure that each of the iteration propels the design closer to its optimal form. This iterative journey positions the product for success by aligning it with user expectations, addressing emerging challenges, and cultivating a design that resonates with stakeholders and end-users.

2.4. Functionality and Manufacturability

In creating innovative products, entrepreneurs must navigate the delicate balance between functionality, which ensures the product meets its intended purpose, and manufacturability, which addresses the practicalities of production. The following discussion explores the principles and strategies behind balancing functionality and user experience to optimize the overall design.

2.4.1 Balancing Functionality and User Experience

Balancing functionality and user experience necessitates a holistic design philosophy where considerations for both seamlessly integrate. Entrepreneurs prioritize features and capabilities that directly contribute to the user's needs and expectations, ensuring a user-centric approach to functionality. This integration ensures that the end product functions effectively and delivers an exceptional user experience. Incorporating a user experience-centred design approach involves iterative usability testing. Entrepreneurs continuously seek user feedback to understand their interactions with the product, identifying pain points and areas for improvement. Based on this feedback, the design undergoes iterations to optimize the user experience while maintaining core functionality. Scalable functionality is crucial to adapt the product to varying user needs and preferences. Entrepreneurs design a flexible architecture that allows for adding features or modules based on evolving requirements. This future-proof design approach ensures that the product can accommodate advancements without requiring a complete overhaul, aligning with user needs over time. Usability heuristics guide user-centred design, addressing learnability, efficiency, and user satisfaction issues. Entrepreneurs apply these heuristics to evaluate the product's usability and conduct periodic heuristic evaluations to inform design adjustments. This ensures the product's functionality aligns with established usability principles, enhancing the overall user experience.

Balancing functionality and user experience necessitates trade-off analysis, where entrepreneurs identify situations where optimizing one aspect may entail compromises in another. Informed decisions are made based on the overall impact of finding optimal solutions that enhance functionality without undermining the user experience and vice versa. This delicate balance contributes to the overall success of the product. Integration of manufacturability principles into the design process is essential. Entrepreneurs incorporate Design for Manufacturing (DFM) principles from the detailed design phase, considering material selection, production processes, and assembly methods. Collaborative engagement with production teams ensures alignment between design aspirations and practical production constraints, bridging the gap between design and manufacturing. Prototyping plays a crucial role in validating both functionality and manufacturability. Entrepreneurs go beyond validating functionality to assess manufacturability by creating physical prototypes. These prototypes undergo iterative manufacturing tests to address scalability, material compatibility, and cost-effectiveness challenges, ensuring the design can be successfully translated into mass production.

Iterative refinement is not limited to functionality alone but extends to user-centric considerations. Entrepreneurs embrace user feedback to refine functional aspects and user experience, ensuring a harmonious integration. The design adapts based on real-world usage patterns and manufacturing insights, resulting in a product that meets functional requirements and exceeds user expectations. Balancing functionality and user experience is an art that requires continuous refinement and a keen understanding of both technological possibilities and user needs. Entrepreneurs who master this delicate equilibrium create products that excel in performance and resonate with users on a profound level, establishing a foundation for sustained success in the market.

2.4.2 Design for Manufacturability

Design for manufacturability is a strategic imperative in product development, ensuring a seamless and efficient transition from design concepts to mass production. This approach encompasses various techniques and principles to optimize the manufacturing process, focusing on the integration of design and manufacturing aspects from the outset. The integration of design and manufacturing is essential for ensuring that products are well-designed and manufacturable at scale. This integration begins with collaborative design teams that bring together engineers, designers, and production specialists. These teams work closely to align design choices with manufacturing feasibility. Manufacturing experts are involved from the initial stages of the design process, providing valuable insights into material selection, production processes, and assembly considerations. Their early involvement helps in identifying potential manufacturing challenges and incorporating solutions during the design phase, thereby preventing costly modifications later.

Design for Assembly (DFA) principles is crucial in simplifying assembly processes. Entrepreneurs focus on designing components and interfaces that minimize the number of parts, reduce complexity, and streamline assembly. By reducing the number of parts, the assembly process becomes less complex and more cost-effective. Additionally, considerations for automated assembly are integrated into the design, ensuring that the product can be efficiently assembled using automated systems. This approach not only optimizes manufacturing efficiency but also enhances product reliability and consistency by reducing the likelihood of assembly errors. A modular design approach further enhances the integration of design and manufacturing. Modular designs allow for interchangeable components, facilitating ease of manufacturing and assembly. Entrepreneurs create modules that can be produced independently and assembled seamlessly, reducing complexity in the manufacturing process. This approach is particularly beneficial for large or complex products, as it allows distinct parts of the product to be developed and tested simultaneously. Moreover, modular designs enhance scalability, enabling manufacturers to adjust production volumes by simply adjusting the number of modules produced. This flexibility ensures that production can adapt to changing demand while maintaining efficiency and quality.

Additionally, Design optimization for production is crucial for ensuring efficient and cost-effective manufacturing processes. Entrepreneurs employ various strategies to streamline production and enhance manufacturability while maintaining product quality. One key strategy is the use of cost-effective production techniques like value engineering. Entrepreneurs identify cost-effective alternatives without compromising quality, optimizing the design to reduce production costs. For certain products, batch production considerations are integrated into the design, allowing for the optimization of resource utilization through the batch manufacturing of specific components. This approach not only lowers costs but also improves the efficiency of production processes.

Simplicity and consistency in design are essential principles for manufacturability. Entrepreneurs streamline unnecessary complexity in the design, simplifying intricate features and structures to enhance ease of production. By reducing complexity, the likelihood of manufacturing errors decreases, and the production process becomes more straightforward and reliable. Consistent manufacturing standards ensure uniformity across components, further streamlining manufacturing processes and reducing the chances of errors. This consistency is vital for maintaining high quality and reducing variability in the final products. Compatibility with tooling and equipment is another critical consideration in design optimization. The design process involves careful consideration of the tooling required for manufacturing processes, ensuring alignment with design specifications for efficient production. Entrepreneurs prioritize compatibility with existing manufacturing equipment to minimize the need for significant capital investment. This approach helps to avoid unnecessary expenses and ensures that the production process can commence smoothly without delays caused by the need for new equipment. Integration of quality control measures into the design is vital for ensuring product quality during production. Design choices consider the need for inspection and quality assurance, with components and features designed for easy inspection. Error-proofing features are also integrated into the design to minimize the impact of human error during manufacturing, further enhancing product quality. These measures ensure that products meet the required standards and specifications, reducing the risk of defects and enhancing customer satisfaction. Supply chain considerations play a crucial role in design optimization for production. Entrepreneurs collaborate with suppliers during the design phase to align product specifications with their capabilities, enhancing supply chain efficiency and minimizing delays. Logistics optimization is also a priority, with entrepreneurs optimizing packaging and transportation to minimize costs and environmental impact throughout the supply chain. By addressing these supply chain factors early in the design process, entrepreneurs can ensure a smooth flow of materials and products, reducing bottlenecks and improving overall efficiency.

Conclusively, design for manufacturability is a multidimensional endeavour requiring a comprehensive understanding of design principles and manufacturing processes. Entrepreneurs, who adopt a collaborative and integrated approach, incorporating feedback from manufacturing experts and optimizing design choices for production efficiency, enable a smooth and cost-effective transition from concept to mass production. This approach not only reduces costs and improves efficiency but also ensures that the final product meets quality standards and is delivered to the market successfully.

2.4.3 Materials Selection and Process Optimization

The selection of materials and the optimization of manufacturing processes play a pivotal role in ensuring the success of a product. In selecting materials, entrepreneurs prioritize functionality by assessing mechanical, thermal, electrical, and chemical properties necessary for optimal product performance. Materials must meet specific functional requirements to ensure the product operates effectively and safely. Additionally, durability and longevity are essential to ensure that materials can withstand environmental conditions and usage scenarios over the product's lifecycle. By prioritizing these functional aspects, entrepreneurs ensure that their products meet performance expectations and offer long-term reliability.

Materials selection also considers manufacturability, focusing on ease of processing during manufacturing. Entrepreneurs evaluate mould ability, machinability, and formability to ensure efficient production processes. Compatibility with chosen manufacturing techniques is essential, as materials should behave predictably during cutting, moulding, casting, or any other manufacturing operation. By choosing materials that align with manufacturing processes, entrepreneurs streamline production and minimize production costs. Sustainability and environmental impact are also critical considerations in materials selection. Entrepreneurs prioritize eco-friendly and sustainable materials, carefully evaluating their extraction, production, and end-of-life implications. Materials with high recyclability and reusability are favoured, as entrepreneurs aim to minimize the ecological footprint of their products. By choosing sustainable materials, entrepreneurs contribute to environmental conservation and align with consumer preferences for eco-conscious products. Finally, materials selection considers cost-effectiveness, balancing performance requirements with budgetary constraints. Entrepreneurs aim to optimize material costs through value engineering principles without compromising essential functionalities. They explore alternative materials to identify options that offer comparable performance at a lower cost. By prioritizing cost-effectiveness, entrepreneurs ensure that their products remain competitive while maintaining profitability. By carefully considering these factors—functional requirements, manufacturability, sustainability, and cost-effectiveness—entrepreneurs can make informed decisions that enhance the overall success of their products.

Further, process optimization enhances manufacturing efficiency, ensures product quality, and promotes sustainability. Entrepreneurs implement various strategies to streamline operations and drive continuous improvement in their manufacturing processes. Entrepreneurs continuously analyse their manufacturing processes to identify bottlenecks, redundancies, or inefficiencies. Through value stream mapping and process flow analysis, they gain insights into the flow of materials, information, and activities within their operations. By optimizing layouts, sequencing tasks, and standardizing work methods, they streamline production and increase throughput. Additionally, entrepreneurs invest in advanced technologies such as robotics, IoT sensors, and data analytics to automate repetitive tasks, minimize human error, and accelerate cycle times. Quality control is not merely a final checkpoint but an integral part of the production process. Entrepreneurs also implement Total Quality Management (TQM) principles, empowering employees to take ownership of quality. They establish robust inspection procedures, set clear quality standards, and provide ongoing training to ensure adherence to specifications. Moreover, they leverage advanced quality control tools such as Six Sigma and Statistical Process Control (SPC) to monitor process variability, identify root causes of defects, and implement corrective actions proactively. In today's dynamic business environment, adaptability is the key to success. Entrepreneurs design their manufacturing systems with modular layouts, flexible equipment configurations, and agile production lines. By adopting principles of lean manufacturing and Just-in-Time (JIT) production, they minimize inventory levels, reduce lead times, and respond quickly to changing customer demands. Furthermore, they invest in versatile machinery and digital manufacturing technologies that enable rapid reconfiguration and retooling, allowing seamless scalability without significant disruptions. Sustainability is a growing concern for businesses worldwide, and entrepreneurs increasingly focus on reducing their environmental footprint. They conduct energy audits to identify opportunities for conservation and efficiency improvements across their operations. By investing in energy-efficient equipment, optimizing process parameters, and implementing waste heat recovery systems, they minimize energy consumption and greenhouse gas emissions. Additionally, entrepreneurs explore renewable energy sources such as solar, wind, and biomass to power their manufacturing facilities, reducing reliance on fossil fuels and mitigating climate change impacts.

Continuous improvement is cultivated through effective leadership, employee engagement, and organizational learning. Entrepreneurs promote open communication, encourage collaboration, and recognize and reward innovative ideas from employees at all levels. They establish cross-functional improvement teams to tackle specific challenges, conduct regular Gemba walks to observe operations first-hand, and facilitate knowledge sharing through training programs and workshops. By institutionalizing a mind-set of kaizen (continuous improvement), entrepreneurs develop a culture of innovation, resilience, and adaptability that drives sustained success in their manufacturing endeavours. Materials selection and process optimization are intertwined in creating a successful and sustainable product. Entrepreneurs ensure that their products meet functional requirements and align with broader sustainability and market viability goals by carefully evaluating material properties, environmental considerations, and cost implications, and optimizing manufacturing processes for efficiency, quality, and adaptability.

2.5. Bill of Materials and Components Supply Chain

Effectively managing the bill of materials (BOM) and establishing robust components supply chain is critical to ensuring a smooth and efficient manufacturing process. The following discussion researches the strategies entrepreneurs employ to create a comprehensive BOM.

2.5.1 Creating a Comprehensive Bill of Materials (BOM)

Holistic Component Identification: Entrepreneurs embark on a meticulous process of identifying every component necessary for the product. This involves thoroughly analysing the product design and functionality to ensure every essential part is noticed. Each item is meticulously documented, whether it is an electronic component, mechanical part, or consumable. Additionally, entrepreneurs prioritize standardization to leverage economies of scale, reduce complexity, and simplify inventory management. By standardizing components where feasible, they streamline procurement processes and minimize the risk of compatibility issues during assembly.

Functional Grouping: Once all components are identified, entrepreneurs organize them into logical groups based on their functional roles within the product. This hierarchical structure helps break down the assembly process into manageable units for complex products. Sub-assemblies are defined to delineate modular components that can be assembled independently before integration into the final product. Clear delineation of sub-assemblies simplifies assembly and aids in troubleshooting and maintenance activities.

Detailed Specifications: Each component listed in the BOM is accompanied by comprehensive technical specifications. These specifications provide detailed information about each component's physical attributes, performance characteristics, and quality requirements. For example, dimensions specify a part's exact size and shape, while material specifications detail the material composition and properties required for its intended function. Tolerance levels are defined to ensure precision and consistency in manufacturing processes. Quality standards outline the expected level of quality for each component, setting benchmarks for suppliers and manufacturing teams to meet.

Supplier Information: Supplier details play a crucial role in the BOM, enabling entrepreneurs to manage the procurement process effectively. Each component in the BOM is linked to its respective supplier, along with relevant contact information and contractual terms. Entrepreneurs maintain a comprehensive supplier database, which includes information on supplier capabilities, performance history, and compliance with regulatory requirements. By diversifying their supplier base and identifying alternative sources for critical components, entrepreneurs mitigate the risk of supply chain disruptions and fluctuations in supplier performance.

Cost Breakdown: Besides listing components, the BOM features a detailed breakdown of costs associated with each component. This breakdown enables entrepreneurs to gain insights into the factors driving production costs and facilitates informed decision-making. By analysing cost allocations at the component level, entrepreneurs can identify opportunities for cost optimization, negotiate better pricing with suppliers, and develop strategies to enhance overall profitability. Moreover, entrepreneurs actively seek cost-effective alternatives for components, leveraging their understanding of material properties, performance requirements, and market dynamics to identify substitutions that offer comparable quality at lower costs.

Lifecycle Considerations: Recognizing the importance of considering the lifecycle of each component, entrepreneurs integrate end-of-life planning into the BOM management process. This involves anticipating potential obsolescence risks, identifying alternative sources or replacements for components, and implementing strategies to ensure continuity of supply. Revision control mechanisms are established to manage changes to the BOM over time, facilitating version control and ensuring stakeholders have access to the most up-to-date information. By proactively addressing lifecycle considerations, entrepreneurs minimize disruptions to production and maintain product continuity throughout its lifecycle.

Interconnected Database Systems: Entrepreneurs integrate the BOM with Product Lifecycle Management (PLM) systems to streamline BOM management and ensure data accuracy. This integration enables seamless synchronization of BOM data with design updates, version changes, and other relevant modifications. Real-time updates to the BOM are facilitated through interconnected databases, providing stakeholders with timely and accurate information for decision-making. By leveraging interconnected database systems, entrepreneurs enhance collaboration, improve data integrity, and optimize BOM management processes.

Regulatory Compliance: Entrepreneurs prioritize regulatory compliance within the BOM, ensuring that components meet relevant industry regulations and standards. The BOM includes documentation for compliance with regulatory requirements, such as safety certifications, quality standards, and environmental regulations. Environmental considerations, including RoHS compliance and sustainability, are factored into component selection decisions. By adhering to regulatory standards and environmental best practices, entrepreneurs mitigate compliance risks, enhance product quality and safety, and demonstrate commitment to responsible business practices.

Overall, a well-structured and comprehensive BOM is a central repository of information that guides the entire product lifecycle—from design and development to production and distribution. Entrepreneurs lay the foundation for efficient manufacturing processes, optimized supply chain management, and successful product launches by investing time and effort into creating and maintaining an accurate BOM. Creating a comprehensive BOM is foundational in orchestrating a seamless manufacturing process. Entrepreneurs, who approach BOM management strategically, considering functionality, supplier relationships, cost dynamics, and compliance requirements, establish a resilient foundation for efficient production and supply chain management.

2.5.2 Strategic Components Sourcing

Strategic component sourcing is crucial to ensuring a reliable and efficient supply chain. The following discussion explores entrepreneurs' methodologies and considerations for strategically sourcing product components.

Supplier Relationship Management: Entrepreneurs understand that the success of their supply chain heavily relies on the relationships they establish with suppliers. They conduct thorough evaluations to ensure that selected suppliers meet quality and cost standards and align with the company's values and long-term goals. By forging strong partnerships with key suppliers, entrepreneurs cultivate an environment of trust and collaboration, substituting mutual growth and innovation. These enduring relationships enable open communication channels for efficient problem-solving and continuous improvement initiatives.

Risk Mitigation Strategies: In today's dynamic business environment, entrepreneurs recognize the importance of mitigating risks within their supply chains. Diversifying their supplier base reduces vulnerability to disruptions caused by unforeseen events, such as natural disasters or geopolitical tensions. Regular risk assessments help entrepreneurs anticipate potential challenges and develop proactive contingency plans to maintain continuity in the supply of critical components. These strategies ensure resilience and adaptability amid uncertainty, safeguarding operations against unforeseen disruptions.

Global Sourcing Considerations: As businesses expand their operations globally, entrepreneurs must navigate the complexities of sourcing components from diverse regions. Strategic assessments of geographical locations consider logistical factors like proximity and transportation costs and broader considerations such as geopolitical stability and regulatory compliance. By gaining insights into local cultures and regulations, entrepreneurs can effectively manage relationships with global suppliers, mitigate risks, and optimize supply chain efficiency across international boundaries.

Supply Chain Visibility: Real-time monitoring capabilities empower entrepreneurs with comprehensive insights into their supply chains, allowing them to track the movement of components and anticipate potential bottlenecks or disruptions. Advanced tracking systems, analytical tools, and communication platforms provide stakeholders with up-to-date information, enabling proactive decision-making and rapid response to be changing circumstances. By harnessing the power of data analytics, entrepreneurs gain actionable insights that drive continuous optimization and enhance overall supply chain performance.

Cost Optimization Strategies: Entrepreneurs understand the importance of optimizing costs throughout the supply chain to maintain competitiveness. Collaborative value engineering initiatives with suppliers involve joint efforts to identify cost-effective alternatives and enhance production efficiency while upholding quality standards. Effective negotiation strategies enable entrepreneurs to secure favourable pricing, payment schedules, and delivery terms, balancing cost-effectiveness, and supplier profitability.

Quality Assurance Measures: Maintaining product quality is paramount for entrepreneurs, necessitating robust assurance measures. Regular supplier audits ensure compliance with quality standards and manufacturing practices while promoting transparency and accountability. Entrepreneurs establish clear quality expectations and collaborate closely with suppliers to promptly address deviations. Feedback mechanisms encourage continuous improvement, developing a culture of excellence and driving enhancements in product quality over time.

Agile Supply Chain Practices: In today's dynamic business landscape, agility is essential for navigating uncertainties and rapid changes. Agile procurement processes empower entrepreneurs to adapt to evolving market conditions and product requirements quickly. Collaborative forecasting practices enable the alignment of production schedules with supplier capabilities, minimizing the risk of inventory imbalances and ensuring optimal resource utilization. By embracing agility, entrepreneurs maintain responsive and resilient components supply chain capable of efficiently meeting shifting demands.

Ethical and Sustainable Sourcing: Ethical and sustainable sourcing practices align with the values of responsible entrepreneurship. Entrepreneurs prioritize suppliers that adhere to fair labour practices, environmental sustainability, and social responsibility standards, raising a positive impact on communities and the environment. Implementing traceability initiatives enhances transparency in the sourcing process, providing stakeholders with visibility into the origins of components and promoting ethical sourcing practices throughout the supply chain.

Strategic components' sourcing is a dynamic and multifaceted process that requires a combination of foresight, collaboration, and adaptability. Entrepreneurs who implement these strategies effectively establish reliable supply chain components and contribute to their businesses' overall resilience and sustainability.

2.5.3 Supply Chain Management in Product Innovation

Effectively managing the supply chain is crucial for the success of product innovation. In The following discussion, we explore the principles and practices that entrepreneurs employ to ensure a streamlined and efficient supply chain in the context of product innovation.

Integrated Supply Chain Planning: Entrepreneurs understand that integrated supply chain planning is about coordinating various functions and ensuring strategic alignment with the overarching goals of product innovation and market responsiveness. By facilitating collaboration between supply chain, product development, and marketing teams, entrepreneurs create a constructive collaboration that optimizes resource allocation, minimizes time-to-market, and enhances customer satisfaction. Through integrated planning platforms, such as Enterprise Resource Planning (ERP) systems or cloud-based solutions, entrepreneurs gain real-time insights into inventory levels, production capacities, and market trends, empowering informed decision-making at every product lifecycle stage.

Agile and Responsive Supply Chains: In product innovation, agility is paramount. Entrepreneurs leverage agile supply chain frameworks to react swiftly to changes and proactively anticipate and capitalize on emerging opportunities. By embedding agility into the supply chain DNA, entrepreneurs create a dynamic ecosystem capable of adapting to customer preferences, market dynamics, and technological advancements. Robust risk mitigation strategies, including scenario planning, supplier diversification, and contingency stockpiling, bolster the resilience of supply chains, safeguarding against disruptions and ensuring continuity of operations even in turbulent times.

Demand-Driven Approaches: Demand-driven approaches represent a change in thinking from traditional supply chain models, placing the customer at the epicentre of decision-making. Entrepreneurs engage in collaborative demand planning, leveraging data analytics, market intelligence, and predictive modelling to forecast demand precisely. Dynamic inventory management systems, equipped with advanced algorithms and predictive analytics, enable proactive inventory optimization, reducing carrying costs while enhancing service levels. By aligning supply with actual demand in real-time, entrepreneurs minimize the risk of excess inventory or stock outs, thus maximizing operational efficiency and customer satisfaction.

Supplier Collaboration and Innovation: In today's hyper-competitive landscape, supplier collaboration transcends transactional relationships to become strategic partnerships driving mutual growth and innovation. Entrepreneurs cultivate an ecosystem of trust and transparency, substituting open communication channels and knowledge sharing with suppliers. By involving suppliers early in the design phase, entrepreneurs tap into their domain expertise to co-create innovative solutions, optimize product designs, and improve manufacturing processes. Furthermore, supplier collaboration extends beyond product development to encompass sustainability initiatives, ethical sourcing practices, and social responsibility commitments, reflecting a shared commitment to environmental stewardship and societal well-being.

Technology Integration for Visibility: Entrepreneurs leverage innovative technologies like the Internet of Things (IoT) and sensors to enhance supply chain visibility. By embedding IoT devices and sensors throughout the supply chain network, entrepreneurs gain real-time insights into inventory levels, shipment statuses, and storage conditions. This technology enables proactive decision-making, allowing entrepreneurs to optimize transportation routes, prevent stock outs, and mitigate risks associated with inventory management. Furthermore, block chain technology is harnessed to ensure transparency and traceability across the supply chain. Through block chain-enabled platforms, entrepreneurs establish immutable records of transactions, enhancing trust and accountability while minimizing the risk of fraud or counterfeiting.

Circular Supply Chain Principles: In line with the global shift towards sustainability, entrepreneurs embrace circular supply chain principles to minimize environmental impact and promote resource efficiency. Sustainable practices, such as recycling, repurposing, and waste reduction, are integrated into supply chain operations. Entrepreneurs explore innovative strategies for extending the life of products, including refurbishing, remanufacturing, and recycling initiatives. By adopting a circular economy mind-set, entrepreneurs reduce waste and carbon footprint, unlock new revenue streams, and enhance brand reputation as environmentally responsible stewards.

Continuous Improvement Culture: A culture of continuous improvement lies at the heart of effective supply chain management. Entrepreneurs imbue their organizations with Kaizen principles, encouraging employees at all levels to actively seek out opportunities for optimization and innovation. Feedback loops are established to capture insights and suggestions from suppliers, logistics partners, and internal teams. Through ongoing evaluation and refinement of supply chain processes, entrepreneurs drive operational excellence, enhance efficiency gains, and adapt to evolving market dynamics with agility and resilience.

Resilience and Contingency Planning: Entrepreneurs prioritize resilience and contingency planning to safeguard supply chain operations against disruptions in an increasingly volatile and unpredictable business environment. Scenario planning exercises are conducted to assess various risk scenarios, including natural disasters, geopolitical tensions, and economic downturns. Based on these scenarios, entrepreneurs develop robust contingency plans and response strategies to mitigate risks and ensure business continuity. Diversification strategies, such as multi-sourcing and multi-location distribution, are employed to reduce dependency on single suppliers or regions, enhancing the resilience and adaptability of the supply chain network.

Supply chain management in product innovation requires a holistic and adaptive approach. Entrepreneurs who prioritize collaboration, agility, sustainability, and continuous improvement in their supply chain practices position themselves to navigate the complexities of product innovation successfully.

2.6. Manufacturing and Assembly Plan

Creating an effective manufacturing and assembly plant is pivotal for transforming design concepts into tangible products. The following discussion explores entrepreneurs' strategic considerations when choosing the right manufacturing processes.

2.6.1 Choosing the Right Manufacturing Processes

Product Complexity Analysis: Entrepreneurs inquire more deeply into the analysis of product complexity by considering various aspects, such as the interaction between different components, assembly intricacies, and the overall system architecture. By understanding these differences, they can better categorize components based on their criticality to the product's functionality and performance. This distinct approach allows for a more tailored selection of manufacturing processes, ensuring that each component is produced in a manner that optimizes both quality and efficiency.

Material Compatibility: Entrepreneurs explore advanced manufacturing techniques that leverage material synergies besides considering material properties. For instance, they may study composite materials or hybrid manufacturing processes that combine traditional and additive manufacturing to achieve enhanced performance or novel functionalities. By pushing the boundaries of material science and manufacturing technology, entrepreneurs can unlock innovative design possibilities and create products that surpass conventional limitations.

Production Volume and Scalability: Entrepreneurs conduct in-depth analyses to forecast production volumes across different market scenarios, considering factors such as seasonality, market trends, and potential disruptions. This comprehensive approach allows them to develop agile manufacturing strategies that can flexibly accommodate fluctuations in demand while maintaining cost efficiency. Additionally, entrepreneurs explore decentralized manufacturing models and distributed production networks to enhance agility and resilience in the face of supply chain disruptions or geopolitical uncertainties.

Precision and Tolerance Requirements: Entrepreneurs leverage advanced metrology tools and quality control methodologies to ensure that components meet the most stringent precision and tolerance requirements. They invest in state-of-the-art inspection technologies, such as coordinate measuring machines (CMMs) and optical metrology systems, to perform thorough dimensional analysis and validate component accuracy. Moreover, entrepreneurs implement closed-loop feedback mechanisms that continuously monitor manufacturing processes and make real-time adjustments to maintain optimal precision levels throughout production.

Lead Time Considerations: Entrepreneurs leverage rapid prototyping techniques beyond 3D printing, such as rapid tooling and injection moulding, to expedite product development cycles. These advanced prototyping methods allow for rapid iteration and refinement of product designs and manufacturing processes, accelerating time-to-market while minimizing development costs. Furthermore, entrepreneurs establish strategic partnerships with logistics providers and implement just-in-time (JIT) inventory management systems to streamline supply chain operations and minimize lead times from raw material procurement to final product delivery.

Cost-Benefit Analysis: Entrepreneurs conduct a meticulous cost-benefit analysis considering immediate production expenses and long-term implications. They explore the intricacies of cost evaluation by factoring in variables like equipment depreciation, labour efficiency, and potential economies of scale. By adopting a Total Cost of Ownership (TCO) approach, entrepreneurs gain a holistic understanding of the financial implications of each manufacturing process, enabling informed decision-making regarding investment allocation and resource optimization.

Environmental Impact and Sustainability: Entrepreneurs embrace sustainability as a core principle in manufacturing process selection. Beyond mitigating environmental harm, they actively seek processes that contribute positively to ecological stewardship. Entrepreneurs minimize resource consumption, reduce carbon emissions, and create a more circular economy by incorporating sustainable practices such as lean manufacturing, renewable energy utilization, and closed-loop material recycling. Through comprehensive life cycle assessments, they quantify the environmental impact of manufacturing processes, ensuring alignment with sustainability goals and regulatory requirements.

Regulatory Compliance: Entrepreneurs strictly adhere to regulatory standards and industry norms throughout the selection of manufacturing processes. They meticulously evaluate the compliance of chosen processes with regulatory frameworks governing worker safety, product quality, and environmental protection. By proactively engaging with regulatory authorities and industry watchdogs, entrepreneurs navigate certification processes seamlessly, earning the trust of consumers and stakeholders alike. Compliance becomes a cornerstone of their manufacturing strategy, laying the groundwork for long-term success and market competitiveness.

Flexibility for Design Changes: Entrepreneurs prioritize manufacturing processes that offer inherent flexibility to accommodate design iterations and refinements. By leveraging advanced digital manufacturing technologies like 3D printing and computer numerical control (CNC) machining, they empower design teams to iterate rapidly, test prototypes, and implement changes with minimal disruption to production schedules. This iterative prototyping approach accelerates product development cycles and enhances innovation by creating a culture of experimentation and continuous improvement. Through agile manufacturing methodologies, entrepreneurs maintain a competitive edge in dynamic market environments and drive sustained business growth.

Choosing the right manufacturing processes is a strategic decision that directly impacts product quality, cost-efficiency, and overall success. Entrepreneurs who carefully analyse the unique requirements of their products and align them with appropriate manufacturing methods set the stage for a robust and effective production plan.

2.6.2 Assembly Line Planning and Optimization

Efficient assembly line planning and optimization are essential components of successful manufacturing. The following discussion explores entrepreneurs' strategic considerations when planning and optimizing assembly lines.

Product Flow Analysis: Entrepreneurs implement sophisticated tools and methodologies for product flow analysis, such as value stream mapping and process simulation software. These tools provide detailed insights into the movement of materials and components throughout the assembly process, enabling entrepreneurs to identify inefficiencies and optimize workflows. Entrepreneurs can proactively address bottlenecks, minimize wait times, and improve efficiency by continuously monitoring and analysing the product flow.

Workstation Design and Layout: Entrepreneurs utilize advanced ergonomic principles and simulation software to design workstations prioritizing worker comfort and safety. They consider workstation height, reach distances, and tool placement to minimize physical strain and fatigue. Additionally, entrepreneurs leverage lean manufacturing principles to optimize workstation layouts, ensuring efficient material flow and minimizing wasted motion. By creating ergonomic work environments, entrepreneurs enhance employee satisfaction, reduce absenteeism, and improve overall productivity.

Automation Integration: Entrepreneurs invest in state-of-the-art automation technologies, such as robotic arms, automated guided vehicles (AGVs), and vision systems, to automate repetitive and labour-intensive tasks on the assembly line. They collaborate with automation experts to design custom solutions tailored to their production needs. Moreover, entrepreneurs implement advanced control systems and machine learning algorithms to optimize the performance of automated processes, enabling adaptive and responsive production systems. By embracing automation, entrepreneurs increase throughput, reduce cycle times, and improve product quality while minimizing labour costs.

Flexible Assembly Systems: Entrepreneurs adopt lean manufacturing principles, such as single-piece flow and just-in-time production, to create flexible assembly systems that quickly adapt to changing demand and product requirements. They design modular workstations and assembly cells that can be easily reconfigured to accommodate different product variants or assembly processes. Additionally, entrepreneurs implement cross-training programs and job rotation schemes to develop a versatile workforce capable of performing multiple tasks within the assembly line. By embracing flexibility, entrepreneurs enhance agility, responsiveness, and resilience in their manufacturing operations, enabling them to thrive in dynamic and uncertain market environments.

Quality Control Measures: Entrepreneurs deploy advanced quality control measures, including computer vision systems and machine learning algorithms, to automate inspection processes and detect defects with high accuracy. They leverage innovative technologies such as AI-powered image recognition and sensors to perform non-destructive testing and ensure product integrity. Additionally, entrepreneurs implement statistical process control (SPC) techniques to monitor process variability and maintain consistent product quality throughout the assembly line.

Optimized Production Scheduling: Entrepreneurs implement advanced production scheduling algorithms and optimization models to balance workload distribution and minimize production bottlenecks. They utilize predictive analytics and machine learning algorithms to forecast demand, optimize production sequences, and allocate resources effectively. Moreover, entrepreneurs employ advanced scheduling software and real-time monitoring systems to adapt quickly to changing demand patterns and production constraints, ensure optimal resource utilization, and maximize throughput.

Worker Training and Empowerment: Entrepreneurs invest in comprehensive training programs and skill development initiatives to empower assembly line workers with the knowledge and expertise to perform their tasks effectively. They leverage virtual reality (VR) and augmented reality (AR) technologies to provide immersive training experiences and simulate real-world assembly scenarios. Additionally, entrepreneurs develop a culture of continuous learning and improvement, encouraging workers to participate in cross-functional teams and share their insights and suggestions for process optimization and innovation.

Lean Manufacturing Principles: Entrepreneurs embrace lean manufacturing principles, such as 5S methodology and value stream mapping, to identify and eliminate waste in the assembly process. They implement visual management techniques, such as Kanban systems and Andon lights, to enhance transparency and facilitate continuous improvement. Moreover, entrepreneurs leverage lean tools and techniques, such as root cause analysis and Poka-Yoke (error-proofing), to prevent defects and streamline operations, resulting in higher efficiency and productivity.

Environmental Sustainability: Entrepreneurs integrate sustainable practices into their assembly line operations, such as energy-efficient lighting systems, renewable energy sources, and waste recycling programs. They invest in environmentally friendly technologies, such as regenerative braking and closed-loop water recycling systems, to minimize resource consumption and reduce environmental impact. Additionally, entrepreneurs collaborate with suppliers to source eco-friendly materials and adopt green manufacturing processes, contributing to a more sustainable and environmentally responsible supply chain.

Efficient assembly line planning and optimization are integral to achieving high productivity, product quality, and competitiveness. Entrepreneurs who embrace an integrated approach, combining technological advancements, human factors, and continuous improvement strategies, position their assembly lines for sustained success in the dynamic manufacturing landscape.

2.6.3 Cost-effective Manufacturing Strategies

Strategically managing costs in the manufacturing process is vital for the success and competitiveness of a product. In The following discussion, we explore key strategies entrepreneurs employ to optimize costs during manufacturing.

Value Engineering: Conducting a thorough functional analysis of product components is foundational to identifying opportunities for cost reduction without compromising performance. Potential inefficiencies or redundancies can be pinpointed by scrutinizing each component's function and necessity. This analysis enables the optimization of the cost-benefit ratio by exploring alternative materials, design modifications, or production processes. For instance, substituting costly materials with more economical yet equally functional alternatives can significantly reduce manufacturing expenses without sacrificing product quality. Likewise, implementing design modifications that streamline production processes or enhance resource efficiency can lead to substantial cost savings over time. By systematically evaluating and refining each aspect of the product, a balanced approach to cost optimization can be achieved, ensuring competitiveness in the market while maintaining product integrity.

Lean Manufacturing Principles: Efficient cost management in production involves eliminating waste and creating continuous improvement. By eliminating waste throughout the production process and applying continuous improvement initiatives, inefficiencies can be identified and addressed systematically. This approach enhances productivity and reduces costs by streamlining operations and maximizing resource utilization. Moreover, developing a culture of on-going optimization encourages employees to proactively seek out opportunities for improvement, driving sustained efficiency gains. Through these concerted efforts, businesses can save costs while maintaining high quality and performance standards in their products and processes.

Supply Chain Collaboration: To optimize procurement and inventory management, businesses can collaborate closely with suppliers to negotiate favourable terms and bulk discounts. Adopting a just-in-time inventory approach minimizes holding costs by ensuring inventory levels are closely aligned with immediate production needs. Additionally, developing strong relationships with suppliers facilitates mutual cost-saving opportunities, such as joint process improvements or shared resources. Figure 2.1 provides a comprehensive overview of the complex supply chain management process, highlighting the interconnectedness of suppliers, manufacturers, distributors, retailers, and consumers. By following and implementing these steps, businesses can streamline procurement processes, reduce inventory-related expenses, and capitalize on cost-saving initiatives throughout the supply chain.

Automation and Technology Integration: To enhance production efficiency and reduce costs, businesses can use automation technologies to streamline manufacturing processes. Companies can increase productivity and minimize labour costs by automating repetitive tasks and optimizing workflows. Additionally, exploring advanced manufacturing technologies, such as robotics or additive manufacturing, offers efficiency gains and cost savings opportunities. By embracing these innovative solutions, businesses can improve operational efficiency, reduce lead times, and enhance their competitiveness in the market.

Energy Efficiency Measures: To minimize operational costs and promote sustainability, businesses can invest in energy-efficient manufacturing equipment. Companies can significantly reduce their energy consumption and related expenses by upgrading to modern machinery designed for energy conservation. Integrating renewable energy sources, such as solar or wind power, into manufacturing processes can reduce energy costs and environmental impact. These investments contribute to cost savings and align with corporate social responsibility initiatives, enhancing the company's reputation and competitiveness in the market.

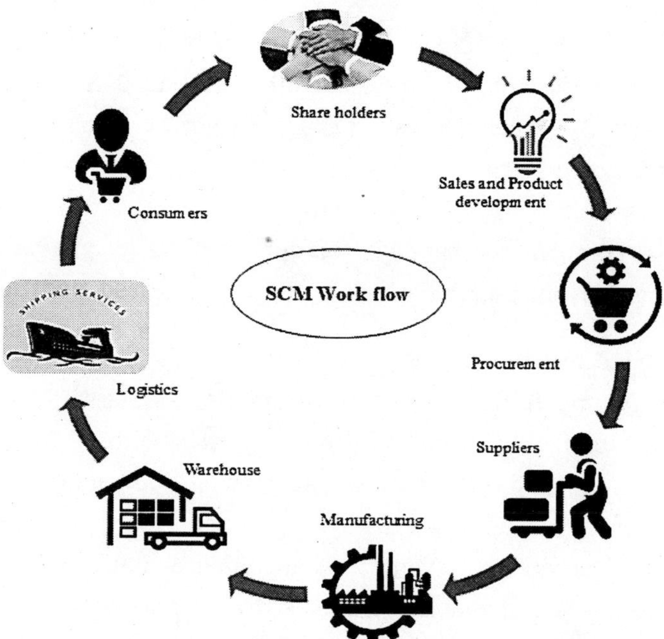

Figure 2.1 Supply chain management workflow

Optimized Workforce Management: Implementing cross-training programs within the workforce promotes flexibility and resilience in operations. By ensuring that employees are proficient in multiple roles, companies can adapt more effectively to changing demands and unexpected absences, minimizing disruptions to productivity. Moreover, raising a positive work environment characterized by open communication, recognition of achievements, and opportunities for professional development encourages employee engagement and enhances overall efficiency. This investment in human capital boosts morale and eventually contributes to higher performance and organizational success.

Cost Analysis and Benchmarking: Conducting detailed cost analyses for each stage of the manufacturing process provides valuable insights into cost drivers and areas ripe for optimization. By benchmarking against industry standards, companies can identify performance gaps and opportunities for improvement. This comparative analysis enables them to implement targeted strategies to reduce costs, enhance efficiency, and remain competitive. Moreover, it facilitates informed decision-making, allowing companies to allocate resources effectively and prioritize initiatives that yield the highest return on investment. Figure 2.2 depicts an optimized manufacturing and assembly workflow, providing a graphical representation of the simplified operations that convert raw materials into completed goods. It demonstrates the efficiency advantages of strategic planning, resource optimization, and innovative production processes.

Economies of Scale: Leveraging economies of scale through optimized production for larger volumes is essential for maximizing efficiency and reducing per-unit costs. By strategically scaling production based on market demand, companies can manage inventory levels and meet growing orders without overproduction or underutilization of resources. This approach ensures that production capacity aligns closely with market needs, minimizing waste and maximizing profitability. Additionally, it enables companies to capitalize on opportunities for growth while maintaining cost-effectiveness and competitiveness in the market.

Risk Management Strategies: Developing robust contingency plans mitigates potential risks and ensures business continuity. By conducting thorough risk assessments, companies can identify vulnerabilities in their supply chain and implement measures to address them effectively. This includes assessing and mitigating suppliers' risks, such as production disruptions or delivery delays. By creating solid relationships with suppliers and implementing backup plans, companies can minimize the impact of unforeseen events and maintain a stable supply chain. This proactive approach enhances resilience and enables companies to respond swiftly to any challenges that may arise.

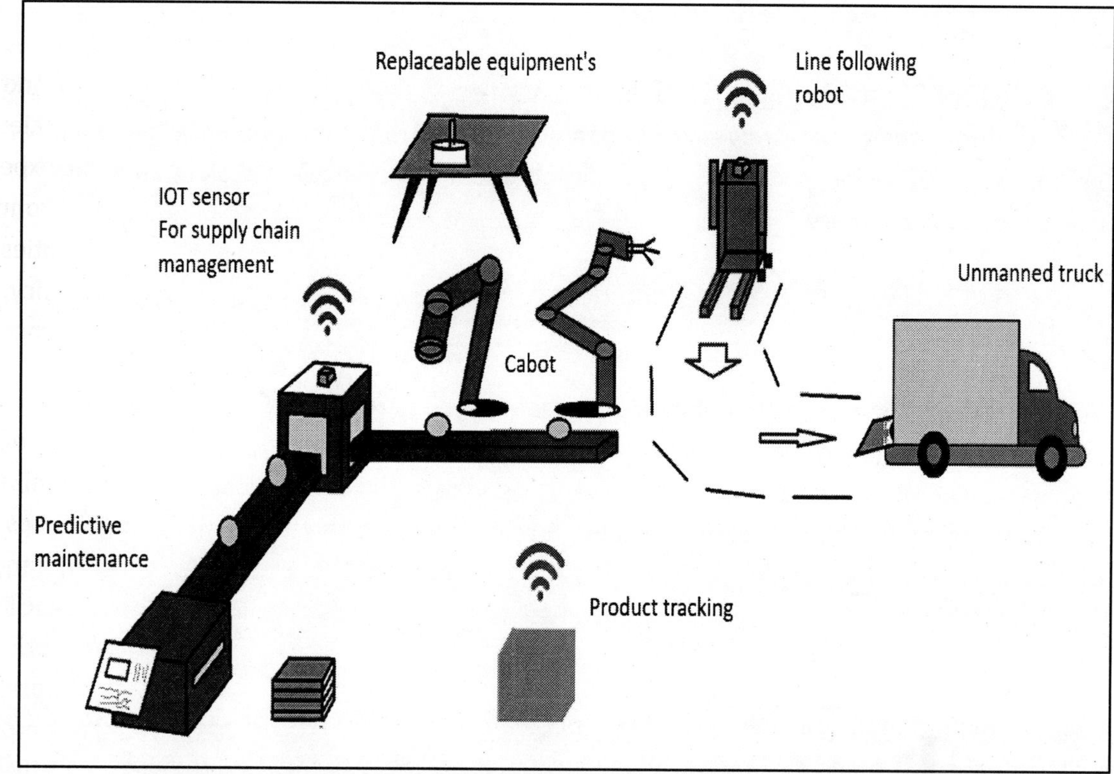

Figure 2.2 Optimized Manufacturing and Assembly Workflow – an example

Regulatory Compliance Efficiency: Streamlining regulatory compliance processes is essential to avoid unnecessary delays and expenses in manufacturing operations. Companies can ensure compliance while minimizing disruptions by proactively adapting manufacturing processes to meet evolving standards. This involves staying informed about regulatory changes and integrating compliance requirements into production workflows. Companies can navigate complex regulatory landscapes more effectively by implementing efficient compliance procedures and developing a culture of regulatory awareness. This proactive approach reduces compliance-related costs, enhances operational efficiency, and develops trust with regulators and customers.

Implementing these cost-effective manufacturing strategies empowers entrepreneurs to produce high-quality products at competitive prices, enhancing financial sustainability and market success. By combining efficiency gains, strategic partnerships, and a proactive approach to cost management, entrepreneurs can navigate the complex manufacturing landscape while maximizing profitability.

2.7. Product Testing and Quality Assurance

Ensuring the quality and reliability of a product is paramount in the manufacturing process. The following discussion explores the significance of rigorous product testing as a fundamental aspect of quality assurance.

2.7.1 Importance of Rigorous Product Testing

1. Customer Satisfaction: Ensuring customer satisfaction is paramount for any business, and rigorous product testing is crucial in achieving this goal. Companies can guarantee that the final product meets or exceeds customer quality, reliability, and performance expectations by subjecting products to thorough testing protocols. When customers receive high-quality products that meet their needs and deliver on promised benefits, it significantly enhances their satisfaction. Satisfied customers are more likely to become repeat buyers, advocate for the brand, and leave positive reviews and feedback, bolstering the company's reputation and strengthening brand loyalty. Therefore, prioritizing product quality through rigorous testing translates into long-term success and sustainable growth for the business.

2. Brand Reputation: Consistently delivering reliable and well-tested products is instrumental in building a positive brand reputation. When customers consistently receive products that meet or exceed their expectations, it develops trust in the brand's reliability and quality. This trust forms the foundation of a strong brand reputation, as customers associate the brand with consistency and excellence. A positive brand reputation, in turn, enhances customer trust and loyalty, as consumers are more likely to choose brands they perceive as trustworthy and reputable. A strong brand reputation can also confer a competitive advantage in the market, as consumers are often willing to pay a premium for products from brands they trust. Overall, prioritizing product reliability and quality testing is essential for cultivating a positive brand image and maintaining a competitive edge in the market.

3. Regulatory Compliance: Rigorous testing is imperative to ensure compliance with industry standards and regulatory requirements. Meeting these standards is not only a legal obligation but also enhances both the product's credibility and the company's reputation. By adhering to regulatory guidelines, businesses demonstrate their commitment to product safety, reliability, and quality. This not only builds trust among consumers but also minimizes the risk of costly recalls or legal issues, contributing to the long-term success and sustainability of the company.

4. Cost Savings in the Long Run: Identifying and rectifying issues during testing is paramount as it prevents costly recalls and post-production defects. By investing in rigorous testing upfront, businesses can mitigate the risk of expensive product failures and warranty claims, safeguarding their finances and reputation. This proactive approach saves costs associated with remediation and raises customer satisfaction and loyalty by delivering high-quality products that meet or exceed expectations.

5. Risk Mitigation: Product testing plays a crucial role in risk mitigation by identifying potential risks and weaknesses in the design or manufacturing process. By addressing these issues early in the testing phase, businesses can significantly reduce the likelihood of defects reaching the market. This proactive approach minimizes the risk of costly recalls and product failures and enhances overall product quality and customer satisfaction. Thorough product testing contributes to a more robust and more resilient business ecosystem.

6. Enhanced Product Durability: Rigorous testing evaluates the durability and longevity of products under various conditions, contributing to enhanced product durability. Items that withstand such testing are more likely to have a longer lifespan and a reduced likelihood of premature failure. This increased durability enhances the product's value proposition and care for customer trust and loyalty. By delivering products that meet or exceed durability expectations, businesses can establish a reputation for reliability and quality in the market.

7. Customer Safety: Thorough product testing ensures customer safety by identifying and addressing potential hazards or risks. Prioritizing customer safety through rigorous testing protects consumers from harm and builds trust and credibility in the marketplace. By demonstrating a commitment to safety, businesses can enhance their reputation and differentiate themselves from competitors, creating stronger relationships with customers and increasing brand loyalty.

8. Differentiation in the Market: Rigorous testing empowers companies to differentiate their products based on quality and reliability, giving them a competitive edge. By consistently delivering high-quality products that have undergone thorough testing, companies can establish themselves as leaders in their industry segments. This differentiation allows them to command premium pricing and attract discerning customers who prioritize quality and reliability. As a result, rigorous testing becomes a means of ensuring product excellence and a strategic tool for market differentiation and long-term success.

9. Continuous Improvement: Testing is pivotal in driving continuous improvement by providing valuable data for refining product design and manufacturing processes. Companies can identify areas for enhancement and optimization through iterative testing and feedback loops. By leveraging insights from testing results, they can iteratively refine their products, making incremental improvements to enhance performance, reliability, and user satisfaction. This commitment to continuous improvement fosters innovation and ensures that products evolve to meet changing market demands and customer expectations, driving long-term success and competitiveness in the industry.

10. Early Detection of Design Flaws: Early testing is a crucial mechanism for detecting design flaws in the nascent stages of product development. By conducting tests during these early phases, companies can promptly identify potential issues and make necessary adjustments before significant investments are committed to mass production. This proactive approach minimizes the likelihood of costly redesigns or recalls later in the product lifecycle, saving time and resources while ensuring that the final product meets quality standards and customer expectations. Thus, early detection of design flaws through testing contributes to overall efficiency and product success.

11. Customer Confidence: Thorough product testing is crucial in instilling confidence in customers by assuring them that the product has undergone rigorous evaluation. This confidence is a crucial driver of repeat business and positive word-of-mouth marketing, as satisfied customers are likelier to recommend the product to others and remain loyal to the brand. By demonstrating a commitment to quality and reliability through comprehensive testing processes, companies can strengthen their relationships with customers and enhance their reputation in the marketplace, leading to increased sales and long-term success.

12. Market Compliance and Acceptance: Rigorous testing is pivotal in ensuring market compliance and acceptance by retailers and distributors. Many markets and retailers have stringent quality and safety standards that products must meet to be accepted for sale. By subjecting products to thorough testing, companies can verify that they meet these requirements, thus facilitating their acceptance by retailers and distributors. This opens opportunities for the products to reach a wider audience and enhances the company's reputation for delivering safe and high-quality products, contributing to its success in the marketplace.

In conclusion, rigorous product testing is not only a quality assurance measure but a strategic investment in the long-term success of a product and the company's reputation. Entrepreneurs, who prioritize and commit to comprehensive testing protocols, position themselves for sustained success in the competitive product development and manufacturing landscape.

2.7.2 Establishing Quality Assurance Protocols

Establishing robust quality assurance protocols is paramount to ensure the reliability and excellence of a product. Defining quality standards is the initial step in ensuring the excellence and consistency of a product's quality. This entails establishing benchmarks based on industry standards, regulatory requirements, and customer expectations. By clearly articulating these standards, entrepreneurs set the foundation for maintaining consistency and meeting or exceeding customer needs. Identifying critical control points within the manufacturing process is crucial for effective quality assurance. These points represent vital stages where deviations from quality standards can occur. Prioritizing testing and inspection at these junctures allow for early detection of potential issues, minimizing the risk of product defects and ensuring adherence to quality standards. Further, developing specific testing criteria is essential to evaluate the product's performance, durability, and safety effectively. These criteria should align closely with the product's intended use and customer expectations. By establishing clear benchmarks for performance and safety, entrepreneurs ensure that the product meets quality standards throughout its lifecycle, enhancing customer satisfaction and loyalty. Integrating quality considerations throughout the product lifecycle is essential for maintaining high standards of quality from design to post-production support. This integrated approach ensures that quality remains a priority at every stage of the process. Encouraging cross-functional collaboration facilitates a comprehensive understanding of quality requirements among team members and enables seamless integration of quality practices into all aspects of the product lifecycle.

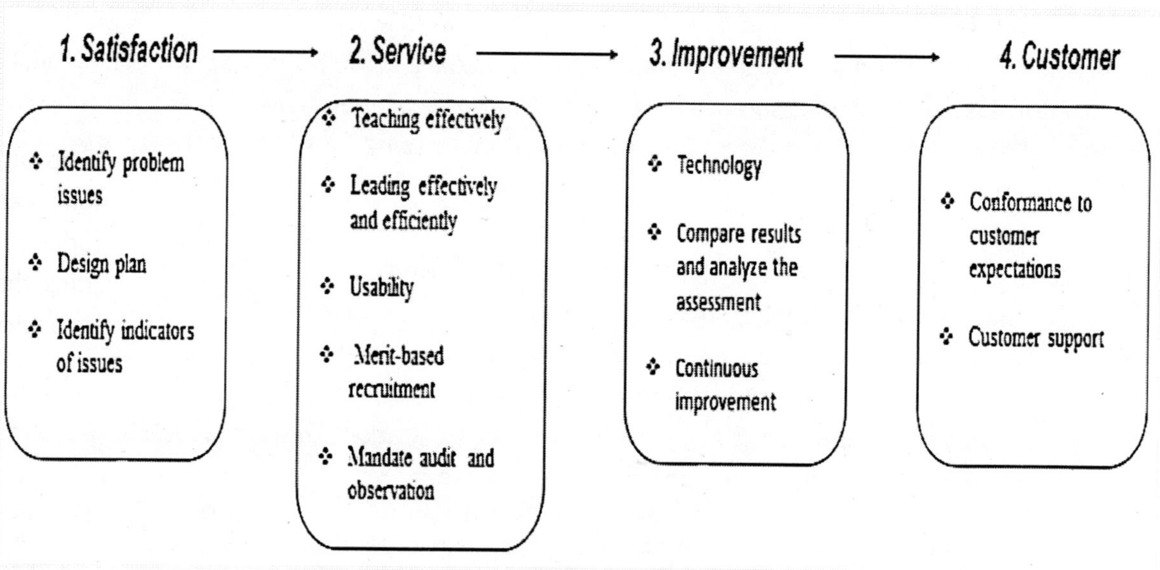

Figure 2.3 Essential Factors of Quality Assurance Framework

Further, implementing standard operating procedures (SOPs) is the first step towards ensuring quality assurance within an organization. SOPs serve as clear guidelines for employees, ensuring consistency and adherence to established quality protocols. By rigorously following SOPs, teams can maintain uniformity and uphold quality standards across all operations. Utilizing innovative testing technologies complements SOPs by improving the precision and efficiency of quality assessments.

Advanced tools such as automated testing equipment and data analytics solutions provide deeper insights into product quality, enabling proactive identification and resolution of potential issues. Regular internal audits are essential for evaluating adherence to quality assurance protocols. These audits identify areas for improvement and detect any deviations from established standards, ensuring consistency and reliability in products or services. Comprehensive employee training programs equip staff involved in quality assurance with the necessary skills to perform effectively, empowering them to uphold quality standards and contribute to continuous improvement efforts. Establishing a feedback mechanism fosters open communication and transparency, enabling organizations to proactively identify and resolve quality issues based on employee insights. Thorough documentation and analysis of test results are crucial components of quality assurance. Meticulously recording test data allows organizations to identify areas for improvement and track the effectiveness of their quality assurance efforts. Cultivating a culture of continuous improvement within the quality assurance team encourages innovation and efficiency. Employees are empowered to propose and implement enhancements based on their experiences and insights, enabling organizations to adapt to evolving challenges effectively.

Partnering with external quality assurance experts or third-party testing laboratories enhances the robustness of quality assurance practices. External collaborations bring objectivity and specialized expertise, complementing internal efforts. Developing an emergency response plan is essential for managing critical quality issues effectively. By preparing for potential emergencies, organizations can minimize the impact of quality incidents and maintain stakeholder trust and confidence. Monitoring and analysing customer feedback is vital for maintaining high standards of quality. Customer insights identify areas for improvement, allowing organizations to proactively address concerns and refine quality assurance processes. Staying updated on industry best practices ensures competitiveness and enhances the effectiveness of quality control measures. Regularly updating protocols to incorporate advancements allows organizations to continuously improve their quality assurance processes and maintain product excellence.

Figure 2.3 depicts the critical components of an effective Quality Assurance Framework, highlighting the important sections required to deliver high-quality goods consistently. This framework includes quality control methods, standardized procedures, continuous improvement activities, and regulatory compliance, improving product reliability, customer satisfaction, and brand reputation. Establishing comprehensive quality assurance protocols requires a proactive and systematic approach. By combining industry standards, innovative technologies, and a commitment to continuous improvement, entrepreneurs can create a quality assurance framework that consistently delivers high-quality products.

2.7.3 Continuous Improvement in Product Quality

Continuous improvement in product quality is a dynamic process that involves on-going assessment, refinement, and optimization. In The following discussion, we explore the fundamental principles and practices for achieving sustained enhancement in product quality. Continuous improvement in product quality is a dynamic process that involves on-going assessment, refinement, and optimization. Establishing a quality culture within the organization is fundamental for achieving sustained enhancement in product quality. By instilling a commitment to quality as a core value and emphasizing its importance at every level, organizations create an environment conducive to continuous enhancement and innovation in quality standards. The Plan-Do-Check-Act (PDCA) cycle serves as a systematic approach to continuous improvement. Through planning, execution, evaluation, and implementation of successful changes, organizations can continuously enhance product quality. Fostering cross-functional collaboration enables organizations to leverage diverse perspectives and effectively address quality challenges comprehensively. Cross-functional teams facilitate effective problem-solving and innovation, enhancing product quality over time. Utilizing Key Performance Indicators (KPIs) establishes measurable benchmarks for performance and guides strategic decision-making. Real-time monitoring systems are crucial for maintaining high product quality standards. By swiftly detecting deviations from quality standards and taking immediate corrective action, organizations minimize potential impacts on product quality and customer satisfaction.

Conducting root-cause analysis helps identify underlying factors contributing to quality issues, allowing organizations to implement corrective actions effectively. Employee involvement and training play a pivotal role in driving continuous improvement efforts and ensuring sustained excellence in product quality. Regular internal audits ensure adherence to quality standards and drive continuous improvement by identifying areas for enhancement. Integrating customer feedback into improvement initiatives provides valuable perspectives on product performance and satisfaction. Lean manufacturing principles aim to eliminate waste and optimize processes, driving product quality and operational excellence enhancements. Embracing the Kaizen philosophy empowers employees to identify and implement small, incremental changes that collectively enhance overall processes and product quality. Exploring and adopting advanced technologies such as automation and data analytics is essential for driving continuous improvement in product quality. Benchmarking against industry leaders provides insights for setting ambitious yet achievable goals for product quality. Transparent communication and regular review meetings facilitate ongoing dialogue, problem-solving, and decision-making, enabling organizations to adapt and refine their improvement strategies effectively.

By weaving continuous improvement into the organization's fabric, entrepreneurs can create a resilient and adaptive approach to enhancing product quality. This iterative and forward-looking mind-set positions the company to meet current standards and continually raise the bar for excellence in the ever-evolving product development and manufacturing landscape.

2.8. Intellectual Property Rights Management

In innovation and entrepreneurship, safeguarding intellectual property (IP) is paramount. The following discussion lays the foundation by delving into the fundamental aspects of understanding intellectual property.

2.8.1 Understanding Intellectual Property (IP)

Intellectual Property plays a crucial role in entrepreneurship, serving as a cornerstone for innovation and business success. Entrepreneurs often invest considerable time, effort, and resources into developing unique ideas, products, and processes. However, without proper protection, these assets are vulnerable to exploitation or imitation by competitors. Intellectual Property rights, such as patents, trademarks, copyrights, and trade secrets, provide entrepreneurs with legal safeguards to safeguard their innovations and creations. By securing exclusive rights to their intellectual assets, entrepreneurs can gain a competitive advantage in the market, attract investors, and establish their brand identity. Moreover, Intellectual Property protection promotes a conductive environment for innovation and encourages entrepreneurs to continue investing in research and development. It also promotes economic growth by incentivizing creativity and entrepreneurship. Therefore, understanding and effectively managing Intellectual Property is essential for entrepreneurs to maximize the value of their innovations and maintain a sustainable competitive edge in the dynamic business landscape.

Patents are most essential for safeguarding inventions and technological advancements, granting exclusive rights to their creators for a specified period. Trademarks play a vital role in protecting symbols, names, and slogans that distinguish goods or services in the marketplace, ensuring brand recognition and consumer trust. Copyrights are indispensable for safeguarding original literary, artistic, and musical works, providing creators with legal protection against unauthorized use or reproduction. Trade secrets are invaluable for protecting confidential business information, offering a competitive edge by safeguarding proprietary knowledge and practices. Additionally, design patents are essential for protecting the ornamental design of functional items, ensuring that unique designs are lawfully copied or imitated. Understanding these several types of intellectual property rights is crucial for entrepreneurs to successfully navigate the complex landscape of innovation and commerce. Intellectual property is pivotal in supporting innovation and competitiveness in the marketplace. IP protection encourages investment in research and development by providing incentives for innovation.

Trademarks and patents are potent market differentiation and exclusivity tools, granting creators a competitive edge. Moreover, IP assets can be monetized through various avenues, contributing to revenue generation. IP rights offer legal protection, allowing creators to enforce their rights and safeguard against unauthorized use or infringement. The intellectual property (IP) lifecycle encompasses several vital stages. It begins with the creation of IP through innovative or creative efforts. Subsequently, the IP is protected through registration or legal safeguards to ensure exclusivity. The commercialization phase involves bringing the IP to market through licensing, sales, or integration into products or services. Vigilant defence against infringement or unauthorized use is crucial to safeguard the IP. Finally, IP rights may expire after a designated period, prompting renewal to maintain exclusivity if desired. Figure 2.4 illustrates the progressive stages of Intellectual Property (IP) life cycle management, beginning with gathering and assessment as the first stage. The focus is identifying and evaluating potential IP assets, including patents, trademarks, and copyrights, to ascertain their strategic value and competitive advantage. Next, the emphasis shifts towards developing strategies to effectively leverage the identified IP assets, encompassing licensing agreements, partnerships, and commercialization plans. Finally, efforts are required to protect and preserve the integrity of IP assets through periodic renewals, enforcement actions, and portfolio optimization strategies. These stages form a structured approach to managing IP assets throughout their life cycle.

1. **Patentable Criteria:** To qualify for a patent, inventions must meet specific criteria. Firstly, they must demonstrate novelty, meaning they must be entirely new and not publicly disclosed before. Additionally, inventions must exhibit non-obviousness, indicating they are not merely apparent improvements over existing knowledge or technology. Lastly, they must possess utility, meaning they must serve a practical purpose or have some proper application. Meeting these patentable criteria is essential for securing patent protection for an invention.

2. **Trademark Basics:** Trademark basics encompass several vital considerations. Firstly, trademarks should be distinctive, allowing consumers to easily distinguish the goods or services they represent from others in the market. While registration is not mandatory, it offers enhanced protection and legal benefits. Finally, trademarks require periodic renewal to maintain their protection, ensuring continued exclusivity and recognition in the marketplace. Understanding these basics is crucial for effectively managing and safeguarding trademarks.

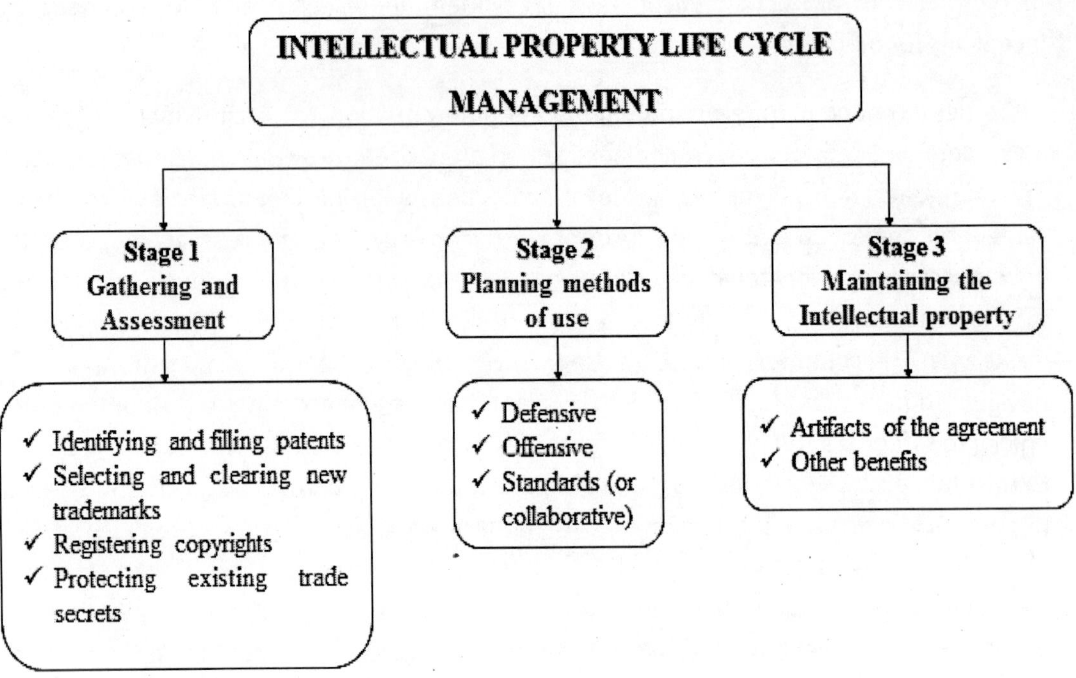

Figure 2.4 Stages of Intellectual Property Life Cycle Management

3. **Copyright Protection:** Copyright protection revolves around several fundamental principles. Firstly, it safeguards original works of authorship, including literary, artistic, and musical creations. Importantly, copyright is automatically granted upon creating qualifying works, providing immediate protection without registration. The concept of fair use also allows for limited use of copyrighted material without permission, typically for purposes such as criticism, commentary, or education. Understanding these aspects is crucial for creators and users to navigate copyright law effectively.
4. **Trade Secret Protection:** Trade secrets rely on the fundamental principle of confidentiality, requiring strict measures to keep proprietary information undisclosed. Unlike patents, trademarks, or copyrights, trade secrets are not registered; proactive protection is essential to prevent unauthorized disclosure. Maintaining secrecy through non-disclosure agreements and restricted access helps safeguard valuable business information from competitors and unauthorized use.
5. **Design Patent Considerations:** Design patents protect the ornamental design of functional items, ensuring exclusive rights to the visual appearance. While utility patents focus on the functionality of inventions, design patents specifically safeguard the unique aesthetic

aspects. Design patents typically have a shorter duration than utility patents but offer crucial protection against unauthorized replication or imitation in the market.

6. **International Considerations:** Intellectual property rights are territorial, meaning protection must be sought in each jurisdiction where rights are desired. Considering key markets and their respective IP regulations is essential for comprehensive protection. International treaties, such as those facilitated by the World Intellectual Property Organization (WIPO), provide frameworks for harmonizing IP laws across different countries, simplifying the process of global IP protection and enforcement.

Understanding the differences in intellectual property is foundational for entrepreneurs navigating the complex landscape of innovation and market competition. In subsequent sections, entrepreneurs explore into strategies for effective IP management, commercialization, and defence against infringement, empowering aspiring entrepreneurs to maximize the value of their intellectual assets.

2.8.2 Types of IP Protection (Patents, Trademarks, etc.)

Intellectual property (IP) protection comes in various forms, each tailored to safeguard creative and innovative work aspects. The following discussion explores the primary types of IP protection, including patents, trademarks, copyrights, and trade secrets. Intellectual property (IP) protection encompasses a variety of mechanisms tailored to safeguard various aspects of creative and innovative work. Among the primary types of IP protection are patents, trademarks, copyrights, trade secrets, industrial designs, plant patents, geographical indications, semiconductor chip protection, and utility models.

In the first category, patents grant inventors exclusive rights to their inventions for a limited period, typically 20 years from the filing date. They are subject to specific criteria, requiring inventions to be novel, non-obvious, and possess practical utility. Utility patents cover new and useful processes, machines, articles of manufacture, or compositions of matter, while design patents protect the ornamental design of functional items. The next category, Trademarks, protects symbols, names, slogans, and other identifiers that distinguish goods or services. To qualify for protection, trademarks should be distinctive and not generic. While registration is not mandatory, it enhances protection and provides a legal presumption of ownership. Trademarks require periodic renewal to maintain their protection.

Copyrights safeguard original works of authorship, including literary, artistic, and musical works. Copyright protection is automatically granted upon creating qualifying works and grants exclusive rights to reproduce, distribute, perform, and display the work. Some uses of copyrighted material may be deemed fair use and not infringing. Trade secrets protect confidential business information that provides a competitive advantage. Criteria for trade secret protection include keeping the information confidential and not known. Unlike patents or trademarks, trade secrets do not require registration and rely on active measures to maintain confidentiality. Industrial designs protect the visual design of objects that are not purely utilitarian. Designs must be novel and non-functional to qualify for protection, offering protection against unauthorized copying or imitation. Plant patents safeguard new and distinct varieties of plants that are asexually reproduced. Criteria include novelty, distinctiveness, and asexual reproduction. Geographical indications identify products as originating from specific geographic locations, ensuring certain quality or characteristics are maintained. Semiconductor chip protection safeguards the layout design or topography of semiconductor chips, requiring originality and novelty in the arrangement of transistors and other circuitry. Utility models, like patents, protect inventions but often have lower inventiveness requirements and provide shorter protection periods than patents.

Understanding the differences among these types of IP protection enables entrepreneurs to leverage the appropriate mechanisms to secure their intellectual assets strategically. The subsequent sections explore strategies for applying, managing, and enforcing these IP protections to maximize their value in the entrepreneurial journey.

2.8.3 Creating and Implementing an IP Strategy

Crafting a robust intellectual property (IP) strategy is essential for entrepreneurs to protect their innovations, establish market differentiation, and maximize the value of their creations. Developing a robust intellectual property (IP) strategy begins with identifying and prioritizing IP assets within the organization. Through a systematic audit, all potential intellectual property, including patents, trademarks, trade secrets, and copyrights, are pinpointed and evaluated based on strategic significance and commercial potential. This prioritization guides resource allocation, ensuring that the most valuable assets receive adequate protection and attention. Aligning the IP strategy with business goals is essential to integrate intellectual property efforts seamlessly into broader organizational objectives. By linking IP protection initiatives with long-term vision and growth plans, organizations strategically leverage their intellectual assets to support market positioning and sustainable competitive advantage. This alignment ensures that IP efforts contribute directly to the company's overarching goals and objectives. Conducting an IP landscape analysis involves assessing the competitive environment to understand existing IP rights and potential areas of conflict. By evaluating industry trends and emerging technologies, organizations position their IP strategy proactively to stay ahead of competitors and remain relevant in dynamic market landscapes. This analysis informs decision-making and ensures that the IP strategy is adaptive and responsive to changing market conditions. Establishing a clear budget and resource allocation framework is crucial for effectively managing intellectual property initiatives. By defining a budget for acquiring, maintaining, and enforcing IP rights, organizations balance the cost of protection with anticipated returns on investment. This ensures optimal resource utilization to safeguard and leverage intellectual assets for business growth and innovation. Determining the appropriate IP protections involves selecting the most suitable safeguards based on the nature of the innovation. Whether through patents, trademarks, or trade secrets, organizations develop a comprehensive strategy to defend against infringement and unauthorized use. Combining these protections provides robust defence mechanisms to safeguard intellectual assets effectively.

Developing an IP filing strategy requires careful planning and alignment with product development milestones. By strategically timing patent applications and considering global expansion plans, organizations optimize their IP protection efforts to support business growth and market competitiveness. This strategic approach ensures that intellectual property is protected in alignment with broader organizational goals and objectives. Implementing in-house IP policies involves establishing internal guidelines and procedures to safeguard confidential information and ensure compliance with IP regulations. By outlining protocols for handling sensitive data and conducting regular training sessions on IP awareness, organizations foster a culture of intellectual property stewardship within the organization. Monitoring and enforcing IP rights are critical for protecting intellectual property assets. By implementing robust monitoring systems and developing proactive enforcement strategies, organizations safeguard against infringement and unauthorized use. Additionally, leveraging licensing and partnerships can maximize the commercialization of IP assets, extending their reach and impact in the market. Creating a defensive IP strategy involves proactive measures to protect against legal challenges and assertions of third-party IP rights. Through freedom-to-operate analyses and regular reviews of the IP strategy, organizations mitigate risks associated with potential infringement claims and ensure continued alignment with evolving business goals and market dynamics. By diligently crafting and implementing an effective IP strategy, entrepreneurs can protect their innovations and strategically leverage their intellectual assets to gain a competitive edge in the market. A well-executed IP strategy contributes significantly to a technology venture's long-term success and sustainability.

Unit summary

This unit immerses students in the dynamic realm of product innovation, guiding them through critical stages of development. Starting with opportunity scanning and need identification, students learn to conduct market surveys and define problems that innovative products can solve. Creative design thinking methodologies are introduced for generating concept ideas, leading to detailed design, and prototyping phases. The unit explores practical considerations, including Bill of Materials creation, supply chain management, and manufacturing planning. Emphasis is placed on rigorous product testing, quality assurance, and the vital aspect of intellectual property rights management.

By the end of the unit, students acquire a holistic understanding of the product innovation lifecycle, from ideation to market-ready solutions, preparing them for the challenges of contemporary product development.

Tutorial questions for practice:

1. Explain the importance of opportunity scanning in the product innovation process. Provide examples to illustrate your answer. Assess the understanding of the significance of opportunity scanning and the ability to apply it in real-world scenarios.
2. Describe the stages of product innovation, from opportunity scanning to intellectual property rights management. Discuss the significance of each stage in the overall process. Evaluate the comprehension of the entire product innovation process and its stages and the ability to analyse their importance.
3. How does creative design thinking contribute to concept generation in product innovation? Provide a step-by-step explanation of the creative design thinking process with examples. Measure the understanding of creative design thinking, its role in generating innovative concepts, and the ability to apply it in practical situations.
4. Discuss the importance of product testing and quality assurance in ensuring the success of a new product launch. Outline the critical steps involved in effective product testing and quality assurance. Evaluate the importance of product testing and quality assurance and the ability to identify and explain key steps in the process with a case study as an example.
5. Why is it essential to manage intellectual property rights during product innovation? Provide examples of intellectual property rights management strategies used by successful companies. Assess the comprehension of the importance of intellectual property rights management and the ability to identify relevant strategies used in real-world scenarios.

Review Questions

1. Define opportunity scanning in the context of product innovation.
2. What is the purpose of conducting market surveys during product development?
3. Define intellectual property rights and their relevance to product innovation.
4. Identify the main components of a creative design thinking process.
5. Define the term "Supply Chain" in the context of product manufacturing.
6. Enumerate the critical components of a manufacturing plan for a new product.
7. Explain the significance of creative design thinking in generating concepts for new products.
8. Discuss the key considerations in creating a product's Bill of Materials (BOM).
9. How does prototyping contribute to the product development lifecycle, and what are its advantages?

10. Analyse the challenges associated with intellectual property rights management in product innovation.
11. Discuss the role of functionality assessment in the prototyping stage of product development.
12. Explain the importance of need identification and problem definition in the context of product innovation.
13. Discuss the role of prototypes in testing and validating the functionality of a new product.
14. Elaborate on the steps involved in the detailed design phase of product innovation.
15. Compare and contrast different methods for product testing and quality assurance.
16. Develop a hypothetical manufacturing and assembly plan for a new innovative product, considering supply chain logistics.
17. Evaluate the impact of market pull and technology push factors on the opportunity scanning process.
18. Develop a comprehensive market survey strategy, including data collection and analysis methods.
19. Compare and contrast different creative design thinking methodologies and their applications in product concept generation.
20. Formulate a hypothetical Bill of Materials (BOM) for a complex product, considering various components and their dependencies.

Multiple Choice Questions (MCQs)

1. Which stage of product innovation involves identifying potential opportunities and understanding market needs?
    a) Creative design thinking
    b) Product testing & quality assurance
    c) Opportunity scanning
    d) Intellectual property rights management
2. What is the primary purpose of conducting a market survey during product innovation?
    a) Detailed design & prototyping
    b) Need identification and problem definition
    c) Bill of materials & components supply chain
    d) Functionality & manufacturability
3. What is the focus of creative design thinking in product innovation?
    a) Opportunity scanning
    b) Concept generation
    c) Manufacturing & assembly plan

d) Product testing & quality assurance

4. Which stage involves creating a detailed plan for manufacturing and assembling the product?
   a) Detailed design & prototyping
   b) Functionality & manufacturability
   c) Manufacturing & assembly plan
   d) Product testing & quality assurance
5. What is the purpose of conducting product testing & quality assurance?
   a) Opportunity scanning
   b) Need identification and problem definition
   c) Product functionality validation
   d) Intellectual property rights management

Fill in the Blanks:

1. ______________ involves understanding market needs and identifying potential opportunities for product development.
2. Creative design thinking is utilized for ______________.
3. The stage of ______________ involves creating a detailed plan for manufacturing and assembly.
4. ______________ ensures that the product meets quality standards and functions as intended.
5. ______________ is responsible for managing and protecting the intellectual property associated with the product.

Answers - multiple Choice Questions:

1. c) Opportunity scanning
2. b) Need identification and problem definition
3. b) Concept generation
4. c) Manufacturing & assembly plan
5. c) Product functionality validation

Answers - Fill in the Blanks:

1. Opportunity scanning

2. Concept generation.
3. Manufacturing & assembly plan.
4. Product testing & quality assurance
5. Intellectual property rights management

References for Suggested Reading

1. Ulrich, Karl T., and Steven D. Eppinger. *Product design and development*. McGraw-Hill, 2016.

2. Rosen, Marc A., and Hossam A. Kishawy. "Sustainable manufacturing and design: Concepts, practices and needs." *Sustainability* 4.2 (2012): 154-174.

3. Weitz, Barton A., and Robin Wensley, eds. *Handbook of marketing*. Sage, 2002.

4. Chelat Bhuvanachandran, Innovision, Khanna Book Publishing, 2022.

5. Kotler, Philip. "Strategies for introducing marketing into nonprofit organizations." *Journal of Marketing* 43.1 (1979): 37-44.

6. Krajewski, Lee J., and Manoj K. Malhotra. *Operations management: Processes and supply chains*. Pearson, 2022.

7. Kamrani, Ali K., and Emad Abouel Nasr. *Engineering design and rapid prototyping*. Springer Science & Business Media, 2010.

UNIT 3 Marketing and Finance

UNIT SPECIFICS: Marketing & Finance Integration

This unit comprehensively explores the dynamic relationship between marketing and finance in the entrepreneurial landscape. Key focus areas include:

1. **Market Segmentation & Market Sizing**
    - Techniques for market segmentation and determining the size of target markets.
    - Understanding how market analysis informs strategic decision-making.
2. **Customer Persona & Value Proposition**
    - Crafting customer personas and developing compelling value propositions.
    - Analysing the intersection between customer needs and the unique value a product or service provides.
3. **Marketing (Go-to-Market) Strategy**
    - Formulating effective marketing strategies for launching products in the market.
    - Understanding the components of a successful go-to-market plan.
4. **Distribution Channels and Sales Network**
    - Exploring various distribution channels and designing an efficient sales network.
    - Analysing the impact of distribution strategies on market penetration.
5. **Funding Requirement and Source of Funding**
    - Evaluating the funding requirements at various stages of the startup lifecycle.

- Identifying diverse funding sources, including angel investors, venture capitalists, and crowdfunding.

6. **Financial Projections and Accounting**

   - Creating robust financial projections for start-up ventures. .
   - Understanding essential accounting principles and practices for sustainable financial management.

7. **Start-up to Scale-Up Financing:**

   - Analysing the financial considerations during the transition from start-up to scale-up.
   - Identifying funding strategies to support the growth and expansion of entrepreneurial ventures.

RATIONALE

This unit is designed to bridge the critical domains of marketing and finance, recognizing their symbiotic relationship in entrepreneurial success. Students will understand how marketing decisions impact financial outcomes by integrating market segmentation, value proposition development, and go-to-market strategies with financial considerations. The unit aims to equip students with the skills to effectively navigate funding landscapes and manage financial aspects at various stages of a start-up's evolution.

PRE-REQUISITES

Understanding of basic marketing strategies and financial principles

UNIT OUTCOMES

Upon completion of this unit, students will be able to:

U3-O1: Develop market segmentation strategies and estimate market sizes for targeted segments.

U3-O2: Create customer personas and articulate compelling value propositions to enhance product-market fit.

U3-O3: Formulate effective marketing strategies and design comprehensive go-to-market plans for entrepreneurial ventures.

U3-O4: Evaluate and select appropriate distribution channels, optimizing sales networks for market penetration.

U3-O5: Analyse funding requirements at different start-up stages and identify diverse funding sources.

Unit-3 Outcomes	Expected Mapping with Programme Outcomes *(1- Weak Correlation; 2- Medium correlation; 3- Strong Correlation)*				
	CO-1	CO -2	CO -3	CO -4	CO -5
U3-O1	3	2	2	2	2
U3-O2	2	1	3	2	2
U3-O3	3	3	2	1	1
U3-O4	3	2	3	2	2
U3-O5	3	3	2	1	1

In the dynamic world of entrepreneurship, success goes beyond innovative ideas and product development. This content, "Marketing and Finance," is designed to equip aspiring entrepreneurs with the essential skills to navigate the intricate terrain of business. From identifying target markets and crafting compelling value propositions to securing financial resources for start-up ventures, this unit explores into the pivotal aspects of bringing a technology venture to completion. Entrepreneurs will gain insights into effectively positioning their products or services in the market by comprehensively exploring marketing strategies, financial planning, and funding sources. Simultaneously, the section offers a deep dive into the intricacies of financial projections, accounting principles, and this diverse landscape of start-up financing.

The journey seamlessly integrates marketing and finance, providing the knowledge and tools to transform innovative concepts into successful, sustainable business ventures. Figure 3.1 depicts the features of sustainable business models, highlighting key elements that contribute to a business's long-term viability and success. These features influence environmental responsibility, social impact, economic resilience, ethical practices, and innovation. The following multifaceted approach and discussion ensure that entrepreneurs create ground-breaking solutions and strategically propel them into the marketplace, securing the foundation for long-term success.

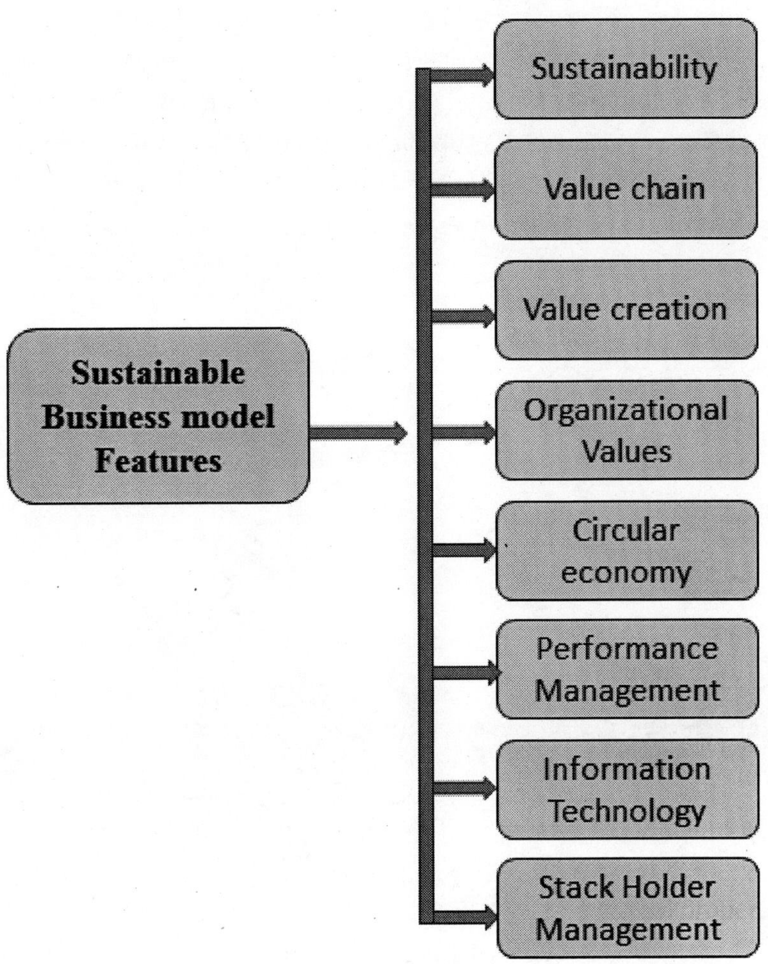

Figure 3.1 Features of sustainable business models

3.1 Market Segmentation and Market Sizing

Market segmentation is a strategic approach that divides a heterogeneous market into distinct, identifiable segments based on shared characteristics. Figure 3.2 illustrates an illustrative example of Market Segmentation Techniques. Market segmentation involves dividing a heterogeneous market into segments based on various criteria such as demographics, geography, behaviour, or psychographic factors. As a result, businesses can better understand different customer groups' diverse needs and preferences, allowing for more targeted and practical marketing efforts. For example, a company may segment its market based on demographic factors like age, gender, income level, or geographic factors such as location or urban-rural divide. Additionally, behavioural segmentation considers customer purchasing behavior, brand loyalty, usage patterns, or product preferences. Moreover, psychographic segmentation explores into consumers' psychological characteristics, lifestyle choices, values, and interests. By employing appropriate segmentation techniques, businesses can tailor their products, services, and marketing messages to meet each segment's specific needs and preferences, enhancing customer satisfaction and driving overall business success. The following sub-topics explore the fundamental concepts of market segmentation and its significance in crafting targeted marketing strategies.

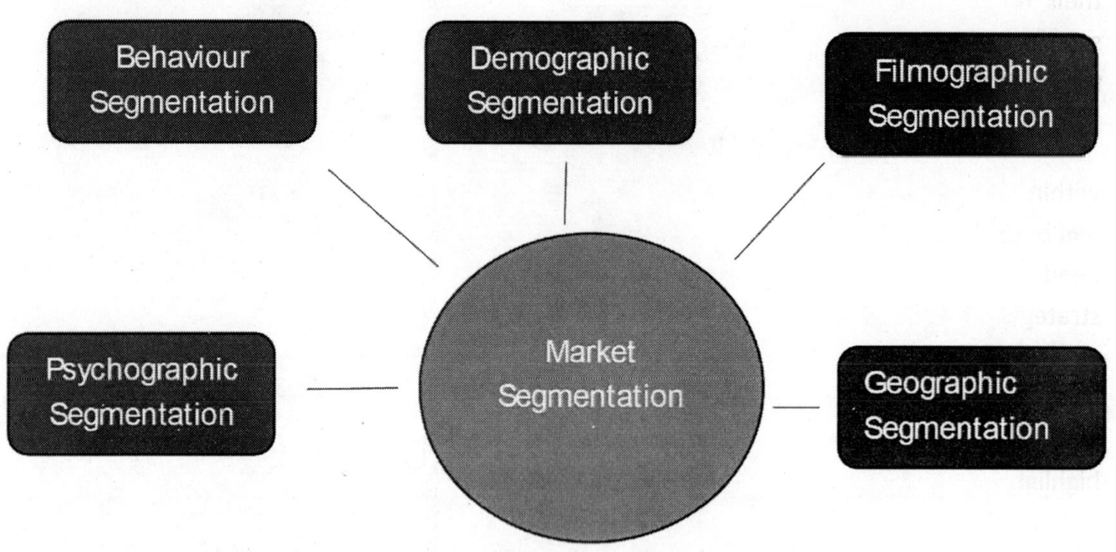

Figure 3.2 An Example of Market Segmentation Techniques

3.1.1 Understanding Market Segmentation

Market segmentation is the process of dividing a market into smaller, more homogeneous groups of customers. These groups are based on shared characteristics, such as demographics, Geographical location, attitudes, behaviour, needs, priorities, shared interests, and other psychographic or behavioural criteria. Market segmentation can help businesses develop products, marketing, advertising, and sales efforts. It can also help businesses determine the selection of marketing strategies by the segment. Market segmentation is crucial for businesses to target their desired audience and tailor their marketing efforts effectively. By dividing a more significant market into smaller groups, companies can create personalized messaging; improve customer satisfaction, and increase sales and revenue. Effective segmentation should be measurable, accessible, substantial, differentiable, and actionable. When a company has segmented its market accordingly, it will eventually become more profitable and successful. Further, in the market segmentation process, the initial step involves defining the overall market and establishing the parameters for the segmentation. Following this, a detailed analysis of existing customers is conducted to understand their characteristics and preferences. Subsequently, buyer persona(s) is created to represent the ideal customer profiles. The process then entails a thorough comparison to identify gaps, distinct groups, and potential opportunities within the market. Once these insights are gathered, the next step is to define and name the segments based on common characteristics and behaviours. The segmentation process continues with dedicated research on each identified segment, examining their unique needs and preferences. Finally, the last steps involve testing and optimizing the segmentation strategy, ensuring it aligns with the dynamic market landscape and effectively targets the identified segments.

For example, the IPhone brand leader 'Apple' exemplifies successful market segmentation within its iPhone product line by acknowledging distinct customer segments' diverse preferences and budgets. This recognition leads Apple to offer a range of iPhone models, each catering to unique needs and price points. This strategic approach aligns with McDonald's market segmentation strategy, where the company adapts its American fast-food style to local ingredients, cultural norms, and preferences when entering new countries. Similarly, Amul employs market segmentation in India by tailoring its products to various age groups. Another notable example is Café Coffee Day, which strategically targets lifestyle-oriented, urban consumers, particularly the youth demographic, highlighting the effectiveness of market segmentation in catering to specific consumer preferences and characteristics.

However, the challenges associated with market segmentation are multifaceted and encompass various aspects of the business process. Limited production capabilities can pose a challenge, restricting the ability to meet the unique demands of segmented markets. Similarly, the expenses incurred in production, along with high marketing costs, can be prohibitive. Access to distribution channels may hinder reaching specific segments effectively, and heavy initial investments could strain resources. Promotion challenges and stock/storage issues further compound these difficulties. Accurately identifying relevant segments, collecting, and analysing reliable data, creating compelling customer profiles, and allocating resources efficiently are integral tasks. Managing overlapping segments and adapting strategies in response to evolving market dynamics are essential components in addressing the complexities associated with market segmentation.

To overcome these challenges, engaging in interactive workshops must be designed for segmenting target markets that align with specific criteria. These workshops facilitate a systematic approach, covering various essential aspects. Defining the workshop's goals and purpose establishes a clear direction for the segmentation process. The subsequent step involves the analysis of relevant data to identify critical segments. Prioritizing these segments follows, emphasizing the significance of each in achieving organizational objectives. Once identified and prioritized, developing comprehensive segment profiles becomes crucial for targeted marketing efforts. Subsequently, crafting effective marketing strategies tailored to each segment ensures a focused and impactful approach. The last step involves creating an action plan and consolidating the workshop outcomes into actionable steps for successful market segmentation implementation. Understanding market segmentation is pivotal for entrepreneurs seeking to position their products strategically in the market.

3.1.2 Techniques for Effective Market Sizing

Market sizing is a critical aspect of strategic planning, providing entrepreneurs with valuable insights into the potential of their target markets. The following discussion details various techniques for effectively estimating market size, helping entrepreneurs make informed decisions and allocating resources judiciously. The Key Techniques for Effective Market Sizing are Top-Down Approach and Bottom-Up Approach.

Top-Down approach is one of the key approaches for market sizing. In this approach, the analysis begins by comprehensively defining the overall market size and narrowing it down to specific segments. Understanding the top-down approach involves recognizing its application in scenarios where a broad market overview is needed before diving into specific details. Practical examples of the top-down approach implementation illustrate its advantages, emphasizing its usefulness in gaining a holistic understanding of market dimensions and facilitating a more focused and targeted segmentation strategy. The Bottom-Up Approach involves delving into the details and estimating the market size by aggregating data from individual segments. Practical applications of the bottom-up approach became known in scenarios where a granular, segment-specific analysis is more appropriate, and real-world illustrations highlight instances where this method proves advantageous in providing accurate and detailed market size estimations. Another crucial technique for adequate market sizing involves Competitor Analysis. This approach relies on leveraging Competitive Intelligence, utilizing information about competitors to gauge market share and extrapolate overall market size. Businesses can refine their market size estimates by understanding competitors' strategies and market presence. Benchmarking against competitors becomes a valuable tool in this process, offering insights into industry standards, best practices, and potential areas for growth. This technique enhances the accuracy of market sizing and provides a strategic perspective by aligning business goals with the competitive landscape. Further, in market analysis, three key concepts are pivotal in shaping a business's strategic approach. The Total Addressable Market (TAM) serves as the foundation, representing the market demand for a specific product or service. Moving forward, the focus narrows to the Serviceable Addressable Market (SAM); this encapsulates the portion of TAM that a business can realistically target, considering numerous factors such as resources, capabilities, and market reach. Finally, the Serviceable Obtainable Market (SOM) explores the business's expectations more deeply, representing the share of SAM that the company aims to capture successfully. TAM, SAM, and SOM form a structured framework guiding businesses in understanding, targeting, and strategically capturing market opportunities.

Also, Surveys and interviews constitute an essential methodology for adequate market sizing. The utilization of surveys involves a meticulous survey design process aimed at gathering comprehensive data from potential customers. This design should encompass thoughtful questions that extract relevant information to gauge market preferences, demands, and potential size. In parallel, interview techniques play a pivotal role. Conducting structured interviews becomes a valuable strategy to extract nuanced insights and validate assumptions about the market. Through direct interactions, businesses can explore customer perceptions, preferences, and behaviours deeper, ensuring a more accurate and well-rounded understanding of the market dynamics. Integrating surveys and interviews into the market sizing process provides a qualitative dimension, complementing quantitative data and enhancing the overall accuracy of market assessments. Further, In the era of advanced market analysis, Data Analytics and Modelling are pivotal techniques for refined market sizing. Utilizing Big Data is integral to this process, involving the exploration of vast datasets to glean valuable insights. Through advanced analytics, businesses can harness the power of Big Data to refine market sizing, gaining a more comprehensive understanding of consumer behaviours, trends, and preferences. Additionally, Predictive Modelling plays a crucial role in enhancing the accuracy of market size projections. Leveraging statistical algorithms and historical data allows businesses to forecast future market trends and dynamics, contributing to more informed decision-making. Integrating Data Analytics and Modelling facilitates precise market sizing and empowers businesses to stay ahead in the dynamic market trends and consumer behavior landscape.

Incorporating Regulatory and Industry Reports is also fundamental to comprehensive market sizing. Businesses can leverage existing reports from regulatory bodies and industry analysts, gaining valuable insights into market trends, growth projections, and competitive landscapes. Accessing Industry Reports provides businesses with a wealth of data compiled by experts, aiding in formulating well-informed market size estimations. Additionally, interpreting Regulatory Guidelines is crucial in understanding how regulatory frameworks may impact market dynamics and size. This awareness ensures businesses account for legal and compliance factors when assessing the market landscape. By integrating insights from regulatory and industry reports, businesses enhance their market sizing strategies' robustness, aligning them with industry standards and regulatory expectations. In addition, Scenario Analysis is a strategic technique for inadequate market sizing, primarily for its role in risk mitigation and decision-making under uncertainty. By incorporating scenario analysis, businesses can account for various uncertainties and potential risks in their market sizing endeavours. This methodology involves developing multiple hypothetical scenarios reflecting different market conditions, enabling businesses to prepare for various potential outcomes. This approach is instrumental in promoting risk resilience and ensuring market sizing strategies remain adaptable to changing dynamics. Furthermore, scenario analysis provides valuable insights for decision-making under uncertainty, offering businesses strategic frameworks for making informed choices in ambiguous market conditions. This technique enhances the robustness of market sizing by acknowledging and addressing the inherent uncertainties within the business landscape. Finally, conducting an Interactive Workshop with a Market Sizing Exercise is a hands-on and immersive approach to applying market sizing techniques tailored to specific ventures. In this dynamic environment, entrepreneurs actively engage in the practical application of market sizing methodologies relevant to their business endeavours. The workshop provides a platform for real-time exploration, allowing entrepreneurs to apply and test various market sizing strategies directly. A crucial component of this workshop is incorporating feedback and refinement sessions. Entrepreneurs receive constructive feedback on their market sizing approaches, enabling them to refine and enhance their strategies based on practical exercises. This interactive and iterative process ensures that market sizing efforts are theoretically grounded and tailored to individual ventures' unique challenges and opportunities.

Mastering the techniques for adequate market sizing empowers entrepreneurs to make well-informed decisions, optimize resource allocation, and strategically position their ventures in the competitive landscape. The following discussion provides entrepreneurs with a toolkit of methodologies and practical insights to navigate the complexities of market sizing.

3.1.3 Market Trends Analysis

Market trends analysis is a crucial component of strategic planning, offering entrepreneur's valuable insights into the dynamics shaping their industry. The following discussion explores the methodologies and importance of analysing market trends, helping entrepreneurs stay ahead of the curve and align their ventures with evolving consumer preferences. In strategic market analysis, the foundational step involves understanding market trends. This necessitates a clear definition of market trends and an appreciation of their crucial role in anticipating shifts in consumer behavior. Market trends are dynamic indicators influenced by technological advancements, societal changes, and economic factors. By comprehending these trends, businesses gain insights into evolving consumer preferences and behaviours, enabling them to adapt their strategies proactively. Recognizing the interconnected impact of technology, society, and economics on market trends forms the bedrock for informed decision-making and formulating agile business strategies. Further, recognizing the importance of market trends analysis is essential for businesses striving for competitiveness and innovation. Staying abreast of dynamic market trends provides a competitive edge by enabling businesses to anticipate consumer preferences and behavior shifts. This proactive approach raises innovation as companies adapt to emerging trends swiftly. Market trends analysis serves as a crucial tool in identifying opportunities for growth and potential threats that may arise. By embracing a forward-looking perspective through trends analysis, businesses position themselves strategically to navigate the evolving market landscape, ensuring sustained competitiveness and the ability to capitalize on emerging opportunities. Also, on the other hand, tapping into diverse data sources is imperative for comprehensive insights when delving into trends analysis. Industry reports, offering expert perspectives, stand as a valuable primary source. Supplementing this with consumer surveys allows direct access to evolving preferences. Social media analytics, a dynamic resource, provides real-time indicators of public sentiment. Integrating primary methods, like surveys, with secondary research from industry reports ensures an integrated approach to identifying trends. This comprehensive strategy harnesses the power of varied data sources, combining expert insights and direct consumer feedback to offer a nuanced understanding of market dynamics and emerging trends.

An integral aspect of market trend analysis involves examining Technology Adoption Trends. This entails meticulously analysing the industry's adoption curve for emerging technologies. By understanding the pace at which technologies are embraced, businesses can anticipate shifts in consumer expectations and adapt to evolving market dynamics. Technology trends exercise a major influence in shaping consumer behavior and expectations. Businesses that grasp and leverage these trends position themselves strategically, ensuring they are at the forefront of technological advancements and are well-prepared to meet changing consumer demands in an increasingly tech-driven landscape. Importantly, Consumer Behaviour and Lifestyle Trends thoroughly examine consumer preferences, lifestyle choices, and purchasing behaviour shifts. Understanding these dynamics allows businesses to effectively adapt their strategies to meet evolving consumer needs. Furthermore, connecting these consumer trends to product or service innovation opportunities becomes a strategic imperative. By aligning offerings with changing consumer behaviours and preferences, businesses can proactively position themselves to cater to emerging market demands, promoting innovation and maintaining relevance in a dynamic consumer landscape. A critical facet of trends analysis involves scrutinizing the impact of Economic and Market Forces. This evaluation encompasses the influence of economic factors like inflation, unemployment, and market saturation on emerging trends. Understanding the intricate interplay between these economic variables and industry trends is essential for making informed business impacts decisions. Additionally, recognizing the broader scope, global and local market forces play a pivotal role in shaping industry trends. By comprehending the intricate dynamics of economic and market forces, businesses can navigate trends with foresight, adapt strategies to mitigate risks, and leverage opportunities arising from dynamic market conditions. In addition, a thorough examination of the Competitive Landscape is paramount. This involves assessing how competitors respond to and even drive market trends. By understanding competitors' reactions, businesses gain valuable insights into the market's shifting dynamics. Moreover, this analysis provides a lens into competitors' strategies for capitalizing on emerging opportunities, offering a benchmark for strategic decision-making. Through a comprehensive understanding of the competitive landscape, businesses can position themselves strategically, ensuring they are responsive to trends and proactive in shaping and capitalizing on evolving market dynamics.

Also, an integral aspect of trends analysis involves scrutinizing Regulatory and Environmental Trends. This encompasses meticulously examining trends influenced by regulatory changes and environmental considerations. Understanding the impact of evolving regulations on industries allows businesses to anticipate shifts in market dynamics. Moreover, identifying opportunities for sustainable and socially responsible business practices is a crucial outcome of this analysis. By aligning strategies with regulatory and environmental trends, businesses ensure compliance and position themselves as socially conscious entities, contributing to long-term sustainability and resilience in an ever-changing business landscape. Further, Implementing Scenario Planning Based on Trends is a proactive strategy for navigating a dynamic business environment. This involves employing scenario planning techniques to anticipate potential developments in response to identified trends. By creating strategic responses for different scenarios, businesses ensure adaptability and resilience. This forward-looking approach prepares organizations for various potential outcomes, developing strategic agility. Through scenario planning based on trends, businesses not only navigate uncertainties effectively but also position themselves strategically to capitalize on emerging opportunities and mitigate risks associated with evolving market dynamics. For example, McDonald's exemplifies successful trend adaptation by tailoring its menu to local tastes. In India, where a significant population is vegetarian, McDonald's introduced vegetarian options, highlighting a keen understanding of and responsiveness to local preferences.

Finally, Interactive content engages users in the trend identification exercise. Using a whiteboard, entrepreneurs brainstorm trends in the fitness industry, creating nodes and branches. Grouping ideas by colour and branch thickness signifies strength. Entrepreneurs then vote on critical trends, leading to in-depth discussions on each. Topics include defining the trend, its importance, its impact on the fitness industry, and associated opportunities and challenges. The session would conclude with action item generation, preparing businesses for the evolving fitness landscape. This adaptable exercise creates forward-thinking and strategy development for various industries, aligning businesses with emerging trends for sustained growth and competitiveness.

Market trends analysis is a powerful tool for entrepreneurs seeking to position their ventures strategically in the marketplace. This enables the entrepreneurs to practice the skills and methodologies necessary to conduct insightful trends analysis, creating an environment of adaptability and innovation within their entrepreneurial journey.

3.2. Customer Persona and Value Proposition

Understanding your target audience is fundamental to crafting effective marketing strategies. The following discussion examines creating customer personas, providing entrepreneurs with a structured approach to developing detailed, actionable representations of their ideal customers. Figure 3.3 illustrates the Components of a Customer Persona. It is a valuable marketing and product development tool to better understand and empathize with target customers. Customer personas, also known as buyer personas or user personas represent fictional characters that symbolize the characteristics, needs, goals, and behaviours of a particular target audience segment. The components of a customer persona typically include demographic information such as age, gender, occupation, income level, and geographic location. Moreover, psychographic details explore into the customer's lifestyle, interests, values, attitudes, and pain points.

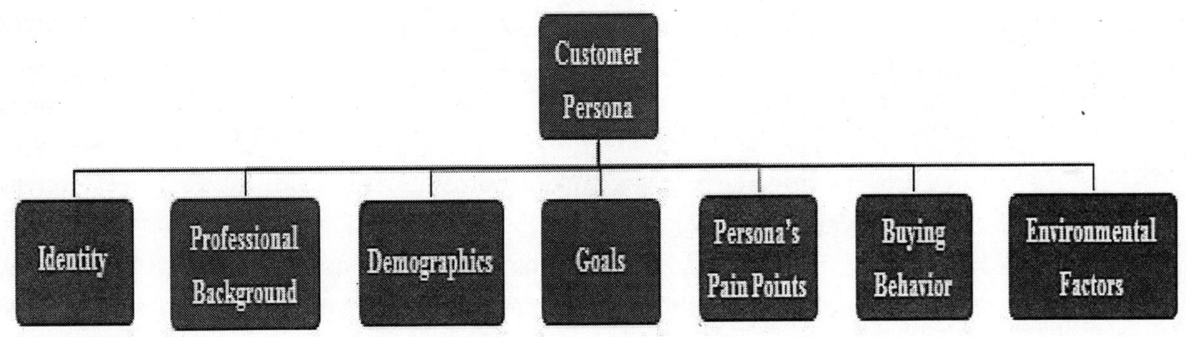

Figure 3.3 Components of a customer persona

3 2.1 Creating Customer Personas

A customer persona is a semi-fictional depiction of the ideal customer, offering a comprehensive profile that encapsulates key characteristics, demographics, behaviours, and preferences specific to the target audience. This detailed representation aids businesses in understanding and empathizing with their customers, facilitating more effective and personalized marketing strategies. By humanizing the target audience through personas, businesses can tailor their products, services, and communication strategies to better resonate with the identified customer segments, enhancing customer engagement and satisfaction. Highlighting their importance underscores their profound impact on aligning marketing strategies with customer needs. Businesses can tailor their approaches to resonate with specific segments by creating detailed representations of the ideal customer, resulting in more effective and targeted marketing efforts. Additionally, customer personas are pivotal in enhancing organizational communication and collaboration. Teams can align their efforts based on a shared understanding of the customer, developing a cohesive approach prioritizing customer-centricity. Using customer personas transcends marketing, becoming a fundamental tool for creating a unified organizational focus on delivering value to the identified target audience.

Creating a customer persona is a strategic process involving several vital steps. Begin by gathering existing customer data to understand the persona's details. Describe the customer's needs and pain points, mapping out the ideal experience they seek. To bring the persona to life, vividly tell their story, emphasizing their goals and behaviours. Organize and refine the information to create a cohesive representation. Sharing the persona across the organization ensures alignment. Consider developing various personas to capture different customer segments. A comprehensive customer persona should encompass details about who the buyers are, their objectives, driving goals, thought processes, behavioural patterns, and the purchasing decision-making process. Examples of customer personas include buyer personas, representing target customers; user personas, reflecting those using a product or service; and website personas, embodying all visitors a website aims to serve. Each persona type aids businesses in tailoring their strategies to meet diverse customer needs effectively.

Effective customer research involves exploring diverse methods, such as surveys, interviews, and analytics tools. Surveys provide quantitative insights, capturing numerical data on customer preferences and behaviours. Interviews, on the other hand, offer qualitative depth by delving into customers' experiences, emotions, and nuanced perspectives. Leveraging analytics tools enables businesses to extract valuable data from online interactions, informing decision-making. The significance lies in gathering quantitative and qualitative data for a comprehensive understanding. Quantitative data offers statistical insights, while qualitative data provides context and customer narratives. Integrating both data types ensures an integrated method, enabling businesses to make informed decisions grounded in numerical trends and nuanced customer insights. Identifying demographics (age, gender, location) and psychographics (values, interests, and lifestyle) is pivotal for persona development. Demographic factors provide a foundational understanding of a customer's essential characteristics, while psychographics explore into their intricate motivations and preferences. Combining demographics and psychographics creates a holistic customer profile, enhancing persona accuracy. This comprehensive approach ensures that personas go beyond surface-level details, enabling businesses to tailor their strategies with a nuanced understanding of customers' diverse needs, behaviours, and aspirations.

Examining into customer pain points and motivations is integral to persona development. Businesses can create more empathetic and tailored personas by investigating customers' challenges (pain points) and understanding their driving forces (motivations). Addressing pain points and aligning with motivations strengthens value propositions, as businesses can offer solutions that directly resonate with customers' needs and desires. Recognizing and addressing these key elements enhances customer satisfaction, loyalty, and engagement, contributing to creating products or services that genuinely meet the unique requirements of the target audience. Businesses use customer journey maps to visually portray the connection points and experiences of various personas as they connect with the company. These maps serve as powerful tools for identifying opportunities for engagement and improvement at various stages of the customer's experience. Businesses can gain insights into customer expectations, pain points, and moments of delight, allowing them to optimize each touch point for a more seamless and satisfying customer journey. Through the strategic use of journey maps, businesses enhance their understanding of customer interactions, enabling them to tailor experiences that resonate with the unique needs of each persona.

Effective persona documentation includes demographics, psychographics, pain points, motivations, and customer journey insights. This holistic template ensures a comprehensive understanding of the target audience. Regularly updating and refining personas based on evolving customer insights is crucial for maintaining accuracy. As customer behaviours and preferences shift, businesses must adapt to stay aligned with their audience. This iterative process ensures that personas remain dynamic and reflective of the ever-changing landscape, enabling businesses to craft strategies that consistently resonate with their evolving customer base.

Examining case studies on effective persona utilization provides valuable insights. Blue Cable's focus on the Software Architect persona reflects tailored solutions for technical professionals. The Administrative Assistant persona in 'Smallpdf' illustrates customized techniques tailored to distinct user roles. 'Clear Voice's' Marketing Director Persona exhibits persona-driven marketing techniques. In the case of the 'Swiggy' App, targeting the Busy Professional persona demonstrates the importance of understanding and meeting the unique needs of time-strapped individuals. These diverse case studies underscore the versatility and efficacy of leveraging customer personas to tailor products, services, and marketing efforts for maximum impact across various industries.

Creating customer personas is a foundational step in developing a robust marketing strategy. Immersing entrepreneurs in the practical persona creation process equips them with the tools and insights necessary to resonate with their target audience and effectively tailor their value propositions. A persona creation exercise must be practised, including diverse stakeholders identifying entrepreneurs, gathering research, defining user segments, and creating persona templates. Connecting personas with user stories and involving the development team enhances cohesion. The iterative process of reviewing and refining ensures that personas align closely with user insights, developing targeted strategies and solutions.

3.2.2 Crafting a Compelling Value Proposition

In the competitive entrepreneurship landscape, a compelling value proposition is the key to capturing the attention of potential customers. The following discussion focuses on the art and science of crafting a value proposition that resonates with your target audience and sets your venture apart from the competition. A value proposition is a concise statement articulating the unique value offered by a product or service to customers. It serves as a beacon, effectively communicating how the offering addresses specific customer needs and stands out from competitors. Central to business strategy, the value proposition encapsulates what sets a product or service apart, compelling customers to choose it over alternatives. By succinctly conveying the benefits and advantages of the offering, a well-crafted value proposition resonates with target audiences and forms the cornerstone of effective marketing and differentiation strategies in competitive markets. A robust value proposition is essential in customer acquisition and retention. By clearly articulating a product or service's unique benefits and value, a strong value proposition effectively attracts prospective customers and convinces them to choose the offering over alternatives. Furthermore, it is pivotal in securing customer loyalty and retention by continuously reaffirming the value delivered. Moreover, a compelling value proposition strengthens brand positioning. It enhances market competitiveness by differentiating the offering from competitors and resonating with the target audience's needs and preferences, establishing a solid foothold in the market landscape. A compelling value proposition comprises several vital elements essential for conveying compelling customer messages. It breaks down into the Unique Selling Proposition (USP), highlighting what sets the product or service apart from competitors. Additionally, it articulates the benefits customers can expect, addressing their pain points and fulfilling their needs. Furthermore, differentiation is crucial, highlighting why the offering is superior or different from alternatives in the market. Examples of well-crafted value propositions across diverse industries illustrate how companies successfully communicate their value to customers, enhancing brand perception and driving competitive advantage in the marketplace. Customer-centric value propositions prioritize alignment with customer needs, preferences, and pain points. They develop trust and engagement by addressing these aspects, as customers feel understood and valued. This approach ensures relevance and resonance, enhancing customer satisfaction and loyalty.

Also, Benefits-oriented messaging in value propositions shifts the focus from product features to customer-centric benefits. Crafting value propositions that emphasize the positive impact on the customer effectively communicates how the product or service fulfils their needs and addresses pain points. By highlighting the value and outcomes experienced by customers, businesses create more compelling messages that resonate with their target audience, driving engagement and conversion. Further, differentiation strategies play a pivotal role in setting apart value propositions from competitors. Businesses can explore various approaches such as innovation, ensuring unique features or functionalities, maintaining superior quality, offering competitive pricing, and prioritizing exceptional customer experiences. By analysing these factors, businesses can craft value propositions that stand out in the market landscape, effectively communicating their unique value and compelling reasons for customers to choose their offerings over alternatives. This differentiation seeks customer loyalty and market competitiveness, driving sustained growth and success. Additionally, the Value Proposition Canvas serves as a dynamic visual tool for designing, testing, and refining value propositions and guiding entrepreneurs through its practical application; businesses can systematically analyse customer segments' needs and pains alongside the features and benefits of their products or services. This collaborative process develops a deeper understanding of customer preferences and enables the creation of compelling value propositions tailored to meet market demands. Through iterative testing and refinement, businesses can optimize their value propositions to resonate effectively with target audiences, driving customer engagement and satisfaction.

Crafting a compelling value proposition is a dynamic process that requires a deep understanding of customer needs and effective communication. The following discussion empowers entrepreneurs to articulate their unique value propositions, ensuring their ventures stand out and resonate meaningfully with their target audience.

3.2.3 Aligning Value Proposition with Customer Needs

Ensuring that your value proposition directly addresses your target customers' needs and desires is essential for building a solid and lasting connection. Figure 3.4 shows the Value Proposition Canvas, a strategic tool entrepreneurs use to visualize and design compelling value propositions for their products or services. It consists of two main elements: the Customer Profile, which outlines the characteristics and needs of the target customers, and the Value Map, which illustrates how the product or service addresses those needs and provides unique value. The following discussion explores strategies for aligning your value proposition with customer needs to create a compelling and irresistible offering. The influencing factors are as follows.

Understanding customer needs requires thorough research to identify their pain points, challenges, and aspirations. This entails empathetic listening and observation to uncover nuanced needs. By delving into customers' experiences and perspectives, businesses gain valuable insights that inform the development of tailored solutions. Empathizing with customers develops deeper connections and enables businesses to address the customers' needs effectively, by enhancing customer satisfaction and loyalty. Through empathetic research practices, businesses can align their offerings more closely with customer preferences, ensuring greater relevance and resonance in the market. Also, Value co-creation involves actively engaging them in product development or service design processes. By soliciting customer feedback, ideas, and preferences, businesses can tailor their offerings to better meet their needs and preferences. This collaborative approach develops a sense of ownership and empowerment among customers and strengthens the relationship between businesses and their customer base. Through value co-creation, businesses can build a loyal and satisfied customer community that actively shapes the direction and evolution of the products or services, leading to enhanced customer satisfaction and long-term success.

Further, by implementing iterative feedback loops is crucial for continuously gathering customer insights and staying informed about evolving needs and preferences. By regularly soliciting feedback through surveys, interviews, or customer interactions, businesses can adapt their value proposition to remain relevant in changing market dynamics. Addressing customer pain points is equally important for enhancing the value proposition's relevance and attractiveness. By integrating solutions directly into their offerings to alleviate customer challenges, businesses demonstrate understanding and commitment, strengthening customer loyalty. Clear communication is paramount to ensure customers understand the tangible benefits they will receive.

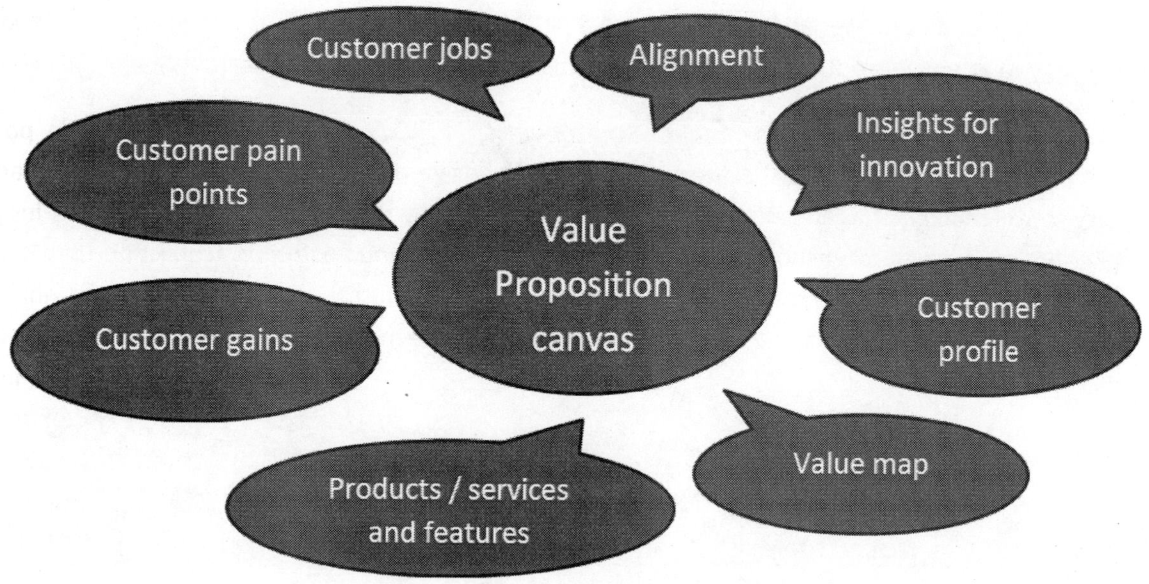

Figure 3.4 Value Proposition Canvas

By using language and messaging that directly address customer pain points and aspirations, businesses can effectively convey the value of their offerings, driving engagement and loyalty. Balancing emotional and functional appeals in the value proposition is key to engaging customers on multiple levels and increasing conversion rates. By resonating with customers' desires and addressing their practical needs, businesses can create meaningful connections and long-term loyalty. Continuous monitoring and adaptation of the value proposition based on real-time feedback and market analysis is essential to staying agile and aligned with evolving customer expectations. Integrating the value proposition with customer personas ensures consistency and resonance with specific audience segments, driving targeted engagement and business success.

By aligning the value proposition closely with customer needs, entrepreneurs can create a powerful connection with their target audience, developing loyalty and sustained success in the marketplace. This enables entrepreneurs to practice practical strategies to ensure that their offerings address customer needs effectively and resonate authentically with their audience.

3.3. Marketing (Go-to-Market) Strategy

A well-crafted Go-To-Market (GTM) strategy is essential for successfully bringing a product or service to market. The following discussion explores the critical components of a comprehensive GTM strategy, guiding entrepreneurs through the strategic planning process to maximize market penetration and customer adoption. Figure 3.5 illustrates the key elements of a go-to-market (GTM) strategy to effectively outline the plan for bringing a product or service to market.

3.3.1 Components of a Go-to-Market Strategy

A Go-to-Market (GTM) strategy is a comprehensive plan that delineates how a product or service will reach its target customers. It is a roadmap for coordinating various marketing, sales, and distribution aspects to ensure effective market penetration and customer acquisition. By defining the GTM strategy, businesses can align their efforts and resources toward achieving their market objectives and maximizing the impact of their offerings in the marketplace.

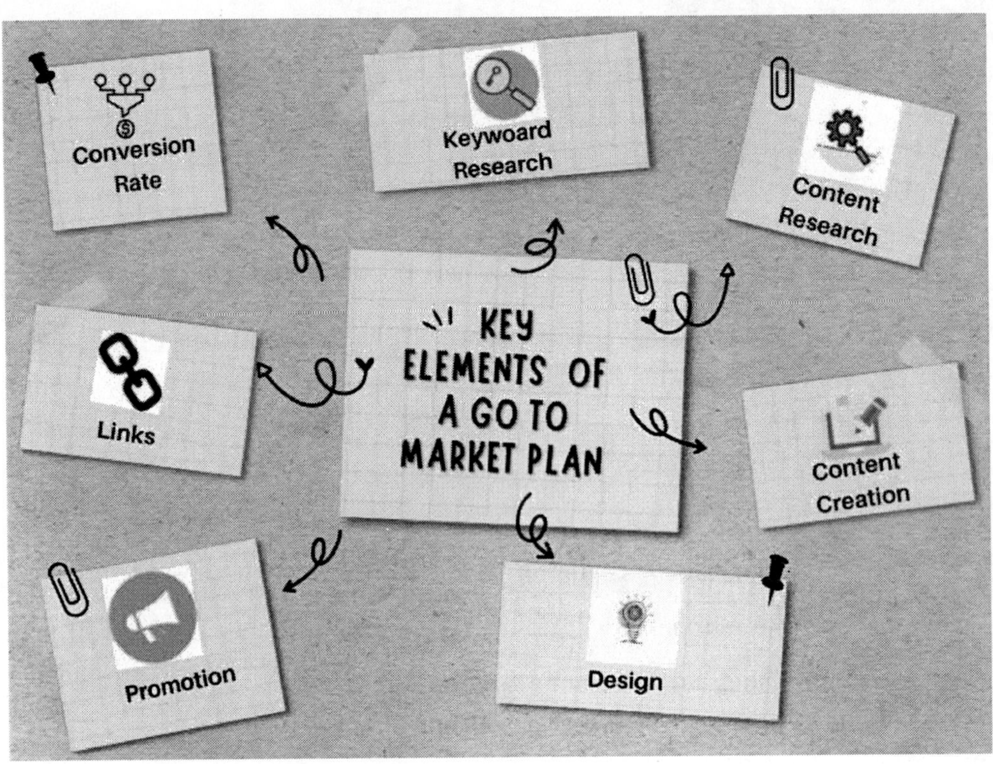

Figure 3.5 Key Elements of a Go-to-Market Strategy

Market segmentation and targeting are crucial steps in developing a successful Go-to-Market (GTM) strategy. By revisiting the importance of market segmentation, businesses can identify distinct customer segments with unique needs, preferences, and behaviours. Selecting target customer segments allows businesses to focus their resources and efforts on the most promising opportunities. Aligning the GTM strategy with the characteristics and preferences of the identified target audience ensures that marketing messages, distribution channels, and sales approaches resonate effectively, maximizing the chances of success in the marketplace. Seamlessly integrating the value proposition into the Go-to-Market (GTM) strategy is essential for its success. By aligning marketing messages with the unique benefits highlighted in the value proposition, businesses can effectively communicate the value of their offerings to target customers. This integration ensures consistency across all touch points and maximizes the impact of marketing efforts. By emphasizing the value proposition throughout the GTM strategy, businesses can differentiate themselves in the marketplace and attract and retain customers more effectively.

Identifying and optimizing distribution channels are integral to a successful Go-to-Market (GTM) strategy. This involves selecting the most suitable channels through which the product or service will reach customers, whether direct, indirect, online, or offline. Businesses can ensure efficient and effective reach to their target market by carefully evaluating and optimizing distribution channels. Additionally, establishing robust sales networks through in-house sales teams, partnerships, or online platforms enables businesses to capitalize on diverse opportunities and maximize market penetration. Figure 3.6 illustrates a Comparison of Distribution Channels, displaying different avenues through which products or services can reach consumers. This comparison allows businesses to evaluate and choose the most suitable distribution channels based on target audience, product characteristics, and market dynamics. Further, a well-defined pricing strategy is essential for aligning the product or service with customer expectations while reflecting its value proposition. Businesses must develop a pricing strategy considering competitive pricing, perceived value, and various pricing models. By carefully balancing these factors, businesses can set prices that capture the value offered and remain competitive.

A thoughtful pricing strategy enhances the perceived value of the offering and contributes to its overall market positioning. A comprehensive marketing communication plan is vital for effectively conveying the value proposition and generating customer interest. This plan should encompass various communication channels, including advertising, public relations, content marketing, and social media. By coordinating communication efforts across these channels, businesses can create a cohesive and impactful brand message that resonates with their target audience. A well-executed marketing communication plan enhances brand visibility, drives customer engagement, and supports the overall success of the GTM strategy. Then, a well-executed launch plan is crucial for the success of a Go-to-Market (GTM) strategy. This involves developing a phased approach encompassing pre-launch, launch, and post-launch activities. Leveraging teaser campaigns, pre-orders, and exclusive previews can help generate anticipation and excitement among the target audience. By carefully arranging each stage of the launch plan, businesses can maximize the visibility, engagement, and adoption of their product or service.

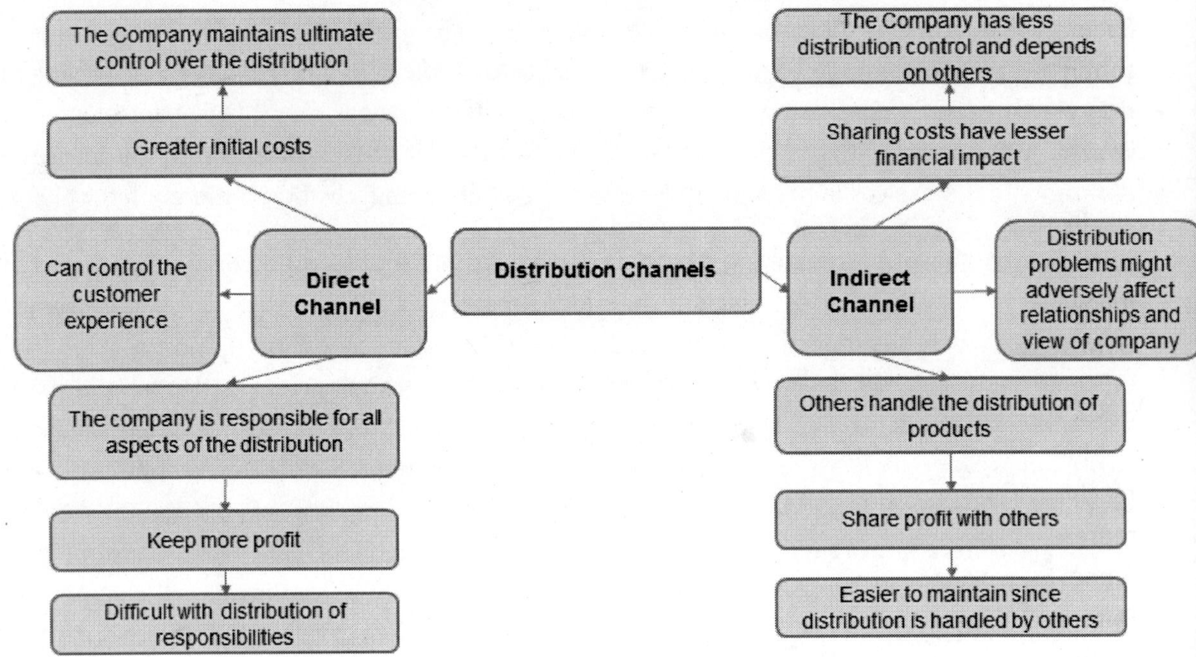

Figure 3.6 Comparisons of Distribution Channels

In continuation, Sales enablement plays a pivotal role in supporting the execution of the GTM strategy. Implementing strategies to equip the sales team with the necessary tools, training, and collateral ensures they are well-prepared to effectively communicate the value proposition to potential customers. By providing sales teams with the resources and support they need, businesses can empower them to drive conversions, build relationships, and contribute to the success of the GTM strategy. Customer acquisition and retention are key objectives of the GTM strategy. This involves outlining tactics for lead generation, conversion strategies, and on boarding processes to attract and on-board new customers. Additionally, developing strategies for customer retention, such as loyalty programs and on-going engagement initiatives, is essential for developing long-term relationships and maximizing customer lifetime value. Businesses can achieve sustainable growth and profitability by prioritizing acquisition and retention efforts. Also, it is important in establishing measurable metrics and key performance indicators (KPIs) which are essential for evaluating the effectiveness of the GTM strategy. By tracking metrics such as sales performance, customer acquisition costs, and customer lifetime value, businesses can gain valuable insights into the performance and impact of their GTM efforts. Monitoring and analysing data allow businesses to make informed adjustments and improvements, optimizing their GTM strategy for continued success. Identifying potential risks and developing contingency plans is critical for mitigating the impact of unforeseen challenges on the GTM strategy. By proactively assessing risks such as market fluctuations, competitive threats, or obstruction in the supply chain, businesses can develop robust contingency plans to minimize disruptions and maintain momentum. Far-sightedness for potential risks ensures businesses can navigate challenges effectively and remain agile in executing their GTM strategy.

By thoroughly exploring the components of a GTM strategy, entrepreneurs can ensure a systematic and practical approach to introducing their products or services to the market. The following discussion provides entrepreneurs practical insights and tools to develop a customized GTM strategy that aligns with their venture's objectives and resonates with their target audience.

3.3.2 Digital Marketing Techniques

In the era of digital connectivity, leveraging effective digital marketing techniques is crucial for reaching and engaging target audiences. Figure 3.7 illustrates the Digital Marketing Funnel, which represents potential customers' journey from awareness to conversion in the online realm. The funnel consists of several stages: Awareness, Interest, Consideration, Conversion, and Retention. Different digital marketing strategies and tactics are employed at each stage to engage and guide customers toward purchasing or taking a desired action. Understanding the digital marketing funnel helps entrepreneurs optimize their marketing efforts and improve conversion rates by delivering targeted and relevant content to prospects at each funnel stage. The following discussion explores various digital marketing strategies and tactics, providing entrepreneurs with insights into harnessing the power of online channels to enhance brand visibility, drive customer engagement, and optimize conversion rates. Digital marketing encompasses a variety of strategies aimed at enhancing online visibility and engaging target audiences effectively. Search Engine Optimization (SEO) is fundamental, involving tactics to optimize content for higher search engine rankings. This includes both on-page and off-page strategies to drive organic traffic and increase website visibility. Complementing SEO efforts, content marketing focuses on creating valuable and relevant content tailored to audience interests. A well-defined content strategy helps establish thought leadership and drive brand awareness by delivering consistent messaging across various channels.

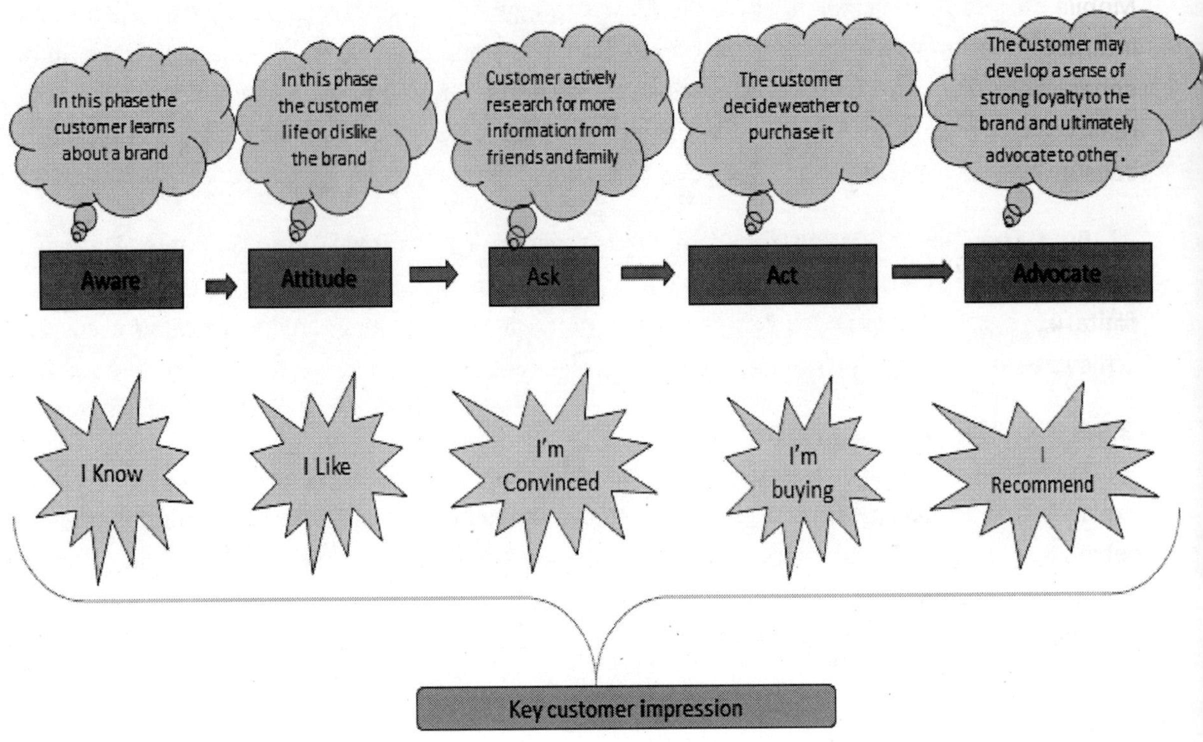

Figure 3.7 Digital marketing funnel

Social media marketing plays a pivotal role in brand promotion and community building, leveraging popular platforms to engage with audiences authentically. Crafting a social media strategy aligned with brand voice and target demographics enhances brand visibility and fosters customer loyalty. Alongside social media, email marketing serves as a direct communication channel with prospects and customers. Effective email campaigns and automation sequences nurture leads, drive conversions, and cultivate long-term relationships with customers. Pay-Per-Click (PPC) advertising complements organic efforts by driving targeted traffic through paid ads. Crafting compelling ad copy and optimizing landing pages are essential for maximizing the impact and return on investment of PPC campaigns. Influencer marketing harnesses the influence of key individuals to amplify brand reach and credibility. By collaborating with influencers aligned with brand values, businesses can extend their reach to new audiences and build trust with consumers. Additionally, online public relations tactics enhance brand visibility and reputation management. Building relationships with industry influencers and online publications generates positive media coverage, bolstering brand credibility in the digital landscape. Data-driven decision-making is crucial for optimizing digital marketing performance. Implementing analytics tools enables tracking and analysis of key metrics, informing strategic decisions to improve ROI and overall effectiveness.

Mobile marketing targets users on smartphones and tablets, optimizing experiences for seamless interaction. Video marketing is another powerful tool for storytelling and brand promotion, enhancing engagement and brand recall. Lastly, exploring emerging trends such as augmented reality and voice search enables businesses to stay ahead of the curve and adapt to evolving consumer behaviours in the digital realm.

By mastering digital marketing techniques, entrepreneurs can amplify their reach, engage with their audience effectively, and drive measurable results. This enables entrepreneurs to understand digital marketing strategies and empowers them to navigate the dynamic online landscape to achieve their business goals.

3.3.3 Building Brand Awareness and Loyalty

Building a solid brand is foundational to the success of any venture. The following discussion explores strategies for creating brand awareness and supporting customer loyalty, providing entrepreneurs with insights into the principles and practices contributing to a memorable and enduring brand. Developing a strong brand identity and positioning strategy is foundational for any business, encompassing both visual and emotional elements that set the brand apart in the market. Consistency in brand messaging across all channels is vital, reinforcing brand values and building recognition and trust among the target audience. By aligning brand messaging with the established identity, businesses can effectively resonate with consumers, fostering deeper connections and loyalty. Multi-channel marketing plays a crucial role in maximizing brand exposure and reach, utilizing both online and offline platforms to reinforce the brand message. Integrated marketing campaigns across diverse channels ensure consistent messaging and increase visibility among potential customers. Additionally, storytelling emerges as a powerful tool for creating emotional connections with the audience, humanizing the brand, and forging stronger bonds with consumers.

As the trend grows towards user-generated content (UGC), it further strengthens community engagement and advocacy, amplifying brand awareness and authenticity. Designing a positive brand experience at every stage of the customer journey is essential for building loyalty and advocacy, ensuring consistent and memorable interactions. Loyalty programs and incentives complement this effort, rewarding and retaining customers while driving long-term engagement. Building a brand community through various engagement initiatives fosters a sense of belonging among customers, while influencer partnerships enhance brand credibility and reach. Effective brand monitoring and reputation management strategies enable proactive responses to customer feedback, maintaining brand credibility and trust. Integrating sustainability and corporate social responsibility (CSR) initiatives into the brand strategy communicates the brand's commitment to societal and environmental concerns, enhancing reputation and loyalty among socially conscious consumers.

Monitoring key brand metrics and impact through analytics provides valuable insights for strategic decision-making, ensuring the effectiveness of brand-building efforts and driving continuous improvement. Developing a strong brand identity and positioning strategy is foundational for any business, encompassing both visual and emotional elements that set the brand apart in the market. Consistency in brand messaging across all channels is vital, reinforcing brand values and building recognition and trust among the target audience. By aligning brand messaging with the established identity, businesses can effectively resonate with consumers, fostering deeper connections and loyalty. Finally, monitoring key brand metrics and impact through analytics provides valuable insights for strategic decision-making, ensuring the effectiveness of brand-building efforts and driving continuous improvement. By strategically building brand awareness and developing customer loyalty, entrepreneurs can create a lasting and positive impact in the market. The following discussion provides entrepreneurs with practical guidance on the principles and techniques that contribute to effective brand building, enabling them to cultivate a solid and enduring brand presence

3.4. Distribution Channels and Sales Network

Selecting the proper distribution channels is critical to bringing a product or service to market. The following discussion explores various distribution channels, guiding entrepreneurs in understanding their options and making informed decisions to optimize their distribution and sales network.

3.4.1 Exploring Different Distribution Channels

The significance of distribution channels cannot be overstated, as they serve as the vital link between products or services and end consumers. Effective distribution expands the market reach and ensures customer accessibility, contributing to overall business success. Entrepreneurs must weigh the options between direct and indirect distribution channels when considering distribution strategies. Direct distribution involves selling products directly to consumers without intermediaries, while indirect distribution utilizes intermediaries like retailers, wholesalers, or distributors. Understanding the nuances between these models is essential for selecting the most suitable distribution approach based on business goals and target market dynamics.

Another critical distinction to consider is between online and offline distribution channels. Contrasting online distribution through e-commerce platforms with traditional offline distribution via brick-and-mortar stores enables entrepreneurs to evaluate the advantages and challenges of each approach. Product nature and target audience preferences inform strategic decisions regarding distribution channels. Entrepreneurs encounter various models within retail distribution, including exclusive, selective, and intensive distribution strategies. It is imperative to consider factors such as brand positioning and market coverage when selecting retail partners and managing relationships within the distribution network. Wholesalers are crucial in expanding market reach and accessing broader customer segments. Establishing and managing distribution partnerships with third-party entities requires careful consideration of factors such as product demand and channel profitability.

Direct-to-consumer (DTC) strategies offer brands opportunities to engage directly with customers, leveraging online platforms, subscription models, and personalized experiences. Assessing the benefits and challenges of DTC approaches aids in designing effective distribution strategies aligned with business objectives. Evaluating the potential of e-commerce platforms like Amazon and Shopify involves optimizing product visibility and sales through strategic positioning and marketing efforts. Leveraging online marketplaces requires understanding platform dynamics and implementing tailored strategies for success. Managing conflicts in multi-channel distribution requires proactive strategies to maintain positive relationships with channel partners. Addressing issues promptly and transparently nurtures cooperation and alignment within the distribution network. Expanding distribution channels internationally necessitates careful consideration of logistics, regulatory compliance, and cultural nuances. Entrepreneurs must navigate challenges such as market entry barriers and adapt distribution strategies to suit diverse global markets. Direct sales strategies offer advantages in specific industries and scenarios, including in-person sales teams and field force operations. Deploying direct sales channels requires adequate training and management to optimize sales performance and customer engagement. Digital distribution platforms play a significant role in reaching global audiences and expanding market presence. Leveraging digital platforms requires understanding platform dynamics and tailoring distribution strategies to capitalize on emerging opportunities in the digital landscape. Analysing case studies of ventures with successful distribution strategies provides valuable insights into considerations, challenges, and outcomes associated with different distribution channels. Learning from real-world examples informs strategic decision-making and enhances the effectiveness of distribution strategies.

By exploring different distribution channels and sales network models, entrepreneurs can strategically position their ventures for success in the market. This enables entrepreneurs to practice the knowledge and tools to evaluate, select, and optimize distribution channels based on their unique products, target audience, and business objectives.

3.4.2 Developing an Effective Sales Network

An effective sales network ensures a product or service's successful distribution and commercialization. The following discussion explores the strategies and considerations for developing a robust sales network, empowering entrepreneurs to establish and manage relationships that drive revenue and market penetration.

A strategic sales network is more than just a means of generating revenue; it is a cornerstone of sustainable business success. By strategically planning and managing a sales network, companies can expand their market reach, drive revenue growth, and maintain a competitive edge in the long term. One of the fundamental aspects of developing a strategic sales network is thorough planning. This involves aligning the sales network with overarching business goals and understanding key market characteristics. Factors such as geographic coverage, customer segments, and product positioning are pivotal in shaping the sales strategy. By carefully analysing these elements, companies can tailor their approach to meet their target audience's needs and preferences. Recruiting and training a skilled sales team is another critical component of a successful sales network. Investing in a structured recruitment process and comprehensive training programs ensures sales representatives have the necessary product knowledge and effective selling techniques. A motivated and well-trained sales team drives revenue and develops positive customer relationships, contributing to long-term business success. Effective territory management is essential for optimizing sales coverage and minimizing overlap within the sales network. By strategically allocating territories to sales representatives, companies can ensure that each representative has a defined and manageable area to focus on, maximizing efficiency and productivity. This approach also helps prevent conflicts and confusion, allowing sales teams to work cohesively towards common goals.

Nurturing relationships with channel partners, such as distributors, retailers, and resellers, is another crucial aspect of sales network development. By developing agreements and incentives that align with the interests of channel partners, companies can substitute mutually beneficial partnerships that drive sales and revenue growth. Effective channel partner management is crucial in expanding market reach and accessing new customer segments. Designing incentive programs and compensation structures is essential for motivating and rewarding sales teams. Balancing fixed and variable components in compensation packages ensures that sales representatives are incentivized to perform at their best while providing stability and security. By aligning incentives with performance, companies can encourage desired behaviours and drive sales effectiveness. Implementing tools and processes for accurate sales forecasting and pipeline management is critical for informed decision-making and resource allocation. Companies can enhance relationship management and improve sales efficiency using CRM systems to centralize customer information and track interactions. Integrating CRM tools with sales processes enables seamless communication and collaboration across sales teams, improving productivity and customer satisfaction.

Developing strategies for managing key accounts and strategic partnerships is essential for nurturing long-term relationships and driving business growth. By allocating resources and attention to high-value customers, companies can ensure they receive the personalized support and service they need to remain loyal and satisfied. Effective key account management is crucial to customer retention and revenue expansion. Identifying key sales metrics and conducting regular performance evaluations provide valuable insights for enhancing individual and team effectiveness. By tracking metrics such as sales conversion rates, customer acquisition costs, and customer lifetime value, companies can identify areas for improvement and take proactive steps to address them. Regular performance evaluations help ensure that sales teams are aligned with business objectives and focused on delivering results. Integrating technology solutions is essential for enhancing sales efficiency and effectiveness in today's digital age. By exploring tools for lead generation, sales automation, and data analytics, companies can streamline sales processes, identify new opportunities, and make data-driven decisions. Sales technology integration enables sales teams to work more efficiently and productively, driving revenue growth and business success.

Exploring considerations and strategies for expanding sales networks internationally is essential for companies looking to tap into new markets and capitalize on global opportunities. By understanding the challenges related to cultural differences, market dynamics, and regulatory compliance, companies can develop tailored approaches to international sales expansion that mitigate risks and maximize returns. Effective international sales expansion requires careful planning, diligent research, and strategic partnerships to navigate unfamiliar territories and succeed in diverse markets. Analysing case studies of successful sales network development provides valuable insights into the strategies employed, challenges faced, and outcomes achieved by companies in various industries. Companies can better understand and apply best practices to their sales efforts by studying real-world examples of effective sales network development. Case studies offer valuable lessons and practical insights that can inform strategic decision-making and drive business success in today's competitive marketplace.

In conclusion, the process of Sales Network Development encompasses several phases, including market research; network planning, partner selection, training, and launch, monitoring and assistance, and adaptation and evolution. By proficiently navigating through these phases, entrepreneurs can ensure the efficient distribution of their products or services and the generation of sustainable revenue. The implementation will enable the entrepreneur's practical guidance and tools to strategize, construct, and oversee a sales network that aligns with their business goals and amplifies their presence in the market.

3.4.3 Channel Management and Optimization

Effectively managing and optimizing distribution channels are essential for maximizing the reach and impact of a product or service in the market. The following discussion explores strategies and best practices for channel management and optimization, guiding entrepreneurs to enhance the efficiency and effectiveness of their distribution networks.

Channel Management Strategies: Developing a comprehensive channel management strategy involves identifying the channels through which your product or service will be distributed. This includes direct channels like selling through your website or physical stores and indirect channels like wholesalers or retailers. Each channel should be evaluated based on its ability to reach your target market effectively and efficiently. The strategy should also outline how each channel will be managed, including responsibilities, incentives, and performance metrics.

Relationship Building with Channel Partners: Building strong relationships with channel partners is essential for successful distribution. This involves effective communication, collaboration, and alignment of goals between your business and your partners. Regular meetings, clear expectations, and mutual support are crucial elements of relationship building. Providing training and resources to help partners understand your product or service and its value proposition can also strengthen relationships.

Performance Monitoring and Evaluation: Implementing tools and metrics for monitoring channel performance allows you to track key indicators such as sales volume, customer satisfaction, and inventory turnover. Regular evaluations help identify areas where channels may be underperforming or opportunities for improvement. This data-driven approach enables you to make informed decisions about optimizing your distribution network.

Inventory and Supply Chain Management: Optimizing inventory levels and supply chain processes ensures that products are available when and where customers want them. Just-in-time (JIT) inventory management can help minimize storage costs and reduce the risk of overstock or stock outs. Efficient supply chain management involves coordinating with suppliers, distributors, and retailers to ensure a seamless flow of goods from production to consumption.

Pricing and Margin Strategies: Developing pricing strategies that balance the need for profitability with the desire to remain competitive is crucial in channel management. This includes setting wholesale and retail prices that provide sufficient margins for your business and partners. Incentive programs and discounts can strategically encourage channel partners to effectively meet sales targets and promote your products.

Conflict Resolution in Channel Management: Conflict is inevitable in any business relationship, but how it is handled can determine its impact on the partnership. Developing conflict resolution mechanisms, such as clear communication channels and formal dispute resolution processes, helps address issues promptly and maintain positive relationships. Open dialogue, compromise, and focusing on finding mutually beneficial solutions are fundamental principles of effective conflict resolution.

Channel Expansion and Contraction: Evaluating opportunities for channel expansion or optimization requires a thorough understanding of market demand and channel performance. This may involve entering new markets, adding new distribution channels, or consolidating existing channels. Considerations such as cost, reach, and alignment with business objectives should guide channel expansion or contraction decisions.

Technology Integration for Channel Optimization: Leveraging technology solutions streamlines channel management processes and improves efficiency. This includes implementing software for order processing, inventory management, and performance analytics. Automation reduces manual tasks and minimizes errors, while data analytics provides insights into channel performance and helps identify areas for improvement.

Data Analytics for Informed Decision-Making: Utilizing data analytics enables you to make informed decisions about channel optimization. By collecting and analysing data on sales, customer behavior, and market trends, you can identify patterns, opportunities, and potential risks. This data-driven approach ensures that decisions about channel management are based on empirical evidence rather than intuition or guesswork.

Channel Training and Support: Providing training and support to channel partners is essential for ensuring they have the knowledge and resources to represent your brand effectively. This may include product training, sales techniques, and marketing support. Regular communication and access to resources such as sales collateral and marketing materials help empower channel partners to promote your products or services successfully.

Compliance and Regulatory Considerations: Staying informed about compliance requirements and regulations relevant to distribution channels is critical for avoiding legal issues and reputational damage. This may include industry-specific regulations, tax laws, and import/export regulations. Developing strategies to ensure compliance, such as regular audits and training programs, helps mitigate risks and build trust with customers and partners.

Customer Feedback Integration: Integrating customer feedback into channel management processes provides valuable insights into customer preferences, satisfaction levels, and areas for improvement. This feedback can be collected through surveys, reviews, and direct communication channels. Analysing customer feedback helps identify opportunities to enhance product offerings, improve service levels, and optimize distribution channels to meet customer needs better.

Continuous Improvement in Channel Management: Establishing a culture of continuous improvement encourages ongoing evaluation and optimization of channel management practices. This involves regularly reviewing channel performance, soliciting feedback from partners and customers, and implementing changes based on lessons learned. Continuous improvement ensures that your distribution network remains agile and responsive to evolving market conditions and customer expectations.

By mastering channel management and optimization, entrepreneurs can ensure that their products or services are delivered to customers efficiently and that their distribution networks contribute to overall business success. The following discussion would provide entrepreneurs with practical guidance and tools to manage and optimize their distribution channels for maximum impact strategically.

3.5 Funding Lifecycle

The funding lifecycle spans from the ideation phase to maturity, with each stage requiring specific financial support. It is essential to align funding needs with the developmental demands of each stage to ensure sustainable growth and success. Figure 3.8 depicts the perspective of the funding lifecycle, illustrating the stages a venture progresses regarding financing. The lifecycle typically includes Seed Funding, Series A, Series B, and so forth, each representing different investment rounds as the venture grows and matures, as discussed below.

During the initial stages of venture development, funding plays a pivotal role in shaping the trajectory of the business. Pre-seed funding, sourced from personal savings, family and friends, and grants, initiates the journey by supporting product ideation and initial market validation. As the venture progresses into the seed stage, funding avenues expand to include angel investors, seed funds, and crowd funding platforms, facilitating product development and proof of concept. This early-stage funding sets the foundation for subsequent growth and expansion. Moving into the early-stage funding phase, capital infusion fuels market expansion, team building, and further product development efforts. Venture capital funding, corporate partnerships and government grants become instrumental in providing the necessary resources to scale operations and solidify market presence. Subsequent series funding rounds (A, B, C) enable startups to scale even further, achieve market dominance, and potentially expand globally, with participation from venture capital firms, private equity investors, and strategic partners.

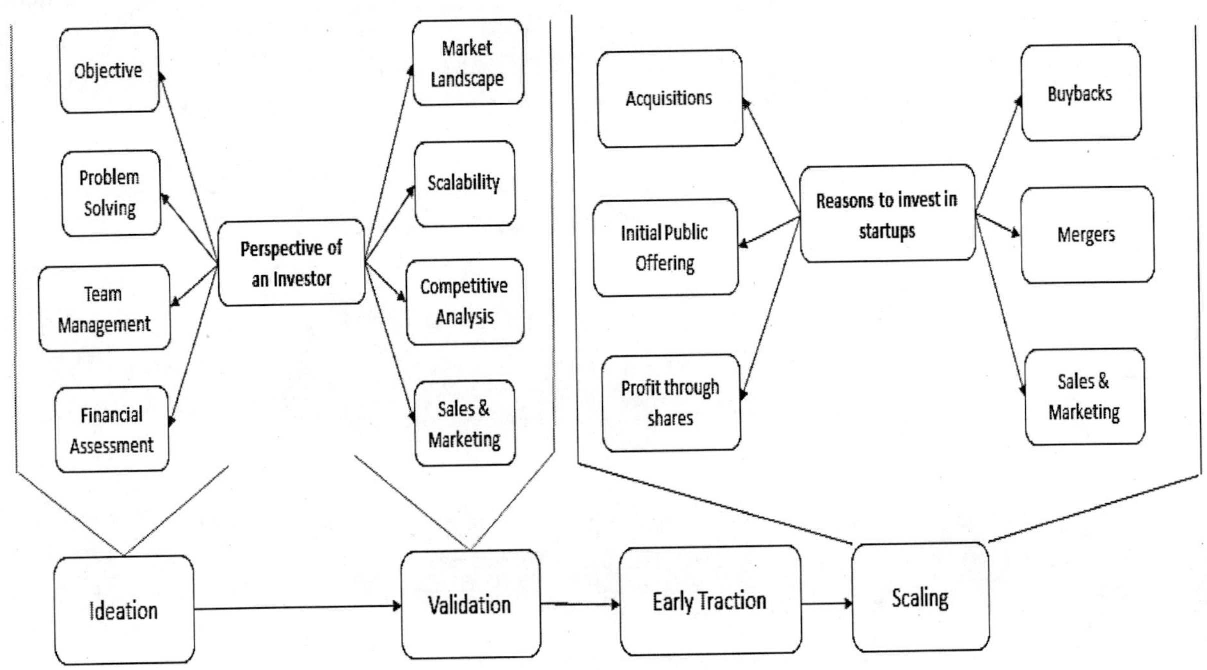

Figure 3.8 Perspective of the Funding Lifecycle

Throughout the funding journey, entrepreneurs must carefully consider the implications of each financing option on equity ownership and control within the venture. Maintaining a balanced and fair equity structure is essential for preserving alignment between founders and investors. Additionally, entrepreneurs need to navigate the complexities of funding documentation and legal considerations, addressing key documents such as term sheets and investment agreements while ensuring compliance with intellectual property protection and regulatory requirements. As ventures mature, investors begin to contemplate withdrawal plans to realize returns on their investments. These strategies may include acquisition and secondary offerings, highlighting the importance of strategic planning for investor exits to maximize value and ensure business continuity. Moreover, fostering positive investor relations through transparent communication and diligent due diligence practices enhances trust and confidence, contributing to the success of the funding journey.

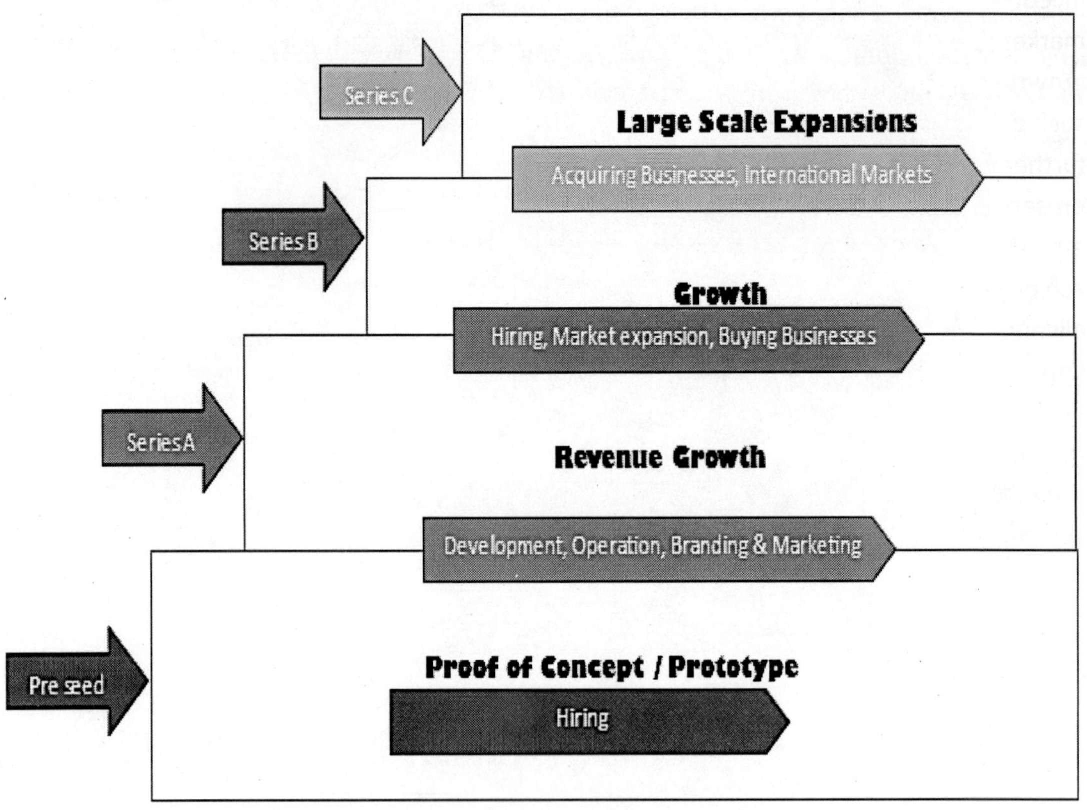

Figure 3.9 Funding Requirements at Different Stages

Figure 3.9 shows the various funding requirements at various stages of the entrepreneurial journey. By comprehensively understanding the funding requirements at various stages, entrepreneurs can strategically secure the necessary capital to drive their ventures forward. This enables entrepreneurs to practice the tools to navigate the complex funding landscape, ensuring they make informed decisions aligned with their business objectives and growth plans.

3.5.1 Aligning Funding with Milestones

Strategic alignment between funding and critical milestones is essential for the success of a technology venture. The following discussion explains the importance of synchronizing funding rounds with specific developmental milestones, empowering entrepreneurs to secure capital at crucial junctures and optimize the trajectory of their ventures. Implementing a milestone-based funding strategy is integral to aligning financial resources with the venture's business objectives, instilling confidence in investors. This structured approach ensures that funding rounds coincide with achieving specific developmental milestones, optimizing the venture's trajectory from its inception. In the pre-seed stage, securing modest funding is pivotal for validating ideas, conducting market research, and initiating initial prototype development, laying the groundwork for subsequent growth and investment attraction. Moving into the seed stage, funding supports critical milestones such as product development, market-entry, and proof of concept, which are essential for attracting further investment. Early-stage funding becomes indispensable as the venture expands its market presence, builds teams, and advances product development to meet evolving market demands effectively. Subsequent series funding rounds (A, B, C) strategically align with scaling operations, achieving market dominance, and expanding globally, fuelling the venture's growth trajectory in alignment with its milestones. Throughout the funding journey, achieving milestones significantly impacts the venture's valuation during funding rounds, influencing dilution and strategic funding decisions. Maintaining transparent communication with investors regarding milestone progress fosters trust and confidence, demonstrating the venture's commitment to achieving goals and optimizing investor returns while preserving founder equity. Moreover, flexible funding strategies accommodate reassessment of milestones in response to market dynamics, unforeseen challenges, or strategic pivots, ensuring continued alignment with business objectives and sustained growth.

Entrepreneurs can strategically navigate the venture development journey by aligning funding with critical milestones. This enables the entrepreneurs to practice developing a milestone-based funding strategy, ensuring that financial resources are allocated efficiently to achieve critical developmental goals at each stage of their technology venture.

3.5.2 Capital Structure Considerations

Optimizing the capital structure is a critical aspect of financial management for technology ventures. This title explores key considerations in determining capital structure, guiding entrepreneurs to make informed decisions that balance equity, debt, and other financial instruments to support sustainable growth.

Understanding capital structure is essential for entrepreneurs as it encompasses both equity and debt financing, impacting various aspects of financial performance, risk, and business strategy. Equity financing involves obtaining funds from investors such as venture capital firms or angel investors. While this route offers benefits like expertise and network access, decisions made in equity financing can significantly influence ownership structures and decision-making dynamics within the company. On the other hand, debt financing involves borrowing capital through bank loans or lines of credit, providing immediate access to funds but comes with repayment obligations. Entrepreneurs must carefully consider the advantages and challenges of debt financing to ensure sustainable growth for their ventures. Additionally, hybrid financing instruments, such as convertible securities, blend elements of both equity and debt. Understanding these instruments empowers entrepreneurs to strategically leverage diverse funding sources based on their specific needs and circumstances. The choices made in capital structure directly impact the risk-return profile of the venture, as they involve analysing trade-offs between equity and debt. By striking a balance between financial stability and growth potential, entrepreneurs can optimize their capital structure to achieve their long-term objectives.

Equity financing rounds may lead to dilution, affecting existing shareholders. Therefore, implementing strategies to manage dilution ensures equitable ownership distribution and alignment with long-term goals. Metrics like financial leverage and debt-to-equity ratio provide insights into capital structure efficiency, reflecting the proportion of debt and equity utilized. Maintaining a healthy balance between the two is crucial for sustaining financial health and stability. A flexible capital structure is vital for adapting to dynamic business environments. It allows for strategic adjustments, fostering agility and resilience in response to market shifts. Navigating regulatory and compliance requirements are imperative across different financing forms to ensure adherence to legal obligations and reporting standards, mitigating associated risks. For technology ventures, tailoring capital structure guidelines is essential for determining optimal financing strategies. Drawing insights from industry benchmarks and best practices informs decisions, aligning financing strategies with organizational goals. Capital structure concerns play a pivotal role in supporting growth ambitions and fostering innovation. Strategic finance creates an environment conducive to innovation, enhancing competitiveness and flexibility in the ever-evolving landscape of technology. Also analysing the case studies illuminates effective capital structure strategies. Insights from successful ventures inform decision-making, guiding entrepreneurs in balancing equity, debt, and hybrid financing for sustainable growth.

By navigating capital structure considerations strategically, entrepreneurs can position their technology ventures for sustainable growth and resilience. This enables the entrepreneurs to practice making informed decisions regarding the composition of equity, debt, and hybrid financing, ensuring that their capital structure aligns with their business goals and market dynamics.

3.6. Source of Funding for Start-up Ventures

Entrepreneurs often explore various funding sources to fuel their growth in the initial stages of a start-up venture. Bootstrapping and self-financing are integral components of this early funding landscape. The following discussion provides insights into the advantages, challenges, and strategic considerations of bootstrapping and self-financing.

3.6.1 Bootstrapping and Self-financing

Bootstrapping is a funding approach adopted by start-ups wherein the initial capital is sourced from personal savings, generated revenue, or minimal external investment. This method exemplifies the entrepreneurial resourcefulness and resilience crucial for success in the competitive business landscape. By relying on internal resources, entrepreneurs demonstrate their ability to navigate challenges independently and bootstrap their way to growth.

Self-Financing Strategies: Self-financing strategies encompass a variety of approaches tailored to the individual entrepreneur's circumstances. These strategies may include utilizing personal savings, leveraging assets such as property or investments, and reinvesting profits the business generates. By opting for self-financing, entrepreneurs maintain control and ownership of their ventures while avoiding the dilution of equity that comes with external investment. This aligns with their desire for autonomy and enables them to chart their course towards success.

Advantages of Bootstrapping and Self-Financing: Bootstrapping is a funding approach adopted by start-ups wherein the initial capital is sourced from personal savings, generated revenue, or minimal external investment. This method exemplifies the entrepreneurial resourcefulness and resilience crucial for success in the competitive business landscape. By relying on internal resources, entrepreneurs demonstrate their ability to navigate challenges independently and bootstrap their way to growth.

Challenges and Considerations: Bootstrapping presents specific challenges that entrepreneurs must navigate despite its benefits. Limited resources and slower growth potential are common hurdles when relying solely on internal funding. Entrepreneurs must balance leveraging the advantages of bootstrapping, such as autonomy and independence, while addressing the limitations, such as resource constraints. Effective management of these challenges ensures bootstrapped ventures' long-term success and sustainability.

Sustainable Growth Strategies: In bootstrapping, sustainable growth is not merely about expanding quickly at any cost. It is about strategically pacing expansion efforts to align with available resources and market opportunities. Bootstrapped ventures can grow steadily by adopting incremental expansion strategies while maintaining financial stability. Efficient resource utilization is another cornerstone of sustainable growth, where every resource, whether financial, human, or technological, is utilized optimally to maximize the output. Additionally, prioritizing objectives ensures that the limited resources are directed toward achieving the most critical goals, thereby enhancing the long-term viability and resilience of the venture.

Resource Optimization Techniques: Resource optimization techniques are essential for bootstrapped ventures to make the most out of limited resources. Cost-effective marketing strategies, such as leveraging social media and content marketing, allow start-ups to reach their target audience without breaking the bank. Lean operations methodologies help streamline processes and eliminate unnecessary overhead costs, enabling efficient utilization of resources. Moreover, adopting agile and iterative approaches to product development ensures that resources are allocated to features and functionalities that provide the most value to customers, thereby enhancing the sustainability and competitiveness of the venture.

Bootstrapping Success Stories: Success stories of bootstrapped start-ups serve as invaluable sources of inspiration and learning for aspiring entrepreneurs. By analysing these stories, entrepreneurs can gain insights into practical strategies, innovative solutions to everyday challenges, and the key milestones achieved along the journey. These success stories also highlight the resilience and creativity of entrepreneurs who have successfully navigated the complexities of boot strapping, proving that self-funded ventures can thrive in today's competitive market landscape.

Alternative Funding Sources during Bootstrapping: While bootstrapping remains the primary funding approach for start-ups, exploring alternative funding sources can provide additional capital and support to fuel growth. Crowd funding platforms offer an opportunity for start-ups to raise funds from a large pool of backers who believe in their vision and product. Grants from government agencies or non-profit organizations can provide non-dilutive funding to support specific projects or initiatives. Strategic partnerships with complementary businesses or investors can also provide access to capital, expertise, and resources, further augmenting bootstrapped ventures' sustainability and growth prospects.

Building Investor Confidence: Successfully bootstrapping a venture demonstrates resilience and self-reliance, prudent financial management, and strategic decision-making. These qualities instil confidence in potential investors, signalling that the venture is well-managed and has a record of accomplishment of achieving results with limited resources. As a result, bootstrapped ventures are often viewed favourably by investors, positioning them for potential future funding rounds or strategic partnerships that can further accelerate growth and expansion.

Strategic Exit Considerations: Bootstrapped ventures approaching an exit must carefully evaluate their options and consider several factors, such as acquisition offers, growth trajectories, and market dynamics. Bootstrapped ventures can negotiate favourable exit scenarios that maximize stakeholder value by leveraging their sustainable growth and profitability record of accomplishment. Strategic exits allow founders and investors to realize the value they have created while ensuring a smooth transition for the business and its employees. Additionally, successful exits can further enhance the reputation and credibility of the founding team, opening new opportunities for future endeavours or investments.

By understanding the nuances of bootstrapping and self-financing, entrepreneurs can navigate the preliminary stages of their ventures with resilience and strategic acumen. The following discussion provides entrepreneurs with practical insights and actionable strategies to leverage personal resources, achieve sustainable growth, and position their start-ups for long-term success.

3.6.2 Angel Investors and Venture Capital

As start-up ventures progress beyond the initial stages, external funding becomes crucial for scaling operations and realizing ambitious growth plans. The following discussion explores the roles of angel investors and venture capital in providing essential capital injections, mentorship, and strategic guidance to start-ups.

Angel Investors: Angel investors are high-net-worth individuals who offer capital and mentorship to early-stage start-ups, often drawn by the potential for high returns and the opportunity to contribute to entrepreneurial success actively. Their involvement goes beyond financial support, providing valuable industry insights, networking opportunities, and strategic guidance that can significantly benefit start-ups as they navigate the challenges of growth and expansion.

Venture Capital (VC) Firms: Venture capital firms are institutional investors that pool funds from various sources, such as high-net-worth individuals, corporations, and pension funds, to invest in high-potential start-ups to achieve significant returns on investment. These firms typically have specific investment criteria based on factors like industry sector, stage of development, and growth potential. They often provide capital, strategic guidance, industry expertise, and networking opportunities to help start-ups scale and succeed.

Angel Investment Process: Securing angel investment typically involves several steps, starting with entrepreneurs pitching their business ideas to angel investors. If interested, angel investors can determine the start-up's viability and potential. Once both parties are satisfied, funding agreements are negotiated and finalized. Critical considerations for start-ups seeking angel investment include crafting a compelling pitch, demonstrating market traction, and aligning with the investor's objectives and expertise.

Venture Capital Investment Process: The venture capital investment process typically consists of several stages, beginning with deal sourcing, where VC firms identify and evaluate investment opportunities. Due diligence follows, during which thorough research and analysis are conducted to assess the start-up's business model, market potential, and team. If the investment is considered viable, terms and conditions are discussed. Finally, the deal is closed, and funding is provided to the start-up. VC firms have specific expectations and requirements at each stage, often focusing on scalability, market opportunity, and potential for high returns.

Equity Financing Terms: Equity financing terms associated with angel investments and venture capital funding vary but often include vital concepts such as valuation, equity ownership, and convertible instruments. Valuation determines the worth of the start-up and influences the percentage of equity offered to investors in exchange for their capital. Equity ownership refers to the portion of the company investors own after the investment round. Convertible instruments, such as convertible notes or convertible preferred stock, allow investors to convert their investment into equity at a later stage, typically upon reaching predefined milestones or during a future financing round. Understanding and negotiating these terms is essential for start-ups seeking equity financing.

Angel Investor Networks: Angel investor networks play a significant role in the start-up ecosystem, where angel investors pool their resources, expertise, and networks to evaluate and fund start-ups. These networks offer start-ups access to a broader range of investors with diverse backgrounds and industry expertise, increasing the chances of securing funding. Additionally, angel networks provide start-ups valuable mentorship, guidance, and support throughout their growth journey.

Venture Capital Funding Rounds: Venture capital funding rounds, such as Seed, Series A, B, C, etc., represent various stages of financing for start-ups as they progress from early-stage development to growth and expansion. Each funding round serves specific objectives, such as product development, market expansion, or scaling operations, and typically involves increasing amounts of capital and higher valuations as start-ups achieve milestones and demonstrate progress.

Due Diligence in Angel and VC Investments: Due diligence is crucial for angel investors and venture capital firms to assess the viability and potential risks of investing in start-ups. Factors considered during due diligence include market potential, team capabilities, competitive landscape, intellectual property, financial health, and regulatory compliance. Thorough due diligence helps investors make informed investment decisions and mitigate risks associated with start-up investments.

Mentorship and Strategic Guidance: Angel investors and venture capital firms often provide mentorship and strategic guidance to start-ups beyond financial investment. This support includes industry insights, business advice, networking opportunities, and introductions to potential partners or customers. Mentorship and guidance from experienced investors can significantly enhance a start-up's chances of success by helping founders navigate challenges, make strategic decisions, and capitalize on growth opportunities.

Exit Strategies and Returns: Exit strategies for angel investors and venture capital firms typically involve realizing investment returns through acquisitions or initial public offerings (IPOs). Successful exits result in liquidity events where investors can sell their equity stake in the start-up and realize profits. The timing and method of exit depend on several factors, including market conditions, company performance, investor objectives, and the start-up's growth trajectory.

Balancing External Investment with Founder Control: One of the challenges that start-ups face when seeking external investment is balancing the need for capital while maintaining founder control and vision. While external funding can fuel growth and expansion, it may also entail relinquishing some control or decision-making authority to investors. Founders must carefully consider the investment agreements and negotiate terms that align with their long-term vision while still attracting the necessary capital.

By understanding the dynamics of angel investment and venture capital, entrepreneurs can strategically approach external funding to accelerate their growth. The following discussion provides entrepreneurs with valuable insights and practical knowledge to navigate the complex external funding landscape, fostering collaborations with investors and positioning their start-ups for sustainable success.

3.6.3 Crowd funding and Alternative Funding Models

Entrepreneurs can access diverse funding models beyond traditional sources in the ever-evolving start-up funding landscape. The following discussion explores crowdfunding and alternative funding models, offering insights into their mechanisms, advantages, and considerations for start-ups seeking innovative ways to finance their ventures.

Crowd funding is a funding model where many individuals contribute lesser amounts of capital to support a project or venture. It encompasses several types, including reward-based, equity-based, and debt-based crowd funding. Reward-based crowd funding involves backers receiving non-monetary rewards or products in return for their contributions, while equity-based crowd funding offers backers equity stakes in the funded venture. Debt-based crowd funding involves backers providing loans to the venture, which are repaid with interest over time.

Mechanisms of Crowd funding: Popular crowd funding platforms facilitate fundraising for start-ups by providing online platforms where entrepreneurs can create campaigns to highlight their projects or ventures. These platforms typically offer tools and resources to help entrepreneurs set fundraising goals, create compelling pitches, and engage with potential backers. Backers can browse campaigns, contribute funds, and interact with entrepreneurs directly through the platform. The platform acts as an intermediary, handling transactions and providing support throughout the fundraising process.

Advantages of Crowd funding: Crowd funding offers several advantages for start-ups, including access to a global pool of investors, market validation, and marketing opportunities. By engaging directly with backers, entrepreneurs can gather feedback, build a community around their venture, and generate buzz and awareness. Successful crowd funding campaigns can attract additional investors, partnerships, and media attention, further fuelling the venture's growth and visibility.

Challenges and Considerations: Despite its benefits, crowd funding presents challenges for entrepreneurs, including campaign preparation, fulfilment of rewards, and maintaining investor relations. Successful campaigns require careful planning, compelling storytelling, and effective marketing strategies. Fulfilling rewards and meeting backers' expectations can be time-consuming and costly, requiring careful budgeting and logistics management. Additionally, entrepreneurs must prioritize transparency, communication, and accountability to maintain trust and credibility with backers throughout the campaign.

Equity Crowd funding Regulations: Equity crowd funding is subject to regulations and frameworks governing securities offerings and investor protections. These regulations vary by jurisdiction and may include requirements related to disclosure, investor accreditation, fundraising limits, and reporting obligations. Entrepreneurs must navigate these regulatory requirements carefully to ensure compliance and mitigate legal risks. The evolving regulatory landscape presents opportunities and challenges for equity crowd funding platforms and start-ups seeking investment.

Peer-to-peer lending platforms facilitate direct lending between individuals, bypassing traditional financial institutions. Start-ups can access capital through peer-to-peer lending by borrowing from individual investors willing to lend money in exchange for interest payments. These platforms provide an alternative source of financing for start-ups that may not qualify for traditional bank loans or prefer more flexible terms and lower interest rates.

Revenue-Based Financing: Revenue-based financing offers start-ups a flexible funding option where capital is repaid based on a percentage of the venture's revenue over time. Unlike traditional loans, revenue-based financing does not require fixed monthly payments or collateral. Instead, investors receive a share of the venture's revenue until a predetermined repayment cap is reached. This model aligns the interests of investors and entrepreneurs, as repayment is directly tied to the venture's financial performance.

Corporate Sponsorship and Partnerships: Corporate sponsorship and partnerships provide start-ups financial support, resources, and market access through strategic collaborations with established companies. These partnerships can take various forms, including co-marketing agreements, product integrations, and joint ventures. Start-ups can leverage corporate sponsorships and partnerships to access capital, tap into existing networks, and accelerate growth through shared expertise and resources.

Government Grants and Subsidies: Government grants and subsidies offer start-ups alternative funding sources, particularly in sectors or research areas supported by government initiatives. These funding programs provide financial assistance, research grants, tax incentives, and other support to eligible start-ups. Accessing government funding requires entrepreneurs to navigate application processes, meet eligibility criteria, and comply with reporting and accountability requirements.

Impact Investment and Social Funding: Impact investment and social funding models prioritize positive social or environmental outcomes alongside financial returns. These funding models attract investors and backers passionate about making a meaningful impact through their investments. Start-ups with a social impact focus can access funding from impact investors, philanthropic organizations, and socially responsible funds that align with their mission and values.

Hybrid Funding Approaches: Hybrid funding approaches involve start-ups combining multiple funding models to diversify their capital sources and mitigate risks. By blending crowdfunding with other alternative funding methods, start-ups can leverage the strengths of each model to optimize their fundraising efforts. Hybrid funding approaches offer flexibility, scalability, and resilience, enabling start-ups to navigate evolving market conditions and investor preferences effectively.

By exploring crowd funding and alternative funding models, entrepreneurs can tap into innovative financial avenues that align with their venture's goals and values. This enables the entrepreneurs to practice navigating these diverse funding landscapes, creativity, and adaptability in securing capital for their start-ups.

3.7. Financial Projections and Accounting

Accurate financial projections are indispensable for guiding the strategic decision-making of technology ventures. The following discussion details building realistic financial projections, offering entrepreneurs practical insights into forecasting revenue, expenses, and overall financial performance.

3.7.1 Building Realistic Financial Projections

Importance of Financial Projections: Financial projections are crucial in business planning, fundraising, and day-to-day operations. Realistic projections provide a sustainable growth and financial health roadmap, guiding strategic decision-making and resource allocation. By forecasting future revenues, expenses, and cash flows, entrepreneurs can anticipate challenges, seize opportunities, and navigate uncertainties effectively. Figure 3.10 shows the Scale Financial Planning Roadmap, outlining the strategic steps involved in scaling up a business financially.

Revenue Forecasting: Forecasting revenue involves detailing methods and considerations such as market analysis, pricing strategies, and sales projections. Understanding market dynamics and customer behaviours is essential for accurate revenue forecasting. Entrepreneurs can develop realistic revenue projections that align with business objectives and growth targets by analysing market trends, competitor performance, and customer preferences.

Expense Projections: Expense projections encompass various categories, including operating costs, marketing expenses, personnel costs, and capital expenditures. Accurate expense projections are critical for effective budgeting and resource allocation. Entrepreneurs can identify cost-saving opportunities, prioritize spending, and optimize financial performance by estimating expenses based on historical data, industry benchmarks, and future growth plans.

Cash Flow Projections: Cash flow projections define the inflow and outflow of cash over a specified period, providing insights into the liquidity and solvency of the venture. Managing cash flow is essential for meeting day-to-day obligations and sustaining operations. By aligning revenue and expense projections with cash flow requirements, entrepreneurs can ensure sufficient liquidity to support growth initiatives and weather financial challenges.

Financial Assumptions and Sensitivity Analysis: Financial projections are based on various assumptions that underpin revenue, expense, and cash flow forecasts. Conducting sensitivity analysis allows entrepreneurs to assess the impact of changing assumptions on financial outcomes. Entrepreneurs can identify potential risks, uncertainties, and opportunities by testing different scenarios and variables, enabling informed decision-making and proactive risk management.

Pro Forma Financial Statements: Pro forma financial statements, including the income statement, balance sheet, and cash flow statement, provide a comprehensive view of a venture's financial position and performance. These statements project future financial outcomes based on assumptions and historical data. By analysing pro forma financial statements, entrepreneurs can evaluate profitability, solvency, and growth potential, facilitating strategic planning and investor communication.

Integration with Business Strategy: Financial projections should be aligned with overall business strategy and objectives. By integrating projections with strategic plans, entrepreneurs can evaluate the feasibility of business initiatives, assess resource requirements, and monitor progress toward goals. Financial projections support strategic decision-making by providing insights into the financial implications of different courses of action and guiding resource allocation priorities.

Accounting Principles and Practices: Fundamental accounting principles and practices, such as accrual vs. cash accounting, revenue recognition, and expense classification, are essential for maintaining accurate financial records and compliance with regulatory requirements. Entrepreneurs should understand basic accounting concepts to effectively interpret financial statements, evaluate performance, and make informed financial decisions.

Compliance and Reporting Obligations: Start-ups must comply with regulatory requirements and reporting obligations, including financial statement audits, tax filings, and disclosures. Maintaining accurate financial records is essential for legal and financial transparency, facilitating compliance with regulatory standards and investor expectations. By adhering to reporting obligations, start-ups can build credibility, instil investor confidence, and mitigate legal risks.

Financial Management Tools and Software: Financial management tools and software assist in building, analysing, and updating financial projections. These tools automate data entry, perform complex calculations, and generate customizable reports, streamlining financial modelling and reporting processes. By leveraging technology, entrepreneurs can improve financial management efficiency, accuracy, and scalability, enabling better decision-making and resource allocation.

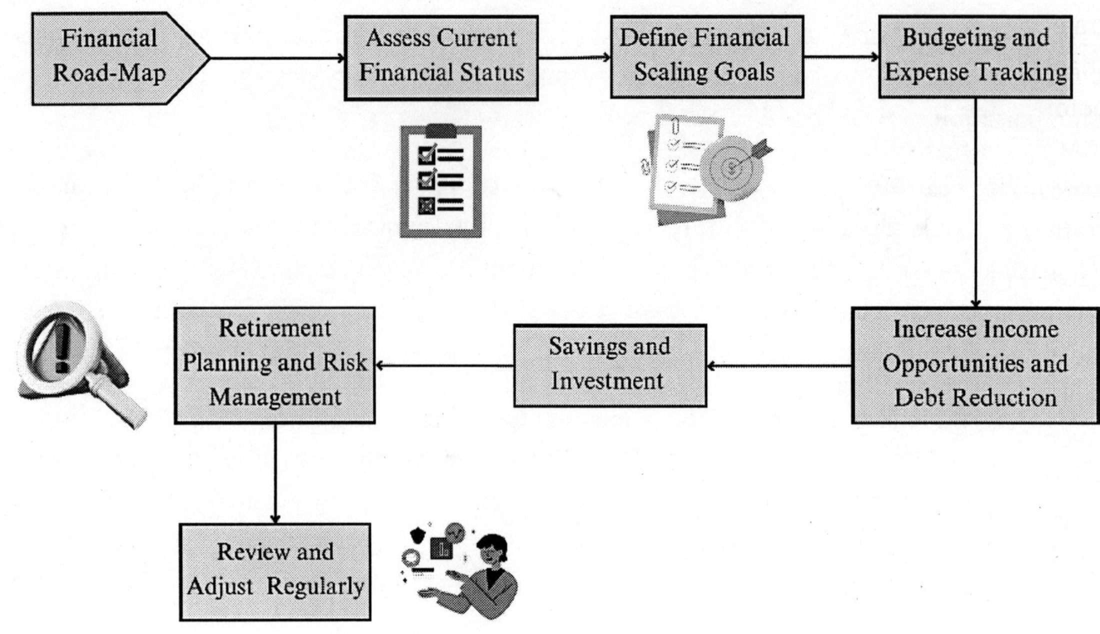

Figure 3.10 Scale-Up Financial Planning Roadmap

Continuous Monitoring and Adjustment: Financial projections are iterative and require continuous monitoring and adjustment to reflect changing business conditions. By regularly reviewing actual performance against projected outcomes, entrepreneurs can identify variances, trends, and anomalies, enabling timely adjustments and course corrections. Continuous monitoring enhances the accuracy and reliability of projections, improving forecasting capabilities and supporting agile decision-making.

By mastering the art of building realistic financial projections, entrepreneurs can confidently make informed decisions, secure funding, and navigate their ventures' financial landscape. This enables entrepreneurs to practice creating projections that serve as valuable tools for guiding their technology ventures toward sustained success.

3.7.2 Key Financial Metrics for Start-ups

Understanding and effectively utilizing critical financial metrics is vital for the success of start-ups. The following discussion explores the essential financial metrics entrepreneurs should monitor and analyse to assess their technology ventures' financial health, performance, and sustainability.

Key revenue metrics such as Monthly Recurring Revenue (MRR), Annual Recurring Revenue (ARR), and Gross Revenue offer valuable insights into a start-up's revenue generation and growth trajectory. MRR and ARR are particularly pertinent for subscription-based businesses, providing a snapshot of recurring revenue streams, while Gross Revenue portrays the total revenue generated before deductions. Complementing these metrics is the assessment of Customer Acquisition Cost (CAC), which quantifies the expenses associated with acquiring new customers, thus enabling a critical evaluation of marketing and sales efficiency. Effective optimization of CAC is instrumental in crafting cost-effective customer acquisition strategies. Moreover, understanding Customer Lifetime Value (CLV) helps gauge the potential revenue each customer may generate throughout their relationship with the company, informing targeted marketing and retention efforts. Equally vital is the monitoring of the Burn Rate, which illustrates the pace at which a start-up is depleting its capital. This metric is pivotal for maintaining optimal cash flow and ensuring expenditures align with revenue generation goals, thus facilitating sustainable operations. Lastly, assessing Runway, which denotes the duration a start-up can operate with its existing cash reserves before exhausting funds, is crucial for strategic financial planning and fundraising. By leveraging these metrics collectively, start-ups can navigate their financial landscape more effectively, make informed decisions about resource allocation, and enhance their prospects for long-term success and sustainability.

Further, gross Margin is a critical metric for start-ups, representing the percentage of revenue that surpasses the cost of goods sold. It is a fundamental gauge of profitability and cost efficiency, offering insights into the startup's ability to generate profits from its core business activities. On the other hand, Churn Rate measures the percentage of customers who discontinue using a product or service within a specified time limit. Minimizing churn is essential for bolstering customer retention and sustaining long-term revenue growth, pinpointing areas for improvement in product/service offerings and customer experiences. Metrics such as Monthly Active Users (MAU) and Daily Active Users (DAU) provide valuable insights into user engagement, reflecting the impact and popularity of the start-up's offerings while indicating the level of user interaction and satisfaction. Conversion Rate, another crucial metric, denotes the percentage of users who complete a desired action, such as purchasing or signing up for a service. This metric is a critical indicator of marketing and sales effectiveness, shedding light on the efficiency of conversion strategies and user experiences. Lastly, the Cash Conversion Cycle (CCC) represents the duration for a start-up to convert investments in inventory and resources into cash flow from sales. It profoundly influences liquidity and operational efficiency, guiding inventory management and optimization of working capital to ensure smooth operations and financial stability. By leveraging these metrics collectively, start-ups can gain comprehensive insights into various aspects of their business performance, enabling informed decision-making and strategic planning for sustainable growth.

Quick Ratio and Current Ratio serve as essential liquidity ratios for start-ups, evaluating their capability to fulfil short-term obligations. These metrics offer crucial insights into financial stability and solvency, aiding start-ups in managing liquidity risks and maintaining robust cash reserves to navigate uncertainties effectively. Return on Investment (ROI) emerges as a pivotal metric, gauging the profitability of investments undertaken by start-ups. It facilitates informed decision-making regarding resource allocation, directing funds towards initiatives with the potential for optimal returns and sustainable long-term growth. Moreover, examining case studies spotlighting start-ups' strategic utilization of financial metrics unveils valuable insights. Through analysing these real-world examples, entrepreneurs gain practical knowledge of the correlation between metric-driven strategies and positive outcomes. Such case studies provide a rich source of learning, enabling entrepreneurs to grasp the significance of integrating financial metrics into their decision-making processes and supporting a culture of data-driven strategic planning. By leveraging these metrics alongside insightful case studies, start-ups can enhance their financial acumen, optimize resource allocation, and bolster their prospects for enduring success in a dynamic business landscape.

Creating a Financial Metrics Dashboard: By creating a financial metrics dashboard, the entrepreneurs can collaborate to develop personalized dashboards tailored to their start-ups' needs. This would allow entrepreneurs to identify and prioritize critical financial metrics relevant to their business objectives and industry dynamics. Facilitators must guide entrepreneurs through selecting, calculating, and interpreting key metrics and encouraging discussions on best practices, common challenges, and strategic implications. By actively engaging in creating their financial metrics dashboard, entrepreneurs gain a deeper understanding of how financial metrics drive strategic decision-making and performance monitoring. Throughout the session, entrepreneurs can share insights, exchange ideas, and receive feedback from peers and facilitators, enhancing their ability to leverage financial metrics to drive business success effectively. Finally, entrepreneurs will have a comprehensive financial metrics dashboard, a valuable tool for informed decision-making and performance evaluation in their start-ups.

By mastering vital financial metrics, entrepreneurs would gain actionable insights into the performance and sustainability of their start-ups. This enables the entrepreneurs to practice leveraging metrics effectively, supporting informed decision-making and steering their technology ventures toward financial success.

3.7.3 Best Practices in Start-up Accounting

Effective accounting practices are foundational to the financial health and sustainability of start-ups. The following discussion explores best practices in start-up accounting, providing entrepreneurs with insights and strategies to maintain accurate financial records, ensure compliance, and make informed financial decisions.

Importance of Accurate Accounting: Accurate accounting serves as the backbone of financial decision-making, enabling entrepreneurs to assess the financial health of their start-ups, make informed strategic choices, and comply with regulatory requirements. Reliable financial records support transparency and build trust among investors, stakeholders, and regulatory bodies, laying a solid foundation for sustainable growth and success.

Adopt Cloud-Based Accounting Software: Cloud-based accounting software offers start-ups numerous advantages, including streamlined financial processes, enhanced accessibility, real-time collaboration, automated workflows, and robust data security measures. By leveraging cloud-based solutions, start-ups can efficiently manage their finances, access critical financial information from anywhere, and scale their operations as they grow.

Chart of Accounts Design: Designing a tailored Chart of Accounts is essential for organizing financial transactions and generating accurate financial reports. Start-ups should customize their Chart of Accounts to reflect their business's unique needs and structure, ensuring that expenses, revenues, assets, and liabilities are appropriately categorized for clear and comprehensive reporting.

Accrual vs. Cash Accounting: Choosing between accrual and cash accounting methods requires careful consideration of factors such as revenue recognition timing and financial reporting objectives. Accrual accounting records revenues and expenses when they are earned or incurred, providing a more accurate depiction of a start-up's financial performance over time, while cash accounting records transactions when cash is received or paid, offering simplicity and ease of use.

Expense Tracking and Categorization: Implementing best practices for tracking and categorizing expenses is crucial for maintaining transparency and accuracy in financial reporting. Start-ups should establish clear guidelines for expense tracking, ensuring that all expenses are recorded promptly, categorized accurately, and supported by appropriate documentation. Detailed expense records facilitate budgeting, cost management, and strategic decision-making.

Bank Reconciliation: Bank reconciliation is vital for identifying discrepancies between a startup's accounting records and bank statements. By regularly reconciling bank accounts, start-ups can ensure the accuracy of their financial data, detect errors or fraudulent activities, and maintain confidence in their financial reporting. Timely reconciliation enhances financial transparency and supports informed decision-making.

Budgeting and Forecasting: Proactive budgeting and forecasting enable start-ups to anticipate financial needs, allocate resources effectively, and align financial planning with strategic goals. By developing realistic budgets and forecasts, start-ups can identify potential challenges, seize growth opportunities, and make informed decisions to drive long-term success. Budgeting promotes discipline, accountability, and financial stability within the organization.

Regular Financial Audits: Regular internal and external financial audits are essential for start-ups to ensure compliance with regulations, accuracy in financial reporting, and identifying areas for improvement. Internal audits help evaluate financial controls, detect errors, and strengthen internal processes, while external audits provide independent verification of financial statements, enhancing credibility and investor confidence.

Compliance with Tax Regulations: Local and national tax regulations are critical for start-ups to avoid legal issues and financial penalties. Effective tax planning and reporting strategies enable start-ups to optimize their tax liabilities, maximize deductions, and maintain compliance with changing tax laws. By adhering to tax regulations, start-ups can mitigate risks and preserve financial resources for growth.

Financial Reporting Standards: Adherence to financial reporting standards such as GAAP or IFRS enhances the credibility and comparability of financial statements. By following established reporting frameworks, start-ups ensure transparency, consistency, and accuracy in financial reporting, facilitating investor trust and regulatory compliance. Compliance with financial reporting standards also improves access to capital and fosters investor confidence.

Segregation of Duties: Segregating accounting duties is essential for preventing fraud and errors within start-ups. By separating responsibilities such as recording transactions, authorizing payments, and reconciling accounts, start-ups establish adequate internal controls and reduce the risk of financial mismanagement. Clear guidelines and oversight mechanisms help ensure accountability and integrity in financial operations.

Documentation and Record Retention: Thorough documentation and record retention support the accuracy and integrity of financial transactions and decisions. By maintaining organized financial records, start-ups can track financial activities, provide evidence of compliance, and facilitate audits or investigations. Documented records also serve as valuable historical data for analysis, planning, and decision-making.

Training and Skill Development: Continuous training and skill development for accounting teams are essential for staying updated on accounting principles, regulations, and software tools. By investing in professional development, start-ups equip their accounting staff with the knowledge and skills to perform their roles effectively, adapt to changing requirements, and leverage technology for improved efficiency and accuracy.

Cyber security for Financial Data: Implementing cyber security measures is crucial to protect financial data from unauthorized access and breaches. Start-ups should employ encryption, secure access controls, and employee training programs to safeguard sensitive financial information. By prioritizing cyber security, start-ups can mitigate the risk of data breaches, preserve trust with stakeholders, and ensure the confidentiality and integrity of financial data.

By embracing best practices in start-up accounting, entrepreneurs can establish a robust financial foundation, enhance transparency, and make informed decisions. This enables the entrepreneurs to practice optimizing their accounting processes, ensuring the financial well-being of their technology ventures.

3.8 Start-up to Scale-up Financing

The transition from start-up to scale-up marks a pivotal phase in the growth journey of technology ventures. The following discussion explores the financial considerations, funding strategies, and critical milestones in successfully transitioning from the start-up stage to scale-up operations.

3.8.1 Transitioning from Start-up to Scale Up

Understanding the Start-up to Scale-up Transition: The transition from start-up to scale-up represents rapid growth and expansion for technology ventures. Characterized by increased market presence and scalability, this transition brings challenges and opportunities. Start-ups must navigate the complexities of scaling operations while maintaining agility and innovation. Understanding the dynamics of this transition is crucial for laying the foundation for sustainable growth and long-term success.

Financial Landscape in Scale-up Operations: As start-ups transition to scale-up operations, the financial landscape undergoes significant changes. The demands for resources, capital, and infrastructure increase as companies strive to capitalize on growth opportunities and enter new markets. Strategic financial planning is paramount to effectively allocating resources, managing cash flow, and supporting accelerated growth while maintaining financial stability and flexibility.

Identifying Scale-up Milestones: Key milestones act as a checkpoint in the scale-up path while indicating the progress and preparedness for business growth. Achieving product-market fit, expanding the customer base, and increasing revenue are pivotal scale-up milestones. These milestones signify growth and inform strategic decisions regarding resource allocation, market penetration, and operational scaling.

Funding Considerations for Scale-up: Scale-ups require larger funding rounds and strategic investments to fuel their expansion initiatives. Venture capital, private equity, and other financing options provide the capital necessary to scale operations, enter new markets, and drive innovation. Start-ups must align their funding strategies with their growth objectives and investor expectations to secure the resources needed for successful scale-up.

Venture Debt and Growth Financing: Venture debt offers scale-ups an alternative financing option to complement equity funding. Leveraging debt alongside equity allows scale-ups to access additional capital while minimizing equity dilution. Growth financing strategies, including venture debt and growth capital, provide flexible funding solutions to support expansion plans, product development initiatives, and market penetration efforts.

Strategic Partnerships and Alliances: Strategic partnerships and alliances support scale-up objectives by providing access to resources, markets, and expertise. Collaborations with industry leaders, distribution channels, or complementary businesses can accelerate growth, enhance market reach, and facilitate innovation. Scale-ups should actively pursue strategic partnerships that align with their growth strategy and contribute to achieving their scale-up milestones.

International Expansion and Global Financing: Expanding the business internationally presents scale-up opportunities and challenges. Considerations include cultural differences, regulatory requirements, and market dynamics. Global financing strategies may involve accessing capital from international investors, establishing partnerships with foreign entities, or exploring government funding programs in target markets.

IPO Readiness and Public Financing: Preparing for an Initial Public Offering (IPO) requires meeting stringent financial performance, governance, and compliance criteria. Going public can provide access to substantial capital, enhance visibility and credibility, and facilitate further growth through acquisitions or strategic investments. However, it also entails regulatory scrutiny, shareholder expectations, and ongoing reporting obligations.

Managing Risks in Scale-up Financing: Scale-up financing comes with inherent risks, including over-leverage, dilution of ownership, and exposure to market volatility. Effective risk management involves diversifying funding sources, maintaining a balanced capital structure, and prudent financial planning. Strategies may include stress-testing financial models, implementing hedging mechanisms, and maintaining adequate reserves.

Investor Relations and Communication: Transparent communication with investors is critical during the scale-up phase to develop trust and confidence. Effective investor relations strategies involve regular updates on financial performance, strategic initiatives, and milestone achievements. Clear and consistent communication helps align investor expectations with the company's growth trajectory and minimizes the risk of misunderstandings or conflicts.

Scaling-up of Operations Efficiently: Efficient scaling up of activities is critical for growth management and momentum sustainability. This involves optimizing processes, expanding teams strategically, and enhancing infrastructure to accommodate increased demand. Leveraging technology and automation can streamline operations, improve productivity, and drive cost efficiencies, enabling scale-ups to scale rapidly while maintaining operational excellence.

Figure 3.11 illustrates the Pros and Cons of Different Funding Sources, providing entrepreneurs with valuable insights into the diverse options for financing their ventures. Understanding the advantages and disadvantages of each funding source is crucial for making informed decisions and developing a robust financial strategy. By navigating the complexities of scale-up financing, entrepreneurs can position their ventures for sustained growth and market leadership. This enables the entrepreneurs to practice navigating the financial landscape of scale-up operations and secure the funding needed to propel their technology ventures to new heights.

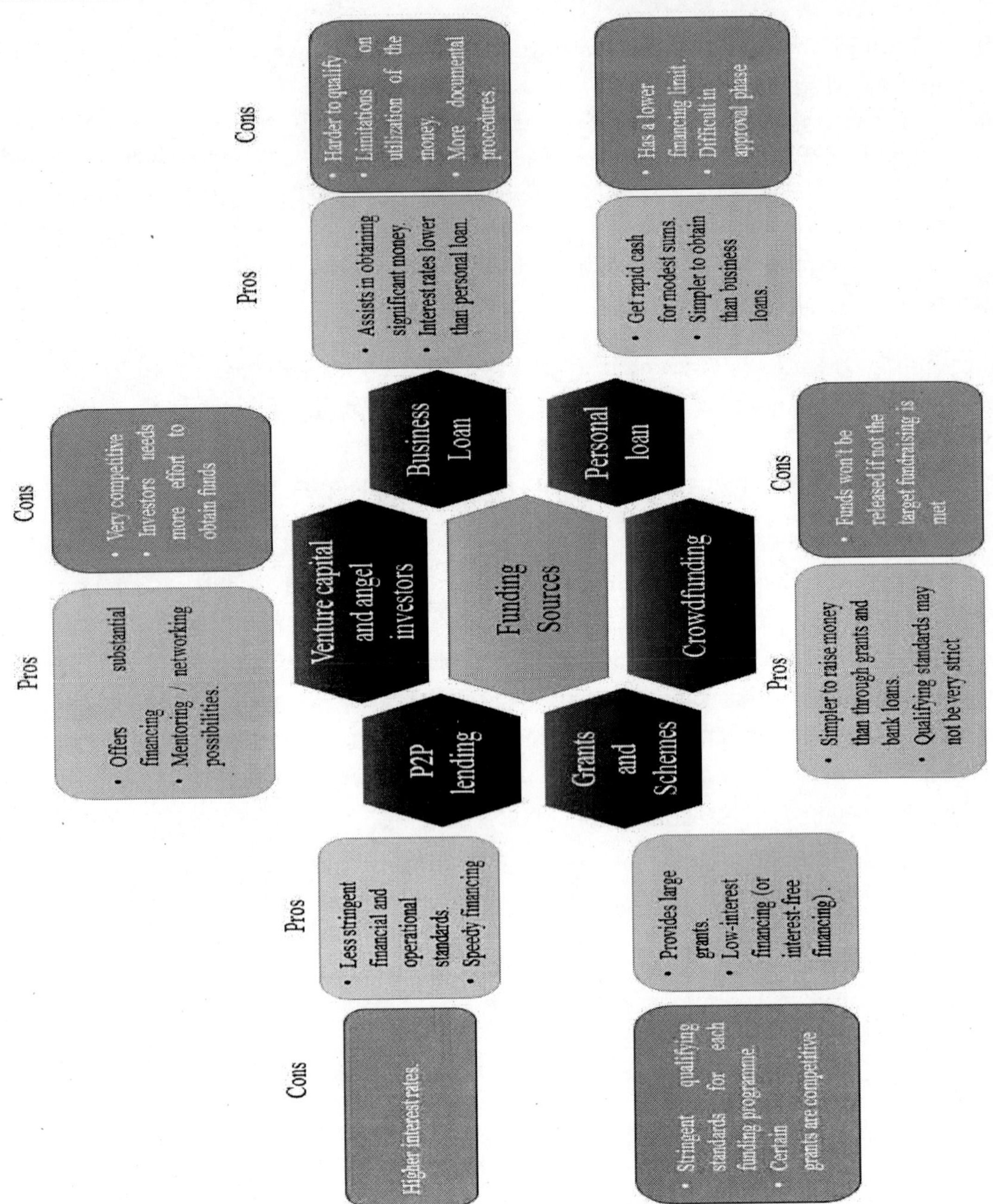

Figure 3.11 Pros and Cons of Different Funding Sources

3.8.2 Series Funding and Scaling Strategies

Series funding is crucial to scaling a technology venture, providing the necessary capital to fuel growth and expansion. The following discussion explores the dynamics of series funding rounds and outlines effective scaling strategies for entrepreneurs looking to propel their ventures to the next level. It consists of a sequence of investment rounds, each serving distinct purposes and fuelling various aspects of a start-up's development and expansion. These rounds, including Seed, Series A, Series B, and beyond, represent significant milestones in a start-up's journey, allowing it to secure the resources needed to progress and thrive. Figure 3.12 illustrates Scaling Strategies and Corresponding Financing Options by guiding entrepreneurs to identify their target audience. It also addresses the importance of hiring experienced management, improving customer service, and developing strategic partnerships while optimizing the sales funnel.

Seed Funding and Proof of Concept: Seed funding represents the initial injection of capital into a start-up, typically used to validate its concept and demonstrate its market potential. At this stage, entrepreneurs develop prototypes, conduct market research, and attract early customers or users. Securing seed funding is often crucial for start-ups to move from ideation to execution, and it involves engaging with angel investors, venture capital firms, or accelerators. The primary goal of seed funding is to provide the resources necessary to establish a proof of concept and lay the groundwork for future growth and fundraising efforts.

Series A - Scaling Operations: The Series A funding round marks a significant milestone in a start-up's journey, signalling its transition from the early stage to the growth stage. Now, the focus shifts towards scaling operations, expanding the customer base, and achieving product-market fit. Series A funding enables start-ups to invest in team expansion, aggressive marketing strategies, and infrastructure development to support increased demand and growth. By securing Series A funding, start-ups validate their market traction and gain the resources needed to accelerate their growth trajectory and establish a solid foundation for future success.

Series B - Accelerated Growth: Series B funding represents a pivotal stage in a start-up's growth journey, characterized by accelerated expansion, market penetration, and scaling of business processes. With the capital raised in the Series B round, start-ups can further enhance their product offerings, enter new markets, and build a sustainable customer base. This stage focuses on optimizing operations, scaling revenue generation, and solidifying the start-up's position as a market leader. Series B funding allows start-ups to capitalize on their initial successes and propel themselves towards greater market dominance and long-term sustainability.

Series-C and Beyond - Scaling to Maturity: As start-ups progress beyond Series-B funding, later-stage rounds like Series-C and beyond are instrumental in scaling to maturity and achieving market dominance. These rounds enable companies to execute ambitious growth strategies, including strategic acquisitions, international expansion initiatives, and preparations for potential initial public offerings (IPOs). By solidifying their market position and driving sustainable long-term growth, start-ups aim to establish themselves as industry leaders and capture significant market share.

Investor Relations in Series Funding: Effective investor relations are paramount during series funding rounds, creating trust and confidence among investors. Start-ups must communicate transparently with investors, regularly updating financial performance, strategic initiatives, and milestone achievements. Building long-term relationships with investors facilitates successful fundraising and ensures continued support for the company's growth journey. By maintaining open and transparent communication channels, start-ups can navigate a series of funding rounds with confidence and maximize investor confidence.

Scaling Strategies for Different Industries: Tailoring scaling strategies to the unique characteristics of various industries is crucial for start-up success. Industries such as technology, healthcare, and consumer goods present distinct challenges and opportunities in scaling operations, requiring customized approaches to address specific market dynamics, regulatory requirements, and consumer preferences. By understanding the nuances of their respective industries and adapting their scaling strategies accordingly, start-ups can effectively navigate growth challenges and capitalize on emerging opportunities.

Balancing Growth and Financial Health: Achieving a delicate balance between aggressive growth and maintaining financial health is paramount during funding rounds. Start-ups must carefully manage burn rates, optimize operational efficiency, and implement prudent financial management practices to ensure sustainable growth. Balancing growth objectives with financial stability is essential for long-term success, as it enables start-ups to weather economic downturns, withstand market volatility, and position themselves for continued growth and expansion. By prioritizing growth and financial health, start-ups can create a solid foundation for long-term success and sustainability.

Technology and Innovation in Scaling: Technology and innovation play pivotal roles in efficiently scaling start-up operations. By leveraging innovative technologies and embracing digital transformation, start-ups can streamline processes, automate workflows, and enhance productivity. Innovations in product development, customer engagement, and data analytics enable start-ups to gain a competitive edge in their respective markets and drive rapid growth. By harnessing the power of technology and innovation, start-ups can optimize their operations and position themselves for sustainable long-term success. Also, by examining key strategies, challenges faced, and lessons learned from their scaling journeys, entrepreneurs can glean actionable insights and apply best practices to their ventures. Case studies offer real-world examples of how start-ups have navigated a series of funding rounds, implemented effective scaling strategies, and overcome obstacles to achieve significant growth and market traction. By learning from the experiences of successful technology ventures, entrepreneurs can make informed decisions and increase their chances of success in the competitive start-up landscape.

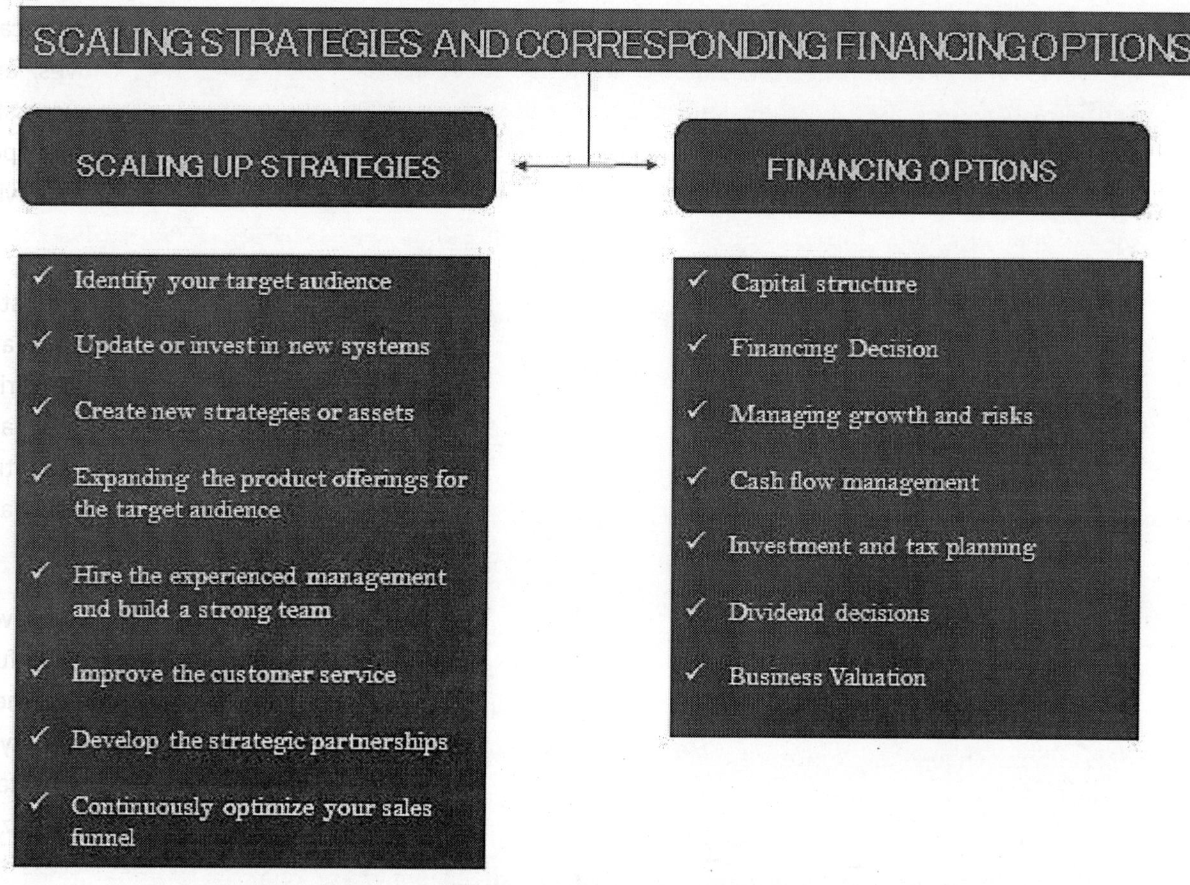

Figure 3.12 Scaling Strategies and Corresponding Financing Options

By mastering the intricacies of series funding and implementing effective scaling strategies, entrepreneurs can navigate the complexities of each funding round and position their ventures for sustained growth and success. This enables the entrepreneurs to practice confidently approaching series funding and scaling their technology ventures to new heights.

3.8.3 Managing Finances in the Growth Phase

Effectively managing finances during the growth phase is critical for sustaining momentum and positioning a technology venture for long-term success. Financial planning is paramount during this phase, requiring entrepreneurs to leverage financial forecasting, budgeting, and scenario analysis to anticipate challenges and opportunities. This proactive approach enables effective resource allocation and decision-making, helping entrepreneurs navigate the complexities of growth while maintaining a strategic focus on long-term objectives.

Efficient capital allocation is essential for supporting various growth initiatives. Entrepreneurs must prioritize investments in product development, marketing, talent acquisition, and infrastructure based on their impact on growth objectives and the overall business strategy. Strategic allocation of capital maximizes returns and drives sustainable growth, ensuring that the venture remains on a path of steady progress. Simultaneously, optimizing resources and enhancing operational efficiency through technology, automation, and lean processes enable startups to achieve cost-effectiveness and scalability. Streamlining workflows and eliminating inefficiencies allows for the strategic allocation of resources, driving growth effectively. Scaling operations and infrastructure to meet increased demand presents both challenges and opportunities. Entrepreneurs need practical strategies for expanding teams, enhancing production capacity, and improving logistics to sustain growth momentum. Investing in scalable infrastructure and agile processes is crucial for adapting to evolving market dynamics and ensuring the venture can handle the complexities of rapid expansion. Effective working capital management is also critical for sustaining day-to-day operations during this period. Optimizing inventory levels, managing receivables, and negotiating favourable payment terms help ensure adequate liquidity and mitigate cash flow risks, supporting sustainable growth and financial stability.

Rapid growth introduces various risks, including market volatility, competition, and operational challenges. Entrepreneurs must implement robust risk management strategies to identify, assess, and mitigate potential threats. Proactive risk management practices, such as contingency planning and diversification, safeguard the business against uncertainties and ensure resilience during periods of growth. By effectively managing these financial considerations and employing strategic practices, entrepreneurs can navigate the growth phase successfully, positioning their technology ventures for long-term success. Robust financial controls and governance structures are imperative during this period to ensure accountability and mitigate financial risks. Implementing internal controls, compliance frameworks, and regular financial audits helps maintain integrity and transparency in financial operations, safeguarding the business against fraud and mismanagement. By ensuring that financial operations are transparent and accountable, entrepreneurs can build a solid foundation for sustainable growth.

Sustaining growth requires on-going funding strategies, including follow-on investments, debt financing, and strategic partnerships. Entrepreneurs must carefully balance debt and equity to maintain a healthy capital structure and support expansion initiatives effectively. While seeking external funding, it is crucial to consider long-term financial sustainability and the potential impact on equity ownership. Efficient capital allocation, prioritizing investments in product development, marketing, talent acquisition, and infrastructure based on their impact on growth objectives, maximizes returns and drives sustainable growth. International expansion during the growth phase requires meticulous financial planning and strategic execution. Entrepreneurs must navigate currency fluctuations, regulatory complexities, and cultural differences while exploring global financing options. Effective management of international finances, including risk mitigation strategies for currency and regulatory issues, ensures successful expansion and reduces associated risks. Scaling operations and infrastructure to meet increased demand in international markets presents both challenges and opportunities that require careful planning and investment in scalable infrastructure and agile processes. Additionally, transparent communication with investors is paramount for maintaining trust and confidence during the growth phase. Entrepreneurs should prioritize effective investor relations strategies by providing timely updates, financial performance insights, and growth projections. Building strong relationships with investors facilitates future fundraising efforts and ensures continued support for the venture. Additionally, adhering to best practices in financial reporting and compliance is essential for meeting stakeholder expectations and regulatory requirements. Transparent reporting enhances credibility and trust among investors, customers, and other stakeholders, further supporting sustainable growth. Entrepreneurs should also consider exit strategies, such as mergers, acquisitions, and potential IPOs, which require careful financial planning and consideration of several factors, including valuation, market conditions, and strategic objectives.

By mastering the art of managing finances during growth, entrepreneurs can sustain momentum, capitalize on opportunities, and position their technology ventures for long-term success. This enables entrepreneurs to practice navigating the financial complexities of growth and make informed decisions that drive sustained financial success.

Unit summary

The following discussion explores the intersection of marketing and finance, which are crucial aspects of any technology venture's success. The unit begins by exploring market segmentation and sizing, which is essential for understanding target audiences and identifying growth opportunities. It then explores into creating customer personas and value propositions, key elements in crafting compelling messages and offerings that resonate with potential customers. The discussion expands to marketing strategy, covering go-to-market strategies that outline how products or services will be introduced to the market. Distribution channels and sales networks are also explored, highlighting the importance of efficient and effective methods for reaching and engaging customers. On the finance side, the unit addresses funding requirements based on the stage of the venture, providing insights into the diverse funding sources available to start-up ventures. Financial projections and accounting practices are discussed in detail, emphasizing the importance of accurate forecasting and transparent financial records.

The unit concludes by examining the transition from start-up to scale-up financing, outlining strategies for securing funding during different growth phases. Throughout the unit, marketing and finance strategies are integrated, highlighting their symbiotic relationship in driving sustainable growth and long-term success for technology ventures.

Tutorial questions for practice:

1. Market Segmentation Exercise:
    - Divide the class into groups and give them a hypothetical product or service.
    - Ask each group to identify and define different market segments for the product or service based on demographic, geographic, psychographic, and behavioural characteristics.
    - Have each group present their segmentation strategy and rationale to the class, followed by a discussion on the effectiveness of their approach.
2. Market Sizing Analysis:
    - Present the students with a real-world scenario of a start-up entering a specific market.
    - Task them with conducting market sizing analysis to estimate the potential revenue and size of the target market.
    - Guide them through gathering relevant data, analysing market trends, and applying various methods (e.g., top-down, bottom-up) to determine market size.
    - Discuss the findings as a class and explore implications for the start-up's growth strategy.
3. Customer Persona Development:
    - Provide students with case studies or personas representing different customer segments.

- In groups, ask them to develop detailed customer personas, including demographics, preferences, pain points, and buying behaviours.
- Encourage students to brainstorm value propositions tailored to each persona and identify how the start-up's product or service can address their needs.
- Facilitate a group discussion on understanding customer personas in crafting effective marketing strategies.

4. Go-to-Market Strategy Simulation:

   - Divide students into teams and assign each team a unique startup idea or product.
   - Task them with developing a comprehensive go-to-market strategy, including product positioning, pricing, distribution channels, and promotional tactics.
   - Have each team present their strategy to the class, emphasizing their rationale and critical decision points.
   - Encourage peer feedback and discussion on the strengths and weaknesses of each strategy, as well as potential opportunities and threats.

5. Financial Projections Workshop:

   - Provide students with financial data for a start-up and guide them through creating financial projections.
   - Walk them through vital financial concepts such as revenue forecasts, cost estimation, cash flow analysis, and profit margins.
   - Encourage students to discuss the assumptions and risks associated with their projections and how they can mitigate potential challenges.
   - Facilitate a discussion on the importance of accurate financial planning for startup success and the role of financial projections in attracting investors.

Review Questions

1. Define market segmentation and its importance in entrepreneurial marketing.
2. Identify one component of a go-to-market strategy.
3. Discuss the factors influencing the creation of customer personas and their role in marketing.

4. Explain the concept of value proposition and its significance in attracting customers.
5. Evaluate the impact of market segmentation on the financial success of an entrepreneurial venture.
6. Develop a comprehensive go-to-market strategy for a hypothetical product, considering key marketing components.
7. Define distribution channels and their role in sales networks.
8. Identify one source of funding for start-up ventures.
9. Compare and contrast different funding sources, such as angel investors and venture capitalists.
10. Discuss the importance of financial projections in the planning and execution of a start-up.
11. Formulate a market sizing strategy for a niche product, considering relevant factors.
12. Analyse the impact of distribution channel selection on sales network efficiency and market reach.
13. Define value proposition and its connection to customer needs.
14. Identify a key consideration when transitioning from start-up to scale-up financing.
15. Discuss the role of financial projections in attracting potential investors.
16. Analyse the benefits and challenges of crowd funding as a source of start-up funding.
17. Consider demographics and psychographics to Formulate a comprehensive customer persona for a specific product.
18. Develop a financial plan for start-up to scale-up financing, incorporating key growth considerations.
19. Define go-to-market strategy.
20. Identify one financial principle relevant to sustainable financial management.
21. Discuss the importance of marketing strategies in influencing funding decisions.
22. Explain the concept of market sizing and its relevance in developing a business plan.
23. Evaluate the role of distribution channels in reaching diverse market segments.
24. Formulate a value proposition for a product that addresses the unique needs of a specific customer segment.

Multiple Choice Questions (MCQs)

1. Market segmentation involves dividing the market into distinct groups based on:
    a) Product Features
    b) Demographic characteristics
    c) Geographic location
    d) All the above

2. Market sizing is the process of:
    a) Estimating the potential revenue of a market
    b) Determining the number of competitors in a market
    c) Calculating the cost of marketing campaigns
    d) Analysing customer feedback

3. Customer personas are fictional representations of:
    a) Actual customers
    b) Competitors' customers
    c) Potential investors
    d) Market trends

4. A value proposition describes:
    a) The unique benefits a product or service offers to customers
    b) The cost of a product or service
    c) The number of units sold in a given period
    d) The total revenue generated by a product or service

5. A Go-to-Market strategy outlines:
    a) How a product or service will be launched and promoted to customers
    b) The distribution channels used to deliver products to customers
    c) The financial projections for a startup venture
    d) The stages of funding required for startup growth

Fill in the Blanks:

1. Distribution channels and sales networks are essential components of a start-up's __________ strategy.
2. Funding requirement for a start-up is often determined by its ____________________.
3. ________________________ is the process of predicting a company's future financial performance based on current data and assumptions.
4. Start-up to scale-up financing involves securing ________________________ to support rapid growth and expansion.

Answers: Multiple Choice Questions (MCQs)

1. b) Demographic characteristics

2. a) Estimating the potential revenue of a market
3. a) Actual customers
4. a) The unique benefits a product or service offers to customers
5. a) How a product or service will be launched and promoted to customers

Answers: Fill in the Blanks:

1. Go-to-market
2. stage of growth
3. Financial projections and accounting
4. funding or investment

References for Suggested Reading

1. Meyer, Marc H., and Frederick G. Crane. *Entrepreneurship: An innovator's guide to start-ups and corporate ventures*. Sage, 2010.

2. Grinberg, A. (2016). The development of a start-up from idea to feasible business concept.

3. Chishti, Susanne, and Thomas Puschmann. *The Wealthtech book: The FinTech handbook for investors, entrepreneurs and finance visionaries*. John Wiley & Sons, 2018.

4. Denault, Jean-Francois. *The handbook of marketing strategy for life science companies: formulating the roadmap you need to navigate the market*. CRC Press, 2018.

5. Turner, Stephen, and Stan DeVaughn. *Net value: How to develop a winning value proposition for marketing in the digital culture*. Lulu. Com, 2008.

6. Arthur, Lisa. *Extensive data marketing: engage your customers more effectively and drive value*. John Wiley & Sons, 2013.

UNIT 4 Venture Creation

UNIT SPECIFICS

This unit offers a comprehensive examination of the venture creation process within the context of sustainable business practices. Key areas of focus include:

1. **Sustainable Business Options & Pathways**
   - Exploration of sustainable business models and pathways for entrepreneurial ventures.
   - Understanding the principles of sustainability and their integration into business strategies.
2. **Business Model & Business Canvas**
   - Development of robust business models and business canvases tailored to sustainable ventures.
   - Analysis of critical components such as value proposition, revenue streams, and cost structure.
3. **Startup Team & Business Partners**
   - Strategies for assembling and managing startup teams committed to sustainability.
   - Collaboration and partnership models with stakeholders aligned with sustainable goals.
4. **Start-up Ecosystem and Stakeholders**
   - Examination of the broader start-up ecosystem and the role of various stakeholders in sustainable ventures.

- Networking strategies for engaging with investors, mentors, and industry partners supportive of sustainability.

5. **Technology Business Incubators & Parks**

   - Understanding the role of technology business incubators and parks in nurturing and supporting sustainable start-ups.
   - Accessing resources and support services available within incubation ecosystems.

6. **Proposal Pitching & Agreements**

   - Techniques for effectively pitching proposals to investors and partners, emphasizing sustainability goals.
   - Negotiation and drafting agreements aligning with sustainable business practices and objectives.

7. **Start-up Company Incorporation**

   - Guidance on the legal and procedural aspects of incorporating a startup company focusing on sustainability.
   - Compliance with regulations and standards relevant to sustainable ventures.

8. **Social Impact & Responsibility**

   - Integrating social impact considerations into sustainable ventures' core mission and operations.
   - Strategies for measuring and communicating social impact to stakeholders and the wider community.

These focus areas collectively provide learners with the knowledge and tools to conceptualize, launch, and sustain entrepreneurial ventures prioritizing sustainability and social responsibility.

RATIONALE

This unit is designed to equip learners with the knowledge and skills necessary for venture creation in the context of product innovation and entrepreneurship. Understanding sustainable business options, developing effective business models, assembling, and managing startup teams, and navigating the startup ecosystem are crucial for successfully launching and sustaining new ventures. Additionally, knowledge of legal aspects such as company incorporation, pitching proposals, agreements, and social impact and responsibility considerations are essential for aspiring entrepreneurs.

PRE-REQUISITES

1. Basic understanding of product innovation and entrepreneurship concepts
2. Familiarity with business fundamentals such as marketing, finance, and operations
3. Knowledge of market research techniques and analysis
4. Understanding of technology and its applications in business
5. Awareness of legal and regulatory frameworks relevant to start-ups and businesses

UNIT OUTCOMES

Upon completion of this unit, learners will be able to:

U4-O1: Evaluate and select sustainable business options and pathways suitable for their ventures.

U4-O2: Develop comprehensive business models and business canvases to guide the start-up initiatives.

U4-O3: Formulate strategies for building effective start-up teams and collaborating with business partners.

U4-O4: Navigate the start-up ecosystem and engage with various stakeholders, including investors, mentors, and advisors.

U4-O5: Understand the role and function of technology business incubators and parks in supporting startup ventures.

Unit-4 Outcomes	Expected Mapping with Programme Outcomes *(1- Weak Correlation; 2- Medium correlation; 3- Strong Correlation)*				
	CO-1	CO -2	CO -3	CO -4	CO -5
U4-O1	3	2	2	2	1

Unit-4 Outcomes	Expected Mapping with Programme Outcomes *(1- Weak Correlation; 2- Medium correlation; 3- Strong Correlation)*				
	CO-1	CO -2	CO -3	CO -4	CO -5
U4-O2	3	1	3	1	2
U4-O3	2	3	2	2	2
U4-O4	3	2	3	2	1
U4-O5	3	3	2	1	1

Venture creation marks the culmination of entrepreneurial efforts, transforming innovative ideas into tangible, sustainable businesses. This unit explores the multifaceted landscape of launching and establishing a technology venture. From crafting a robust business model to navigating the intricacies of start-up ecosystems, it provides a comprehensive guide for aspiring entrepreneurs to create impactful and successful ventures. Drawing on real-world examples, strategic frameworks, and practical insights, Unit 4 explores the dynamic journey of venture creation, offering a roadmap for navigating the challenges, seizing opportunities, and laying the foundation for a thriving technology enterprise. Whether you envision a ground-breaking start-up or seek to enhance your understanding of the venture creation process, this unit serves as a valuable resource for translating entrepreneurial visions into tangible business realities.

4.1. Sustainable Business Options and Pathways

In an era where societal and environmental considerations are integral to business practices, exploring sustainable business models is not just a strategic choice but a necessity. The following discussion explores into sustainable entrepreneurship, examining various business models prioritizing economic, social, and environmental sustainability. Figure 4.1 illustrates the key components of a business model, delineating essential elements that form the foundation of a successful enterprise.

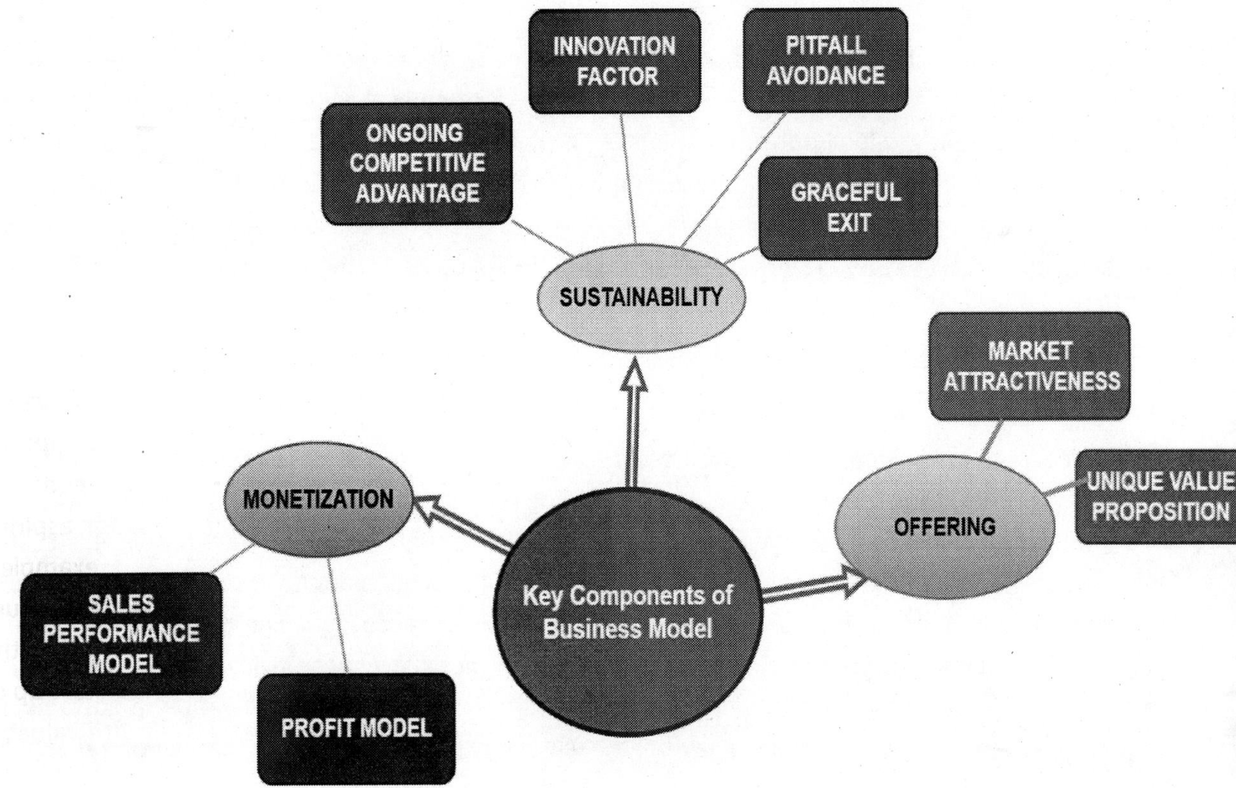

Figure 4.1 Key Components of a Business Model

4.1.1 Exploring Sustainable Business Models

Understanding sustainability in business entails comprehending its broader impact on society and the environment. It involves defining sustainability within business operations and acknowledging its significance beyond mere profitability. This involves adopting the triple bottom line approach, which integrates economic, social, and environmental dimensions into business practices. By considering these three pillars, businesses strive to achieve financial success, social responsibility, and environmental stewardship, for long-term sustainability and contributing to a more sustainable future.

Sustainable business models are crucial in ensuring businesses' long-term viability and positive societal impact. By integrating sustainability into core business strategies and decision-making processes, companies can align their operations with environmental and social responsibility objectives. This integration allows businesses to mitigate adverse impacts on the environment and society and unlock opportunities for innovation and growth. Sustainable business models prioritize the efficient use of resources, reduce waste, and initiate responsible practices throughout the value chain. They enable businesses to thrive economically while contributing to environmental preservation and societal well-being. Various sustainable business models have emerged to address environmental and social challenges while supporting economic growth. One prominent model is the circular economy, which prioritizes minimizing waste and maximizing the value of resources by promoting reuse, recycling, and regeneration. Another model is the shared economy, where resources are shared or utilized more efficiently, reducing overall consumption and environmental impact. Additionally, regenerative business models focus on restoring ecosystems and enhancing natural capital while delivering economic value. Each model offers unique business opportunities across industries to align with sustainability goals and respond to evolving market demands.

In addition, circular economy models advocate eliminating waste and continuously using resources in a closed-loop system. Businesses can adopt principles such as designing products for longevity, promoting reuse and repair, and embracing recycling and remanufacturing processes. For instance, companies can offer products with modular designs that facilitate easy repair and upgrades, extending their lifespan. Examples of successful circular economy models include clothing rental services, where garments are leased and returned for reuse, reducing the demand for new clothing production, and minimizing textile waste. Such models reduce environmental impact and offer economic benefits by optimizing resource utilization and nurturing innovation in sustainable practices. Shared economy models leverage technology to facilitate the sharing of resources, enabling more efficient utilization and reducing overall consumption.

Platforms such as 'Airbnb' and 'Uber' exemplify this model by connecting individuals with underutilized assets, such as spare rooms or vehicles, with those needing temporary accommodation or transportation. Similarly, co-working spaces allow individuals and businesses to share office facilities, promoting collaboration and reducing the environmental footprint of maintaining separate office spaces. The shared economy extends beyond physical assets to include shared access to services like peer-to-peer lending and crowd-funding platforms, which democratize access to capital while promoting community engagement and resource efficiency. Regenerative business models represent a change in thinking from merely minimizing harm to actively restoring and replenishing natural and social ecosystems. Unlike traditional business models that focus solely on profit generation, regenerative models prioritize the creation of positive environmental and social impacts. These models seek to harness business activities as a force for good, leveraging innovative approaches to address pressing global challenges such as climate change, biodiversity loss, and social inequality. By integrating principles of sustainability and regeneration into their core operations, businesses can play a transformative role in fostering ecological resilience, enhancing community well-being, and creating shared value for all stakeholders.

Further, sustainable businesses prioritize innovation and product development strategies that minimize environmental impact throughout the product lifecycle. They employ design thinking methodologies and life cycle assessments to identify opportunities for eco-friendly materials, energy-efficient manufacturing processes, and recyclable packaging. These businesses also embrace concepts like bio mimicry and cradle-to-cradle design to create products that mimic nature's efficiency and circularity. Examples include companies developing renewable energy technologies, biodegradable packaging solutions, and sustainable fashion lines that minimize waste and pollution while maximizing resource efficiency. Effective measurement of sustainable impact is crucial for businesses committed to sustainability. Key performance indicators (KPIs) often include carbon footprint reduction, water and energy usage efficiency, waste diversion rates, and social impact metrics such as fair labour practices and community engagement. Transparent reporting on sustainability metrics, such as through sustainability reports aligned with global standards like the Global Reporting Initiative (GRI) or the Sustainability Accounting Standards Board (SASB), enhances accountability and trust with stakeholders. By tracking and disclosing their sustainability performance, businesses can demonstrate their commitment to creating positive environmental and social change while driving long-term value creation.

Entrepreneurs embracing sustainable business models face challenges, including higher initial investment costs, limited access to sustainable materials, and uncertainty regarding consumer willingness to pay premiums for eco-friendly products. However, these challenges present opportunities for differentiation and market leadership. Sustainable businesses can capitalize on growing consumer demand for ethically sourced and environmentally friendly products, access niche markets, and build strong brand loyalty based on shared values with eco-conscious consumers. By adopting sustainable practices, businesses can also enhance operational efficiency, reduce long-term costs, and mitigate risks associated with resource scarcity and environmental degradation. The regulatory landscape for sustainable business practices continues to evolve globally, with governments enacting policies and regulations to address climate change, resource depletion, and social equity issues. To avoid legal penalties and reputational damage, businesses must stay abreast of these regulations and ensure compliance. Compliance involves adhering to environmental standards, labour laws, product safety regulations, and ethical sourcing practices. By proactively integrating sustainability into their operations and supply chains, businesses can navigate regulatory complexities, build trust with stakeholders, and contribute to positive societal and environmental outcomes. Entrepreneur's may learn from the examples from various industries, such as renewable energy, organic food production, and eco-friendly apparel. By examining the experiences of these ventures, entrepreneurs can learn about innovative business models, successful marketing strategies, supply chain management practices, and stakeholder engagement initiatives that drive sustainable entrepreneurship. Extracting critical lessons from these case studies helps entrepreneurs navigate challenges and capitalize on opportunities in their sustainable business endeavours.

By exploring sustainable business models, entrepreneurs can contribute to positive societal and environmental outcomes and enhance their long-term resilience and success. This provides a comprehensive overview, empowering participants to navigate the landscape of sustainable entrepreneurship and create ventures that thrive economically and ethically.

4.1.2 Aligning with Environmental and Social Responsibility

In pursuing sustainable business practices, aligning with environmental and social responsibility becomes paramount. The following discussion details into the crucial aspects of how businesses can embrace responsibility towards the environment and society, developing a positive impact alongside economic growth.

Environmental responsibility is increasingly recognized as a core component of modern business practices. It involves acknowledging and addressing the ecological impact of business operations, products, and services. By understanding the environmental consequences of their activities, businesses can implement strategies to minimize harm to ecosystems, natural resources, and biodiversity. This includes reducing carbon emissions, minimizing waste generation, conserving energy, and water resources, and adopting sustainable practices throughout the product lifecycle. Moreover, businesses must comply with environmental regulations and continuously strive to improve their environmental performance. Sustainable supply chain management focuses on integrating environmental and social considerations into every stage of the supply chain, from sourcing raw materials to delivering products to consumers. This approach emphasizes transparency, accountability, and collaboration among supply chain partners to address environmental challenges such as pollution, deforestation, and climate change. Sustainable supply chain management strategies include adopting green procurement policies, engaging with suppliers committed to sustainability, optimizing transportation and logistics to reduce emissions, and implementing circular economy principles to minimize waste. Businesses increasingly embrace eco-friendly practices to minimize their environmental footprint and differentiate themselves in the market. These practices encompass various initiatives such as using renewable energy sources, implementing energy-efficient technologies, reducing packaging waste, and promoting recycling and reuse. Innovation plays a crucial role in driving eco-friendly practices by enabling the development of sustainable products, processes, and business models. Through research and development, businesses can create innovative solutions prioritizing environmental sustainability while meeting consumer demands and regulatory requirements.

Importantly, Social responsibility in business extends beyond economic considerations to encompass ethical labour practices, environmental stewardship, and community engagement. Businesses are responsible for upholding ethical standards in their operations, including fair treatment of employees, suppliers, and stakeholders. Community engagement involves actively participating in and contributing to the well-being of local communities where businesses operate. This can include supporting education and healthcare initiatives, investing in infrastructure development, and collaborating with local organizations to address social challenges such as poverty and inequality. Also, Diversity, equity, and inclusion (DEI) are essential to social responsibility and contribute to building a more equitable and just society. Businesses play a crucial role in promoting DEI by developing diverse and inclusive workplace cultures where all employees feel valued, respected, and empowered to contribute their unique perspectives and talents. Strategies for promoting DEI include implementing non-discriminatory hiring and promotion practices, training on unconscious bias and cultural sensitivity, and creating affinity groups or employee resource networks to support underrepresented groups.

Corporate philanthropy involves businesses allocating resources, such as financial donations, volunteer hours, or in-kind contributions, to support social causes and community development initiatives. Businesses can address pressing social issues through corporate philanthropy, strengthen stakeholder relationships, and enhance their corporate reputation. Examples of corporate philanthropy include donating to charitable organizations, sponsoring community events, funding educational scholarships, and participating in disaster relief efforts. By giving back to society, businesses demonstrate their commitment to being responsible corporate citizens and making a positive impact beyond profit generation.

Effective stakeholder communication is essential for businesses to demonstrate their environmental and social responsibility commitment. Transparent communication builds trust and credibility with customers, employees, investors, and other stakeholders. Businesses can engage stakeholders through various channels, including corporate reports, social media platforms, and direct communication channels. Strategies for stakeholder engagement may include soliciting feedback, hosting community events, and providing regular updates on sustainability initiatives and progress. Figure 4.2 illustrates the strategies employed for stakeholder engagement, highlighting the importance of building solid relationships with key stakeholders to support business objectives. Ethical marketing practices align with environmental and social responsibility by promoting honesty, transparency, and integrity in advertising and promotional activities. Ethical marketers avoid deceptive or manipulative tactics and instead focus on providing accurate information and raising consumer trust. Consumer awareness is vital in driving demand for socially responsible products and services. Consumers increasingly seek businesses that demonstrate a commitment to sustainability and ethical practices as they become more informed about environmental and social issues.

Impact investing and socially responsible investing (SRI) are investment approaches that consider environmental, social, and governance (ESG) factors alongside financial returns. Impact investors seek to generate positive social or environmental outcomes while achieving financial goals. Businesses can attract investment from impact investors and SRI funds by demonstrating strong ESG performance, transparent reporting on sustainability metrics, and a clear commitment to environmental and social responsibility. Access to impact capital can support businesses in scaling their sustainability initiatives and driving positive change. Compliance with industry standards and obtaining certifications for responsible business practices are essential for demonstrating a commitment to environmental and social responsibility. Adhering to standards ensures businesses operate ethically and sustainably, minimizing negative environmental and societal impacts. Certifications provide third-party validation of responsible practices and can enhance credibility and trust among stakeholders. Well-known certifications, such as Fair Trade, B Corp, and LEED, signal a business's dedication to sustainability, ethical labour practices, and social impact.

Businesses face various challenges in aligning with environmental and social responsibility, including the costs associated with implementing sustainable practices and overcoming operational hurdles. However, embracing responsible practices also presents significant differentiation and competitive advantage opportunities. By prioritizing sustainability and social impact, businesses can attract environmentally and socially conscious consumers, strengthen brand reputation, and develop long-term relationships with stakeholders. Additionally, responsible practices can drive innovation, efficiency improvements, and access to new markets and opportunities.

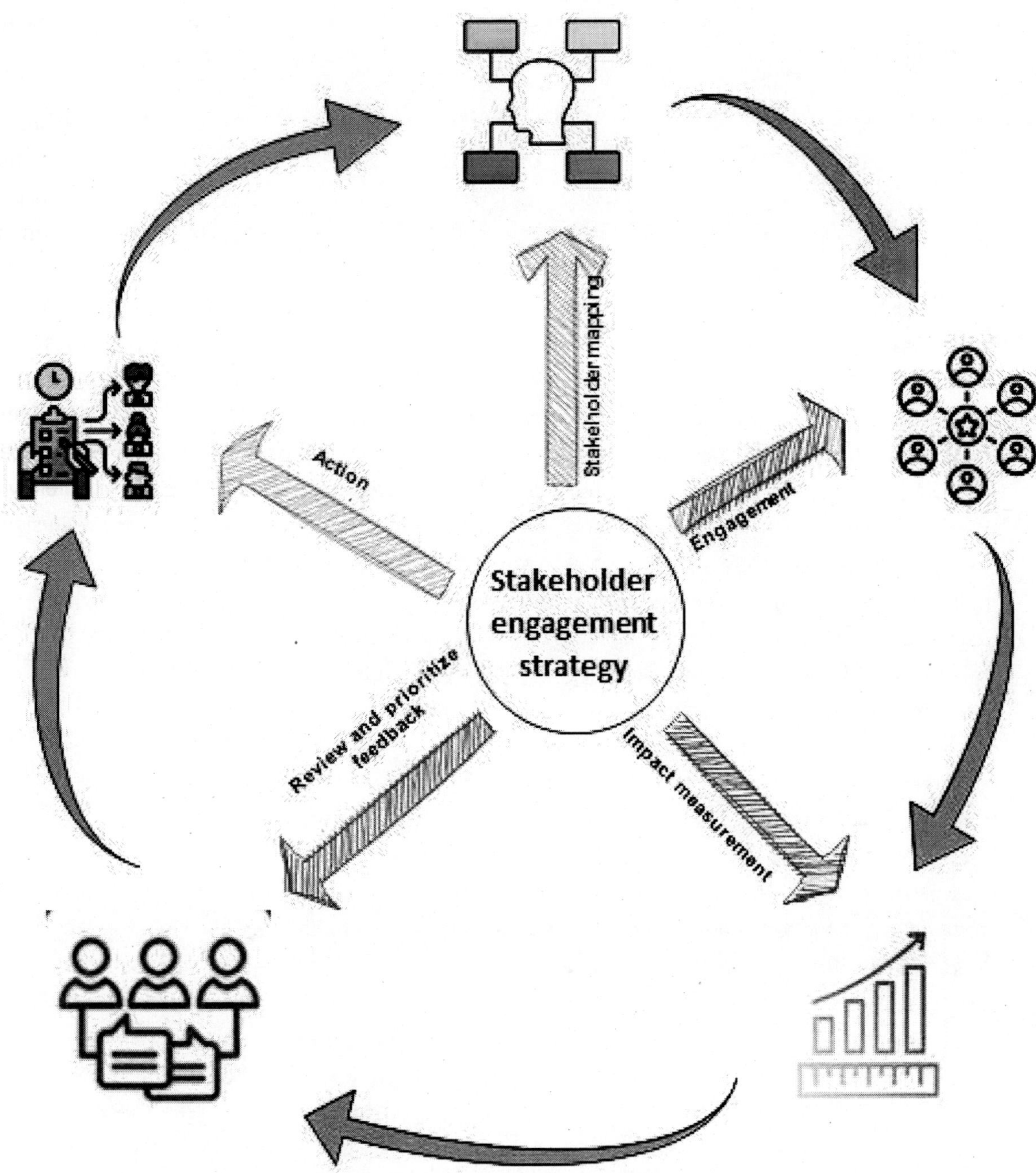

Figure 4.2 Stakeholder Engagement Strategies

By aligning with environmental and social responsibility, businesses contribute to positive societal and environmental outcomes and a solid ethical foundation. The following discussion provides insights and practical guidance, empowering participants to navigate the complex landscape of responsible business practices and integrate them seamlessly into their venture creation journey.

4.1.3 Pathways to Sustainable Venture Creation

Embarking on the journey of sustainable venture creation involves navigating diverse pathways that align with ecological and societal well-being. The following discussion explores the various routes and strategies entrepreneurs can undertake to infuse sustainability into the DNA of their ventures, ensuring a harmonious coexistence of profitability and responsibility. The pathway starts with Integrating Sustainability into the Business Model. Entrepreneurs strategically integrate sustainability into the core of their business models by aligning mission, vision, and values with sustainable practices. They explore innovative approaches to address environmental and social challenges while delivering value to stakeholders. By embedding sustainability into every aspect of their operations, entrepreneurs create resilient and impactful ventures that contribute to a sustainable future. Then, forging collaborative partnerships with like-minded organizations and stakeholders is essential for amplifying the impact of sustainable ventures is essential. Entrepreneurs leverage partnerships to access complementary resources, expertise, and networks, enhancing their ability to address complex sustainability challenges. Working together supports collective responsibility and drives meaningful change across industries and communities. Further, Innovation is pivotal in creating sustainable products, services, and solutions. Entrepreneurs leverage technological advancements, creative thinking, and interdisciplinary approaches to develop innovative solutions that address environmental and social issues. By embracing a culture of continuous innovation, they drive progress towards sustainability goals while unlocking new opportunities for growth and positive impact. Also, sustainable ventures prioritize green technologies and eco-friendly practices to minimize their environmental footprint. They explore renewable energy sources, utilizing efficient energy systems, and integrating sustainable materials to reduce resource consumption and greenhouse gas emissions. By integrating eco-friendly practices into their operations, these ventures contribute to resource conservation and environmental preservation, supporting a more sustainable future for future generations. Sustainable ventures embrace the principles of the circular economy to redesign production processes, minimize waste generation, and maximize resource efficiency. They adopt product lifecycle extension, resource recovery, and closed-loop systems to promote circularity throughout the value chain. By implementing circular economy practices, these ventures reduce waste and environmental impact and create new opportunities for innovation and economic growth.

Social enterprises and impact-driven ventures prioritize social and environmental impact alongside financial returns. These ventures often have a clear mission to address pressing societal or environmental challenges by integrating sustainability into their core business strategies. By leveraging innovative business models and partnerships, they aim to create positive change while generating revenue. Through their commitment to social and environmental causes, these ventures contribute to building more equitable and sustainable societies. Further, securing sustainable finance and funding is essential for ventures committed to responsible business practices. These ventures explore various pathways for financing, including impact investment, green bonds, and socially responsible funds. Impact investors prioritize ventures with measurable social and environmental impact, aligning their investment goals with sustainability objectives. By accessing sustainable finance options, ventures can accelerate their growth while staying true to their values and mission. Then, implementing corporate social responsibility (CSR) programs within sustainable ventures involves integrating initiatives that benefit society and the environment. These programs align with the venture's mission and values, aiming to make a positive impact beyond financial returns. By investing in causes such as community development, environmental conservation, or employee well-being, sustainable ventures demonstrate their commitment to social responsibility. Strategic alignment ensures that CSR efforts complement the venture's objectives, enhancing its reputation and promoting stakeholder relationships. Importantly, Sustainable product lifecycle management encompasses practices that minimize environmental impact throughout a product's journey, from design to disposal. Ventures prioritize eco-friendly materials, energy-efficient manufacturing processes, and recyclable packaging to reduce carbon footprint. By considering environmental factors at every stage, from sourcing raw materials to end-of-life disposal, sustainable ventures aim to create products with minimal ecological impact. These practices reflect a commitment to environmental stewardship and contribute to building a more sustainable future. Ethical sourcing and responsible supply chain practices are fundamental to the operation of sustainable ventures. These ventures prioritize transparency and traceability in their supply chains, ensuring that materials and components are sourced ethically and sustainably. By partnering with suppliers who uphold fair labour practices and environmental standards, sustainable ventures mitigate risks associated with unethical practices like child labour or deforestation. Ethical sourcing practices align with the venture's values, promoting integrity and accountability throughout the supply chain. Also, B Corp certification and adherence to industry standards play a crucial role in validating the commitment of sustainable ventures to social and environmental responsibility. B Corp certification, awarded by the non-profit B Lab, evaluates companies based on their performance in governance, community impact, and environmental stewardship. Adherence to industry standards demonstrates a venture's alignment with best practices and benchmarks set by relevant sectors. Certification requires rigorous assessment and compliance with established criteria, signalling a venture's dedication to sustainable business practices and accountability. Finally, scaling the impact of sustainable ventures beyond local boundaries involves strategic planning and collaboration on a global scale. Ventures explore opportunities for expanding their reach and influence by leveraging networks, partnerships, and technology platforms. Global outreach initiatives enable ventures to address sustainability challenges on a broader scale, tapping into diverse markets and resources. Collaboration with international organizations, governments, and communities facilitates knowledge sharing and collective action toward achieving global sustainability goals.

Entrepreneurs can tailor their approaches to align with their unique missions and goals by exploring diverse pathways to sustainable venture creation. The following discussion provides insights and practical guidance, empowering participants to embark on a journey that ensures their ventures' success and contributes positively to the environment and society.

4.2. Business Model and Business Canvas

The foundation of any successful venture lies in its business model — a strategic framework that outlines how a company creates, delivers, and captures value. In The following discussion, we dissect the critical components of a business model, providing entrepreneurs with the essential building blocks to craft a robust and sustainable foundation for their ventures.

4.2.1 Components of a Business Model

The components of a business model start with Value Proposition. The value proposition forms the cornerstone of a business model, defining the unique benefits and solutions offered to customers. Entrepreneurs must articulate a compelling value proposition that resonates with target audiences, addressing their needs, desires, and pain points. Developing a compelling value proposition involves thorough market research, customer feedback analysis, and differentiation from competitors. By clearly communicating the value delivered, ventures can attract and retain customers, driving revenue and growth. Then, identifying and segmenting the target customer base is essential for understanding market dynamics and tailoring products or services accordingly. Entrepreneurs must delineate distinct customer segments based on demographics, behaviours, and preferences. By gaining insights into customer profiles, ventures can customize marketing efforts, product features, and pricing strategies to meet the diverse needs of different segments. Understanding the nuances of each customer segment enables ventures to optimize resource allocation and maximize customer acquisition and retention efforts. Importantly, Channels encompass the pathways through which a venture delivers its products or services to customers. Entrepreneurs explore distribution channels, including direct sales, online platforms, retail partnerships, and distribution networks, to optimize efficiency and extend customer reach. By understanding customer preferences and market dynamics, ventures can strategically select and leverage channels that align with their value proposition and target audience, ensuring seamless delivery and enhanced customer experience.

Further, customer relationships define the interactions and connections between a venture and its customers throughout the customer lifecycle. Entrepreneurs establish strategies for cultivating meaningful relationships, encompassing customer support, feedback mechanisms, and personalized communication. By prioritizing customer satisfaction and engagement, ventures can develop long-term loyalty, advocacy, and repeat business, driving sustained revenue growth and market success. Also, Revenue streams delineate the sources through which a venture generates income from its offerings. Entrepreneurs diversify revenue streams to mitigate risk and optimize financial sustainability, incorporating strategies such as product sales, subscription models, licensing agreements, advertising revenue, and ancillary services. By aligning revenue streams with value creation and customer willingness to pay, ventures can capitalize on monetization opportunities and maximize profitability while delivering exceptional customer value. In addition, Key resources encompass the essential assets and inputs for a venture's operations and value-creation process. Entrepreneurs identify critical resources such as physical infrastructure, technological tools, human capital, intellectual property, and financial reserves. By strategically allocating and managing resources, ventures optimize efficiency, minimize waste, and enhance competitiveness. Effective resource management ensures that ventures possess the capabilities to deliver value to customers and sustain long-term growth and profitability.

In continuation, Key activities delineate the core processes and operations that drive the execution of a venture's value proposition. Entrepreneurs outline vital activities such as product development, manufacturing, marketing and sales, customer service, and strategic planning. By aligning critical activities with overarching business objectives and value-creation strategies, ventures streamline operations, optimize resource utilization, and enhance overall performance. Well-defined and focused key activities enable ventures to deliver exceptional customer value, achieve competitive advantage, and drive sustainable growth. Key partnerships also involve strategic collaborations with external entities that complement and enhance a venture's capabilities, resources, and reach. Entrepreneurs identify and cultivate partnerships with suppliers, distributors, technology providers, research institutions, and industry peers. By leveraging synergies and combined resources, ventures expand market access, accelerate innovation, mitigate risks, and capitalize on growth opportunities. Selecting partners based on shared values, mutual benefits, and aligned objectives develop trust, collaboration, and long-term success in the competitive business landscape. Most importantly, cost structure encompasses all expenses incurred in a venture, including fixed and variable costs. Entrepreneurs analyse and categorize production costs, marketing expenses, personnel salaries, overheads, and administrative costs. By understanding cost drivers and dynamics, ventures can implement cost optimization strategies to improve efficiency, reduce waste, and enhance profitability. Effective cost management ensures that ventures operate within budgetary constraints while delivering value to customers and stakeholders, thus supporting sustainable growth and resilience in competitive markets.

The Business Model Canvas is a visual framework for entrepreneurs to develop, analyse, and iterate on their business models. Comprising nine fundamental building blocks, including value proposition, customer segments, channels, customer relationships, revenue streams, essential resources, key activities, key partnerships, and cost structure, the canvas provides a holistic view of the venture's business model. By leveraging the canvas, entrepreneurs can visualize the interdependencies among different components, identify areas for improvement, and communicate their business model effectively to stakeholders. Innovation and iteration are crucial to refining and evolving business models to adapt to changing market dynamics and customer preferences. Entrepreneurs embrace innovation by experimenting with new value propositions, revenue streams, customer segments, and distribution channels. By continuously iterating and refining their business models based on feedback and market insights, ventures remain agile, responsive, and competitive in dynamic business environments. Case studies of successful ventures highlight the importance of innovation and iteration in achieving sustainable growth and market leadership. Importantly, Industry-specific considerations play a pivotal role in shaping the design and efficacy of a business model. Each industry has unique characteristics, market dynamics, regulatory requirements, and customer expectations that influence the choice of business model components and strategies. Entrepreneurs must analyse industry trends, competitive landscapes, and customer behaviours to tailor their business models accordingly. By understanding industry-specific nuances, ventures can optimize their value proposition, customer segments, channels, and revenue streams to capitalize on market opportunities and mitigate industry-specific risks effectively. Also, analysing the real-time examples of ventures with successful business models provides valuable insights into the strategies and practices that contribute to their success. By examining diverse ventures across different industries and market segments, entrepreneurs gain a deeper understanding of practical business model design, implementation, and optimization. Case studies highlight innovative approaches, strategic partnerships, customer-centric strategies, and scalability initiatives that drive sustainable growth and competitive advantage. Extracting critical lessons from these case studies enables entrepreneurs to implement proven strategies and best practices in creating sustainable and scalable business models.

Understanding and strategically crafting the components of a business model are pivotal steps for entrepreneurs aiming to build ventures that survive and thrive in dynamic market landscapes. The following discussion equips participants with the knowledge and tools to design business models that align with their vision, resonate with customers, and drive sustained success.

4.2.2 Business Canvas: A Visual Framework

In the realm of entrepreneurship, clarity and coherence are paramount. The Business Model Canvas emerges as a powerful visual tool, providing entrepreneurs with a structured framework to articulate, analyse, and iterate on their business model. The following discussion explores the intricacies of the Business Canvas, offering insights into its components and how entrepreneurs can leverage this visual framework to navigate the complexities of venture creation.

The Business Model Canvas, conceived by Alexander Osterwalder and Yves Pigneur, is a concise visual representation of a venture's business model. It condenses complex business concepts into a single-page framework, improving clarity and coherence in entrepreneurial endeavours. The canvas is a structured tool for articulating, analysing, and iterating on various business model aspects, enabling entrepreneurs to conceptualize their ventures comprehensively. The canvas comprises nine key components, each representing a critical aspect of the venture's business model. These components include Customer Segments, Value Propositions, Channels, Customer Relationships, Revenue Streams, Key Resources, Key Activities, Key Partnerships, and Cost Structure. Entrepreneurs utilize the canvas to systematically examine and define these components, understanding their interdependencies and strategic implications. Customer Segments and Value Propositions are foundational elements of the Business Model Canvas. Identifying and comprehensively understanding customer segments directly informs the creation of a compelling value proposition. Entrepreneurs explore strategies for aligning value propositions with target customer segments' specific needs, preferences, and pain points, ensuring their offerings resonate deeply with the intended audience. This alignment enhances the overall effectiveness and attractiveness of the business model, laying the groundwork for sustainable customer relationships and revenue generation.

Though it may appear repetitive, channels are extremely important in providing products or services to clients, making their selection a vital part of the company strategy. Entrepreneurs must carefully consider various distribution channels to ensure efficient and effective delivery while maximizing customer reach. Moreover, customer relationships are intricately tied to the chosen channels, with different channels easing several types of interactions and engagement levels with customers. Understanding this relationship is essential for building and supporting meaningful customer connections. Revenue streams represent the avenues through which a venture generates income, with each stream aligned with the value created for customers. Entrepreneurs explore diverse monetization strategies, such as product sales, subscriptions, licensing, and advertising, ensuring that revenue streams complement the value propositions offered to customers. Additionally, cost structures are influenced by the chosen activities, resources, and partnerships, with entrepreneurs striving to optimize costs while maintaining operational excellence and value delivery. Importantly, essential resources, activities, and partnerships drive the venture's value proposition and business model. Identifying and leveraging critical resources, such as physical assets, intellectual property, and human capital, enables entrepreneurs to deliver their value propositions effectively. Similarly, key activities encompass the core processes and operations contributing to value creation and customer satisfaction. Moreover, strategic partnerships enhance the venture's capabilities and reach, enhancing innovation, efficiency, and growth. Together, these interconnected elements contribute to the efficiency and effectiveness of the business model, laying the groundwork for sustainable success.

The Business Model Canvas is a powerful tool for entrepreneurs to visualize and comprehend the complex interdependencies between business model components. By mapping out essential elements such as customer segments, value propositions, channels, and revenue streams on a single canvas, entrepreneurs understand how these components interact and influence each other. Moreover, entrepreneurs can observe how changes made in one area of the canvas can have ripple effects across the entire business model, highlighting the interconnected nature of their venture's operations and strategy. One of the defining features of the Business Model Canvas is its iterative nature, which encourages entrepreneurs to refine and adapt their business models continuously. As market dynamics evolve and new insights are gained, entrepreneurs can revisit and adjust the canvas to reflect changes in their strategy, value proposition, or target market. This iterative approach supports agility and responsiveness, aligning entrepreneurs with customer needs and competitive pressures. Regularly revisiting and refining the canvas ensures the business model remains relevant and adaptable in an ever-changing landscape. While the Business Model Canvas provides a universal framework for articulating business models, its adaptability allows entrepreneurs to tailor it to suit different industries' specific requirements and nuances. By incorporating industry-specific considerations into the canvas, such as regulatory constraints, technological trends, or customer preferences, entrepreneurs can create a more tailored and effective representation of their business model. Examples of industry-specific adaptations may include modifications to customer segments, revenue streams, or key partnerships to better align with the dynamics of a particular industry or market segment.

Effectively utilizing the Business Model Canvas requires adherence to certain best practices in individual and team settings. Firstly, ensuring that all stakeholders clearly understand the canvas's components and how they interrelate is crucial. Encouraging active participation and collaboration among team members enhances diverse perspectives and insights. Additionally, maintaining focus on the customer and continuously validating assumptions through market research enhances the accuracy and relevance of the canvas. Common pitfalls include oversimplification, neglecting to update the canvas in response to latest information, and failing to consider external factors that may impact the business model. Finally, analysing examples of ventures that have effectively leveraged the Business Model Canvas provides valuable insights into its real-world applications. Key learning's and strategies emerge by examining how these ventures utilized the canvas to refine and optimize their business models. These examples highlight the versatility of the canvas across diverse industries and contexts, highlighting its effectiveness in guiding strategic decision-making and innovation. Extracting actionable insights from successful applications of the canvas enables entrepreneurs to apply similar principles and techniques to their ventures, increasing the likelihood of success.

The Business Model Canvas serves as a dynamic compass for entrepreneurs, enabling them to navigate the complex landscape of venture creation with clarity and strategic insight. The above discussion empowers participants to harness the visual power of the canvas, turning abstract ideas into tangible, actionable business models that form the bedrock of successful ventures.

4.2.3 Iterative Development of Business Models

The journey from ideation to a robust business model is seldom linear in the ever-evolving entrepreneurship landscape. The following discussion explores the iterative nature of business model development, emphasizing the importance of continuous refinement and adaptation. Entrepreneurs are guided through a dynamic process that allows them to respond to market feedback, changing dynamics, and emerging opportunities.

Successful business models are characterized by their dynamic and adaptive nature, which makes them capable of evolving in response to changing circumstances. The following discussion underscores the importance of recognizing that developing a business model is not a one-time event but an on-going process. Entrepreneurs must continuously evaluate and adjust their models to remain relevant and competitive. This iterative approach enables them to adapt to evolving consumer preferences, technological advancements, and industry trends. By embracing the dynamic nature of business models, entrepreneurs can position their ventures for long-term success. Next, feedback loops are invaluable for gathering insights from various stakeholders, including customers, partners, and industry experts. The following discussion explores how entrepreneurs can establish feedback loops to collect data, assess market responses, and validate assumptions about their business model. Customer validation is pivotal in refining value propositions and ensuring alignment with market needs. By soliciting feedback early and often, entrepreneurs can iteratively improve their business models, enhance customer satisfaction, and increase the likelihood of sustainable growth. Importantly, The Lean Start-up methodology revolutionizes business model development by advocating for iterative experimentation and rapid adaptation. Entrepreneurs are introduced to the core principles of Lean Start-up, emphasizing the importance of validated learning, quick iterations, and a relentless focus on delivering customer value. Central to this methodology is the Build-Measure-Learn feedback loop, where entrepreneurs iteratively build prototypes, measure customer responses, and learn from feedback to refine their business models. By embracing Lean Start-up practices, entrepreneurs can efficiently navigate uncertainty, mitigate risks, and accelerate the development of successful ventures.

Next, minimum Viable Product (MVP) is a foundational concept in Lean Start-up methodology, enabling entrepreneurs to test their assumptions and gather feedback with minimal resources. This definition of MVP as a basic version of a product or service contains only essential features. Prototyping and MVPs provide tangible representations of the venture's value proposition, allowing entrepreneurs to validate assumptions, gather user feedback, and iterate based on real-world insights. By leveraging MVPs and prototyping, entrepreneurs can efficiently validate market demand, mitigate product development risks, and accelerate time-to-market. Further, continuous testing and experimentation are integral components of Lean Start-up methodology, facilitating data-driven decision-making and iterative refinement. Entrepreneurs are guided through the importance of designing controlled experiments to test hypotheses and validate critical assumptions about their business models. By systematically collecting and analysing data from experiments, entrepreneurs gain valuable insights into customer preferences, market dynamics, and competitive landscapes. This iterative approach empowers entrepreneurs to make informed decisions, optimize business model components, and enhance the likelihood of achieving product-market fit. In addition, Pivoting emerges as a strategic maneuver in the iterative development process, allowing entrepreneurs to navigate uncertainties and adapt to validate learning's. The following discussion explores pivoting as a deliberate shift in business strategy or direction based on insights gained from experimentation and customer feedback. Moreover, it underscores the significance of perseverance and resilience in the entrepreneurial journey, highlighting the need to remain steadfast in pursuing the venture's vision despite setbacks and obstacles. By embracing pivoting and perseverance, entrepreneurs can iterate towards success, evolving their business models to better align with market realities and opportunities.

Importantly, data-driven decision-making is a cornerstone of the iterative development process, enabling entrepreneurs to make informed choices based on empirical evidence rather than intuition or assumptions. Entrepreneurs are introduced to various tools and metrics for measuring key performance indicators (KPIs) and gathering actionable insights from experimentation and user feedback. By leveraging data analytics and rigorous measurement techniques, entrepreneurs can identify trends, validate hypotheses, and optimize their business models for greater effectiveness and customer value. Then, agility and flexibility emerge as essential attributes for navigating the uncertainties and complexities of the entrepreneurial landscape. The following discussion emphasizes the importance of maintaining an agile mind-set, characterized by responsiveness to changing market conditions and readiness to adapt to added information and challenges. Entrepreneurs are encouraged to cultivate a culture of flexibility within their organizations, empowering teams to experiment, iterate, and pivot as needed. By embracing agility and flexibility, entrepreneurs can proactively respond to emerging opportunities, mitigate risks, and drive continuous improvement in their business models.

Stakeholder engagement and co-creation emerge as pivotal elements in the iterative development process, developing collaboration and enhancing the effectiveness of business model refinement is the notable part of this discussion. It explores into the benefits of involving stakeholders in the co-creation process, including customers, partners, and investors. By soliciting feedback, ideas, and insights from diverse perspectives, entrepreneurs can gain valuable inputs that inform decision-making and drive innovation. Moreover, collaborative approaches promote a sense of ownership and commitment among stakeholders, leading to greater alignment with the venture's objectives and increased stakeholder satisfaction. Failures and setbacks are reframed as invaluable learning opportunities in the iterative development journey, underscoring the importance of resilience and adaptability in entrepreneurship. The following discussion encourages entrepreneurs to embrace failure as a natural part of the innovation process and to view challenges as opportunities for growth and refinement. By adopting a growth mind-set and learning from past mistakes, entrepreneurs can identify areas for improvement, iterate on their business models, and enhance their chances of success. Moreover, incorporating lessons from failures creates a culture of continuous improvement and innovation within the entrepreneurial ecosystem. By acknowledging various industries' unique characteristics and challenges, entrepreneurs can tailor their iterative approaches to align with specific industry dynamics. Discussions explore how market maturity, regulatory frameworks, and consumer behaviour influence the iterative process. Insights are provided on adapting iterative methodologies to suit the nuances of different industries, emphasizing the importance of flexibility and industry awareness in driving successful business model refinement.

By embracing the iterative development approach, entrepreneurs refine their business models and develop resilience and adaptability. The following discussion guides participants through a dynamic process, empowering them to navigate the uncertainties of entrepreneurship with a strategic and iterative mind-set.

4.3. Start-up Team and Business Partners

In the complicated setup of entrepreneurship, the composition and dynamics of the start-up team play a pivotal role in determining the venture's success. The following discussion explores into the art and science of building a dynamic start-up team, exploring the key considerations, strategies, and best practices contributing to a harmonious and high-performing entrepreneurial ensemble. Figure 4.3 represents the various roles and responsibilities within a team, demonstrating the diverse functions and tasks necessary for the success of a venture. From leadership to operational roles, each member contributes uniquely to the team's objectives and overall mission. A clear description of roles and responsibilities promotes efficient collaboration and effective communication and maximizes individual strengths within the team dynamic.

4.3.1 Building a Dynamic Start-up Team

Building a dynamic start-up team is pivotal for determining a start-up's success trajectory. By embracing diverse skill sets, backgrounds, and perspectives, start-ups can cultivate a team capable of tackling multifaceted challenges and seizing opportunities with agility. A heterogeneous team enhances innovation, problem-solving, and adaptability, significantly improving the start-up's capacity to navigate the entrepreneurial journey's complexities. Identifying and delineating key roles and responsibilities within the start-up team is crucial for operational efficiency and achieving goals. Clearly defining these roles streamlines decision-making processes, optimizes resource allocation, and fosters a culture of accountability. Aligning roles with the start-up's objectives ensures that each team member contributes meaningfully to the collective vision while leveraging their expertise and strengths. Additionally, exploring various leadership approaches and their impact on team dynamics highlights the importance of a shared vision, common values, and effective communication among founders. Cultivating mutual respect, resolving conflicts constructively, and leveraging complementary strengths are essential for nurturing a harmonious and productive leadership dynamic within the start-up ecosystem.

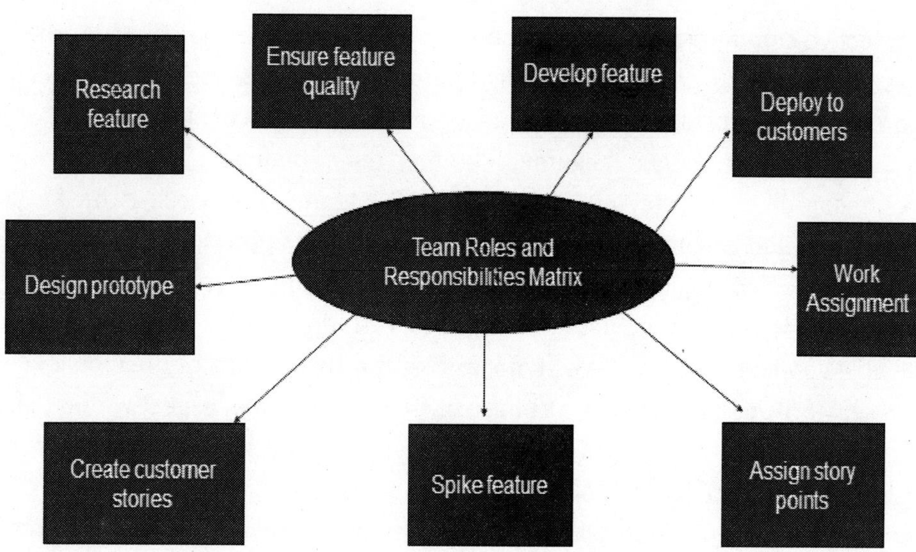

Figure 4.3 Team Roles and Responsibilities

Recruiting and attracting top talent is crucial for start-ups, as their success heavily depends on the calibre of their team. Innovative recruitment strategies are essential, focusing on highlighting the start-up's vision, culture, and growth opportunities to potential recruits. Leveraging social media platforms, networking events and industry connections can amplify the start-up's appeal and ensure alignment between the venture's objectives and the aspirations of prospective team members. Furthermore, ensuring a cultural fit and values alignment is vital for fostering a positive and collaborative work atmosphere. Assessing cultural fit during recruitment and promoting shared values among team members' catalyses constructive collaboration, trust, and mutual understanding within the start-up ecosystem. Also, nurturing a culture of innovation is imperative for start-ups aiming to thrive in dynamic markets. This involves creating an environment where creativity can flourish through continuous learning initiatives, encouraging experimentation, and maintaining open communication channels. Emphasizing risk-taking, iteration, and cross-functional cooperation enables start-ups to unlock their full potential for disruptive innovation and long-term success. Additionally, focusing on team development and training ensures that teams are well-equipped to adapt to evolving industry trends and technological advancements. Investing in skill development and knowledge enrichment allows start-ups to effectively tackle emerging challenges and seize new opportunities, ensuring sustained growth and competitiveness.8. Effective Communication and Collaboration:

Effective communication and collaboration are indispensable pillars for the success of start-up teams, especially for geographically distributed or diverse setups. The details in the following discussion have the pivotal role of transparent and efficient communication in developing constructive collaboration and alignment among team members. Discussing various tools and strategies tailored to address the needs of diverse teams, the focus is on facilitating seamless information flow and collaborative efforts, thereby enhancing productivity and cohesion within the start-up ecosystem. Managing conflict and structuring healthy team dynamics are critical aspects of team management within start-ups. This involves exploring approaches for identifying, addressing, and resolving conflicts constructively. Emphasizing the significance of open dialogue, empathy, and compromise, start-ups can cultivate a culture of trust and mutual respect within the team. Proactive conflict management strategies not only help in resolving issues but also harness the transformative potential of conflicts to spur innovation, enhance team resilience, and foster collective growth. Further, diversity and inclusion within start-up teams hold transformative potential by fostering creativity and innovation through varied perspectives. Creating an inclusive environment that values diverse viewpoints ensures that every team member feels heard, respected, and empowered to contribute their unique insights. By embracing diversity intentionally, start-ups can unlock new avenues for problem-solving, drive innovation, and strengthen their competitive edge in the marketplace. Additionally, cultivating external networks and partnerships is vital for expanding the horizons and capabilities of start-up teams. Networking with industry peers, investors, mentors, and other stakeholders allows start-ups to access new opportunities, gain market insights, and overcome challenges more effectively, thereby enhancing competitiveness and accelerating growth. Equitable equity distribution and well-designed incentive structures are crucial for fostering motivation, alignment, and long-term commitment within start-up teams. Fair compensation, equity allocation, and incentive mechanisms tailored to the start-up's stage and goals promote a culture of shared ownership and accountability. Transparent and merit-based reward systems contribute to team motivation, retention, and cohesion, aligning team interests with organizational success. Through these practices, start-ups can drive sustained performance and collective growth. Building a dynamic start-up team is like gathering a group of musicians in a symphony, with each member contributing a unique ability to create a harmonious masterpiece that flourishes in the dynamic world of business.

4.3.2 Roles and Responsibilities of Team Members

In the intricate tapestry of a start-up team, delineating roles and responsibilities form the foundational structure upon which the venture's success is built. The following discussion intricately explores the crucial aspect of defining and assigning roles within the team, ensuring clarity, efficiency, and a seamless collaboration that propels the start-up towards its goals.

Role Definition and Clarity highlight how unambiguous role definitions bolster efficiency and teamwork. Through discussions on effective strategies for articulating responsibilities and expectations for individual team members, the focus is on developing a shared understanding of each member's contributions to the collective endeavour. By establishing clear role boundaries and objectives, start-ups can minimize confusion, streamline decision-making, and maximize productivity, laying a solid groundwork for organizational success. Further, founder and leadership roles form the bedrock of start-up teams, shaping the venture's vision, direction, and culture. The following discussion explores into the multifaceted responsibilities and challenges inherent in these pivotal positions, from setting strategic objectives and promoting innovation to nurturing talent and navigating uncertainties. By discussing the unique dynamics of founder-led start-ups and the evolving roles of leaders as the venture scales, the focus is on equipping entrepreneurs with insights and strategies to steward their teams through the complexities of start-up growth effectively. Through visionary leadership and effective stewardship, founders can inspire, guide, and empower their teams to achieve ambitious goals and realize the full potential of their ventures.

Then, technical and Non-Technical Role illuminates the nuanced differences between technical and non-technical roles within start-up teams, recognizing the diverse skill sets required for comprehensive team functionality. By delving into the significance of striking a harmonious balance between technical expertise and non-technical proficiencies, the focus is on developing a well-rounded team capable of addressing multifaceted challenges. Through discussions on leveraging complementary skill sets and encouraging cross-functional collaboration, start-ups can harness the collective strengths of their team members to drive innovation, problem-solving, and sustainable growth.

Within the realm of product development and engineering, specific roles play instrumental parts in bringing concepts to fruition and ensuring technical alignment with overarching business objectives. This segment provides a detailed exploration of the roles and responsibilities associated with product development and engineering functions, shedding light on the critical intersections between technical expertise, innovation, and market needs. By emphasizing the importance of constructive collaboration between technical roles and broader business strategies, start-ups can optimize product development processes, accelerate time-to-market, and cultivate competitive advantages in dynamic market landscapes. Sales and marketing are vital for start-up success, driving market penetration, brand visibility, and revenue generation. This segment identifies key responsibilities within sales and marketing teams, spanning customer acquisition, market research, branding, and promotional activities. Through discussions on strategic alignment between sales and marketing efforts and overarching business objectives, start-ups can optimize resource allocation, enhance customer engagement, and maximize return on investment. By nurturing cohesive sales and marketing teams, start-ups can effectively convey their value proposition, cultivate customer relationships, and gain a competitive edge in saturated market environments. Importantly, Operations and Project Management Roles unveil the pivotal roles dedicated to overseeing day-to-day operations and project management, which are crucial for ensuring streamlined processes and achieving organizational objectives. By delving into the intricate responsibilities of these roles, start-ups gain insights into the essential functions of operational efficiency, resource allocation, and milestone tracking. Through discussions on the importance of effective project management methodologies, start-ups can navigate complexities, mitigate risks, and drive progress toward strategic goals. By empowering operations and project management teams with the necessary tools and resources, start-ups can enhance productivity, develop collaboration, and lay the groundwork for scalable growth.

Importantly, in customer-centric start-ups, customer support and success roles are fundamental in nurturing strong customer relationships and driving satisfaction and retention. This segment explores the multifaceted responsibilities within customer support and success teams, emphasizing proactive engagement, issue resolution, and value-driven interactions. Start-ups can cultivate loyalty, advocacy, and long-term partnerships by discussing strategies for building robust customer relationships and addressing evolving customer needs. Through a customer-centric approach to role delineation and resource allocation, start-ups can elevate their brand reputation, differentiate themselves in competitive markets, and sustainably scale their customer base. Research and development (R&D) function's drive innovation and differentiation within start-up ecosystems, while driving continuous evolution and competitive advantage. The roles and responsibilities of R&D activities, spanning ideation, experimentation, and product iteration must be more focused. By emphasizing the significance of encouraging a culture of innovation and knowledge creation, start-ups can unlock new market opportunities, address unmet needs, and stay ahead of industry trends. Through discussions on the strategic alignment of R&D initiatives with business objectives, start-ups can optimize resource allocation, minimize time-to-market, and develops a culture of creativity and exploration. Also, within start-ups, roles concerning financial management and administrative functions form the backbone of organizational stability and fiscal responsibility. The key roles responsible for financial planning, budgeting, and overseeing administrative operations must be focused. By delving into strategies for effective financial management, start-ups can ensure prudent resource allocation, mitigate financial risks, and maintain fiscal transparency. Through discussions on streamlining administrative processes and optimizing operational efficiency, start-ups can create a culture of accountability, productivity, and regulatory compliance, laying the groundwork for sustainable growth and resilience.

Navigating the legal landscape and ensuring compliance with regulatory requirements are critical imperatives for start-ups. This segment delineates the roles tasked with legal and compliance matters, underscoring the importance of upholding ethical standards, and safeguarding the organization's legal interests. By detailing the responsibilities of legal and compliance roles, start-ups can proactively mitigate legal risks, protect intellectual property, and ensure adherence to industry regulations. Through discussions on the significance of legal, due diligence and contract management, start-ups can fortify their legal foundations, enhance risk management practices, and cultivate trust with stakeholders and partners. In the dynamic ecosystem of start-ups, cross-functional collaboration emerges as a prerequisite for driving innovation, constructive collaboration, and organizational agility. The necessity of developing collaboration and communication across diverse teams and functional areas needs to be focused. By exploring strategies for breaking down storage and developing a culture of collaboration, start-ups can harness the collective expertise and creativity of their teams, driving holistic problem-solving and innovation. Through discussions on leveraging collaborative tools, promoting knowledge sharing, and a spirit of inclusivity and respect, start-ups can cultivate a collaborative ethos that fuels collective success, adaptability, and resilience.

Within the fluid landscape of start-ups, the ability to adapt and evolve is paramount for sustained success. This segment underscores the imperative of flexibility and adaptability in roles as start-ups navigate their entrepreneurial journey. By emphasizing the need for dynamic roles that can pivot in response to evolving market dynamics and organizational priorities, start-ups can cultivate resilience and agility within their teams. Through discussions on developing a culture of experimentation, learning, and adaptation, start-ups can empower team members to embrace change as an opportunity for growth and innovation, positioning the venture for long-term viability and competitiveness. Further, effective performance management optimizes individual and team contributions within start-ups. The following discussion explores into establishing performance metrics to assess individual and collective effectiveness in fulfilling role responsibilities. By detailing strategies for defining clear performance indicators, start-ups can align expectations, track progress, and identify areas for improvement. Through discussions on providing constructive feedback, recognizing achievements, and addressing performance gaps, start-ups can create a culture of accountability, motivation, and continuous improvement. By leveraging performance data to inform decision-making and resource allocation, start-ups can optimize team performance and drive organizational success.

Assembling a team with well-defined roles is akin to assembling a puzzle where each piece contributes to the overall picture. The above discussion equips entrepreneurs with the insights and tools to meticulously craft roles and responsibilities, fostering a team that collaboratively works towards the shared vision of the start-up.

4.3.3 Collaborating with Business Partners for Success

In the dynamic landscape of entrepreneurship, the success of a start-up often hinges on effective collaboration with external entities. The following discussion explores the intricate art of forging partnerships and collaborations that propel the start-up toward its goals. Entrepreneurs are guided through the nuances of identifying, establishing, and nurturing strategic business partnerships that enhance capabilities, expand reach, and drive mutual success.

In the dynamic world of entrepreneurship, strategic partnerships serve as vital threads binding diverse entities toward common goals. By highlighting how partnerships extend the start-up's capabilities, amplify its market reach and innovation, entrepreneurs gain insights into the transformative potential of collaborative ventures. Through discussions on leveraging complementary strengths, accessing novel resources, and mitigating risks, start-ups can harness the power of partnerships to navigate challenges, capitalize on opportunities, and accelerate their journey toward success. Identifying and assessing potential business partner is like prospecting for valuable gems in a rich mine of opportunities. The purpose is to elucidate strategies for discerning and evaluating prospective collaborators with precision and insight. By delineating criteria for compatibility, shared values, and strategic alignment, entrepreneurs gain clarity on the attributes that underpin fruitful partnerships. Through discussions on conducting due diligence, building rapport, and creating trust, start-ups can navigate the complexities of partner selection with confidence and discernment. By aligning with partners who complement their vision, culture, and objectives, start-ups can forge alliances that fortify their foundation and propel them toward sustained growth and success. In the intricate part of entrepreneurship, partnerships emerge as versatile threads that weave diverse entities together toward common objectives. Entrepreneurs gain insights into the spectrum of collaborative possibilities available within the start-up ecosystem by illuminating strategic alliances, joint ventures, and collaborations. Through discussions on the benefits of shared resources, complementary expertise, and expanded market access, start-ups can discern the most fitting partnership model to propel their growth trajectory. By weighing the nuances of each partnership type, start-ups can embark on alliances that amplify their strengths, mitigate their weaknesses, and develop innovation, resilience, and mutual success.

The negotiation table becomes a crucible of opportunity where start-ups forge the foundational agreements that underpin successful partnerships. By elucidating strategies for articulating goals, defining roles, and delineating responsibilities, entrepreneurs navigate the complexities of partnership agreements with clarity and acumen. Through discussions on crafting win-win solutions, anticipating contingencies, and facilitating flexibility, start-ups can build collaborations that yield mutual benefits and mitigate potential risks. By leveraging legal expertise, market insights, and negotiation prowess, start-ups architect agreements that lay the groundwork for enduring partnerships characterized by trust, constructive collaboration, and shared prosperity. Also, at the heart of every successful partnership lies a foundation of trust, nurtured through open communication channels and mutual respect. By exploring strategies for transparency, cultivating empathy, and resolving conflicts constructively, start-ups create an environment conducive to collaboration and innovation. Through discussions on regular check-ins, honest feedback, and shared goals, start-ups forge bonds of trust that transcend transactional exchanges and engender enduring relationships. By prioritizing active listening, empathy, and integrity, start-ups cultivate a culture of trust and communication that forms the bedrock of resilient, collaborative partnerships.

Within the intricate ecosystem of business partnerships, the fusions of complementary strengths catalyse innovation and growth. It explores into the art of identifying and harnessing synergies between partners, illuminating pathways to amplify the collective capabilities of the start-up. Entrepreneurs unlock the full potential of collaborative endeavours by elucidating strategies for conducting thorough assessments, recognizing expertise gaps, and aligning complementary skill sets. Through discussions on shared resources, specialized knowledge, and diversified networks, start-ups orchestrate partnerships that augment their competitive edge and enrich their value proposition. By embracing the diversity of perspectives and competencies, start-ups cultivate alliances that propel them towards shared objectives, fortified by a tapestry of complementary strengths. Managing Risks and Mitigating Challenges navigates the terrain of risk management within partnerships, equipping start-ups with the tools and foresight to pre-emptively address potential pitfalls. By identifying common risks such as misaligned objectives, communication breakdowns, and contractual ambiguities, entrepreneurs lay the groundwork for proactive risk mitigation strategies. Through discussions on contingency planning, conflict resolution mechanisms, and contractual safeguards, start-ups fortify their partnerships against adversities that may arise along their collaborative journey. By developing transparency, trust, and resilience, start-ups cultivate partnerships that weather storms and emerge stronger, united by a shared commitment to mutual success. Entrepreneurs unleash the creative potential inherent in collaborative endeavours by exploring avenues for joint ideation, iterative refinement, and shared experimentation. Through discussions on open innovation platforms, co-development initiatives, and knowledge exchange networks, start-ups spark synergies that catalyse breakthrough innovations and disruptive solutions. By embracing a mind-set of openness, adaptability, and collective creativity, start-ups forge partnerships that serve as crucibles for innovation, driving joint initiatives that redefine industry standards and inspire market evolution.

By meticulously delineating expectations, tasks, and accountabilities, start-ups lay the groundwork for seamless collaboration and effective execution. Through discussions on transparency, alignment, and accountability, entrepreneurs cultivate an environment conducive to trust, constructive collaboration, and mutual understanding. By articulating roles with precision and clarity, start-ups mitigate the risk of misunderstandings, conflicts, and inefficiencies, thus fortifying the foundation of their partnerships and paving the way for shared success. By elucidating key performance indicators (KPIs) and metrics tailored to partnership dynamics, start-ups gain insights into the efficacy and impact of their collaborative efforts. Through discussions on tracking performance, soliciting feedback, and adapting strategies in response to changing circumstances, entrepreneurs foster a culture of continuous improvement and adaptation. By embracing the ethos of on-going evaluation and iteration, start-ups optimize their partnerships for mutual benefit, resilience, and sustained growth in the dynamic landscape of entrepreneurship.

By delving into considerations of scalability, resource allocation, and alignment of objectives, entrepreneurs build partnerships that evolve in tandem with the expanding aspirations of their ventures. Through discussions on flexibility, innovation, and nurturing trust, start-ups cultivate partnerships capable of navigating the complexities of rapid growth and seizing emergent opportunities. By embracing the ethos of strategic expansion and collaboration, start-ups amplify their capabilities, market reach, and competitive advantage, thus accelerating their journey toward enduring success and impact.

Educating effective business partnerships is an art that requires a delicate balance of strategic thinking, effective communication, and a shared commitment to success. The above discussion empowers entrepreneurs with the insights and tools to navigate the landscape of business collaborations, nurturing relationships that elevate the start-up to new heights of achievement.

4.4. Start-up Ecosystem and Stakeholders

In the complex setup of entrepreneurship, the start-up ecosystem serves as both a nurturing ground and a dynamic stage for ventures to thrive. The following discussion explores into the multifaceted landscape of the start-up ecosystem, unravelling its essential components and providing entrepreneurs with a comprehensive understanding of the stakeholders, resources, and opportunities that shape the entrepreneurial journey. The flowchart in Figure 4.4 visually represents the interconnected elements of the start-up ecosystem.

4.4.1 Understanding the Start-up Ecosystem

The understanding the Start-up Ecosystem highlights the ever-evolving nature of the start-up ecosystem, where change is constant and a driving force propelling ventures towards new frontiers of success. Through discussions on the impact of external factors, market trends, and global dynamics, entrepreneurs gain insights into the fluidity and complexity inherent in the entrepreneurial landscape. By embracing the ethos of adaptability, resilience, and foresight, start-ups navigate the ebbs and flows of the ecosystem, harnessing emerging opportunities and surmounting unforeseen challenges on their journey towards growth and impact. Components of the Start-up Ecosystem range from incubators and accelerators to co-working spaces and funding organizations. Through detailed explorations of each component, entrepreneurs gain a nuanced understanding of the interconnectedness and synergies that underpin the ecosystem. By leveraging the diverse array of resources, mentorship, and networks available within the ecosystem, start-ups harness the collective power of collaborative innovation, driving their ventures toward growth, sustainability, and success.

Further, through discussions on the tailored support, mentorship, and resources provided by incubators and accelerators, entrepreneurs gain insights into the transformative impact of these entities on the trajectory of early-stage ventures. By tapping into the expertise, networks, and funding opportunities facilitated by these organizations, start-ups accelerate their growth, refine their strategies, and overcome the hurdles inherent in the entrepreneurial journey. In the bustling landscape of the start-up ecosystem, co-working spaces and collaborative hubs emerge as vibrant epicentres of creativity, collaboration, and community. Through discussions on accidental encounters, knowledge exchange, and networking opportunities facilitated by co-working spaces, entrepreneurs gain insights into the transformative power of collaborative environments. By immersing themselves in these dynamic ecosystems, start-ups forge meaningful connections, gain access to valuable resources, and embark on collaborative ventures that propel their growth and amplify their impact on the entrepreneurial landscape.

Within the journey of entrepreneurship, access to capital emerges as a pivotal factor shaping the trajectory of start-ups. It explains the diverse array of funding organizations, venture capitalists, angel investors, and financial entities that populate the start-up ecosystem. Through explorations of the roles, investment criteria, and funding mechanisms employed by these stakeholders, entrepreneurs gain insights into the intricate dynamics of the funding landscape. By cultivating relationships, refining their pitches, and demonstrating traction and potential, start-ups position themselves to attract the financial support necessary to fuel their growth, scale their operations, and realize their visions of success. Also, in the mixture of the start-up ecosystem, government initiatives and policies play a pivotal role in shaping the contours of entrepreneurial activity. The impact of supportive policies, incentives, and regulatory frameworks on the vibrancy and resilience of the ecosystem is to be understood. Through initiatives such as tax incentives, grants, and incubation programs, entrepreneurs gain insights into how governments nurture innovation, entrepreneurship, and economic development. By leveraging the resources and support provided by government initiatives, start-ups navigate regulatory landscapes, access funding opportunities, and accelerate their growth trajectories, thus contributing to the overall vitality and competitiveness of the entrepreneurial ecosystem.

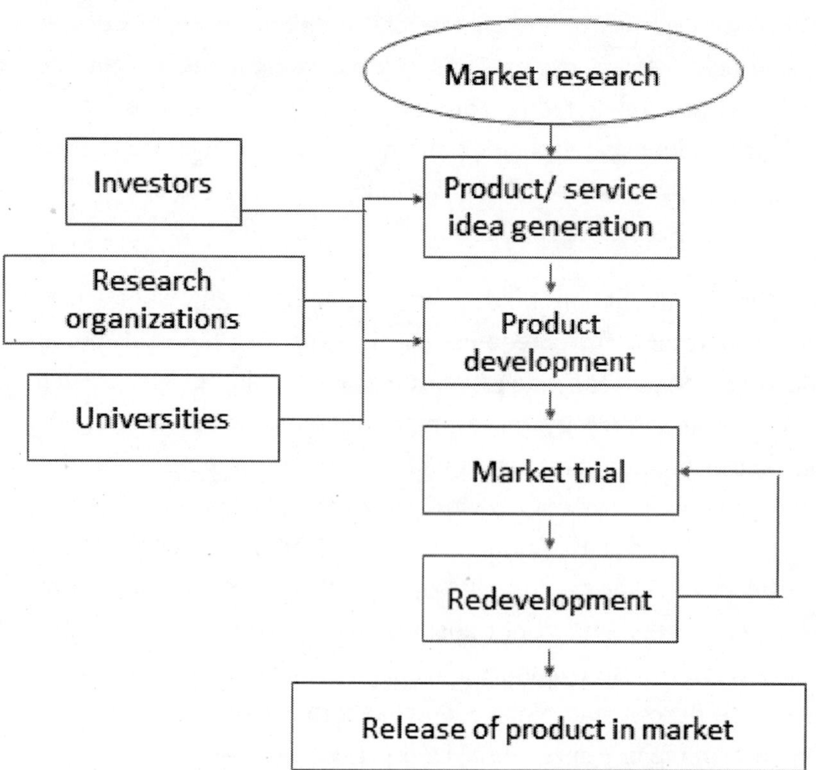

Figure 4.4 Mapping the Start-up Ecosystem

In the nexus of innovation and academia, collaborations between start-ups and educational or research institutions emerge as fertile grounds for knowledge exchange, talent acquisition, and technological innovation. The symbiotic relationship between start-ups and educational or research institutions is to be understood, where interdisciplinary collaborations and research partnerships flourish. Through explorations of knowledge transfer mechanisms, research commercialization initiatives, and talent acquisition strategies, entrepreneurs gain insights into the transformative potential of these collaborations. By tapping into the expertise, resources, and talent pools available within educational and research institutions, start-ups catalyse innovation, drive technological advancements, and forge pathways toward sustainable growth and impact in the entrepreneurial ecosystem. Corporate partnerships and innovation hubs serve as vital conduits between established industries and the agile, disruptive world of start-ups. These partnerships bridge the gap, facilitating knowledge exchange, resource sharing, and collaborative innovation initiatives. By detailing how corporate entities and start-ups collaborate on joint projects, co-development ventures, and innovation challenges, entrepreneurs gain insights into the symbiotic relationships that drive mutual growth and innovation. Both parties leverage their strengths and expertise through strategic collaborations to create innovative solutions, enters new markets, and unlocks value across industries.

Importantly, networking events and conferences act as dynamic platforms for entrepreneurs to connect with mentors, investors, and industry experts, securing invaluable relationships and opportunities for growth. By exploring the role of these events in facilitating knowledge exchange, idea sharing, and strategic partnerships, entrepreneurs gain a deeper understanding of how participation can elevate their visibility and open doors to new opportunities. Entrepreneurs leverage pitching competitions, panel discussions, or informal networking sessions and events to highlight their ventures, gain feedback, and forge meaningful connections that propel their ventures forward. Also, supporting organizations, industry associations, and specialized resources are pivotal in providing tailored support and resources to start-ups, enhancing their capabilities and competitiveness in various sectors. By detailing these entities' unique offerings and support mechanisms, entrepreneurs gain insights into how access to specialized resources, mentorship programs, and industry-specific knowledge accelerates their growth and success. Through access to research facilities, sector-specific grants, or mentorship networks, start-ups leverage these resources to overcome challenges, seize opportunities, and thrive in dynamic ecosystems. The start-up ecosystem is a diverse tapestry woven with variations and similarities on a global scale, influenced by cultural, economic, and regional factors. By exploring these nuances, entrepreneurs gain a deeper appreciation for the complexities and opportunities of different entrepreneurial landscapes. Discussions on how cultural attitudes towards risk-taking, government policies, and access to capital shape the entrepreneurial environment provide valuable insights for entrepreneurs seeking to navigate global markets and expand their ventures beyond borders.

Entrepreneurs navigate the start-up ecosystem with a blend of strategy, resilience, and relationship-building. The following discussion provides practical insights and strategies and equips entrepreneurs with the tools and mind-set needed to leverage the ecosystem effectively. By discussing considerations for building meaningful relationships with ecosystem stakeholders, identifying strategic partnership opportunities, and navigating regulatory landscapes, entrepreneurs gain a roadmap for success in the dynamic and ever-evolving entrepreneurial landscape. Understanding the intricacies of the start-up ecosystem is akin to deciphering a complex puzzle where each piece plays a crucial role. The above discussion equips entrepreneurs with a holistic view, enabling them to navigate and harness the diverse opportunities within the dynamic landscape of the start-up ecosystem.

4.4.2 Identifying and Engaging with Stakeholders

In the vibrant tapestry of entrepreneurship, stakeholders form the threads that weave the intricate pattern of a start-up's journey. The following discussion explores into the art of identifying and engaging with stakeholders, separating the diverse network of individuals and entities that play a pivotal role in shaping the success and sustainability of a venture.

Stakeholders in the start-up ecosystem encompass a broad spectrum, extending beyond investors to customers, employees, partners, and the community. By emphasizing this expansive view of stakeholders, entrepreneurs recognize the multifaceted relationships that underpin their ventures and the diverse interests they must navigate to succeed. Through stakeholder mapping and analysis, entrepreneurs gain insights into the interests, influence, and expectations of key players in the ecosystem. This process enables a strategic approach to engagement, ensuring that efforts are directed toward building productive relationships with stakeholders who can drive the venture's growth and sustainability. Internal stakeholders, including founders, employees, and management, play a pivotal role in shaping the culture and direction of the start-up. By exploring strategies for a positive and collaborative internal stakeholder environment, entrepreneurs lay the foundation for a cohesive team aligned with the venture's vision and goals. External stakeholders such as customers, investors, partners, and the community contribute significantly to the success and impact of the start-up. Understanding their needs, expectations, skills, and flexibility is essential for cultivating mutually beneficial relationships that drive the venture forward.

Managing relations with investors requires effective communication, transparency, and trust-building. Entrepreneurs strengthen investor confidence and support for their ventures by exploring strategies for providing timely updates and developing open communication channels. Customer engagement goes beyond transactions; it involves building meaningful relationships, collecting feedback, and building brand loyalty. Entrepreneurs explore approaches for understanding customer needs, addressing pain points, and delivering value that exceeds expectations. Strategic partnerships and alliances can enhance a start-up's capabilities, reach, and innovation potential. By exploring the dynamics of collaborating with external partners, entrepreneurs uncover opportunities to leverage complementary strengths and drive mutual growth. Start-ups have a unique opportunity to contribute positively to the community and make a social impact. By detailing strategies for incorporating social responsibility into their operations and engaging with local and global communities, entrepreneurs align their ventures with values that resonate with stakeholders.

Further, engaging with government entities and understanding regulatory frameworks are essential for long-term sustainability and compliance. By discussing the importance of collaboration with regulatory bodies, entrepreneurs navigate complex legal landscapes and ensure that their ventures operate ethically and responsibly. Participation in industry associations and networking events provides valuable visibility, credibility, and collaboration opportunities. Entrepreneurs explore the benefits of engaging with professional networks and leveraging these platforms to build relationships and access resources that support their ventures' growth. During challenging times, effective crisis communication and stakeholder management are paramount. By discussing strategies for maintaining trust and transparency, entrepreneurs navigate crises resiliently and preserve valuable relationships with stakeholders. Creating stakeholder engagement plans tailored to the unique needs of the start-up ensures that efforts are focused, strategic, and responsive to evolving dynamics. Entrepreneurs gain insights into stakeholder engagement's iterative nature and adaptability's importance in building and maintaining productive relationships. Identifying and engaging with stakeholders is a dynamic and iterative process that requires skill, flexibility, and adaptability. The following discussion equips entrepreneurs with the knowledge and tools to navigate the intricate network of stakeholders, nurturing relationships that contribute to the resilience and success of the start-up.

4.4.3 Navigating Ecosystem Challenges

In the dynamic realm of entrepreneurship, challenges within the start-up ecosystem are inevitable. The following discussion provides entrepreneurs with insights and strategies to navigate and overcome these challenges, ensuring resilience and adaptability in the face of external pressures. From regulatory hurdles to market dynamics, this exploration equips entrepreneurs with the tools to turn challenges into opportunities for growth.

The first step towards overcoming any challenge is acknowledging its existence. Navigating regulatory hurdles and compliance challenges is paramount for start-ups seeking to operate within legal frameworks while building innovation. In an ever-evolving regulatory landscape, start-ups must remain vigilant and adaptive to ensure compliance with industry standards and government regulations. Proactively staying abreast of regulatory changes and engaging in open dialogue with regulatory bodies can mitigate potential risks and develop a culture of compliance within the organization. By integrating compliance measures into their operational strategies, start-ups can mitigate regulatory risks and establish a foundation for sustainable growth.

Navigating regulatory hurdles and compliance challenges is paramount for start-ups seeking to operate within legal frameworks while building innovation. In an ever-evolving regulatory landscape, start-ups must remain vigilant and adaptive to ensure compliance with industry standards and government regulations. Proactively staying abreast of regulatory changes and engaging in open dialogue with regulatory bodies can mitigate potential risks and develop a culture of compliance within the organization. By integrating compliance measures into their operational strategies, start-ups can mitigate regulatory risks and establish a foundation for sustainable growth. Managing funding constraints and maintaining positive investor relations are critical components of the start-up journey, particularly during uncertain financial periods. Start-ups often need help securing adequate funding to support their growth objectives while managing investor expectations and concerns. By implementing transparent communication channels and demonstrating a clear roadmap for growth, start-ups can cultivate trust and confidence among investors. Additionally, optimizing financial resources through strategic budgeting and diversifying funding sources can help mitigate the impact of funding constraints and ensure continued progress toward long-term goals.

Adapting to the dynamic landscape of market dynamics and competitive pressures is essential for sustaining growth and relevance in an increasingly crowded marketplace. Start-ups must continuously monitor market trends, consumer preferences, and competitive activities to identify opportunities for differentiation and innovation. By conducting thorough market analysis and leveraging data-driven insights, start-ups can identify untapped market segments and develop targeted strategies to capitalize on emerging trends. Furthermore, developing a culture of agility and innovation within the organization enables start-ups to adapt quickly to changing industry landscapes and maintain a competitive edge in the marketplace. Also, attracting and retaining skilled talent within the start-up ecosystem poses significant challenges for entrepreneurs seeking to build high-performing teams. Start-ups often compete with established companies for top talent, facing resource constraints and limited brand recognition. To overcome these challenges, start-ups must prioritize building a strong organizational culture that values diversity, creativity, and continuous learning. Offering competitive benefits, opportunities for professional development, and a supportive work environment can help attract and retain talented individuals aligned with the company's mission and values. By investing in their people and develops a culture of growth and development, start-ups can position themselves as employers of choice within the competitive talent landscape.

Navigating the ever-changing landscape of technology adoption and innovation barriers presents significant challenges for start-ups aiming to stay ahead in rapidly evolving industries. From limited resources for research and development to technological obsolescence, start-ups must overcome various hurdles to remain competitive. Embracing technological advancements and developing a culture of innovation within the start-up is essential for driving sustainable growth. This entails investing in innovative technologies, encouraging cross-functional collaboration, and encouraging experimentation and iteration. By leveraging emerging technologies and embracing a culture of innovation, start-ups can position themselves as industry leaders and disruptors in their respective markets. Expanding into international markets introduces numerous challenges related to global expansion, cross-cultural communication, and navigating diverse business environments. Start-ups must navigate cultural differences, language barriers, and regulatory complexities to successfully establish a foothold in foreign markets. Tailoring approaches to diverse markets and investing in cross-cultural competency training are essential for building trust and credibility with international stakeholders. Developing a diverse and inclusive workplace culture enables start-ups to leverage their team members' unique perspectives and experiences, driving innovation and facilitating successful global expansion strategies.

Incorporating environmental sustainability into business practices presents challenges and opportunities for start-ups seeking to align with eco-friendly initiatives. Environmental concerns are increasingly shaping consumer preferences and regulatory landscapes, from resource scarcity to climate change. Start-ups must navigate the complexities of sustainability by integrating environmentally responsible practices into their operations and supply chains. This may involve adopting renewable energy sources, minimizing waste generation, and sourcing ethically produced materials. By prioritizing sustainability and aligning business practices with eco-friendly initiatives, start-ups can mitigate environmental risks, enhance brand reputation, and appeal to environmentally conscious consumers. Effectively managing crises and mitigating reputation risks are critical aspects of safeguarding the long-term viability of start-ups. Unforeseen events can harm the brand's reputation and stakeholder trust, from product recalls to public relations crises. Start-ups must develop proactive communication strategies and establish robust crisis management protocols to respond swiftly and effectively to crises as they arise. Building resilience in the face of adversity involves cultivating a culture of transparency, accountability, and ethical leadership within the organization. By prioritizing reputation management and implementing proactive crisis preparedness measures, start-ups can minimize the impact of negative perceptions and emerge stronger from challenging situations.

Establishing and maintaining successful collaborations and partnerships present unique challenges for start-ups operating in dynamic ecosystems. Misaligned goals, communication breakdowns, and conflicting priorities can hinder the effectiveness of partnerships and jeopardize collaborative initiatives. Start-ups must prioritize effective communication, establish clear expectations, and to develop a culture of trust and mutual respect within partnerships. Proactively addressing conflicts and establishing dispute resolution mechanisms can strengthen collaborative relationships and drive shared value creation. By aligning goals, leveraging complementary strengths, and fostering open communication channels, start-ups can maximize the potential for successful collaborations and partnerships.

Navigating government policies and political instability poses significant challenges for start-ups operating in uncertain business environments. Regulatory changes, trade tensions, and geopolitical risks can disrupt operations and impact market dynamics. Start-ups must stay informed about evolving policies and geopolitical developments to anticipate potential risks and opportunities. Developing contingency plans and diversifying market exposure can help mitigate the impact of political instability and safeguard against regulatory uncertainties. By engaging with policymakers, industry associations, and legal experts, start-ups can advocate for policies that support innovation and entrepreneurship while managing political risks effectively. Resilience and adaptability within the start-up ecosystem are essential for navigating uncertainties and sustaining long-term success. Start-ups must anticipate challenges, embrace change, and continuously learn and iterate to remain competitive in dynamic markets. This involves developing a culture of resilience, where failure is viewed as an opportunity for learning and growth. Proactive problem-solving, agility, and strategic foresight enable start-ups to pivot quickly in response to market disruptions and emerging trends. By nurturing collaboration, knowledge sharing, and collective problem-solving within the ecosystem, start-ups can enhance their capacity to adapt to changing circumstances and thrive in an ever-evolving business landscape.

Navigating ecosystem challenges is an integral part of the entrepreneurial journey. The above discussion empowers entrepreneurs with the knowledge and strategies to confront and overcome challenges, ensuring their ventures' sustained growth and success within the dynamic start-up ecosystem.

4.5. Technology Business Incubators and Parks

In the ever-evolving landscape of innovation and entrepreneurship, Technology Business Incubators (TBIs) emerge as catalysts for the growth and success of start-ups. The following discussion explores into the crucial role played by TBIs within the entrepreneurial ecosystem, unravelling their functions, benefits, and the invaluable support they offer nascent ventures. Figure 4.5 outlines the advantages of technology incubators, displaying their pivotal role in nurturing start-ups and innovation. These advantages include access to mentorship and expertise, shared resources and infrastructure, networking opportunities, funding support, and access to potential investors. Technology incubators facilitate an ecosystem conducive to growth and development, offering valuable support to entrepreneurs as they navigate the challenges of launching and scaling their ventures.

TBIs play a pivotal role in facilitating access to funding opportunities for start-ups at various stages of their development. By connecting ventures with investors, venture capitalists, angel investors, government grants, and other financial resources, TBIs help bridge the funding gap and fuel the growth of technology-driven ventures. Additionally, TBIs provide support in preparing funding proposals, pitching to investors, and negotiating investment terms, enhancing the likelihood of securing investment. TBIs develop a vibrant ecosystem of networking and collaboration among start-ups, mentors, industry partners, and other stakeholders. By facilitating networking events, workshops, seminars, and collaborative initiatives, TBIs create opportunities for knowledge exchange, partnerships, and synergies. Through collaboration within the TBI community, start-ups can leverage collective expertise, resources, and networks to accelerate their growth and scale their businesses more effectively. TBIs establish connections with industries and provide start-ups with access to market insights, industry networks, and potential customers. TBIs help start-ups validate their solutions, access new markets, and scale their businesses by developing partnerships with industry leaders, corporate partners, and market experts. Industry connects programs, market access initiatives, and corporate innovation partnerships enable start-ups to gain traction, build credibility, and accelerate their path to commercial success within competitive markets.

Importantly, TBIs offer comprehensive training and skill development initiatives tailored to the specific needs of entrepreneurs and their teams. These programs cover diverse topics, including business management, technology development, marketing strategies, financial planning, and leadership skills. TBIs empower entrepreneurs to enhance their capabilities and equip their teams with the necessary skills to successfully navigate the complexities of running a technology-driven venture by providing access to expert-led workshops, seminars, online courses, and mentoring sessions. Through hands-on learning experiences and practical insights, these programs enable entrepreneurs to develop competencies essential for innovation, growth, and sustainable business development. TBIs employ robust monitoring and evaluation mechanisms to assess the progress and effectiveness of their support programs. By establishing clear performance metrics, milestones, and goals, TBIs track the development and growth of supported ventures over time. Regular progress reviews, feedback sessions, and performance evaluations enable TBIs to identify areas of improvement, measure the impact of their support interventions, and make data-driven decisions to optimize program delivery. TBIs maintain alignment with their objectives by ensuring accountability and transparency in monitoring and evaluation processes and continuously strives to enhance the quality and effectiveness of their support services.

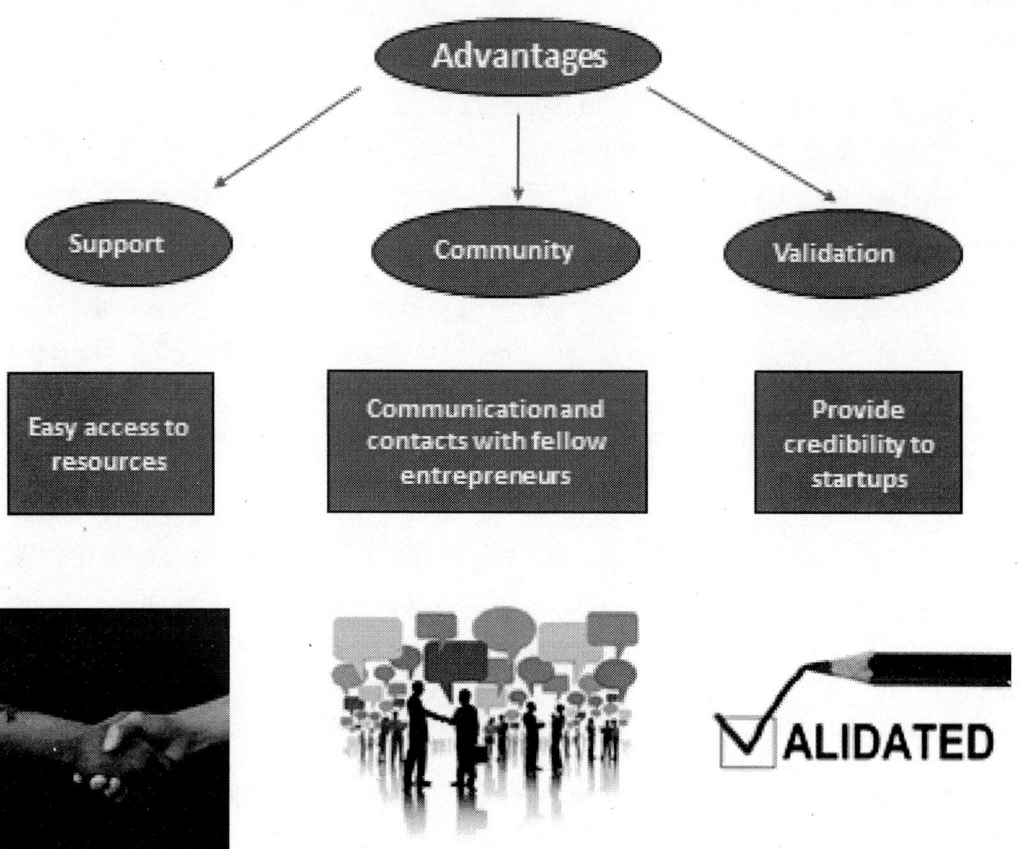

Figure 4.5 Advantages of Technology Incubators

TBIs recognize technology-driven ventures' unique needs and challenges and tailor their support programs accordingly. These initiatives are designed to address the specific requirements of sectors such as information technology, biotechnology, advanced manufacturing, and other emerging technology domains. Specialized programs and initiatives offer targeted support in product development, intellectual property management, regulatory compliance, and market penetration strategies. By catering to technology ventures' distinct characteristics and requirements, TBIs enable entrepreneurs to leverage their core competencies and drive innovation, competitiveness, and sustainable growth within their respective industries. TBIs have a proven track record of nurturing successful start-ups significantly contributing to their respective industries. Critical elements of TBI assistance can be identified by analysing the success stories of ventures that have flourished under TBI support. These may include access to funding opportunities, mentorship from experienced professionals, networking and collaboration opportunities, access to specialized infrastructure and resources, and tailored support programs addressing specific business needs. By highlighting the journeys of successful start-ups, TBIs inspire and motivate aspiring entrepreneurs while displaying the tangible impact of their support on innovation, entrepreneurship, and economic growth. Collaborative initiatives between TBIs and academic institutions play a vital role in knowledge transfer, research, and innovation. TBIs often collaborate with universities, research institutes, and academic experts to leverage their expertise, resources, and facilities. Joint research projects, technology transfer programs, and industry-academic partnerships enable TBIs to access innovative research and expertise while providing academic institutions with opportunities for real-world application and commercialization of their innovations. By bridging the gap between academia and industry, these collaborations facilitate the creation of a vibrant innovation ecosystem conducive to entrepreneurial success and societal impact.

While engaging with TBIs offers numerous benefits, start-ups may encounter challenges such as limited access to TBI resources, competition for TBI support, and mismatched expectations regarding the level of assistance provided. To maximize the benefits of TBI engagement, start-ups must proactively identify and address potential hurdles by establishing clear objectives, communicating their needs effectively, and actively participating in TBI programs and activities. Developing solid relationships with TBI staff, mentors, and fellow entrepreneurs can enhance collaboration, create mutual learning, and support opportunities. By leveraging the strengths of TBIs while navigating potential challenges, start-ups can unlock the full potential of TBI support and accelerate their journey toward success in the competitive landscape of innovation and entrepreneurship.

Understanding the pivotal role of Technology Business Incubators is crucial for entrepreneurs seeking to thrive in technology-driven sectors. The above discussion gives start-ups insights into how TBIs can serve as instrumental partners in their journey, providing essential support for innovation, growth, and market success.

4.5.2 Benefits of Incubator Programs

Participating in incubator programs can be a transformative experience for start-ups, offering various advantages beyond conventional support structures. The following discussion explores the diverse benefits of incubator programs, providing entrepreneurs with valuable insights into how these programs can catalyse growth and pave the way for long-term success. Figure 4.6 outlines the essential components of an incubator program lifecycle, providing a structured framework for nurturing start-up ventures from inception to maturity.

Incubator programs are designed to accelerate start-ups' growth and development by providing access to various resources, mentorship, and networking opportunities. Through intensive support and guidance, incubators help start-ups navigate challenges, overcome obstacles, and scale their businesses more rapidly than they could. By leveraging the collective expertise and networks of incubator staff, mentors, and fellow entrepreneurs, start-ups can capitalize on opportunities, iterate on their products or services, and gain traction in their target markets more efficiently. One of the significant benefits of participating in incubator programs is gaining access to specialized infrastructure and facilities. Incubators typically provide start-ups with state-of-the-art laboratories, equipment, co-working spaces, and other physical resources they may need access to otherwise. By leveraging these resources, start-ups can enhance their operational capabilities, conduct research and development activities, and prototype innovations more effectively. Access to specialized infrastructure enables start-ups to reduce costs, accelerate product development timelines, and improve the quality of their offerings, positioning them for long-term success. Incubator programs offer start-ups various funding opportunities and direct connections to investors. Through networking events, pitch sessions, and investor matchmaking programs, incubators facilitate introductions between start-ups and angel investors, venture capitalists, corporate investors, and other funding sources. By exposing start-ups to potential investors and helping them refine their pitch decks and investment strategies, incubators increase the likelihood of securing funding and fuelling growth. Access to funding opportunities enables start-ups to invest in product development, marketing initiatives, talent acquisition, and other critical areas of their business, driving sustainable growth and expansion.

Incubator programs offer entrepreneurs personalized mentorship and expert guidance, providing them invaluable insights and support across strategic, operational, and leadership dimensions. Experienced mentors, who often have backgrounds in entrepreneurship, technology, finance, marketing, and other relevant fields, offer guidance on business strategy, market positioning, product development, customer acquisition, and other vital areas. By working closely with mentors, entrepreneurs can gain access to diverse perspectives, tap into industry knowledge, and make more informed decisions. Mentorship also helps entrepreneurs build confidence, develop leadership skills, and navigate the challenges of building and scaling a successful start-up.

Incubator programs develop a collaborative environment where start-ups can interact with fellow entrepreneurs, share ideas, and collaborate on projects. By bringing together like-minded individuals with diverse backgrounds and skill sets, incubators create a supportive ecosystem where innovation thrives. Networking events, workshops, and collaborative initiatives enable start-ups to expand their professional networks, forge partnerships, and access new opportunities. Collaboration within the incubator community nurtures creativity, accelerates learning, and gives start-ups access to knowledge and resources to help them overcome challenges and achieve their goals.

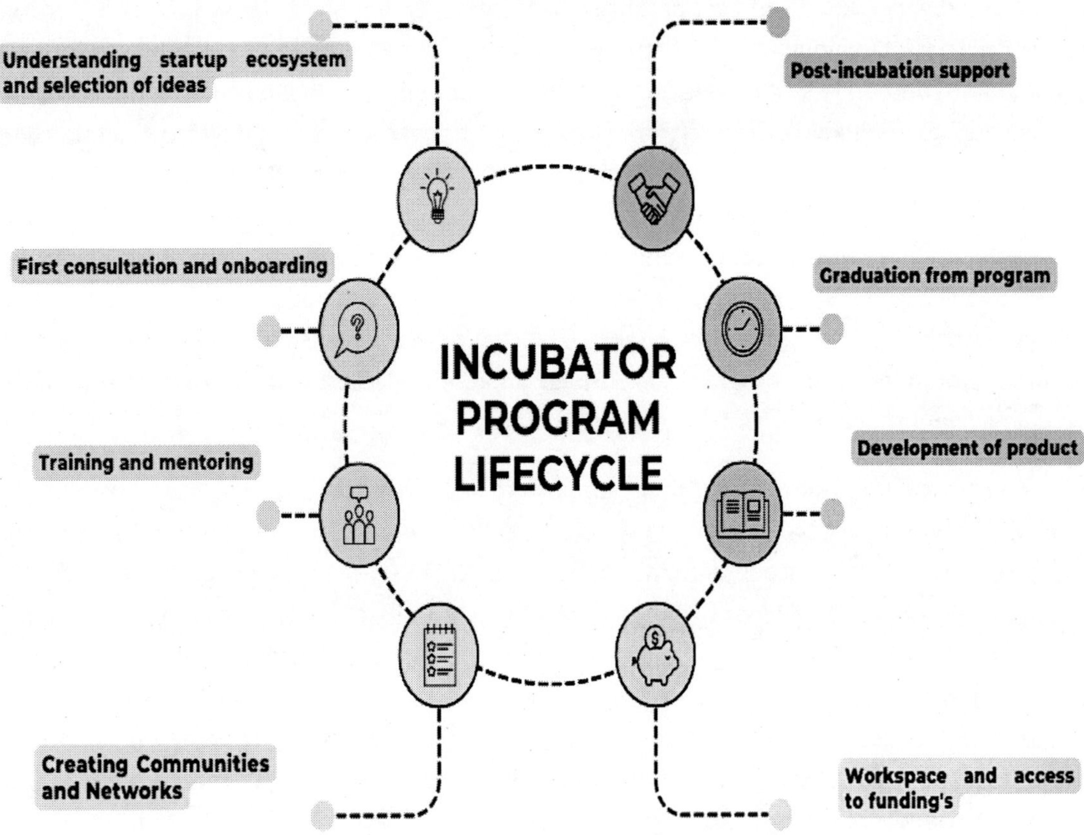

Figure 4.6 Components of Incubator Program Lifecycle

Incubator programs provide start-ups with opportunities for market validation and exposure to industry stakeholders, potential clients, and strategic partners. Through market research, customer discovery exercises, and product validation workshops, incubators help start-ups refine their value proposition, validate product-market fit, and identify growth opportunities. Additionally, incubators often facilitate connections with industry experts, corporate partners, and potential customers, providing start-ups with valuable feedback, insights, and validation. Exposure to industry stakeholders and market influencers increases start-ups' visibility, credibility, and opportunities for collaboration, positioning them for success in competitive markets.

Incubator programs offer skill enhancement and training programs to equip entrepreneurs and their teams with the knowledge and capabilities needed to succeed in the start-up ecosystem.

These programs cover several topics, including business management, entrepreneurship, marketing, finance, product development, and leadership. By participating in workshops, seminars, and hands-on training sessions, entrepreneurs can enhance their skills, acquire new competencies, and stay abreast of industry trends and best practices. Skill enhancement and training programs contribute to the professional development of entrepreneurs, empowering them to tackle challenges, seize opportunities, and drive sustainable growth within their ventures. Incubator programs provide start-ups access to valuable research and development resources, facilitating innovation and technological advancement. By collaborating with academic institutions, research centres, and specialized experts, start-ups can leverage innovative research, technical expertise, and state-of-the-art facilities to drive product development and technology innovation. These collaborations enable start-ups to tap into a vast network of researchers, scientists, and industry professionals, facilitating knowledge transfer and cross-disciplinary collaboration. By accessing research and development resources within incubator programs, start-ups can accelerate innovation, enhance product quality, and gain a competitive edge in their respective markets.

Incubator programs tailor their support to meet the unique needs of technology-driven ventures. They offer specialized initiatives to address the challenges and opportunities specific to IT, biotechnology, and advanced manufacturing sectors. These tailored programs provide targeted support in product development, intellectual property management, regulatory compliance, and market entry strategies. By leveraging industry-specific expertise, resources, and networks, incubator programs enable technology ventures to overcome barriers to growth and capitalize on emerging opportunities within their respective industries. By providing customized support tailored to the needs of technology ventures, incubator programs empower entrepreneurs to realize their full potential and drive innovation-led growth. Participation in incubator programs enhances the visibility and recognition of start-ups within the entrepreneurial ecosystem and beyond. Incubators provide platforms for start-ups to highlight their innovations, achievements, and milestones through events, competitions, demo days, and industry highlights. These opportunities enable start-ups to gain exposure to investors, potential customers, strategic partners, and media outlets, enhancing their brand visibility and credibility. By leveraging visibility and recognition opportunities provided by incubator programs, start-ups can attract investment, forge strategic partnerships, and differentiate themselves in competitive markets. Additionally, increased visibility can facilitate access to talent, resources, and market opportunities, positioning start-ups for long-term success and growth.

Incubator programs implement continuous monitoring and evaluation processes to assess the progress and effectiveness of the incubation journey. By establishing clear performance metrics, milestones, and goals, incubators track the development and growth of supported ventures over time. Regular progress reviews, feedback sessions, and performance evaluations enable incubators to identify areas of improvement, measure the impact of their support interventions, and make data-driven decisions to optimize program delivery. By ensuring accountability and transparency in monitoring and evaluation processes, incubators maintain alignment with their objectives and continuously strive to enhance the quality and effectiveness of their support services. Incubator programs embody flexibility and adaptability, evolving to meet start-ups' changing needs, dynamics, and broader entrepreneurial ecosystem. Incubators continually refine their support offerings, program structures, and service delivery models to address emerging trends, market shifts, and evolving industry landscapes. By remaining agile and responsive to the needs of start-ups, incubator programs ensure relevance and effectiveness in supporting entrepreneurial ventures at various stages of development. This flexibility enables start-ups to access tailored support that aligns with their evolving needs and growth trajectories, empowering them to navigate challenges and capitalize on opportunities in dynamic market environments.

Further, joining an incubator's alum network offers numerous benefits for start-ups, including access to a valuable community of peers, mentors, and industry experts. Alum networks provide opportunities for continued collaboration, knowledge sharing, and networking, enabling start-ups to leverage the collective expertise, resources, and networks of fellow alums. Additionally, incubators often offer alums post-incubation support programs and services, including access to funding opportunities, mentorship, networking events, and on-going business development assistance. By staying connected with the incubator community post-incubation, start-ups can continue to access support, leverage opportunities, and growth beyond the initial incubation period.

Understanding the multitude of benefits of incubator programs empowers entrepreneurs to make informed decisions about their participation. The above discussion serves as a guide, shedding light on how incubators can propel start-ups toward success and sustained growth.

4.5.3 Choosing the Right Incubation Environment

Selecting the most suitable incubation environment is a critical decision for entrepreneurs embarking on their start-up journey. The following discussion explores into the key considerations and factors entrepreneurs should consider when choosing an incubator program. From aligning with the venture's goals to assessing the available resources, this exploration guides entrepreneurs in making informed choices that align with the unique needs of their ventures.

Emphasizing the importance of clearly defining the goals and needs of the start-up is foundational in choosing the right incubation environment. Entrepreneurs must articulate their product development, market expansion, or technology innovation objectives. These goals will shape the criteria for selecting an incubation environment, ensuring that the chosen program aligns with the venture's strategic direction and growth trajectory. Detailing the significance of choosing an incubation environment aligned with the industry focus of the start-up is crucial. Entrepreneurs should seek out incubators specializing in their respective sectors, such as technology, biotechnology, or advanced manufacturing. Specialized incubators offer domain-specific expertise, resources, and networks tailored to the unique needs and challenges of ventures operating within those industries. Also, exploring the infrastructure offered by potential incubators is essential for supporting the operational requirements of the start-up. Entrepreneurs should assess the facilities, laboratories, equipment, and workspaces provided by incubators to ensure they meet the specific needs of their ventures. Access to state-of-the-art infrastructure can enhance productivity, innovation, and collaboration within the incubation environment.

Detailing the role of mentorship and advisory support within the incubation environment is critical for the success of start-ups. Entrepreneurs should seek out programs that offer access to experienced mentors and advisors who can provide guidance, feedback, and strategic insights. Experienced mentors contribute to the start-up's strategic, operational, and leadership aspects, accelerating its growth and mitigating potential risks. Exploring how potential incubators facilitate access to funding opportunities is essential for sustaining the growth and scalability of start-ups. Entrepreneurs should evaluate the incubation environment's track record in connecting ventures with angel investors, venture capitalists, and other sources of financial support. Access to funding can provide the necessary capital to fuel product development, market expansion, and operational scaling. Discussing the importance of networking and collaboration within the incubation environment highlights the value of a vibrant ecosystem of peers, mentors, and industry stakeholders. Entrepreneurs should seek out programs that offer opportunities for networking, knowledge exchange, and collaborative initiatives. A collaborative ecosystem enhances the start-up's visibility, recognition, and growth potential by developing partnerships, strategic alliances, and business opportunities.

Exploring success stories of start-ups that have thrived within specific incubators offers valuable insights into the program's effectiveness and impact. Entrepreneurs should review the track record of incubators in nurturing successful ventures and inquire about the achievements and milestones of their alums. Joining an incubator with a successful record of accomplishment and an active alum network offers access to a supportive community, mentorship opportunities, and potential partnerships, enhancing the start-up's chances of success.

Detailing the flexibility and adaptability of incubator programs is crucial for entrepreneurs assessing potential options. Incubator programs must be flexible enough to accommodate start-ups' evolving needs and dynamics as they progress through various stages of development. Discussing how programs evolve to meet changing needs involves examining how incubators adjust their offerings, resources, and support mechanisms based on feedback from participating start-ups. A flexible and adaptive programme may better serve the different requirements and growth trajectories of start-ups by adjusting mentorship programmes, extending networking opportunities, and offering extra resources. Discussing the time and resource commitments associated with different incubation programs helps entrepreneurs make informed decisions about their participation. Entrepreneurs should evaluate the time and resource investment required by each program and assess whether it aligns with their venture's stage and growth trajectory. This involves considering factors such as program duration, intensity of mentorship and support, and any financial or equity commitments. By understanding the time and resource requirements upfront, entrepreneurs can ensure that they can fully commit to and derive maximum value from the chosen incubation program.

Exploring the evaluation criteria and milestones set by incubators is essential for entrepreneurs to understand how their progress will be assessed throughout the program. Incubators typically establish clear criteria and milestones to monitor the progress of participating start-ups and ensure alignment with program goals. These criteria may include product development milestones, market validation metrics, revenue targets, or key performance indicators. By understanding the evaluation criteria upfront, entrepreneurs can track their progress effectively and leverage support resources to address any areas needing improvement. Detailing the post-incubation support and opportunities potential incubators offer is crucial for assessing participation's long-term impact and sustainability. While incubation programs provide valuable support during the initial stages of start-up development, entrepreneurs should also consider what support they will receive after graduation. This may include access to alum networks, continued mentorship, networking events, funding opportunities, or other resources to support the sustained success and growth of the start-up beyond the incubation period. Discussing the importance of conducting site visits and interacting with current and past participants of potential incubators highlights the value of first-hand experiences and testimonials. Site visits allow entrepreneurs to assess the incubation environment, facilities, and resources firsthand and gain insights into the culture and dynamics of the program. Interactions with current and past participants provide valuable perspectives on the level of support, quality of mentorship, and overall experience within the incubator. By gathering first-hand information, entrepreneurs can make more informed decisions about which incubator aligns best with their venture's needs and aspirations. Exploring the alignment of the incubator's values and culture with those of the start-up emphasizes the importance of developing a positive and collaborative environment. Entrepreneurs should seek out incubators that share their values, vision, and culture, as this facilitates a supportive and conducive ecosystem for growth and innovation. A shared vision between the start-up and the incubator enhances communication, trust, and collaboration, facilitating a more productive and rewarding incubation experience for all parties involved.

Choosing the right incubation environment is a pivotal step in the entrepreneurial journey. The above discussion equips entrepreneurs with the tools and insights needed to navigate the selection process, ensuring that the chosen incubator aligns seamlessly with the goals and aspirations of their ventures.

4.6. Proposal Pitching and Agreements

In the competitive entrepreneurship landscape, articulating and presenting a compelling business proposal is crucial for start-ups seeking partnerships, funding, or collaborations. The following discussion explains the art and science of crafting a business proposal that communicates the venture's vision and captures the attention and interest of potential stakeholders. From structure to content, entrepreneurs will gain insights into creating persuasive proposals that pave the way for successful agreements. Figure 4.7 demonstrates the essential elements of a compelling business proposal by emphasizing the key components necessary for effectively communicating a venture's value proposition and potential. These elements should include a clear problem statement, a detailed solution or product description, market analysis and opportunity assessment, a comprehensive business model, financial projections, and a strategic execution plan.

4.6.1 Crafting a Compelling Business Proposal

Defining a business proposal's primary objectives and purposes sets the foundation for effective communication and persuasion. A well-crafted proposal serves as a tool for articulating the venture's vision, goals, and strategies while developing collaboration and alignment with potential stakeholders. By clearly outlining the problem addressed, the solution offered, and the expected outcomes, entrepreneurs can convey the value proposition of their venture and inspire confidence in its potential for success.

Detailing the essential components of a compelling business proposal ensures comprehensive coverage of critical aspects that resonate with stakeholders. These components typically include an executive summary, problem statement, solution overview, unique value proposition (UVP), market analysis, competitive landscape, business model, financial projections, and call to action. Each section is critical in conveying the venture's story, value proposition, and potential impact, providing a holistic view of the opportunity presented. Discussing the importance of a clear and concise executive summary highlights its role as a hook to capture stakeholders' attention and interest. The executive summary is a snapshot of the venture, providing a concise overview of its purpose, value proposition, market opportunity, and anticipated outcomes. Entrepreneurs should highlight critical elements, such as the problem addressed, the innovative solution offered, the market potential, and the team's expertise, compellingly and concisely to pique stakeholders' curiosity and encourage further proposal exploration.

Detailing how to effectively present the problem statement and highlight the venture's innovative solution emphasizes the importance of addressing market needs and demonstrating a deep understanding of the problem landscape. Entrepreneurs should clearly articulate the pain points faced by the target audience, supported by data and evidence, to underscore the urgency and relevance of the problem. Subsequently, presenting the innovative solution compellingly, highlighting its uniqueness, feasibility, and potential impact, reinforces the value proposition and enhances stakeholder buy-in. Discussing the significance of a Unique Value Proposition (UVP) in differentiating the venture underscores the importance of clearly communicating what sets the venture apart from existing solutions. Entrepreneurs should identify and articulate the distinctive features, benefits, and advantages of their offering that resonate with the target audience. By emphasizing how the venture addresses unmet needs, delivers superior value, or offers innovative solutions, entrepreneurs can effectively differentiate their proposition and create a compelling case for stakeholder engagement. Detailing the components of a comprehensive market analysis within the business proposal underscores the importance of market research, target audience identification, and competitive landscape analysis. Entrepreneurs should conduct thorough market research to gain insights into market size, trends, growth drivers, customer preferences, and competitive dynamics. By demonstrating a deep understanding of the market opportunity and positioning their venture strategically within the competitive landscape, entrepreneurs can enhance the credibility and attractiveness of their proposal to potential stakeholders.

Discussing how to outline a feasible and realistic implementation plan involves detailing the phases, milestones, and timelines that demonstrate a practical approach to executing the proposed solution. Entrepreneurs should break down the implementation process into manageable phases, each with clearly defined objectives, tasks, and deliverables. Entrepreneurs can display a structured and systematic approach to achieving project goals by establishing realistic milestones and timelines. Additionally, outlining dependencies, resource requirements, and contingency plans ensures preparedness to navigate unforeseen challenges and maintain project momentum, instilling confidence in potential stakeholders regarding the feasibility and viability of the proposed solution. Including financial projections and Return on Investment (ROI) analysis in the business proposal underscores the importance of demonstrating the venture's financial viability and potential for generating returns. Entrepreneurs should provide realistic and data-driven financial projections, including revenue forecasts, expense breakdowns, cash flow statements, and profitability analysis.

By quantifying the expected financial outcomes and articulating the projected ROI, entrepreneurs can illustrate the attractiveness of the investment opportunity to potential stakeholders. Realistic financial projections build credibility and transparency, instilling confidence in stakeholders regarding the venture's ability to deliver tangible value and generate sustainable returns over time.

Figure 4.7 Elements of a Compelling Business Proposal

Discussing the importance of addressing potential risks and providing mitigation strategies highlights the proactive approach to risk management within the business proposal. Entrepreneurs should conduct a comprehensive risk assessment to identify and prioritize potential threats to project success, including market, operational, financial, and regulatory risks. By acknowledging challenges upfront and articulating proactive mitigation strategies, such as risk diversification, contingency planning, and insurance coverage, entrepreneurs can demonstrate resilience and preparedness to navigate uncertainties effectively. Addressing risks and mitigation strategies enhances the credibility and robustness of the proposal, reassuring stakeholders of the venture's ability to manage and mitigate potential setbacks. Detailing the incorporation of social impact and sustainability elements in the business proposal emphasizes the venture's commitment to ethical practices, environmental responsibility, and positive societal contributions. Entrepreneurs should articulate how their venture aligns with sustainability goals, promotes responsible business practices, and contributes to social welfare. By quantifying social impact metrics, such as job creation, community engagement, environmental conservation, and ethical sourcing, entrepreneurs can highlight the broader value proposition of their venture beyond financial returns. Incorporating social impact and sustainability considerations enhances the attractiveness of the proposal to stakeholders who prioritize environmental, social, and governance (ESG) factors, facilitating alignment with values-driven investors and partners.

Discussing strategies for crafting an engaging and visually appealing business proposal presentation emphasizes the importance of storytelling, visuals, and graphics in capturing stakeholders' attention and interest. Entrepreneurs should structure their presentations to tell a compelling narrative highlighting the venture's unique value proposition, market opportunity, and impact potential. Utilizing visuals, info graphics, and multimedia elements can enhance the clarity and impact of key messages, making the presentation more engaging and memorable. By incorporating storytelling techniques that resonate with the audience and evoke emotion, entrepreneurs can create a memorable and persuasive presentation that effectively communicates the essence and value of their venture. Exploring the importance of tailoring proposals for different stakeholders underscores the need to customize content and messaging based on the interests and priorities of specific audiences. Entrepreneurs should adapt their proposals to address stakeholders' concerns, preferences, and decision-making criteria, such as investors, customers, partners, and regulatory bodies. By conducting audience analysis and understanding stakeholders' motivations and expectations, entrepreneurs can tailor their proposals to highlight relevant benefits, address potential objections, and raise resonance with each audience segment. Tailoring proposals for different stakeholders enhances relevance, alignment, and receptiveness, increasing the likelihood of securing buy-in and collaboration from diverse stakeholders.

A compelling business proposal is essential for entrepreneurs navigating the competitive business landscape. The above discussion provides a comprehensive guide, equipping start-ups with the tools and insights to create persuasive proposals that captivate stakeholders and pave the way for successful agreements and partnerships.

4.6.2 Effective Pitching Techniques

The art of pitching is a critical skill for entrepreneurs aiming to convey their venture's vision, garner support, and secure agreements. The following discussion explores into the techniques that make a pitch compelling, engaging, and persuasive. From storytelling to delivery, entrepreneurs will gain insights into effective pitching strategies that captivate audiences, whether they are potential investors, partners, or collaborators.

Delving into the psychological aspects that influence the effectiveness of a pitch is crucial for crafting a persuasive presentation. By understanding the audience's mind-set, entrepreneurs can tailor their pitch to resonate with their emotions, motivations, and decision-making processes. Addressing cognitive biases, emotional triggers, and social dynamics enables entrepreneurs to craft a pitch that captures attention, evokes empathy, and inspires action. Emphasizing the power of storytelling in making a pitch memorable highlights the importance of structuring a narrative that engages and resonates with the audience. Entrepreneurs should craft a compelling story that conveys the venture's journey, challenges, successes, and aspirations. By incorporating elements of conflict, resolution, and transformation, entrepreneurs can create a narrative arc that captures attention, provokes emotion, and communicates the venture's value proposition in a memorable and relatable way. Discussing the importance of a solid and impactful opening in setting the tone for the pitch underscores the need to grab attention and create immediate engagement. Entrepreneurs should employ compelling anecdotes, thought-provoking questions, or startling statistics to captivate the audience. By sparking curiosity and creating an emotional connection with the audience, entrepreneurs can lay the foundation for a persuasive and memorable pitch.

Detailing the significance of conveying passion and authenticity during a pitch highlights the importance of genuine enthusiasm and belief in the venture. Entrepreneurs should communicate their passion for their venture with sincerity and conviction, as it enhances credibility, builds trust, and inspires confidence in potential stakeholders. By sharing personal anecdotes, demonstrating vulnerability, and expressing authentic enthusiasm, entrepreneurs can establish a genuine connection with the audience and leave an impression. Discussing the importance of adapting pitch content and style to the dynamics of the audience underscores the need for flexibility and responsiveness in communication. Entrepreneurs should tailor their pitch based on specific stakeholders' interests, priorities, and preferences, whether they are investors, customers, or partners. Entrepreneurs can customize their pitch to resonate with each audience segment's unique needs and perspectives by understanding audience demographics, motivations, and decision-making criteria. Detailing the effective use of visuals, multimedia, and supporting materials in a pitch emphasizes the importance of creating a visually compelling and engaging presentation. Entrepreneurs should leverage well-designed slides, images, videos, and interactive elements to enhance the impact and clarity of their message. Visuals capture attention, aid comprehension, evoke emotion, and reinforce key points, making the pitch more memorable and persuasive. By incorporating visuals that complement and reinforce the narrative, entrepreneurs can create a more immersive and impactful pitch experience for the audience.

Emphasizing the importance of maintaining clarity and conciseness in a pitch underscores the need to convey critical messages succinctly while avoiding information overload. Entrepreneurs should focus on distilling complex ideas into simple, digestible concepts that are easy for the audience to understand and remember. Techniques such as using understandable language, structuring content logically, and prioritizing essential information help maintain clarity and conciseness. By keeping the pitch concise, entrepreneurs can ensure that the audience remains engaged and retains the most critical aspects of the presentation. Discussing strategies for effectively addressing questions and concerns raised during a pitch highlights the importance of preparedness and thoughtful responses. Entrepreneurs should anticipate potential questions and objections and prepare well-reasoned and evidence-based responses. Listening to the audience's concerns, acknowledging their perspectives, and providing transparent and honest answers build credibility and trust. By demonstrating a thorough understanding of the venture and its market, entrepreneurs can address questions confidently and reassure stakeholders, building confidence in the venture's viability and potential for success. Detailing the incorporation of relevant data and metrics to substantiate claims and projections emphasizes the importance of presenting a compelling and evidence-based pitch. Entrepreneurs should leverage information, such as market research, customer testimonials, and financial projections, to support critical assertions and illustrate the venture's value proposition. By presenting data and metrics in a clear, accessible manner, entrepreneurs can enhance credibility, mitigate uncertainty, and build confidence in the feasibility and potential of the venture. Incorporating quantitative evidence strengthens the persuasive impact of the pitch and reinforces the credibility of the entrepreneur's assertions.

Discussing the elements of a memorable closing in a pitch highlights the importance of leaving an impression and issuing a call to action. Entrepreneurs should summarize key points, reiterate the value proposition, and articulate a clear and compelling call to action that aligns with the objectives of the pitch. By inspiring the audience with a vision of the venture's potential and inviting them to take specific next steps, entrepreneurs can motivate stakeholders to engage further and support the venture's objectives. A memorable closing reinforces the key messages of the pitch and leaves the audience with a sense of excitement and urgency.

Detailing the importance of rehearsing and refining the delivery of a pitch underscores the value of practice in enhancing confidence, fluency, and overall impact. Entrepreneurs should rehearse their pitch repeatedly to refine their delivery, timing, and body language. Practicing in front of a trusted audience or mentor can provide valuable feedback and help identify areas for improvement. By rehearsing effectively, entrepreneurs can build confidence, develop a natural and engaging delivery style, and deliver a polished and compelling pitch that resonates with the audience. Discussing strategies for handling unexpected challenges, objections, or curveballs during a pitch emphasizes the importance of adaptability and composure in overcoming obstacles. Entrepreneurs should remain calm, composed, and flexible in responding to unforeseen challenges, reframing objections as opportunities to provide further clarification or address concerns. Active listening, empathy, and resilience are essential in navigating unexpected situations and maintaining credibility and rapport with the audience. Entrepreneurs can effectively overcome pitching challenges by demonstrating adaptability and problem-solving skills and leaving a positive impression on stakeholders.

Mastering effective pitching techniques is a transformative skill for entrepreneurs navigating the dynamic landscape of business presentations. The above discussion equips start-ups with actionable strategies, enabling them to deliver pitches that resonate with audiences and create lasting impressions, driving success in securing agreements and partnerships.

4.6.3 Negotiating and Drafting Agreements

Negotiating and drafting agreements are pivotal in formalizing partnerships, collaborations, and investment deals for a start-up. The following discussion explores the intricacies of negotiation strategies, legal considerations, and the art of crafting comprehensive agreements that protect the interests of all parties involved. Entrepreneurs will gain insights into navigating the negotiation table and drafting agreements that establish clear expectations, responsibilities, and terms.

Researching the stages and dynamics of the negotiation process is crucial for achieving successful outcomes. Entrepreneurs should understand the critical negotiation phases, from preparation and opening offers to bargaining and reaching a final agreement. Discussing the importance of preparation, effective communication, and strategic thinking in negotiations highlights the need for thorough research, clear objectives, and flexibility to adapt to changing circumstances. Discussing the importance of setting clear negotiation objectives and priorities underscores the need for a well-defined negotiation strategy. Entrepreneurs should align their negotiation objectives with the venture's goals and long-term vision, prioritizing key outcomes and concessions. By establishing clear objectives and priorities, entrepreneurs can focus their efforts and resources on negotiating favourable terms that advance the interests of the venture. Detailing practical communication skills essential for successful negotiations emphasizes the importance of clear and persuasive communication. Entrepreneurs should hone their ability to articulate their needs, listen actively to the concerns of other parties, and convey information effectively. Techniques such as active listening, asking probing questions, and using assertive but respectful language facilitate open dialogue and promote understanding between negotiating parties. Discussing the role of trust and rapport-building in negotiation highlights the importance of creating a positive and collaborative atmosphere. Entrepreneurs should build rapport with negotiating counterparts, demonstrate integrity, and develop mutual respect. By establishing trust and rapport, entrepreneurs can create an environment conducive to open communication, creative problem-solving, and reaching mutually beneficial agreements.

Detailing different negotiation styles and approaches enables entrepreneurs to adapt their strategies to varying negotiating counterparts. Whether facing competitive, collaborative, or accommodating negotiation styles, entrepreneurs should recognize and understand the motivations and preferences of other parties. By flexibly adjusting their approach and tactics, entrepreneurs can navigate differences in negotiation styles and maximize the potential for positive outcomes. Equipping entrepreneurs with strategies for handling conflicts and challenges during negotiations prepares entrepreneurs to address obstacles and maintain progress toward reaching agreements. Entrepreneurs should develop techniques for managing conflicts constructively, such as remaining calm, actively listening, and reframing issues to find common ground. By maintaining composure and seeking mutually acceptable solutions, entrepreneurs can overcome impasses and preserve the integrity of the negotiation process. Detailing the legal considerations and elements crucial for agreement drafting underscores the importance of precision and clarity in formalizing agreements. Entrepreneurs should work closely with legal advisors to ensure that agreements address vital legal requirements, mitigate risks, and protect the interests of all parties involved. By adhering to legal standards and incorporating appropriate clauses and provisions, entrepreneurs can create agreements that withstand legal scrutiny and provide a solid foundation for successful partnerships and collaborations.

Discussing the components of comprehensive and transparent agreements highlights the importance of creating documents that accurately reflect the intentions and obligations of all parties involved. Entrepreneurs should ensure that agreements include essential sections such as definitions, scope of work, responsibilities, payment terms, confidentiality provisions, and dispute resolution mechanisms. By detailing each aspect of the agreement in unambiguous language, entrepreneurs can minimize ambiguity and prevent misunderstandings or disputes down the line. Detailing the importance of clearly defining roles, responsibilities, and expectations in agreements underscores the need for explicit terms that leave no room for interpretation. Entrepreneurs should outline each party's duties and obligations, including timelines, deliverables, and performance metrics. By setting clear expectations upfront, agreements can help prevent misunderstandings, mitigate risks, and accountability among all parties involved. Discussing the inclusion of contingencies and exit strategies in agreements emphasizes the importance of planning for unforeseen circumstances and ensuring long-term stability. Entrepreneurs should anticipate potential challenges such as breaches of contract, changes in ownership, or market disruptions and outline contingency plans and exit mechanisms accordingly. By addressing contingencies and exit strategies upfront, agreements can provide a framework for resolving disputes and facilitating smooth transitions in the event of unforeseen events.

Detailing specific considerations for negotiating funding and investment terms highlights the complexities involved in financial agreements. When negotiating funding agreements, entrepreneurs should carefully consider valuation, equity distribution, investment milestones, and exit clauses. By seeking expert guidance and conducting thorough due diligence, entrepreneurs can negotiate terms that align with the venture's financial objectives while protecting the interests of all parties involved. Also, discussing the importance of ensuring compliance with regulatory standards in agreements underscores the legal obligations that govern business transactions. To lessen legal risks and liabilities, entrepreneurs should ensure that agreements adhere to applicable laws, regulations, and industry standards. By seeking legal advice and conducting compliance checks, entrepreneurs can safeguard the interests of all parties involved and avoid potential legal disputes or penalties. Discussing the importance of continuous review and agreement amendments acknowledges the dynamic nature of business relationships and evolving regulatory landscapes. Entrepreneurs should regularly review and update agreements to reflect changes in business dynamics, market conditions, or regulatory requirements. By proactively addressing emerging issues and revising agreements as necessary, entrepreneurs can ensure that agreements remain relevant, enforceable, and supportive of the venture's objectives over time.

Negotiating and drafting agreements are integral aspects of entrepreneurial ventures. The following discussion equips entrepreneurs with the knowledge and skills needed to navigate the negotiation table effectively, ensuring that agreements are comprehensive, legally sound, and aligned with the strategic goals of the start-up.

4.7. Start-up Company Incorporation

Incorporating a start-up involves navigating various legal considerations to establish a solid foundation for business operations. The following discussion explores the legal aspects of start-up incorporation, guiding entrepreneurs through the essential steps and considerations. From choosing the proper legal structure to compliance requirements, entrepreneurs will gain insights into the legal framework underpinning their ventures' formal establishment. Figure 4.8 outlines the legal considerations for start-up incorporation, highlighting key aspects entrepreneurs must address when establishing their businesses.

4.7.1 Legal Aspects of Start-up Incorporation

Detailing different legal structures available for start-up incorporation is crucial for entrepreneurs to make informed decisions about the structure that best suits their business goals and circumstances. Discussing the characteristics, advantages, and disadvantages of structures such as sole proprietorship, partnership, limited liability company (LLC), and corporation enables entrepreneurs to assess liability protection, taxation, management flexibility, and administrative requirements. By understanding the implications of each legal structure, entrepreneurs can select the most appropriate option to establish their ventures. Discussing the legal requirements and documentation necessary for start-up incorporation guides entrepreneurs through the procedural aspects of the incorporation process. Detailing the steps involved in preparing and submitting necessary paperwork, such as articles of incorporation, ensures entrepreneurs are equipped with the knowledge and resources to navigate the incorporation process efficiently and compliantly. By adhering to legal requirements, entrepreneurs can establish a solid legal foundation for their ventures and mitigate the risk of potential legal challenges or complications in the future.

Further, detailing the content and significance of articles of incorporation and bylaws emphasizes their role in defining the start-up's fundamental principles, structure, and governance. Articles of incorporation establish essential information about the company, such as its name, purpose, registered agent, and authorized shares of stock. Bylaws, on the other hand, outline the internal rules and procedures governing the operation and management of the company, including roles and responsibilities of directors, shareholder rights, meeting protocols, and decision-making processes. Ensuring clarity and precision in these foundational documents lays the groundwork for effective corporate governance and operational efficiency. Additionally, discussing the importance of obtaining relevant licenses and permits for legal compliance highlights the regulatory obligations that start-ups must fulfil to operate lawfully. Detailing the types of licenses and permits applicable to different industries and business activities ensures entrepreneurs are aware of the specific requirements relevant to their operations, such as business licenses, professional licenses, health permits, zoning permits, and environmental permits. By proactively obtaining necessary licenses and permits, entrepreneurs can demonstrate commitment to legal compliance and mitigate the risk of regulatory violations or penalties that could impede business operations.

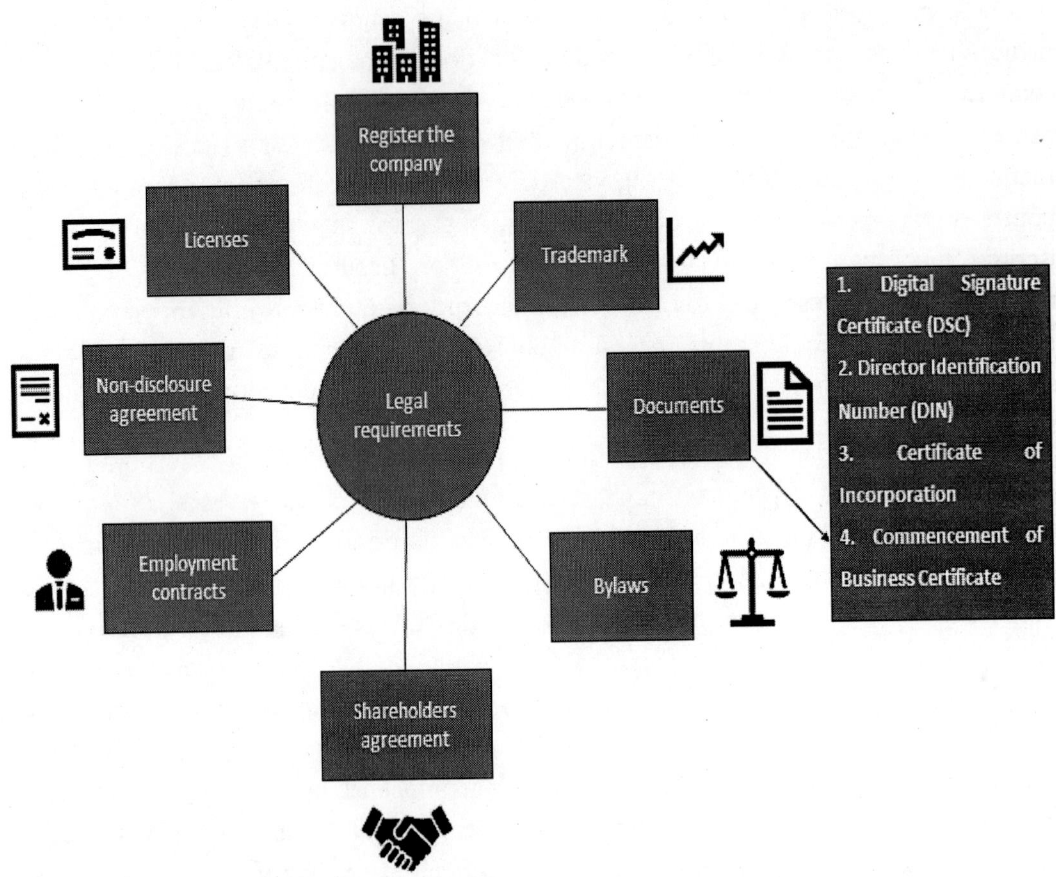

Figure 4.8 Legal Considerations for Start-up Incorporation

Detailing the legal considerations for protecting intellectual property during business operations underscores the importance of safeguarding valuable intangible assets such as trademarks, patents, copyrights, and trade secrets. Discussing strategies for intellectual property protection, such as conducting thorough IP searches, filing trademark and patent applications, implementing confidentiality agreements, and developing IP management protocols, enables entrepreneurs to preserve their competitive advantage and mitigate the risk of IP infringement or misappropriation. By prioritizing intellectual property protection from the outset, entrepreneurs can enhance the value and resilience of their ventures in the marketplace.

Discussing the taxation implications and compliance requirements for start-ups informs entrepreneurs about the tax obligations they must fulfil at the federal, state, and local levels. Detailing considerations related to corporate taxation, such as entity classification, tax filing deadlines, tax deductions, credits, and incentives, empower entrepreneurs to develop effective tax planning strategies and optimize their tax positions. By ensuring compliance with taxation regulations, entrepreneurs can avoid costly tax penalties, maximize tax savings opportunities, and maintain financial transparency through implementing tax laws, regulations, and credibility with stakeholders. Detailing legal considerations related to employment and labour laws is essential for ensuring compliance and minimizing legal risks in hiring and managing personnel. Discussing hiring practices, employment contracts, and compliance with labour regulations informs entrepreneurs about their obligations regarding recruitment, wages, working conditions, employee benefits, anti-discrimination laws, and workplace safety standards. By understanding and adhering to applicable employment and labour laws, entrepreneurs can create a positive work environment, mitigate the risk of legal disputes or penalties, and uphold their responsibilities as employers. Discussing the legal aspects of shareholder agreements and equity distribution underscores the importance of establishing clear terms and expectations among company stakeholders. Detailing considerations for allocating shares, outlining shareholder rights, voting mechanisms, and dividend policies, and addressing potential disputes safeguard the interests of shareholders and promote transparency and fairness in corporate governance. By drafting comprehensive shareholder agreements, entrepreneurs can mitigate the risk of shareholder conflicts, ensure alignment of interests, and facilitate effective decision-making processes within the company.

Detailing ongoing regulatory compliance requirements for incorporated start-ups ensures entrepreneurs know their obligations to regulatory authorities and industry regulators. Discussing reporting obligations, audits, and adherence to industry-specific regulations informs entrepreneurs about the necessary procedures and documentation to maintain compliance with relevant laws and standards. By staying abreast of regulatory requirements and implementing robust compliance measures, entrepreneurs can mitigate the risk of legal violations, financial penalties, reputational damage, and disruptions to business operations. Discussing the importance of corporate governance and maintaining accurate records emphasizes the need for sound organizational practices to uphold transparency, accountability, and compliance. Detailing how corporate governance structures, board responsibilities, meeting protocols, and record-keeping practices contribute to effective decision-making and regulatory compliance guides entrepreneurs in establishing robust governance frameworks. By maintaining comprehensive and accurate records, entrepreneurs can demonstrate adherence to legal and regulatory requirements, facilitate audits and inspections, and enhance investor confidence and trust in the company's management and operations.

Detailing legal considerations for exit strategies such as mergers, acquisitions, or dissolution prepares entrepreneurs for the complex legal processes involved in corporate restructuring or winding down operations. Discussing the legal implications and steps in executing exit plans, including shareholder approvals, asset transfers, contractual obligations, and regulatory filings, enables entrepreneurs to navigate exit scenarios clearly and confidently. By seeking legal advice and developing comprehensive exit plans, entrepreneurs can minimize legal risks, maximize value, and ensure smooth transitions during strategic repositioning or business closure. Discussing the role of legal counsel and professional advice in the incorporation process highlights the importance of seeking expert guidance to navigate complex legal issues and ensure compliance with applicable laws and regulations. Detailing when and how entrepreneurs should seek legal guidance, such as during the incorporation process, contract negotiations, regulatory compliance reviews, or dispute resolution proceedings, empowers entrepreneurs to make informed decisions and mitigate legal risks effectively. By partnering with experienced legal professionals, entrepreneurs can access specialized expertise, mitigate legal liabilities, and safeguard the long-term interests of their ventures. Navigating the legal landscape of start-up incorporation is crucial for establishing a solid legal foundation. The following discussion provides entrepreneurs with a comprehensive understanding of the legal aspects involved, empowering them to make informed decisions and ensure compliance as they embark on the formal journey of incorporating their ventures

4.7.2 Choosing the Right Business Structure

The appropriate business structure is a pivotal decision that significantly influences a start-up's legal, operational, and financial characteristics. The following discussion explores into the various business structures available to entrepreneurs, guiding them through the considerations and implications of each option. From sole proprietorship to corporation, entrepreneurs will gain insights into choosing a structure aligned with their goals, risk tolerance, and long-term vision. Figure 4.9 illustrates the workflow for start-up incorporation, detailing the sequential steps involved in establishing a new venture. Each step is crucial in transforming an idea into a legally recognized entity from the initial ideation phase to the formal registration process.

Detailing the characteristics and considerations of a corporation provides entrepreneurs with insights into the complexities of this formal business entity. C corporations (C corps) and S corporations (S corps) are two common business structures that provide limited liability protection to their owners and shareholders. The main difference between the two is how they are taxed and the rules they must follow to stay compliant with the IRS. Understanding the differences between C corporations and S corporations, including their structures, taxation methods, governance requirements, and shareholder rights, enables entrepreneurs to evaluate the advantages and drawbacks of each option, which is essential. Discussing the factors that influence the choice of a business structure assists entrepreneurs in making informed decisions aligned with their specific circumstances and objectives. Detailing considerations such as liability protection, taxation, operational flexibility, governance, and fundraising capabilities enable entrepreneurs to weigh the relative importance of each factor in selecting the most suitable structure for their ventures.

Detailing how different business structures offer varying levels of liability protection illuminates the implications for entrepreneurs' assets and the separation of business and personal liabilities. Discussing how structures such as corporations and LLCs shield owners from personal liability underscores the importance of asset protection in mitigating risks associated with business operations. Delving into the tax implications associated with different business structures is crucial for entrepreneurs to understand the financial implications of their choices. Detailing how taxation varies for sole proprietorships, partnerships, LLCs, and corporations gives entrepreneurs insights into each structure's potential tax advantages or liabilities. Factors such as pass-through taxation for partnerships and LLCs, double taxation for C corporations, and potential tax deductions or credits for different business expenses equips entrepreneurs to make informed decisions aligned with their tax planning strategies and financial goals. Detailing the operational flexibility and management structures associated with different business structures elucidates how organizational governance and decision-making processes vary across options. Discussing factors such as ownership control, management authority, and voting rights provides entrepreneurs with clarity on the roles and responsibilities within each structure. Exploring how sole proprietorships offer simplicity in management, partnerships allow for shared decision-making among partners, and corporations feature hierarchical structures with boards of directors and executive officers, empowering entrepreneurs to choose a structure that aligns with their preferred management style and organizational needs. Discussing the impact of business structure on fundraising and investor attractiveness highlights how specific structures may be more appealing to investors or suitable for various fundraising stages. Detailing how investors perceive factors such as liability protection, governance transparency, and potential returns informs entrepreneurs about the implications of their structure choice on securing external funding. Exploring how corporations attract venture capital investment due to their scalability and stock offerings, while LLCs may be preferred for closely held businesses seeking flexibility in ownership and management, guides entrepreneurs in aligning their structure with their fundraising objectives and investor preferences.

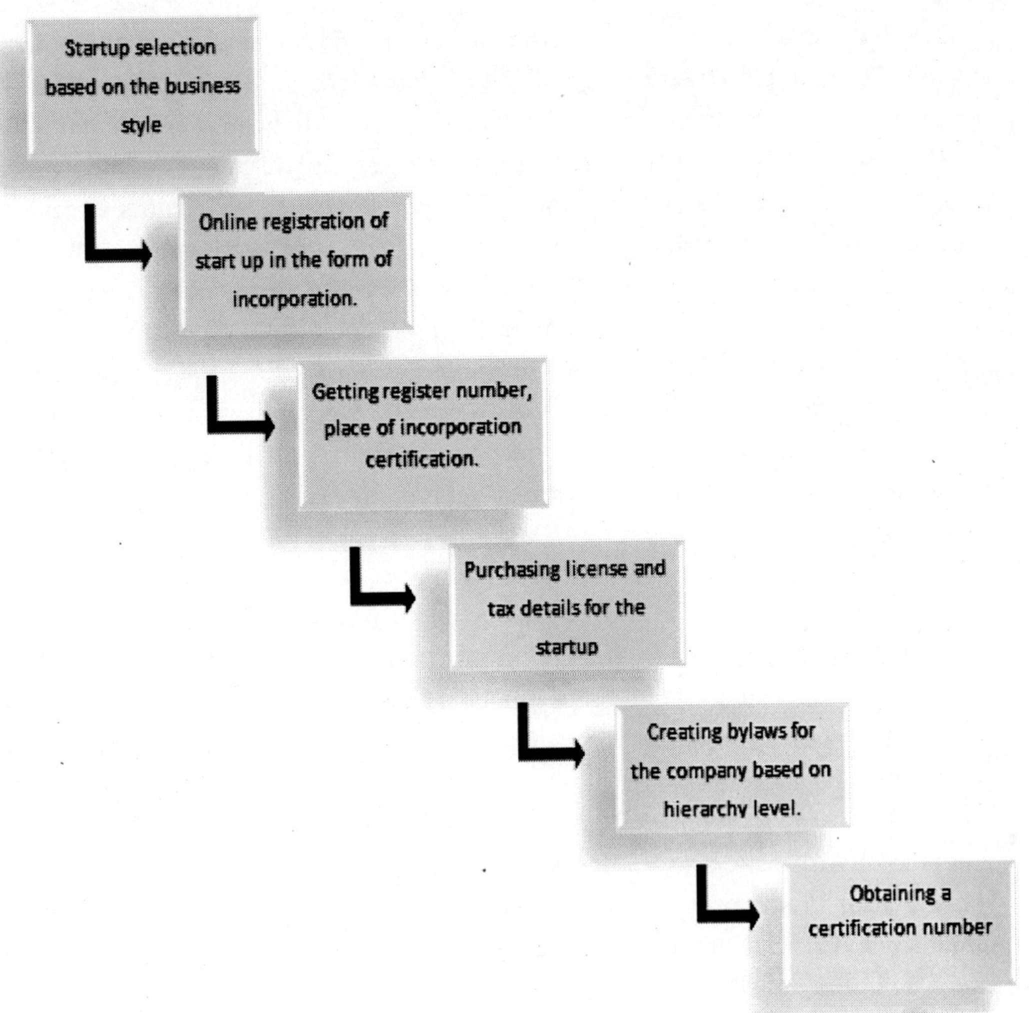

Figure 4.9 Start-Up Incorporation Workflow

Deliberating the possibility of converting or transitioning between business structures addresses the potential for evolving needs and circumstances. Detailing the steps involved, legal considerations, and implications of changing the business structure prepares entrepreneurs for scenarios where restructuring may be necessary to accommodate growth, mitigate risks, or optimize tax efficiency. Exploring factors such as regulatory requirements, tax consequences, and operational disruptions associated with conversion options empowers entrepreneurs to make strategic decisions about structural changes that support their long-term objectives. Analysing case studies of start-ups making strategic decisions about their business structures provides real-world examples for entrepreneurs to learn from. Extracting key considerations, challenges, and outcomes associated with their choices offers valuable insights into the decision-making process. By examining how factors such as industry dynamics, growth projections, and investor expectations influence the selection of a particular structure, entrepreneurs can gain practical insights into the implications of their own structure decisions and anticipate potential challenges or opportunities. Engaging participants in a workshop to evaluate and choose a suitable business structure for a simulated start-up facilitates interactive learning and decision-making. Facilitating discussions on individual venture characteristics, goals, and considerations in the decision-making process encourages participants to apply theoretical knowledge to real-world scenarios. By collaboratively assessing factors such as liability exposure, tax obligations, and operational requirements, participants can weigh the pros and cons of different structures and make informed decisions aligned with the simulated venture's objectives.

Choosing the proper business structure is a foundational decision for entrepreneurs. The above discussion equips start-up founders with the knowledge and considerations needed to make informed choices aligned with their business goals, operational preferences, and long-term vision.

4.7.3 Compliance and Registration Processes

Compliance and registration are integral components of the start-up incorporation process, ensuring that ventures adhere to legal requirements and establish a solid foundation for operations. The following discussion provides a comprehensive guide to the compliance and registration processes, offering entrepreneurs practical insights into navigating regulatory frameworks, submitting required documentation, and fulfilling essential obligations.

Navigating regulatory compliance is a fundamental aspect of the start-up incorporation journey, ensuring legal adherence and operational legitimacy. Entrepreneurs must familiarize themselves with the diverse federal, state, and local business activity regulations. From labour laws to tax regulations, understanding and complying with these requirements is essential for establishing a solid foundation and avoiding potential legal pitfalls. By prioritizing regulatory compliance from the outset, start-ups can mitigate risks and build a reputation for responsible business practices. Industry-specific regulations play a pivotal role in shaping the operating landscape for start-ups, with each sector subject to unique compliance requirements. Whether in healthcare, finance, or technology, entrepreneurs must explore into the specific regulations governing their industry to ensure lawful operations. By comprehensively understanding industry-specific laws, such as data privacy regulations or financial reporting standards, start-ups can proactively address compliance challenges and position themselves for sustainable growth. Registering a business name is foundational in establishing brand identity and ensuring legal recognition. Entrepreneurs must carefully select a business name that reflects their brand essence while complying with naming regulations. This involves conducting thorough research to ensure the chosen name is available and distinct from existing entities. By adhering to naming guidelines and crafting a memorable brand identity, start-ups can lay the groundwork for effective marketing and branding strategies. Obtaining an Employer Identification Number (EIN) is essential for start-ups embarking on hiring processes and conducting business transactions. The EIN serves as a unique identifier for the venture and is required for various tax-related purposes, including payroll processing and tax filings. Entrepreneurs can obtain an EIN through a straightforward application process with the Internal Revenue Service (IRS), enabling them to navigate taxation, banking, and employment matters with ease and compliance.

Obtaining state and local business licenses is imperative for start-ups to operate legally within their jurisdictions. These licenses vary depending on the nature of the business and the geographical location, encompassing permits for specific business activities and regulatory compliance requirements. Entrepreneurs must diligently research and apply for the necessary licenses to avoid potential penalties or disruptions to operations. By prioritizing compliance with state and local regulations, start-ups can develop trust with authorities and stakeholders. Navigating permits and zoning regulations is essential for start-ups engaging in physical operations or property use. Entrepreneurs must comply with local land use and development regulations, from construction permits to zoning approvals. Business activities and location can significantly impact permit requirements and zoning restrictions. By proactively addressing permit and zoning considerations, start-ups can mitigate legal risks and establish a framework for sustainable growth.

Tax registration is a critical aspect of start-up incorporation, encompassing federal, state, and local tax obligations. Entrepreneurs must register for tax purposes with the appropriate authorities and comply with ongoing tax requirements, including income tax, sales tax, and employment tax obligations. By staying abreast of tax regulations and implementing robust compliance measures, start-ups can optimize tax efficiency and avoid potential penalties or audits. Conducting Employment Eligibility Verification is essential for start-ups hiring employees and ensuring workforce legality. This process involves verifying new hires' identity and employment authorization through documentation such as passports or driver's licenses. By meticulously following the Form I-9 procedures outlined by the U.S. Citizenship and Immigration Services (USCIS), start-ups can demonstrate compliance with immigration laws and safeguard against potential legal liabilities related to unauthorized employment.

Ensuring compliance with environmental and safety regulations is paramount for start-ups to uphold workplace safety standards and environmental sustainability. Start-ups must assess and mitigate risks related to hazardous materials, waste disposal, and workplace conditions to protect employees and the environment. Implementing measures such as proper waste management protocols, employee training on safety procedures and regular inspections of facilities can help start-ups maintain compliance with regulations set by environmental protection agencies and occupational safety authorities. Registering intellectual property (IP) during the incorporation process is essential for safeguarding the venture's innovations and branding. Start-ups should pursue trademark registration to protect their unique brand names and logos, patent registration to safeguard inventions and technologies, and copyright registration to protect original works of authorship, such as software code or creative content. By securing IP rights, start-ups can prevent unauthorized use or infringement by competitors and establish a solid foundation for their competitive advantage and market positioning. Addressing data protection and privacy compliance is critical in today's digital age, where the collection and processing of personal information are commonplace. Start-ups must adhere to regulations such as the General Data Protection Regulation (GDPR) or the California Consumer Privacy Act (CCPA) to ensure the lawful handling of customer and employee data. Implementing measures such as data encryption, access controls, and privacy policies can help start-ups mitigate risks associated with data breaches and protect the privacy rights of individuals.

Maintaining accurate corporate records and compliance documentation is essential for demonstrating transparency, accountability, and adherence to regulatory requirements. Start-ups should keep meticulous records of corporate meetings, resolutions, ownership changes, and financial transactions to fulfil legal obligations and facilitate audits or due diligence processes. By documenting compliance efforts comprehensively, start-ups can mitigate legal risks, build investor confidence, and establish a robust corporate governance framework. Sustaining compliance post-incorporation requires a proactive approach to staying informed about regulatory changes and addressing compliance issues promptly. Start-ups should establish processes for monitoring regulatory updates, conducting regular compliance audits, and implementing corrective actions as needed. By developing a culture of compliance and accountability within the organization, start-ups can minimize legal liabilities, maintain operational continuity, and uphold their reputation as responsible corporate citizens.

Analysing case studies of start-ups that successfully navigated compliance challenges offers valuable insights into effective compliance strategies. By examining how start-ups identified regulatory requirements, implemented robust compliance frameworks, and responded to regulatory inquiries or audits, entrepreneurs can glean best practices and lessons applicable to their ventures. Identifying common pitfalls and innovative solutions from real-world examples empowers start-ups to address compliance risks and optimize their regulatory compliance efforts proactively. Engaging participants in a workshop to create a compliance checklist and action plan for a simulated start-up facilitates collaborative learning and practical skill development. By guiding participants through identifying industry-specific regulatory requirements, assessing compliance gaps, and devising proactive compliance measures, the workshop equips entrepreneurs with the tools and knowledge needed to navigate complex regulatory landscapes. By collaboratively developing a tailored compliance strategy, participants can apply theoretical concepts to real-world scenarios and enhance their readiness to address compliance challenges in their ventures.

Navigating compliance and registration processes is vital for start-up success. The above discussion empowers entrepreneurs with the knowledge and practical insights needed to ensure that their ventures adhere to legal requirements, laying a foundation for sustainable growth and operations.

4.8. Social Impact and Responsibility

Social impact and responsibility are integral to modern entrepreneurship, emphasizing businesses' contribution to society. The following discussion explores social impact and responsibility, guiding entrepreneurs to integrate meaningful social initiatives into their ventures. From identifying opportunities for positive change to implementing sustainable practices, entrepreneurs will gain insights into developing a socially responsible and impactful business model.

4.8.1 Integrating Social Impact into Business

Social impact in business refers to the tangible and intangible effects of a company's activities on society and the environment beyond financial profit. It encompasses initiatives and practices to address social, environmental, and economic challenges while generating sustainable value for stakeholders. By adopting a broader perspective of success that considers financial returns and social and environmental outcomes, businesses can contribute to positive change and address pressing societal issues such as poverty, inequality, and climate change. Entrepreneurs can identify opportunities for social impact by aligning business goals with societal needs and market trends. This involves conducting market research, engaging with stakeholders, and assessing business activities' social and environmental impact. By understanding communities' needs and challenges, entrepreneurs can develop innovative solutions, products, and services that address pressing issues and create positive change. Opportunities for social impact may arise in healthcare, education, environmental conservation, and poverty alleviation. Sustainability in business operations involves integrating practices that minimize environmental impact, conserve resources, and promote long-term viability. Entrepreneurs can adopt sustainable practices such as reducing energy consumption, minimizing waste generation, using renewable resources, and promoting responsible supply chain management. By embracing eco-friendly technologies and business models, entrepreneurs can reduce their environmental footprint and enhance operational efficiency and resilience in the face of evolving environmental challenges. Social innovation in entrepreneurship involves developing creative solutions to address social and environmental challenges while creating economic value. Entrepreneurs can engage with local communities, stakeholders, and non-profit organizations to understand community needs and co-create solutions that have a meaningful impact. By building collaboration and partnerships, businesses can leverage local knowledge, resources, and networks to address complex social problems and drive positive change at the grassroots level.

Corporate Social Responsibility (CSR) programs integrate social and environmental considerations into business operations and decision-making processes. Businesses can establish CSR initiatives that align with their core values, business objectives, and stakeholder expectations. These initiatives may include philanthropy, employee volunteering programs, environmental conservation efforts, and community development projects. By investing in CSR programs, businesses can build trust, enhance brand reputation, and contribute to the well-being of society. Ethical business practices involve conducting business that upholds honesty, integrity, fairness, and respect for stakeholders' rights. Entrepreneurs can establish ethical standards and codes of conduct that guide decision-making and behaviour within their organizations. This includes treating employees, customers, suppliers, and communities with dignity and fairness, avoiding unethical practices such as fraud, corruption, and exploitation, and ensuring transparency and accountability in business operations. By prioritizing ethical considerations, businesses can build trust, long-term relationships, and positively impact society.

Measuring and reporting social impact is essential for evaluating the effectiveness of social initiatives and demonstrating accountability to stakeholders. Businesses can employ various strategies, including qualitative and quantitative methods, to measure social impact. Qualitative methods may involve gathering feedback from beneficiaries, conducting case studies, and assessing changes in behaviour or attitudes. Quantitative methods may include tracking key performance indicators (KPIs) such as the number of beneficiaries reached, the amount of resources invested, and the outcomes achieved. By collecting and analysing data on social impact, businesses can assess progress, identify areas for improvement, and communicate results transparently through impact reports and disclosures. Stakeholder engagement promotes social good by collaboration, dialogue, and collective action. Businesses can engage with stakeholders, including employees, customers, suppliers, investors, and the local community, to understand their needs, concerns, and priorities related to social issues. By soliciting input, involving stakeholders in decision-making processes, and seeking feedback on social initiatives, businesses can build trust, enhance credibility, and ensure their efforts align with community needs and expectations. Effective stakeholder engagement can lead to co-creation opportunities and collaborative solutions that maximize social impact. Inclusivity in business practices involves creating a work environment that embraces diversity, equity, and inclusion, ensuring all individuals has fair and equal opportunities for growth and participation. Businesses can implement diversity training, inclusive hiring practices, and employee resource groups to promote diversity and combat discrimination. Businesses can enhance creativity, innovation, and productivity by developing a culture of inclusion where employees feel valued, respected, and empowered to contribute their unique perspectives and talents. Inclusive business practices also extend to customer interactions, product development, and community engagement, ensuring that all stakeholders are represented and supported.

Establishing environmental and social responsibility policies is crucial for guiding business practices and ensuring alignment with sustainability goals and ethical principles. Environmental policies may include commitments to reduce carbon emissions, minimize waste generation, and conserve natural resources through sustainable sourcing and production practices. Social responsibility policies may encompass initiatives to promote diversity, equity, and inclusion within the workplace, support community development projects, and uphold human rights throughout the supply chain. By integrating policies prioritizing environmental stewardship, social justice, and ethical conduct, businesses can demonstrate their commitment to corporate citizenship and responsible business practices. Partnerships and collaborations with non-profits, NGOs, government agencies, and other organizations can amplify the social impact of businesses by leveraging complementary resources, expertise, and networks. Businesses can identify potential partners with similar values and objectives, establish clear goals and expectations, and develop collaborative initiatives that address shared challenges and opportunities. By pooling resources, sharing knowledge, and coordinating efforts, businesses and their partners can achieve grander scale, efficiency, and effectiveness in tackling complex social issues. Impactful partnerships can also facilitate knowledge exchange, capacity-building and collective advocacy efforts that drive positive change at local, national, and global levels. Further, analysing case studies of businesses successfully integrating social impact into their operations can provide valuable insights into practical strategies, challenges, and outcomes. Successful businesses often demonstrate a commitment to social impact embedded in their mission, vision, and values, aligning with core business objectives and priorities. They engage with stakeholders, measure and report on social impact transparently and continuously iterate and improve their initiatives based on feedback and evaluation results. By developing a culture of innovation, collaboration, and accountability, businesses can overcome challenges and achieve meaningful outcomes that benefit society and the bottom line.

Social impact and responsibility are integral to a sustainable and forward-thinking business model. The following discussion equips entrepreneurs with the knowledge and strategies needed to create positive social change through their ventures, creating a business environment that goes beyond profit and contributes to the well-being of society.

4.8.2 Corporate Social Responsibility (CSR)

Corporate Social Responsibility (CSR) is a strategic approach that encourages businesses to embrace responsibility for their impact on the environment, communities, and society. The following discussion explores into the concept of CSR, guiding entrepreneurs in developing and implementing meaningful CSR initiatives. From aligning CSR with business values to measuring the impact of these initiatives, entrepreneurs will gain insights into creating a socially responsible and sustainable business philosophy.

Corporate Social Responsibility (CSR) encompasses businesses' voluntary actions to address social, environmental, and ethical concerns in addition to their legal obligations. CSR has become increasingly significant in today's business landscape as stakeholders demand greater corporate accountability and transparency. This approach represents a shift from a narrow focus on profit maximization to a broader recognition of businesses' impact on society. By integrating CSR into their operations, companies can enhance their reputation, build trust with stakeholders, and contribute to sustainable development. Moreover, CSR initiatives can bring tangible benefits such as improved employee morale, increased customer loyalty, and enhanced long-term profitability. Aligning CSR initiatives with the business's core values is essential for ensuring authenticity and consistency in corporate behaviour. Businesses must identify CSR focus areas that resonate with their mission, vision, and stakeholders' expectations. For example, a company committed to environmental stewardship may prioritize initiatives to reduce carbon emissions, minimize waste, and conserve natural resources. Similarly, a company passionately committed to social equity may focus on initiatives to promote diversity, support underserved communities, and empower marginalized groups. By aligning CSR with business values, companies can demonstrate their commitment to making a meaningful and sustainable impact on their stakeholders in relevant and meaningful areas. Developing a comprehensive CSR strategy involves a systematic approach to setting goals, outlining action plans, and integrating CSR into the overall business strategy. The first step is thoroughly assessing the company's internal and external environment to identify key CSR opportunities and challenges. Based on this assessment, companies can define clear and measurable CSR goals that align with their mission, values, and stakeholder expectations. Next, companies should develop action plans that outline specific initiatives, timelines, responsibilities, and resource allocations. Integrating CSR into the business strategy involves embedding CSR principles and practices into decision-making processes, organizational culture, and performance management systems.

Stakeholder engagement is critical for the success of CSR initiatives as it ensures that all stakeholders' interests, perspectives, and needs are considered and addressed. Businesses can engage with stakeholders, including employees, customers, suppliers, and the local community, through various channels such as surveys, focus groups, town hall meetings, and stakeholder advisory groups. Companies can gain valuable insights, build trust, and develop collaborative relationships by involving stakeholders in the CSR planning and implementation process. Moreover, stakeholder engagement can enhance CSR initiatives' relevance, effectiveness, and credibility by ensuring that they reflect the diverse needs and priorities of the communities and individuals they aim to serve. Incorporating environmental sustainability into CSR initiatives is essential for mitigating environmental impact, promoting conservation, and developing a more sustainable future. Companies can adopt strategies to reduce greenhouse gas emissions, conserve natural resources, and minimize waste generation. For example, companies may invest in renewable energy sources, implement energy-efficient technologies, and adopt sustainable supply chain practices. Moreover, companies can engage in environmental stewardship activities such as reforestation projects, water conservation efforts, and habitat restoration initiatives. By prioritizing environmental sustainability in CSR, companies can address pressing environmental challenges and create a more resilient and sustainable planet for future generations.

CSR initiatives drive social impact and community development by addressing pressing social issues, improving quality of life, and promoting inclusive growth. Companies can support community development through initiatives such as philanthropy, volunteerism, and strategic partnerships with non-profit organizations and community groups. For example, companies may invest in education and vocational training programs, healthcare facilities, and infrastructure projects to enhance community well-being. Moreover, companies can empower local communities by creating economic opportunities, supporting small businesses, and promoting entrepreneurship. By engaging in social impact and community development, companies can build resilient, inclusive, and thriving communities where individuals and families can lead fulfilling and prosperous lives.

Integrating ethical business practices into CSR is paramount for developing a culture of integrity, fairness, and ethical decision-making within the organization. CSR initiatives allow businesses to demonstrate their commitment to ethical conduct and responsible business behaviour. By adhering to ethical principles such as honesty, transparency, and accountability, companies can earn the trust and respect of stakeholders, including employees, customers, investors, and the broader community. Moreover, ethical business practices build a positive corporate reputation, mitigate risks, and enhance long-term sustainability. Companies can establish codes of conduct, ethical guidelines, and compliance mechanisms within CSR programs to ensure their actions align with ethical standards and societal expectations. CSR initiatives can profoundly impact employee engagement and well-being by creating a workplace culture that values social responsibility and employee satisfaction. Employees are increasingly seeking purpose-driven work environments where they can contribute to meaningful causes and make a positive impact beyond their daily tasks. CSR programs that engage employees in volunteer activities, community service projects, and sustainability initiatives can enhance morale, motivation, and job satisfaction. Moreover, companies can support employee well-being by offering benefits such as work-life balance initiatives, wellness programs, and opportunities for professional development. By prioritizing employee engagement and well-being within CSR, companies can attract and retain top talent, boost productivity, and build a cohesive and committed workforce.

Philanthropy and charitable initiatives play a vital role in CSR by allowing businesses to contribute to charitable causes and positively impact society. Through philanthropic efforts, companies can support non-profit organizations, community development projects, and humanitarian relief. Through financial donations, contributions, or volunteerism, businesses can address critical social concerns such as poverty alleviation, education access, healthcare access, and environmental protection. Philanthropic activities not only benefit the recipients of aid but also enhance the reputation and social standing of the company. By aligning philanthropy with the company's values and mission, businesses can demonstrate their commitment to social responsibility and contribute to building more robust and resilient communities. Measuring and reporting the impact of CSR initiatives is essential for evaluating effectiveness, tracking progress, and communicating outcomes to stakeholders. Companies can utilize various strategies, key performance indicators (KPIs), metrics, and reporting frameworks to assess their CSR programs' social, environmental, and economic impact. Common KPIs may include metrics related to environmental sustainability, social impact, employee engagement, community development, and financial performance. By collecting and analysing data on CSR activities, companies can identify areas for improvement, demonstrate accountability, and enhance transparency. Moreover, transparent, and accurate reporting of CSR impact helps build stakeholder trust, attract investors, and differentiate the company in the marketplace.

Businesses can integrate CSR into marketing and branding efforts to enhance brand reputation and consumer loyalty. By effectively communicating CSR initiatives through marketing channels, companies can display their commitment to social responsibility and differentiate themselves from competitors. Strategies for integrating CSR into marketing and branding may include highlighting CSR achievements in advertising campaigns, packaging designs, social media posts, and corporate communications. Moreover, companies can engage consumers in CSR initiatives through cause-related marketing campaigns, corporate partnerships, and customer loyalty programs. By aligning marketing messages with CSR values and objectives, companies can build a strong brand identity, strengthen customer relationships, and drive business growth. Ensuring compliance and ethical standards within CSR is essential for maintaining trust, credibility, and legitimacy. Businesses must ensure their CSR initiatives adhere to legal requirements, industry standards, and ethical principles. This includes complying with relevant laws and regulations and reporting obligations related to CSR activities. Moreover, companies should uphold ethical standards such as integrity, honesty, fairness, and respect for human rights in all CSR programs. Companies can identify and address potential compliance issues, ethical dilemmas, and reputational risks by conducting due diligence, risk assessments, and internal audits. Additionally, businesses should establish mechanisms for receiving feedback, addressing grievances, and remedying any adverse impacts of their CSR initiatives on stakeholders or the environment. Through a commitment to compliance and ethical standards, companies can ensure that their CSR efforts contribute to positive social change while upholding the highest standards of corporate conduct.

Implementing Corporate Social Responsibility is a powerful way for businesses to contribute positively to society while enhancing sustainability. The following discussion provides entrepreneurs with practical guidance on developing and implementing CSR initiatives that align with their business values and creates a positive social impact.

4.8.3 Measuring and Communicating Social Impact

Measuring and communicating social impact is crucial for businesses committed to Corporate Social Responsibility (CSR). The following discussion explores into the methodologies and strategies for effectively measuring the social impact of CSR initiatives and communicating these outcomes to stakeholders. Entrepreneurs will gain insights into selecting meaningful metrics, employing assessment tools, and crafting compelling narratives highlighting the positive change generated by their social responsibility efforts. Figure 4.10 illustrates the components of a social impact assessment, emphasizing the comprehensive approach required to evaluate the broader societal implications of business activities.

Measuring social impact within the realm of CSR is vital as it provides businesses with tangible evidence of their contributions to societal well-being and sustainable development. By quantifying and assessing the outcomes of CSR initiatives, companies can demonstrate accountability to stakeholders, including investors, customers, employees, and the wider community. Impact measurement serves as a mechanism for evaluating the effectiveness of CSR programs, identifying areas for improvement, and optimizing resource allocation. Moreover, it develops a culture of continuous learning and innovation, driving organizational growth and positive social change. Through transparent and data-driven impact measurement practices, businesses can build trust, enhance reputation, and strengthen their social license to operate. Selecting meaningful metrics for social impact measurement is a strategic process that aligns with the objectives and values of CSR initiatives. Businesses must identify key performance indicators (KPIs) that reflect the desired outcomes and intended beneficiaries of their social responsibility efforts. These metrics may encompass various impact dimensions, including environmental sustainability, community development, employee well-being, and stakeholder engagement. By selecting relevant and measurable KPIs, companies can track progress, benchmark performance, and effectively communicate the value of their CSR initiatives. Balancing quantitative and qualitative assessment methods is essential for understanding social impact comprehensively. While quantitative metrics provide numerical data and quantitative insights into the scale and reach of CSR initiatives, qualitative assessments offer nuanced insights into stakeholders' lived experiences, perceptions, and narratives. By combining data-driven metrics with qualitative feedback, companies can capture the multifaceted nature of social impact and uncover hidden dimensions of success or areas for improvement. This comprehensive approach to impact assessment enables businesses to tell compelling stories about the meaningful change generated by their CSR efforts.

Utilizing assessment tools for social impact measurement facilitates systematic evaluation and reporting of CSR outcomes. Various frameworks and methodologies, such as the Social Return on Investment (SROI) methodology and the Global Reporting Initiative (GRI), provide standardized approaches for assessing social, environmental, and economic impacts. These tools enable businesses to quantify the value created by their CSR initiatives, calculate return on investment, and compare performance over time or against industry benchmarks. Additionally, industry-specific standards and certification schemes guide best practices for impact measurement and reporting, enhancing transparency and credibility.

Involving stakeholders in the impact measurement process is essential for capturing diverse perspectives, enhancing transparency, and enhancing the relevance of assessment outcomes. Engaging communities, employees, customers, and other relevant stakeholders allows businesses to gather first-hand insights, validate findings, and ensure that impact measurement efforts are inclusive and participatory. Strategies for stakeholder involvement may include conducting surveys, focus groups, interviews, and participatory workshops to solicit feedback, gather testimonials, and co-create impact narratives. Businesses can build trust, strengthen relationships, and drive continuous improvement in their CSR initiatives by actively involving stakeholders in the impact measurement process. Effectively communicating social impact is crucial for maximizing the visibility and influence of CSR initiatives. Businesses can employ various communication strategies to highlight the outcomes of their social responsibility efforts and engage stakeholders. These strategies may include crafting compelling narratives highlighting the human stories behind CSR initiatives, using visuals such as info graphics, photographs, and videos to convey impact visually appealingly, and leveraging storytelling techniques to evoke empathy and connection with the audience. By tailoring communication messages to resonate with different stakeholders and channels, businesses can amplify the reach and relevance of their social impact stories, creating awareness, support, and engagement.

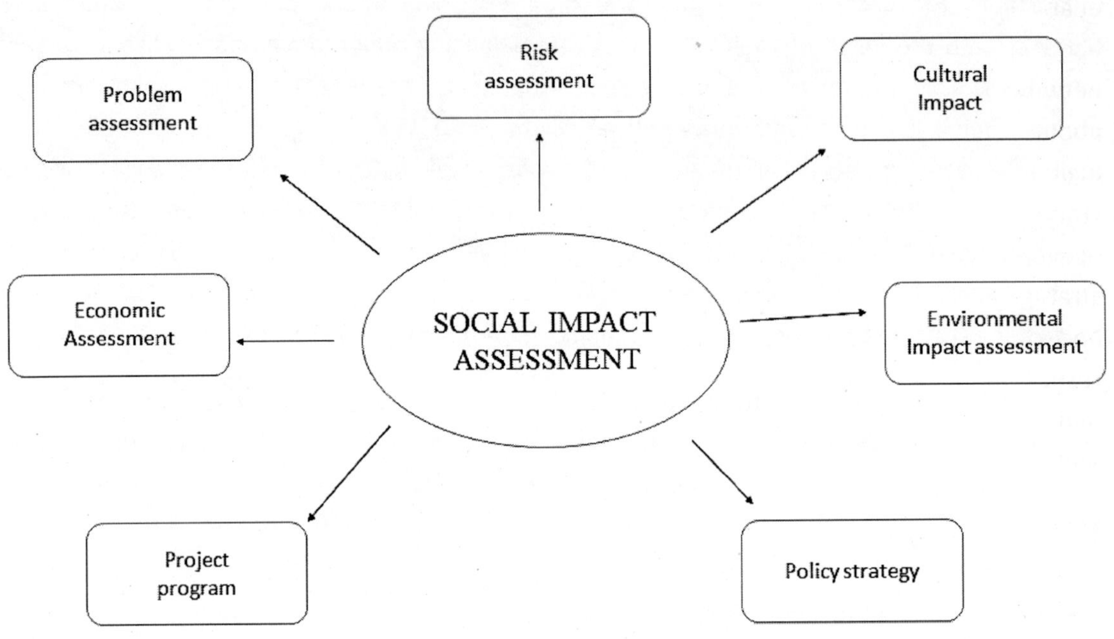

Figure 4.10 Components of Social Impact Assessment

Transparency and accountability are foundational principles in social impact reporting, demonstrating a commitment to openness, integrity, and responsible stewardship. Businesses can build trust with stakeholders by embracing transparency in their communication practices and openly sharing successes and challenges encountered in their CSR initiatives. By providing clear, honest, and timely information about social impact outcomes, businesses can demonstrate accountability for their actions, decisions, and performance. Additionally, businesses can cultivate a culture of continuous improvement by transparently communicating lessons learned and areas for future development, developing trust, credibility, and long-term stakeholder relationships. Integrating social impact reporting into annual reports allows businesses to present a comprehensive performance overview, combining financial results with non-financial metrics related to social, environmental, and governance (ESG) factors. By including social impact indicators alongside traditional financial measures, businesses can give stakeholders a holistic view of their value creation and sustainable practices. This integrated approach to reporting allows businesses to highlight their commitment to corporate citizenship, responsible business practices, and long-term value creation, enhancing transparency, credibility, and stakeholder trust.

Digital platforms and social media offer potent channels for communicating social impact, enabling businesses to reach a wider audience, engage stakeholders, and meaningful conversations about CSR initiatives. By leveraging online channels such as corporate websites, blogs, social networking sites, and multimedia platforms, businesses can share stories, updates, and insights about their social impact efforts in real time. Strategies for effective impact communication on digital platforms may include creating engaging content, utilizing multimedia formats to enhance storytelling, leveraging user-generated content and influencer partnerships to amplify reach, and actively engaging with followers through comments, shares, and interactive features. Through the strategic use of digital platforms and social media, businesses can enhance their visibility, credibility, and influence in CSR. Effectively measuring and communicating social impact is a pivotal aspect of responsible business practices. The following discussion equips entrepreneurs with the knowledge and tools needed to assess the outcomes of CSR initiatives and share these results with authenticity and transparency, reinforcing the positive contributions of their ventures to society.

Unit summary

The unit on Venture Creation: Sustainable Business Options & Pathways offers a comprehensive exploration of the process of establishing and managing entrepreneurial ventures with a focus on sustainability. Throughout the unit, learners explore into various aspects of sustainable entrepreneurship, starting from understanding sustainable business models and pathways. They gain insights into developing robust business models and canvases tailored to sustainable ventures while learning about assembling and managing start-up teams committed to sustainability. The unit emphasizes the importance of collaboration and partnership models with stakeholders aligned with sustainable goals and guiding navigating the broader start-up ecosystem.

Furthermore, learners explore the role of technology business incubators and parks in nurturing sustainable start-ups and gain practical skills in proposal pitching, negotiation, and drafting agreements that prioritize sustainability objectives. The unit also covers essential legal and procedural aspects of start-up company incorporation, ensuring compliance with regulations and standards relevant to sustainable ventures. Integrating social impact considerations into sustainable ventures' core mission and operations is central to the unit. Learners are equipped with strategies for measuring and communicating social impact to stakeholders and the wider community, emphasizing the significance of social responsibility in entrepreneurship. The unit prepares learners to conceptualize, launch, and sustain entrepreneurial ventures prioritizing sustainability, social impact, and responsible business practices. Through theoretical knowledge and practical skills, learners are empowered to navigate the complex landscape of sustainable entrepreneurship with confidence and efficacy.

Tutorial questions for practice

1. Business Model Canvas Workshop:
   - Introduce students to the Business Model Canvas (BMC) framework and its components.
   - Provide students with case studies or hypothetical startup ideas.
   - Guide students through filling out the BMC for their chosen startup, considering customer segments, value propositions, revenue streams, and cost structures.
   - Facilitate group discussions to share and analyse different BMCs, allowing students to gain insights into various business models and their effectiveness.
2. Start-up Ecosystem Exploration:
   - Organize a panel discussion or invite guest speakers from different sectors of the start-up ecosystem, such as entrepreneurs, investors, incubator managers, and government representatives.
   - Allow students to ask questions and interact with the panellists to understand the roles and dynamics of various stakeholders in the start-up ecosystem.
   - Assign students to research and present case studies of successful start-ups and their interactions with the ecosystem, highlighting key partnerships, funding sources, and support services utilized.
3. Proposal Pitching Simulation:
   - Divide students into teams and assign each team a hypothetical start-up idea.
   - Task teams with developing a pitch deck and presenting their business idea to the class or a panel of judges.
   - Provide feedback and constructive criticism to each team, focusing on elements such as clarity of the value proposition, market opportunity, competitive analysis, and financial projections.
   - Encourage teams to refine their pitches based on feedback and present improved versions in subsequent sessions.

4. Social Impact Business Model Workshop:

    - Discuss social impact and corporate social responsibility (CSR) with students, emphasizing the importance of incorporating social and environmental considerations into business models.

    - Present case studies of social enterprises and businesses that have successfully integrated social impact into their operations.

    - Challenge students to develop business models for social impact ventures, considering factors such as mission alignment, stakeholder engagement, and measuring impact metrics.

    - Encourage students to think creatively about how their start-up ideas can generate positive social or environmental outcomes while remaining financially sustainable.

5. Start-up Company Incorporation Process:

    - Walk students through incorporating a start-up company, including legal requirements, registration procedures, and necessary documentation.

    - Provide resources and guidance on choosing the appropriate legal structure (e.g., sole proprietorship, partnership, and corporation) based on the nature of the business and future growth plans.

    - Discuss the implications of incorporation on liability, taxation, and governance, helping students understand the legal and financial responsibilities of starting a business.

    - Allow students to simulate the incorporation process by completing relevant forms and paperwork in a workshop, providing hands-on experience and practical knowledge.

Review questions

1. What are the critical components of a sustainable business model, and why are they essential for entrepreneurial ventures?

2. How do sustainable business models differ from traditional business models regarding objectives and strategies?

3. Describe the pathways available for entrepreneurs to establish sustainable ventures and discuss the factors influencing their choice.

4. What role do startup teams play in the success of sustainable ventures, and how can they be assembled effectively?

5. Explain the significance of collaboration and stakeholder partnerships in sustainable entrepreneurship.

6. How do technology business incubators and parks support the growth and development of sustainable start-ups?

7. What are the essential elements of a business canvas for a sustainable venture, and how does it differ from a traditional business canvas?

8. Discuss the importance of incorporating social impact considerations into the mission and operations of sustainable ventures.

9. What legal and procedural aspects should entrepreneurs consider when incorporating a sustainable start-up company?

10. How can entrepreneurs effectively pitch proposals and negotiate agreements prioritizing sustainability objectives?

11. Describe the process of measuring and communicating social impact for sustainable ventures.

12. What strategies can entrepreneurs use to ensure compliance with regulations and standards relevant to sustainable ventures?

13. Explain the concept of responsible business practices in the context of sustainable entrepreneurship.

14. How do sustainable ventures assess and manage risks associated with their operations and business models?

15. Discuss the challenges and opportunities of financing sustainable ventures at various stages of their lifecycle.

16. What are the various funding sources available to sustainable start-ups, and how do entrepreneurs choose between them?

17. Describe the role of financial projections and accounting principles in ensuring the sustainability of entrepreneurial ventures.

18. How do entrepreneurs transition from start-up to scale-up financing while maintaining their sustainability objectives?

19. Explain the importance of aligning financial goals with sustainability objectives in entrepreneurial ventures.

20. What are the critical considerations for sustainable ventures when selecting distribution channels and designing sales networks?

21. Discuss the role of strategic partnerships and alliances in supporting the growth and expansion of sustainable ventures.

22. How do sustainable ventures navigate the startup ecosystem to access resources, networks, and support services?

23. What are sustainable ventures' potential social and environmental impacts, and how can they be maximized?

24. Describe the process of incorporating feedback and iterative improvement into the operations of sustainable ventures.

25. How can sustainable ventures leverage technology and innovation to enhance their competitiveness and impact?

26. Discuss the role of leadership and organizational culture in fostering sustainability within entrepreneurial ventures.

27. What strategies can sustainable ventures employ to build resilience and adaptability in the face of environmental and market uncertainties?

28. Explain the concept of circular economy principles and their application in sustainable entrepreneurship.

29. How do sustainable ventures balance profitability with social and environmental responsibility in their decision-making processes?

30. Describe the potential long-term benefits of investing in sustainability for entrepreneurs and society.

Multiple Choice Questions:

1. Sustainable business options refer to:
   a) Short-term profit-maximizing strategies
   b) Long-term environmentally friendly practices
   c) Rapid expansion plans
   d) Cost-cutting measures
2. The Business Model Canvas is a framework used to:
   a) Map out a start-up's organizational structure
   b) Identify potential business partners
   c) Visualize and analyse a start-up's business model
   d) Develop marketing strategies
3. A startup team typically consists of:
   a) Only technical experts
   b) Only business professionals
   c) Diverse individuals with complementary skills
   d) Investors and shareholders
4. Technology business incubators and parks provide start-ups with:
   a) Physical space and infrastructure
   b) Funding opportunities
   c) Legal advice
   d) Marketing support
5. Proposal pitching is the process of:
   a) Presenting a business idea to potential investors or partners
   b) Negotiating terms of a business agreement
   c) Developing a marketing campaign
   d) Hiring new team members

Fill in the Blanks:

1. Start-up ______________ and business partners play crucial roles in the success of a new venture.
2. The Business Model Canvas helps entrepreneurs visualize and analyse the critical components of their ______________.
3. Start-up ______________ provide valuable resources and support to early-stage ventures.
4. Proposal pitching is an essential step in securing ______________ and agreements with investors or partners.

5. Start-up company ______________ involves registering the business entity with the appropriate authorities.

Answers - Multiple Choice Questions:

1. b) Long-term environmentally friendly practices
2. c) Visualize and analyse a start-up's business model
3. c) Diverse individuals with complementary skills
4. a) Physical space and infrastructure
5. a) Presenting a business idea to potential investors or partners

Answers - Fill in the Blanks:

1. team & business partners
2. business model
3. ecosystems
4. funding
5. incorporation

References for Suggested Reading

1. Soltanifar, Mariusz, Mathew Hughes, and Lutz Göcke. *Digital entrepreneurship: Impact on business and society*. Springer Nature, 2021.
2. Timmons, Jeffry A., Stephen Spinelli, and Yinglan Tan. *New venture creation: Entrepreneurship for the 21st century*. Vol. 6. New York: McGraw-Hill/Irwin, 2004.
3. Amabile, Teresa M. "A model of creativity and innovation in organizations." *Research in organizational behavior* 10.1 (1988): 123-167.
4. George, Gerard, and Adam J. Bock. *Models of opportunity: How entrepreneurs design firms to achieve the unexpected.* Cambridge University Press, 2012.

UNIT 5 Course Project

UNIT SPECIFICS: Course Project

This unit focuses on developing a comprehensive Product Innovation & Entrepreneurship course project. Key components include:

1. Need Identification: Identifying a specific problem or opportunity in the market or society that warrants innovative solutions.
2. Innovative Solution: Developing a novel and feasible solution to address the identified need, leveraging creative thinking and design principles.
3. Business Plan: Creating a detailed business plan outlining the value proposition, market analysis, revenue model, and operational strategy for the proposed venture.
4. Go-to-Market Strategy: Formulating a strategic plan for launching the product or service into the market, including marketing, distribution, and sales strategies.

RATIONALE

The course project provides students with a hands-on opportunity to apply the concepts and frameworks learned throughout the course to a real-world scenario. By engaging in the entire process of identifying a need, developing an innovative solution, creating a business plan, and devising a go-to-market strategy, students gain valuable experience in entrepreneurship and innovation. This practical exercise enhances their critical thinking, problem-solving, and decision-making skills, preparing them for future entrepreneurial endeavours.

PRE-REQUISITES

Fundamental market analysis, financial modelling, and project management proficiency are desired. Prior coursework or experience in related fields such as marketing, design thinking, and new product development would be beneficial.

UNIT OUTCOMES

Upon completing this unit, students will be able to:

U5-O1: Identify market needs and opportunities through systematic research and analysis.

U5-O2: Develop innovative solutions that address identified needs, applying creative problem-solving techniques and design thinking principles.

U5-O3: Create a comprehensive business plan articulating a new venture's value proposition, target market, revenue model, and operational strategy.

U5-O4: Formulate a strategic go-to-market strategy outlining the marketing, distribution, and sales tactics for successfully launching the product or service.

U5-O5: Present their course project effectively, demonstrating a clear understanding of their proposed venture's problem-solution fit, market potential, and business viability.

Unit-5 Outcomes	**Expected Mapping with Programme Outcomes** *(1- Weak Correlation; 2- Medium correlation; 3- Strong Correlation)*				
	CO-1	CO -2	CO -3	CO -4	CO -5
U5-O1	3	2	3	2	3
U5-O2	3	1	2	1	2
U5-O3	2	3	3	1	2
U5-O4	3	2	3	2	3
U5-O5	3	3	2	3	1

The Course Project represents the culmination of the knowledge and skills acquired through exploring product innovation and entrepreneurship. In this unit, students embark on a comprehensive endeavour that integrates the principles, strategies, and methodologies covered in previous units. They will apply their understanding of market needs identification, innovative solution development, business planning, and go-to-market strategies as they navigate the project. This practical application solidifies their comprehension of the subject matter and cultivates their ability to synthesize and implement entrepreneurial concepts. The Course Project serves as a testament to their growth as aspiring entrepreneurs, providing a platform to highlight their proficiency in addressing real-world challenges and contributing innovative solutions to the entrepreneurial landscape.

5.1. Introduction to the Course Project

The Course Project is the pinnacle of the "Product Innovation and Entrepreneurship" journey, providing students with a dynamic platform to synthesize theoretical knowledge into practical application. This introductory section aims to provide a comprehensive overview of the Course Project, offering students insight into the structure, objectives, and significance of this culminating experience.

5.1.1 Overview of the Course Project

The Course Project is designed to provide participants with the opportunity to apply entrepreneurial principles to real-world scenarios, fostering critical thinking, problem-solving, and decision-making skills essential for entrepreneurial success. Through hands-on project work, individuals gain practical experience in identifying market opportunities, developing innovative solutions, and crafting viable business strategies. This experiential learning approach allows participants to move beyond theoretical knowledge, engaging directly with the challenges and opportunities of entrepreneurship. Integrating learning outcomes from each course unit, the Course Project serves as a platform for synthesizing knowledge from various aspects of entrepreneurship, such as market research, innovation processes, business planning, and startup strategies. By connecting theoretical concepts with practical applications, the project reinforces participants' comprehension and retention of course content, providing a holistic understanding of entrepreneurship. This integration ensures that individuals can see the practical relevance of what they have learned and how different elements of entrepreneurship interrelate.

One of the key features of the Course Project is its emphasis on real-world application. Through simulation exercises and practical challenges, participants are exposed to the complexities and uncertainties inherent in the entrepreneurial process. This exposure helps them develop the resilience, adaptability, and creativity required to navigate the entrepreneurial landscape effectively. By grappling with authentic scenarios and decision dilemmas, individuals are better prepared to handle the realities of starting and running a business. The Course Project is intricately linked to the overarching themes of product innovation and entrepreneurship explored throughout the course. It encapsulates the essence of identifying market needs, conceptualizing innovative solutions, and formulating strategic plans for business success. By aligning project objectives with course themes, participants gain a comprehensive understanding of the entrepreneurial journey, from ideation to execution. This cohesive approach ensures that the Course Project not only consolidates the learning experience but also prepares participants to apply their skills and knowledge in real-world entrepreneurial endeavours.

Within the Course Project, a delicate balance exists between individual contributions and collaborative efforts. Participants could leverage their unique strengths and perspectives while actively engaging in collaborative endeavours. By pooling their talents, insights, and resources, individuals can create a comprehensive entrepreneurial solution. This collaborative approach not only supports teamwork and cooperation but also enables participants to capitalize on diverse skill sets and experiences, thereby enhancing the overall quality and depth of the project outcomes. The Course Project unfolds through various stages, mirroring the iterative nature of the entrepreneurial journey. Participants embark on a transformative process that begins with initial ideation, progresses through concept development, validation, and implementation, and culminates in a final presentation. Each stage of the project lifecycle offers unique challenges and opportunities for learning and growth. By providing students with a structured roadmap, the project lifecycle empowers individuals to navigate the complexities of entrepreneurship methodically, ensuring progress and momentum toward their goals. The project deliverables, including the business plan, go-to-market strategy, and innovative solution, hold immense significance within the Course Project. These tangible outputs serve as manifestations of students' understanding and application of entrepreneurial concepts. The business plan provides a comprehensive roadmap for realizing the venture's vision, outlining strategies for sustainable growth and profitability. Similarly, the go-to-market strategy delineates actionable steps for introducing the product or service to the target market effectively. Finally, the innovative solution represents the culmination of creative ideation and problem-solving, highlighting participants' ability to develop novel and impactful solutions to real-world challenges. These deliverables not only demonstrate academic proficiency but also reflect students' capacity to innovate, strategize, and successfully execute entrepreneurial ventures.

The above discussion will serve as a guide, setting the stage for students to immerse themselves in a hands-on entrepreneurial experience. The Course Project is not merely an academic exercise but an opportunity for students to highlight their creativity, critical thinking, and entrepreneurial prowess in addressing authentic challenges within the business landscape.

5.1.2 Importance of Integrating Theory into Practice

Integrating theoretical concepts into practical application holds paramount importance in the entrepreneurial journey of this book. The following discussion aims to underscore the significance of bridging the gap between theory and practice, emphasizing how this integration enriches the learning experience and cultivates essential skills for aspiring entrepreneurs.

Creativity and innovation are pillars of progress and differentiation in the dynamic entrepreneurship landscape. This segment explores into how integrating theory into practice creativity and propels innovation to the forefront of entrepreneurial endeavours. By exploring this nexus, students embark on a journey of discovery, unearthing novel solutions and approaches to address the multifaceted challenges of entrepreneurship. At the heart of this exploration lies the Course Project, a vibrant crucible where theoretical knowledge converges with practical application to ignite sparks of creativity. Here, students are encouraged to transcend the boundaries of traditional thinking, delving into uncharted territories to uncover innovative solutions to real-world entrepreneurial challenges. By harnessing the power of creativity, they reimagine possibilities, challenge norms, and carve out new pathways toward entrepreneurial success. Central to this journey is the hands-on nature of the Course Project, which offers students a canvas to unleash their creative potential. Beyond the confines of traditional classroom settings, students immerse themselves in a dynamic learning experience where theory comes alive through practical application. As they grapple with real-world scenarios, they are empowered to experiment, iterate, and refine their ideas, nurturing a culture of creativity that fuels entrepreneurial innovation. Integral to integrating theory into practice is the cultivation of problem-solving skills, which serve as the bedrock of innovation. By confronting entrepreneurial challenges head-on, students are prompted to think critically, analyse situations, and devise inventive solutions. Through this process, they hone their ability to identify opportunities and develop the resilience and agility to adapt to evolving market dynamics, laying the groundwork for transformative innovation. Figure 5.1 illustrates the Course Project Journey, providing a visual roadmap for entrepreneurs to navigate through the various stages of their project from idea to market reach.

In the crucible of the Course Project, students are called upon to synthesize creativity with theoretical frameworks, forging a symbiotic relationship that propels innovation forward. They are encouraged to draw inspiration from established theories while challenging conventional wisdom to explore new horizons. By blending the rigors of theory with the fluidity of creativity, they create a fertile ground where innovative ideas take root and flourish, driving entrepreneurial endeavours towards uncharted territories of success. Accepting failure as an inherent part of the innovation process is central to the entrepreneurial journey. Through the Course Project, students learn to embrace failure not as a setback but as a stepping stone toward innovation. By developing a culture of experimentation and risk-taking, they cultivate the resilience and adaptability needed to navigate the uncertainties of entrepreneurship, transforming setbacks into springboards for creative breakthroughs. Integrating theory into practice guides students toward the nexus of creativity and innovation.

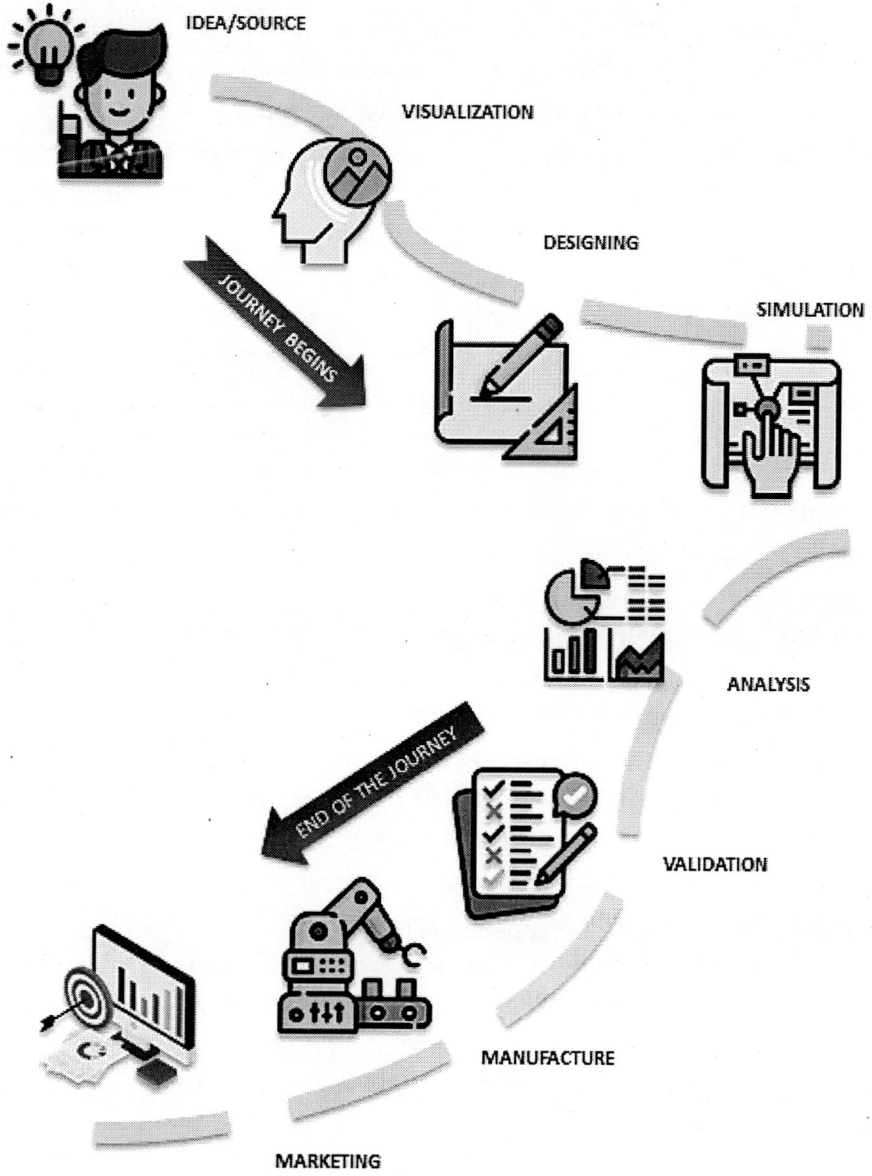

Figure 5.1 Visualizing the Course Project Journey

Through the Course Project, they embark on a transformative journey where theoretical knowledge intertwines with practical application to illuminate new pathways of entrepreneurial success. In this dynamic ecosystem, creativity flourishes, innovation thrives, and the seeds of entrepreneurial brilliance are sown, propelling students toward a future defined by bold ideas and ground-breaking ventures. Embarking on the entrepreneurial journey entails confronting many uncertainties and navigating dynamic environments. In this segment, we acknowledge the inherent complexities of entrepreneurship and emphasize how integrating theory into practice equips students with the resilience and adaptability needed to thrive amidst these challenges. By immersing themselves in real-world scenarios and honing their problem solving skills, students are primed to tackle the unpredictable nature of entrepreneurship with confidence and creativity. Central to preparing for entrepreneurial challenges is the recognition that adaptation and innovation are paramount. By embracing the hands-on nature of the Course Project, students learn to pivot and iterate in response to evolving circumstances, transforming setbacks into opportunities for growth. Through this iterative process, they cultivate the agility and resourcefulness needed to navigate the ever-shifting terrain of entrepreneurship, emerging more robust and more resilient in the face of adversity.

Amidst the uncertainties of entrepreneurship, grounding one's approach in theoretical foundations serves as a guiding light. Students gain invaluable insights into the underlying principles and frameworks that drive entrepreneurial success by integrating theory into practice. Armed with this knowledge, they are better equipped to anticipate challenges, evaluate opportunities, and make informed decisions during ambiguity. Thus, the integration of theory into practice not only prepares students to tackle real-world challenges but empowers them to navigate uncertainties with clarity and conviction. As aspiring entrepreneurs, students must align their skill sets and approaches with industry expectations and entrepreneurial best practices. In The following discussion, we underscore how integrating theory into practice bridges the gap between academic learning and real-world application, ensuring that students are well-prepared to meet the demands of the ever-evolving business landscape. By grounding their approaches in theoretical foundations, students gain a deeper understanding of industry dynamics, market trends, and consumer behaviour. This foundational knowledge enables them to develop strategic insights and innovative solutions that resonate with industry expectations and address emerging challenges. Through the Course Project, students can apply these theoretical frameworks in practical settings, honing their skills and refining their approaches in alignment with industry standards.

In today's fast-paced business environment, adaptability and innovation are key drivers of success. By integrating theory into practice, students learn to embrace change, challenge conventions, and pioneer new pathways for growth. Whether launching a start-up or driving innovation within established organizations, students emerge from the Course Project equipped with the tools and mind-set needed to thrive in a landscape defined by disruption and innovation.

Thus, the integration of theory into practice not only prepares students to meet industry expectations but empowers them to shape the future of entrepreneurship with vision and Vigor. The following discussion underscores that the fusion of theory and practice is not merely an academic exercise but a strategic approach to nurturing well-rounded and resourceful entrepreneurs. As students engage in the Course Project, they embark on a transformative journey beyond textbook knowledge, preparing them to thrive in entrepreneurship's dynamic and challenging realm.

5.1.3 Project Milestones and Deliverables

Understanding the structure and expectations of the Course Project is essential for effective planning and execution. The following discussion outlines the key milestones and deliverables students will encounter throughout the project, providing a roadmap for their entrepreneurial journey.

Embarking on the Course Project begins with the exciting ideation and project initiation phase. Here, you will research into a realm of exploration, brainstorming potential ideas for your entrepreneurial venture. This phase underscores the importance of conducting thorough market research and ideation to establish a robust foundation for your project. Immersing yourself in market trends, consumer preferences, and emerging opportunities will lay the groundwork for an innovative and viable venture that addresses real-world needs. Next, identifying unmet market needs is crucial to success in the entrepreneurship journey. This phase focuses on comprehensively researching and understanding the landscape to uncover areas ripe for innovation. By delving into consumer behaviours, industry dynamics, and emerging trends, you will gain valuable insights that inform the development of your entrepreneurial solution. Through diligent market needs identification, you will be equipped to craft a solution that resonates with your target audience and stands out in the competitive market. Figure 5.2 illustrates the process of identifying market needs, a crucial step in product innovation and entrepreneurship. This process involves conducting thorough market research to understand target customers' pain points, preferences, and unmet needs.

With a solid understanding of market needs, you will transition into the concept development phase and problem-solution fit. Here, you will harness your creativity to develop innovative solutions that address the identified market gaps. This phase emphasizes the iterative process of testing and refining your concepts to ensure alignment with customer needs and preferences. By validating problem-solution fit through user feedback and testing, you will enhance the viability and effectiveness of your entrepreneurial venture. As your entrepreneurial journey progresses, you will transition into the critical business planning and strategy formulation phase.

Here, you will articulate your vision, mission, and strategic goals, laying the groundwork for the success of your venture. This phase encompasses the development of comprehensive marketing strategies, financial projections, and operational plans to guide your venture toward its objectives. By meticulously planning and strategizing, you will set a clear direction for your entrepreneurial endeavour and pave the way for sustainable growth.

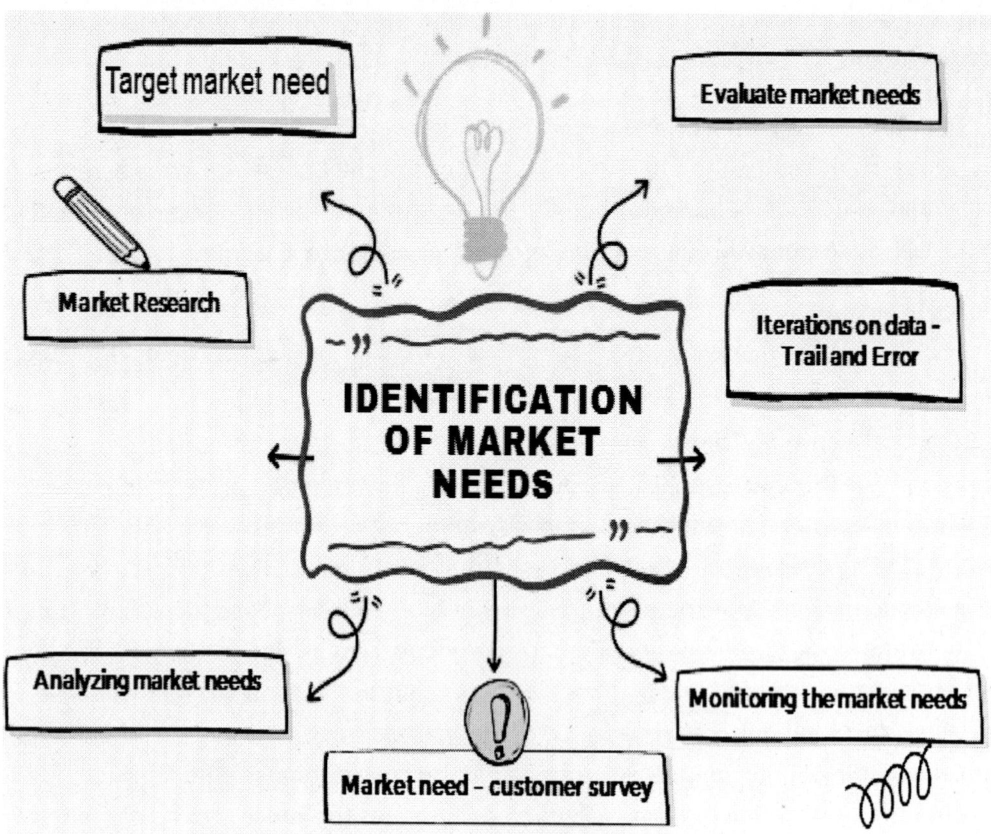

Figure 5.2 Market Need Identification.

In the prototyping stage, you will translate your concepts into tangible prototypes, bringing your entrepreneurial vision to life. This phase emphasizes the iterative nature of prototyping, focusing on functionality and user experience. Through continuous testing and refinement, you will iterate on your prototypes to ensure they meet the needs and expectations of your target audience. By prioritizing user feedback and usability testing, you will create prototypes that resonate with your customers and lay the foundation for a successful product or service. Throughout the Course Project, managing intellectual property rights is paramount to safeguarding your innovations. This phase explores into the importance of protecting your ideas through patents, trademarks, and other protective measures. Understanding intellectual property considerations and implementing appropriate safeguards will protect your innovations from infringement and ensure their long-term viability in the marketplace. Next, as you progress through the Course Project, you will transition into developing a comprehensive go-to-market strategy. This phase explores various marketing channels, distribution networks, and strategies to maximize your venture's market reach. By strategically planning your approach to entering the market, you will position your product or service for success and effectively engage with your target audience. Crafting a compelling business vision and honing practical leadership skills are essential aspects of the Course Project. This phase emphasizes the importance of articulating a clear and inspiring vision for your venture while developing leadership styles that align with the entrepreneurial context. By cultivating leadership skills such as communication, decision-making, and adaptability, you will be a capable leader ready to guide your venture toward success.

Further, effective team collaboration and decision-making play a pivotal role in the success of your entrepreneurial venture. The importance of developing a collaborative team environment, providing strategies for building, and managing dynamic, cross-functional teams must be focussed more. By harnessing the team members' diverse perspectives and skills, entrepreneur can make informed decisions and navigate challenges more effectively throughout the Course Project. Culminating in the presentation of the Course Project provides an opportunity to display your entrepreneurial venture to your peers and instructors. Here, you will discuss the critical components of an impactful presentation and explore strategies for effectively communicating your venture's vision, value proposition, and market strategy. By honing your presentation skills and delivering a compelling pitch, you will leave an impression and garner valuable feedback to refine your venture. Emphasizing the importance of feedback for continuous improvement, you will receive constructive feedback from your peers and instructors to reflect on your entrepreneurial journey. Incorporating feedback into your reflections and future endeavours will enhance your learning experience and prepare you for future entrepreneurial challenges.

Navigating through these milestones and deliverables, the readers will gain practical insights into the entrepreneurial process and develop a comprehensive understanding of how theory translates into impactful business ventures. The structured progression of the project ensures a holistic and immersive experience, preparing students for the challenges and opportunities in their entrepreneurial endeavours.

5.2. Need Identification

Effective market research is the cornerstone of successful need identification in entrepreneurship. The following discussion explores various techniques aspiring entrepreneurs can employ to conduct comprehensive market research, ensuring a deep understanding of consumer needs, industry trends, and market dynamics.

5.2.1 Techniques for Conducting Market Research

1. Surveys and Questionnaires: Embarking on your entrepreneurial journey requires a deep understanding of your target market's preferences, behaviours, and opinions. One effective technique for gathering quantitative data is designing and deploying surveys and questionnaires. Crafted thoughtfully, these tools enable you to collect structured feedback from potential customers, providing valuable insights into their needs and preferences. By formulating well-structured questions, you can extract meaningful data to inform critical decisions throughout your entrepreneurial endeavour.

2. In-depth Interviews: In-depth interviews offer a personalized approach to understanding your target market's needs and motivations. By engaging in one-on-one conversations with potential customers, industry experts, and stakeholders, you can uncover nuanced insights and hidden needs that may not surface through other research methods. Open-ended questions encourage participants to freely share their experiences and perspectives, allowing you to understand their pain points and desires better.

3. Focus Groups: Facilitating focus group discussions allows exploring diverse perspectives within your target market. Combining participants with varied backgrounds and experiences enhances rich discussions and uncover valuable insights into consumer preferences and perceptions. Analysing group dynamics allows you to identify common themes and sentiments, providing valuable direction for product development and marketing strategies.

4. Observational Research: Observational research offers a first-hand glimpse into consumer behaviour in natural settings. By observing and documenting how individuals interact with products or services in their everyday lives, you can identify patterns, preferences, and pain points that may influence purchasing decisions. This direct approach allows you to gather rich qualitative data, complementing other research methods and providing a holistic understanding of your target market.

5. Competitor Analysis: Analysing competitors' products, strategies, and customer feedback is essential for identifying unmet needs and potential market differentiation areas. By studying your competitors' offerings and observing customer reactions, you can gain valuable insights into market trends and consumer preferences. This analysis empowers you to refine your product or service offering, positioning your venture for success in a competitive landscape.

6. Data Analytics and Big Data: In today's data-driven world, leveraging data analytics tools is essential for extracting valuable insights from large datasets. By harnessing the power of big data, aspiring entrepreneurs can uncover trends, predict market shifts, and gain a deeper understanding of consumer behaviour. Through sophisticated analytics techniques, such as data mining and predictive modelling, entrepreneurs can identify patterns and correlations that inform strategic decision-making, giving their ventures a competitive edge in the marketplace.

7. Social Media Listening: Social media platforms serve as rich sources of real-time customer feedback and market intelligence. Entrepreneurs can gain valuable insights into customer sentiments, preferences, and emerging trends by actively monitoring and analysing conversations on platforms like Twitter, Facebook, and Instagram. Social media listening allows entrepreneurs to stay ahead by proactively identifying opportunities and addressing potential issues, enhancing market responsiveness and customer engagement strategies.

8. Prototype Testing: Creating prototypes or minimum viable products (MVPs) is crucial in validating product concepts and gathering user feedback. By developing prototypes early in product development, entrepreneurs can test critical features and functionalities with target users, gaining invaluable insights into usability, desirability, and overall product-market fit. Through iterative testing and refinement, entrepreneurs can tailor their products to meet market needs, increasing the likelihood of success upon launch.

9. Industry Reports and Publications: Accessing industry reports, market studies, and publications provides entrepreneurs with comprehensive insights into market dynamics and competitive landscapes. By tapping into established sources of market intelligence, such as research firms and trade publications, entrepreneurs can gain a deeper understanding of market trends, challenges, and opportunities. With this knowledge, entrepreneurs can make informed decisions about product development, marketing strategies, and business expansion, ensuring their ventures are well-positioned for success in their respective industries.

10. Trend Analyses: Analysing current and emerging trends within the industry is essential for staying ahead of the curve in entrepreneurship. By closely examining shifts in consumer behaviour, technological advancements, and societal influences, entrepreneurs can identify potential needs and opportunities for innovation. Trend analysis enables entrepreneurs to anticipate market demands and proactively align their product offerings with evolving customer preferences, positioning their ventures for long-term success.

11. Online Surveys and Feedback Forms: Utilizing online platforms to distribute surveys and collect feedback offers entrepreneurs a convenient and efficient way to gather insights from a diverse audience. By leveraging the reach of online channels, entrepreneurs can engage with a broader demographic, ensuring a representative sample for their market research efforts. Online surveys and feedback forms enable entrepreneurs to capture valuable data on customer preferences, pain points, and expectations, empowering them to make informed decisions about product development and marketing strategies.

12. Customer Feedback Platforms: Implementing customer feedback platforms and reviews provides entrepreneurs valuable insights into customer satisfaction and product performance. By monitoring online reviews and feedback, entrepreneurs can gain a deeper understanding of customer sentiments, identify improvement areas, and address issues promptly. Customer feedback platforms serve as valuable sources of market intelligence, helping entrepreneurs refine their offerings and enhance the overall customer experience.

13. Expert Consultations: Seeking insights from industry experts, mentors, and advisors can provide entrepreneurs with invaluable guidance and perspective. By tapping into the knowledge and experience of seasoned professionals, entrepreneurs can gain insights into industry trends, best practices, and potential pitfalls to avoid. Expert consultations allow entrepreneurs to validate their ideas, refine their strategies, and navigate challenges more effectively, increasing their chances of success in entrepreneurship.

14. Trend Forecasting: Engaging in trend forecasting activities enables entrepreneurs to anticipate future consumer needs and market dynamics. By analysing historical data, market trends, and emerging technologies, entrepreneurs can identify patterns and opportunities for innovation. Trend forecasting allows entrepreneurs to stay ahead of market shifts and innovations, positioning their ventures to capitalize on emerging trends and gain a competitive edge. Through strategic trend forecasting, entrepreneurs can future-proof their businesses and drive sustainable growth in dynamic market environments.

By combining these market research techniques, entrepreneurs can gain a holistic understanding of the market landscape, identify unmet needs, and lay the foundation for innovative and impactful solutions.

5.2.2 Identifying Unmet Needs and Pain Points

Pursuing innovative solutions, identifying unmet needs, and understanding potential customers' pain points are critical steps. The following discussion explores techniques and strategies to pinpoint where customers face challenges, allowing entrepreneurs to tailor their solutions to address genuine needs.

Conducting in-depth interviews and surveys provides a direct avenue for engaging with potential customers. By asking open-ended questions and actively listening to their responses, entrepreneurs can uncover latent needs and pain points that may not be immediately apparent, enabling them to gain valuable insights into customer preferences, behaviours, and challenges, thereby informing the development of tailored solutions. Furthermore, empathy mapping involves visually representing customer experiences and emotions to better understand their perspectives. By putting themselves in the customer's shoes, entrepreneurs can empathize with their challenges and frustrations, allowing them to identify pain points more intuitively and guide the development of empathetic solutions that address genuine customer needs. Additionally, mapping the customer journey from awareness to post-purchase stages provides entrepreneurs with a holistic view of the customer experience. By documenting touch points and interactions across various stages, they can identify pain points and improvement areas throughout the customer journey, helping to prioritize initiatives that enhance customer experience and drive satisfaction. Observing customers in real-life situations offers valuable insights into the challenges they encounter daily. By noting non-verbal cues and behaviours, entrepreneurs can identify unmet needs that customers may not articulate explicitly, with observational research enabling them to uncover hidden pain points and gain a better understanding of customer preferences and behaviours.

Also, analysing customer complaints, feedback, and reviews provides entrepreneurs with actionable insights into dissatisfaction and unmet needs. By extracting insights from negative feedback, entrepreneurs can identify pain points requiring attention and improvement, empowering them to address customer concerns proactively and enhance the overall customer experience. Additionally, shadowing customers during their daily activities and immersing themselves in their environment offers first-hand insights into their challenges and experiences. By observing customers in their natural settings, entrepreneurs can better understand their needs, behaviours, and pain points. This immersive approach develops empathy and enables entrepreneurs to create solutions that resonate profoundly with customers. Creating a detailed user persona is an invaluable technique for gaining insight into the characteristics and needs of target customers. By developing personas that represent different segments of the target audience, entrepreneurs can tailor their solutions to address the specific pain points of each persona. User persona development ensures that solutions are designed with empathy and precision, enhancing their relevance and resonance with the intended users. Furthermore, considering cultural nuances and sensitivities is essential to ensure solutions resonate with diverse audiences. By conducting a cultural sensitivity analysis, entrepreneurs can identify cultural factors influencing needs and pain points. Adapting solutions to align with diverse cultural perspectives not only enhances their acceptance and effectiveness but also demonstrates a commitment to inclusivity and respect for cultural diversity.

By employing these strategies, entrepreneurs can gain profound insights into the unmet needs and pain points of their target audience, laying the groundwork for the development of solutions that truly resonate with customers

5.2.3 Defining the Scope of the Project

Once unmet needs and pain points are identified, defining the project's scope becomes crucial for effective solution development. The following discussion explores into the key considerations and steps involved in clearly outlining the boundaries and objectives of the entrepreneurial project.

A clear definition of the primary objectives and goals of the project is foundational for its success. Ensuring alignment with the identified unmet needs and pain points, the objectives provide a strategic direction for solution development. Entrepreneurs can maintain focus and coherence throughout the entrepreneurial journey by clearly delineating the project's aims. Then, precise identification and definition of the target audience are essential for tailoring the entrepreneurial solution to meet their specific needs. Understanding the intended users' demographics, behaviours, and preferences enables entrepreneurs to design solutions that resonate with their target market. By defining the target audience, entrepreneurs can refine their approach and enhance the effectiveness of their solution. Next, a concise and specific problem statement is vital for guiding the project and ensuring its relevance to the identified unmet needs. The problem statement serves as a guiding beacon, directing efforts toward addressing the core challenges faced by the target audience. By formulating a clear problem statement, entrepreneurs can align their solution with the identified needs, increasing its impact and effectiveness. Establishing clear boundaries for the project is essential to prevent scope creep and maintain focus on the defined objectives. Entrepreneurs can effectively manage expectations and allocate resources efficiently by outlining what is within the project's scope and what lies outside. Boundary setting ensures that the project remains manageable and achievable within the defined parameters. Assessing the resources available for the project, including workforce, time, and budget, is crucial for determining the project's feasibility. Aligning the scope with available resources ensures the project remains realistic and achievable. Entrepreneurs can mitigate potential challenges and allocate resources effectively to support project goals by conducting a thorough resource assessment. Considering technological constraints and regulatory requirements is essential for ensuring the success and compliance of the project. Addressing technological opportunities and constraints helps entrepreneurs leverage available resources and capabilities effectively. Similarly, identifying and addressing regulatory requirements ensures the project operates within legal and ethical boundaries.

A feasibility analysis is critical to ensure the project goals are realistic and achievable within the defined constraints. Entrepreneurs can assess the project's viability and make informed decisions by identifying potential challenges and developing mitigation strategies. Feasibility analysis helps entrepreneurs anticipate and proactively address obstacles, increasing the likelihood of project success. Assessing the market potential for the proposed solution within the defined scope is essential for understanding its viability and competitiveness. By identifying potential competitors and analysing market positioning, entrepreneurs can gauge the demand for their solution and identify opportunities for differentiation. Establishing a realistic timeline for project completion is crucial for managing resources and expectations. Entrepreneurs can track progress and ensure timely delivery by breaking the project into manageable phases and milestones. A well-defined timeline helps maintain momentum and accountability throughout the project lifecycle. Selecting key performance indicators that align with project goals is essential for measuring progress and success. By establishing metrics for measuring the effectiveness and impact of the entrepreneurial solution, entrepreneurs can track performance and make data-driven decisions. KPIs provide actionable insights that inform strategic direction and drive continuous improvement. Identifying potential risks associated with the project is critical for proactive risk management.

Importantly, entrepreneurs can minimize threats and maximize opportunities by assessing risks and developing mitigation strategies. Effective risk management ensures the project remains on track and resilient when facing challenges. Ensuring alignment with the expectations and requirements of key stakeholders is essential for project success. Entrepreneurs can develop trust and collaboration by transparently communicating the defined scope to stakeholders. Stakeholder alignment facilitates effective decision-making and mitigates conflicts that may arise during the project lifecycle. Acknowledging that the project scope may evolve through iterative refinement allows entrepreneurs to adapt to changing circumstances and insights. By allowing flexibility for adjustments based on ongoing feedback and learning, entrepreneurs can enhance the relevance and effectiveness of their solutions. Iterative refinement enables continuous improvement and innovation throughout the project. Addressing ethical considerations ensures that the project aligns with ethical standards and upholds principles of integrity and responsibility. Entrepreneurs can build trust and credibility with stakeholders by integrating ethical considerations into decision-making processes. Upholding ethical standards demonstrates a commitment to social responsibility and sustainability, enhancing the project's impact and reputation.

By systematically addressing these considerations, entrepreneurs can define a clear and focused project scope, setting the foundation for successful solution development and implementation. The defined scope serves as a roadmap, guiding the entrepreneurial journey toward impactful outcomes

5.3. Innovative Solution Development

Applying creative design thinking principles is instrumental in identifying unmet needs and creating innovative solutions. The following discussion explores the principles and methodologies of design thinking, providing a framework for entrepreneurs to approach problem-solving in a human-centric and innovative manner.

5.3.1 Applying Creative Design Thinking Principles

Understanding the perspective of end-users is fundamental to practical problem-solving. By empathizing with their experiences through user interviews, observations, and immersion, entrepreneurs gain deep insights into user needs, motivations, and pain points. Once these insights are gathered, it is essential to define the problem clearly. Formulating a problem statement based on empathetic understanding lays the groundwork for ideation, ensuring that the solution addresses the root cause of the problem. Generating diverse ideas without judgment is central to the ideation phase. Entrepreneurs explore multiple possibilities and potential solutions by encouraging creativity through brainstorming sessions, mind mapping, and other ideation techniques. Prototyping involves creating tangible representations of ideas to test and refine concepts. Entrepreneurs build rough models or visualizations to bring their ideas to life, allowing for early feedback and iteration. Iteratively testing prototypes with end-users is crucial for validating ideas and gathering feedback. By involving users throughout the testing process, entrepreneurs gain valuable insights that inform refinements and improvements to the solution. Prioritizing the needs and preferences of end-users ensures that the final solution effectively addresses their pain points. By designing with users in mind, entrepreneurs create solutions that resonate with their target audience and deliver meaningful value. Embracing an iterative design approach allows a continuous refinement based on feedback and insights. Entrepreneurs acknowledge that the first iteration may not be the final solution and remain open to feedback-driven improvements throughout the design process. Innovation thrives when diverse perspectives and expertise come together through cross-functional collaboration. This involves mastering teamwork among individuals with varied skills and backgrounds, allowing entrepreneurs to leverage the strengths of a cross-functional team to enrich the ideation and design process, leading to more robust and innovative solutions. Effective design thinking requires a balance between divergent thinking, which involves generating a wide array of ideas, and convergent thinking, which involves selecting the best ideas. Entrepreneurs should avoid premature evaluation to encourage a broad exploration of possibilities before converging on the most promising solutions. Visual tools, such as sketches, diagrams, and storyboards, play a crucial role in the design thinking process. By utilizing visual representations, entrepreneurs can communicate and refine ideas more effectively. Visual thinking enhances communication and understanding, enabling stakeholders to grasp complex concepts and provide valuable feedback.

Design sprints offer a structured, time-constrained approach to solving and testing specific problems. By implementing design sprints, entrepreneurs streamline the design process, allowing for rapid iteration through solutions. This focused approach enables teams to quickly validate ideas, gather feedback, and iterate based on user insights. Embracing a mindset of experimentation is essential for innovation. Entrepreneurs should view challenges as opportunities for growth and improvement, embracing failure as a natural part of the learning process. Mindful experimentation encourages continuous learning and iteration, leading to more refined and impactful solutions. Storytelling is a powerful tool for communicating the narrative of a solution. By crafting compelling stories, entrepreneurs can emotionally engage and resonate with users and stakeholders, effectively conveying the solution's value proposition. Finally, human-centered prototyping prioritizes the human experience, ensuring the solution aligns with user needs, preferences, and behaviours. This involves developing prototypes that are intuitive, user-friendly, and responsive to user feedback, putting users at the centre of the design process to create solutions that truly address their needs and deliver meaningful value. By applying these creative design thinking principles, entrepreneurs can perform innovation, develop solutions that genuinely address user needs, and navigate the iterative refinement process with agility and effectiveness. Design thinking enhances the quality of solutions and cultivates a culture of creativity and adaptability within the entrepreneurial ecosystem.

5.3.2 Prototyping and Iterative Design Process

The prototyping and iterative design process is dynamic and essential in pursuing innovative solutions. The following discussion explores the intricacies of prototyping and outlines the iterative design approach, guiding entrepreneurs through refining their concepts based on user feedback and testing.

Prototypes serve as tangible representations of concepts or ideas, allowing entrepreneurs to test and refine their solutions before full-scale implementation. Clarifying the purpose and scope of the prototype is essential for guiding the development process. Entrepreneurs must identify whether the prototype aims to test functionality, user experience, or both, ensuring alignment with project objectives and user needs. Prototypes come in various forms, each suited to various stages of the design process and testing requirements. Low-fidelity sketches, wireframes, and high-fidelity interactive models are among the common types of prototypes. Entrepreneurs must choose the appropriate type based on the specific goals of the prototype, considering factors such as fidelity, complexity, and usability. User experience lies at the heart of effective prototyping. Prioritizing user-centered design ensures that prototypes align with user expectations and preferences. By incorporating user feedback early in the design process, entrepreneurs can create solutions that resonate with their target audience and address their needs more effectively. Rapid prototyping techniques enable quick iteration and refinement of design concepts. Entrepreneurs embrace tools and methods that facilitate swift and cost-effective prototyping, allowing for rapid experimentation and validation of ideas. Rapid prototyping accelerates the design process, helping entrepreneurs bring innovative solutions to market more efficiently.

Functionality testing focuses on evaluating the core features and functionalities of the prototype. By testing the prototype's technical capabilities, entrepreneurs can identify any technical challenges or limitations that must be addressed. Functionality testing ensures the prototype performs as intended, laying the foundation for further refinement. Usability testing assesses the user-friendliness and effectiveness of the prototype in real-world scenarios. Through usability testing, entrepreneurs gather insights into how users interact with the solution, identifying pain points, friction areas, and opportunities for improvement. Usability testing helps optimize the user experience, enhancing the solution's effectiveness. Establishing mechanisms for collecting user feedback is critical for the iterative design process. Entrepreneurs create a feedback loop that enables continuous improvement based on user insights. By soliciting feedback at each iteration, entrepreneurs ensure that their solutions evolve in response to user needs and preferences, leading to more successful outcomes.

Further, iterative refinement is a crucial aspect of the prototyping process, involving analysing feedback and identifying areas for improvement. Entrepreneurs make iterative adjustments to the prototype based on user feedback and testing results, enhancing its effectiveness, and addressing any identified issues progressively over multiple iterations. Effective collaboration among team members is essential for successful prototyping. Entrepreneurs foster a collaborative environment where team members can contribute ideas, provide feedback, and work together towards refining the prototype. Clear and open communication ensures that all stakeholders are aligned with the evolving design and that feedback is effectively incorporated into the iterative process. Implementing version control measures is crucial for managing multiple iterations of the prototype. Entrepreneurs utilize version control systems to track changes, avoid confusion, and maintain a clear record of design modifications. Version control ensures that the latest version of the prototype is always accessible and that team members can collaborate seamlessly without the risk of overwriting each other's work. During the prototyping phase, entrepreneurs consider scalability issues to anticipate how the solution will perform as it scales. By addressing potential scalability challenges early in the design process, entrepreneurs can ensure that the prototype can accommodate increased usage, data volume, and user interactions without compromising performance or functionality. Accessibility testing ensures that the prototype is inclusive and can be accessed by users with diverse abilities. Entrepreneurs test the prototype for accessibility barriers and address issues hindering users with disabilities from effectively interacting with the solution. By prioritizing accessibility, entrepreneurs create more inclusive and equitable solutions that cater to a broader audience. Cross-platform compatibility is essential to reach users across various devices and platforms. Entrepreneurs verify that the prototype functions seamlessly across different operating systems, browsers, and screen sizes, addressing any discrepancies in user experience to provide a consistent and cohesive interaction regardless of the user's device or environment. Documenting changes and updates during the iterative design process is vital for maintaining a comprehensive record of the prototype's evolution. Entrepreneurs generate extensive documentation that preserves design decisions, feedback, and adjustments made during each iteration. Documentation serves as a valuable reference for future development and knowledge transfer, ensuring continuity and consistency in the prototyping process.

By navigating the prototyping and iterative design process with a strategic and user-centric approach, entrepreneurs can refine their solutions, address potential challenges, and ensure that the final product aligns seamlessly with user needs and expectations. This iterative journey contributes to the development of robust and user-friendly solutions that stand the test of real-world application

5.3.3 Evaluating Feasibility and Viability

As the entrepreneurial journey progresses, evaluating the feasibility and viability of the innovative solution becomes paramount. The following discussion explores the key considerations and methodologies for assessing whether the developed concept is technically feasible, economically viable, and sustainable in the market.

Entrepreneurs embark on a journey of technical feasibility analysis, meticulously examining the solution's technical aspects to gauge its viability. This involves scrutinizing whether the necessary technology for implementation is readily available, scalable, and cost-effective. By delving into the technical requirements, entrepreneurs can discern if the solution aligns with the constraints of available technology resources. Concurrently, they evaluate resource availability, assessing whether the workforce, equipment, and infrastructure required are accessible. Identifying potential resource constraints prompts the development of strategies to address them effectively, ensuring smooth implementation without significant limitations. Conducting a comprehensive cost-benefit analysis is paramount to assess the economic viability of the solution. Entrepreneurs juxtapose anticipated development and implementation costs with expected benefits and returns. By quantifying costs and benefits, they make informed decisions about financial feasibility, weighing whether potential benefits justify the required investment. Additionally, entrepreneurs delve into market viability, analysing the solution's potential to meet market demands effectively. They evaluate if there's genuine market need, alignment with current trends, and consumer preferences, gauging market fit and potential acceptance and adoption by target customers.

A thorough competitive analysis is indispensable to grasp the solution's standing within the market landscape. Entrepreneurs identify competitors, assess their strengths and weaknesses, and analyse challenges in gaining market share. Understanding the competitive landscape enables effective refinement of strategies to differentiate solutions and seize market opportunities. Regulatory compliance is imperative to mitigate legal risks and ensure ethical implementation. Entrepreneurs assess whether the solution complies with relevant regulations and industry standards, addressing potential legal hurdles or ethical considerations. Lastly, scalability assessments are critical to determine if the solution can accommodate growth and increased demand over time. Entrepreneurs anticipate scalability challenges, developing scalable solutions to ensure long-term success and sustainability in the market. Entrepreneurs meticulously evaluate the financial viability of their solutions, analysing revenue generation, cost recovery, and profitability. Through thorough financial analysis, they assess whether the solution can generate sufficient revenue to cover costs and achieve profitability over time, crucial for ensuring long-term sustainability and success. User acceptance testing plays a pivotal role, as entrepreneurs gather feedback from real users to identify and address any usability issues effectively. Involving end-users ensures that the solution meets expectations and effectively addresses their needs, enhancing its acceptance and adoption in the market. Pilot testing is another essential step, involving implementation in a real-world scenario to assess performance and viability. Entrepreneurs select a small-scale test group or pilot environment to evaluate functionality and usability, identifying and resolving any unforeseen challenges or issues. A return on investment (ROI) analysis provides insights into financial performance and profitability, helping entrepreneurs understand the time required to recoup the initial investment and start generating profits. Comprehensive risk analysis is crucial for identifying potential challenges and uncertainties, with entrepreneurs developing mitigation strategies to address and minimize risks effectively. Proactively managing risks enhances the likelihood of achieving objectives and mitigating potential setbacks. Moreover, environmental, and social impact assessments integrate sustainability considerations into business practices. By evaluating the solution's environmental and societal impact, entrepreneurs ensure responsible and ethical conduct while contributing to positive social change.

By systematically evaluating the feasibility and viability of the innovative solution, entrepreneurs can make informed decisions about the path forward. This assessment ensures that the solution aligns with market dynamics, technological capabilities, and ethical considerations, contributing to creating a sustainable and successful venture.

5.4. Business Plan Formulation

In the entrepreneurial journey, formulating a comprehensive business plan is a strategic step toward transforming innovative ideas into viable and successful ventures. The following discussion explores the essential components of a well-rounded business plan, providing entrepreneurs with a structured approach to articulate their vision, strategy, and operational framework. Figure 5.3 outlines the essential components of a business plan, providing entrepreneurs with a structured framework for articulating their vision, strategy, and operational details.

5.4.1 Components of a Comprehensive Business Plan

Executive Summary is one of the important components of a Comprehensive Business Plan. The executive summary serves as a condensed version of the business plan, succinctly encapsulating its core elements. It provides an overview of the business idea, market opportunity, and financial projections, offering stakeholders a glimpse into the venture's potential. Crafting a compelling executive summary is essential as it often serves as the first point of contact for investors and partners, highlighting the venture's viability and attractiveness. Further, a comprehensive business description communicates the essence of the venture, including its mission, vision, and core values. It outlines the unique aspects of the business concept, emphasizing its differentiation and value proposition in the market. The business description sets the tone for the business plan by articulating the fundamental principles guiding the entrepreneurial endeavour, providing context and clarity to stakeholders. Next, conducting a thorough market analysis is crucial for understanding the dynamics of the target market. The following discussion explores into market trends, customer segments, and the competitive landscape, providing insights that inform strategic decision-making. By analysing market data and trends, entrepreneurs can identify opportunities, anticipate challenges, and develop effective marketing and sales strategies to capitalize on market demand. Importantly, defining the venture's organizational structure establishes clarity and accountability within the team. The following discussion outlines critical roles, responsibilities, and reporting lines, ensuring everyone understands their functions and contributions to the business. Entrepreneurs enhance transparency and efficiency by delineating the organizational hierarchy and communication channels, laying the groundwork for effective teamwork and collaboration.

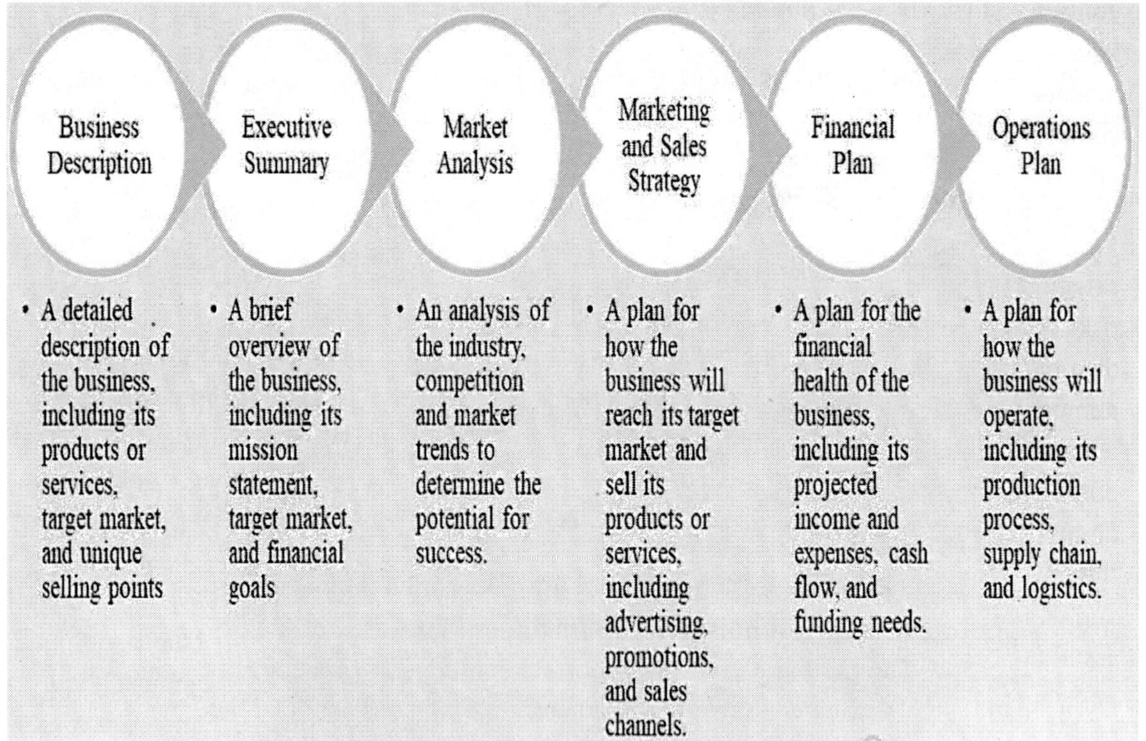

Figure 5.3 Components of a Business Plan

Detailing the features and benefits of the product or service elucidates its value proposition to customers. The following discussion highlights unique selling propositions and competitive advantages, positioning the offering within the market landscape. By articulating the value proposition clearly, entrepreneurs can attract customers and differentiate their offerings from competitors, driving demand and market penetration. The marketing and sales strategy outlines how the venture plans to promote and sell its product or service. By identifying target customer segments, channels, and promotional tactics, entrepreneurs develop a roadmap for reaching and engaging customers effectively. A well-defined marketing and sales strategy aligns with market insights and customer preferences, maximizing the impact of promotional efforts and driving revenue growth. Clearly stating the financial needs of the venture is essential for attracting investors and securing funding. The following discussion outlines the required funding for various stages of development, including startup costs, operational expenses, and expansion plans. By articulating the funding requirements transparently, entrepreneurs demonstrate their understanding of the venture's financial aspects and readiness to capitalize on investment opportunities. Presenting detailed financial forecasts is vital for providing stakeholders with a clear understanding of the venture's financial trajectory. The following discussion includes projected income statements, balance sheets, and cash flow statements, offering insights into revenue generation, expense management, and cash flow dynamics. By outlining financial projections accurately and comprehensively, entrepreneurs demonstrate their ability to plan, budget, and manage resources effectively, instilling confidence in potential investors and partners.

Identifying potential risks and challenges allows entrepreneurs to mitigate threats and safeguard the venture's success proactively. The following discussion thoroughly analyses various risk factors, including market volatility, competition, regulatory changes, and operational disruptions. By developing risk mitigation and contingency planning strategies, entrepreneurs demonstrate their preparedness to navigate uncertainties and adapt to evolving circumstances, enhancing the resilience and sustainability of the venture. Detailing the business's day-to-day operations provides clarity on how the venture will function on a practical level. The following discussion describes processes, resources, and critical suppliers, outlining the operational framework that supports the delivery of products or services. By delineating operational procedures and dependencies, entrepreneurs ensure operational efficiency, resource optimization, and quality assurance, laying the foundation for sustainable growth and scalability. Creating a timeline for implementing critical milestones is essential for guiding the execution of the business plan. The following discussion sets realistic deadlines for product development, market-entry, and other critical activities, ensuring alignment with strategic objectives and resource availability. By establishing an implementation timeline, entrepreneurs track progress, manage dependencies, and mitigate delays, driving momentum and accountability throughout the venture's lifecycle. Defining potential exit strategies clarifies the venture's long-term vision and objectives. The following discussion considers options such as acquisition, merger, or initial public offering (IPO), outlining the mechanisms through which investors or entrepreneurs can realize returns on their investment. Entrepreneurs demonstrate foresight and strategic thinking by proactively planning exit strategies and maximizing stakeholder value creation and liquidity opportunities. Establishing key performance indicators (KPIs) allows entrepreneurs to track and evaluate the venture's progress and success. The following discussion defines metrics for monitoring various aspects of the business, including financial performance, customer satisfaction, and market share. By setting clear and measurable KPIs, entrepreneurs gain insights into their strategies' effectiveness, identify improvement areas, and make data-driven decisions to drive sustainable growth and profitability. Additionally, by including supplementary materials such as market research data, product specifications, or legal documents provides additional context and supporting information for stakeholders. By implementing the salient discussions provide detailed insights into the market landscape, product features, and regulatory compliance, enhancing stakeholders' understanding of the venture's value proposition and operational framework. By providing comprehensive appendices, entrepreneurs bolster the credibility and transparency of the business plan, raising trust and confidence among investors and partners.

By addressing these components, entrepreneurs can create a comprehensive and compelling business plan that serves as a roadmap for the venture's success. A well-structured business plan attracts potential investors and is valuable for guiding decision-making and ensuring alignment with strategic goals throughout the entrepreneurial journey.

5.4.2 Financial Projections and Funding Requirements

In entrepreneurial ventures, meticulous financial planning is pivotal for success. The following discussion explores into the intricacies of financial projections and the determination of funding requirements, offering entrepreneurs a strategic approach to secure the necessary resources to realize their innovative ideas. Forecasting revenue streams is critical for gauging the financial viability of a venture. This involves projecting revenue based on sales forecasts, considering market demand, pricing strategies, and anticipated sales volumes. By differentiating between various product lines or service offerings, entrepreneurs can comprehensively understand their revenue potential and formulate strategies to maximize sales and profitability. Simultaneously, estimating the cost of goods sold (COGS) is crucial for determining the direct expenses associated with production or service delivery. This entails identifying and quantifying materials, labour, and manufacturing costs, enabling entrepreneurs to calculate gross profit margins and make informed decisions regarding pricing, production processes, and resource allocation.

Calculating the gross profit margin offers insights into the profitability of core business operations. By subtracting COGS from revenue, entrepreneurs can determine the gross profit margin percentage, aiding in the evaluation of production efficiency, pricing strategies, and cost management practices. Meanwhile, identifying and categorizing operating expenses, including marketing, sales, administration, and research and development costs, is vital for understanding the overall cost structure of the venture. Accurate estimation of operating expenses facilitates the development of realistic budgetary plans, effective resource allocation, and ensures the sustainability of business operations. Additionally, determining earnings before interest and taxes (EBIT) provides insights into operational profitability, aiding in strategic decision-making to enhance financial performance and profitability. Accounting for interest payments and taxes is essential for ensuring compliance with financial obligations and tax liabilities, enabling entrepreneurs to maintain financial stability and mitigate risks associated with debt management and tax compliance. Finally, calculating net profit offers a comprehensive assessment of the venture's overall profitability, guiding entrepreneurs in measuring performance against strategic objectives and making informed decisions to drive sustainable growth and success.

Developing detailed cash flow projections is essential for managing liquidity and ensuring operational stability. This involves forecasting both inflows and outflows of cash, including revenues, expenses, investments, and financing activities. By analysing cash flow projections, entrepreneurs can anticipate funding needs, identify potential cash shortages, and implement strategies to maintain adequate liquidity to support business operations effectively. Conducting break-even analysis is critical for understanding the point at which the venture's total revenue equals its total costs, resulting in neither profit nor loss. This entails calculating the break-even point based on fixed and variable costs, sales volume, and unit prices. By performing break-even analysis, entrepreneurs can assess the venture's viability, determine pricing strategies, and set sales targets to achieve profitability. Estimating funding needs at various stages of the venture is essential for ensuring adequate capitalization and resource allocation. This aligns funding requirements with critical milestones and development phases, such as product development, market entry, and expansion. By identifying funding needs by stage, entrepreneurs can prioritize resource allocation, secure necessary financing, and effectively manage the venture's growth trajectory. Identifying potential funding sources is crucial for securing the capital to support the venture's growth and development. This involves exploring options such as equity financing, debt financing, grants, or strategic partnerships. By evaluating different funding sources, entrepreneurs can choose the most appropriate financing options based on their financial needs, risk tolerance, and growth objectives. Evaluating the expected return on investment for investors is essential for attracting funding and demonstrating the financial potential of the venture. This involves calculating ROI based on projected financial returns and investment costs. By presenting a compelling case for the financial benefits of supporting the venture, entrepreneurs can attract investors and secure the necessary funding to fuel growth and expansion. Conducting sensitivity analysis helps assess the impact of numerous factors on financial projections and identify potential risks and uncertainties. It involves analysing how changes in key variables, such as sales volume, pricing, and operating costs, affect financial performance. By performing sensitivity analysis, entrepreneurs can develop risk mitigation strategies, enhance financial planning, and make informed decisions to safeguard the venture's financial health. Developing contingency plans for unforeseen financial challenges is essential for maintaining operational resilience and mitigating risks. This involves anticipating potential financial risks and disruptions, such as market downturns, supply chain disruptions, or unexpected expenses.

By proactively identifying and addressing potential risks, entrepreneurs can minimize the impact of adverse events, ensure business continuity, and preserve the venture's long-term viability.

By meticulously crafting financial projections and clearly articulating funding requirements, entrepreneurs enhance their ability to attract investors, secure necessary resources, and confidently navigate the financial landscape. These financial insights not only guide strategic decision-making but also demonstrate the feasibility and sustainability of the venture to potential stakeholders.

5.4.3 Aligning the Business Plan with Project Goals

In the entrepreneurial journey, the business plan serves as a dynamic roadmap, guiding the realization of project goals and the overall success of the venture. The following discussion explores the crucial process of aligning the business plan with project goals, ensuring a harmonious integration of strategic vision and operational execution.

Clear articulation of project goals within the business plan is crucial for providing a roadmap to guide the venture's trajectory. By defining short-term and long-term objectives, entrepreneurs establish a solid foundation for decision-making, resource allocation, and performance evaluation. These goals offer direction and are benchmarks for measuring progress and success throughout the entrepreneurial journey. Ensuring that every component of the business plan contributes harmoniously to the overarching project strategy is critical. Verification that operational plans, financial projections, and marketing strategies align with the project's vision ensures coherence and effectiveness. This alignment facilitates constructive collaboration among different functional areas, maximizing the likelihood of achieving the venture's goals while minimizing potential conflicts or inefficiencies. Establishing measurable Key Performance Indicators (KPIs) allows for ongoing monitoring of progress and performance within the business plan. Entrepreneurs gain valuable insights into the venture's performance by identifying KPIs that directly reflect project goals and integrating them into the plan. These metrics facilitate informed decision-making and enable timely adjustments to optimize outcomes, enhancing the venture's overall success. Effective resource allocation is pivotal for driving project priorities and achieving strategic objectives outlined in the business plan. Aligning financial resources, personnel, and time with project goals maximizes efficiency and effectiveness. Entrepreneurs optimize resource utilization, mitigate risks, and enhance the venture's overall performance and sustainability by directing resources toward strategic priorities. Incorporating project milestones into the business plan signifies progress and achievements, providing a tangible framework for measuring success. Linking milestones to specific plan sections highlights their significance in the venture's development. By integrating milestones, entrepreneurs establish accountability, motivate stakeholders, and ensure the venture stays on track toward goal attainment. Flexibility and adaptability are essential attributes of a robust business plan, enabling entrepreneurs to navigate uncertainties and respond effectively to changing circumstances. Designing the plan with built-in flexibility accommodates adjustments and refinements, enhancing its resilience, agility, and relevance. Anticipating changes and incorporating mechanisms for plan refinement ensures its efficacy in dynamic business environments, increasing the venture's chances of success. Aligning risk mitigation strategies with project goals is essential for safeguarding the venture's success. Within the business plan, entrepreneurs identify potential challenges and outline proactive measures to mitigate risks effectively. By integrating risk mitigation strategies into the plan, entrepreneurs enhance resilience and readiness to address unforeseen obstacles, increasing the venture's chances of achieving its objectives.

Also, establishing mechanisms for continuous monitoring and evaluation of project progress ensures that the venture remains on track toward goal attainment. By incorporating feedback loops into the business plan, entrepreneurs can assess performance regularly and make necessary adjustments. This iterative evaluation process allows for timely course correction, enabling the venture to adapt effectively to changing market conditions and emerging opportunities. Clear communication of the alignment between the business plan and project goals is crucial for ensuring stakeholder understanding and buy-in. Entrepreneurs must articulate the strategic direction and objectives outlined in the plan to all team members and investors. By developing a shared understanding of the venture's goals, entrepreneurs cultivate a sense of purpose and unity, collaboration, and commitment to success. Embracing an iterative approach to business plan refinement enables entrepreneurs to adapt to evolving project goals and market dynamics effectively. By regularly reviewing and updating the plan, entrepreneurs ensure its relevance and responsiveness to changing circumstances. This iterative refinement process allows entrepreneurs to capitalize on new opportunities, address emerging challenges, and optimize the venture's trajectory toward success. Encouraging collaboration across different functional areas enhances constructive collaboration and innovation within the venture. Entrepreneurs harness diverse perspectives and expertise by creating an environment where teams work cohesively towards common project goals. This cross-functional collaboration enables the effective execution of the business plan, driving progress and maximizing the venture's potential for success. Integrating stakeholder perspectives into the business plan ensures alignment with broader project goals and expectations. By addressing concerns and expectations proactively, entrepreneurs build trust and confidence among stakeholders. This integration of stakeholder perspectives develops a sense of ownership and commitment to the venture's success, enhancing collaboration and collective efforts toward goal attainment. Establishing clear communication channels for reporting progress toward project goals keeps stakeholders informed and engaged throughout the venture's development. By regularly communicating progress updates, entrepreneurs maintain transparency and accountability. This open communication develops trust and alignment among stakeholders, ensuring everyone remains informed and involved in the venture's journey toward success.

By meticulously aligning the business plan with project goals, entrepreneurs lay the foundation for a purpose-driven venture. This alignment develops a cohesive and focused organizational culture and enhances the likelihood of achieving strategic milestones and realizing the overarching vision of the entrepreneurial endeavour.

5.5. Go-to-Market Strategy

In the dynamic entrepreneurship landscape, a well-crafted go-to-market (GTM) strategy is essential for successfully introducing innovative products or services. The following discussion explores into the intricacies of crafting a targeted go-to-market plan, providing entrepreneurs with a structured approach to maximize market penetration and achieve sustainable growth. The elements include market segmentation, target audience identification, value proposition development, channel strategy, pricing strategy, sales and distribution plan, marketing tactics, promotional activities, and post-launch evaluation metrics.

5.5.1 Crafting a Targeted Go-to-Market Plan

Crafting a targeted go-to-market plan (refer discussion 3.3) involves a meticulous approach that encompasses several essential components. Initially, market segmentation lays the foundation by dissecting the market into distinct segments, enabling entrepreneurs to focus their efforts and resources effectively. Customer persona development breathes life into these segments, providing empathy and insight to tailor offerings and messaging to resonate deeply with the target audience. A compelling value proposition and strategic positioning strategy further refine the approach, ensuring clarity in communicating the offering's unique benefits and identity amidst competitors. Distribution channels, pricing strategy, and promotional tactics come into play, creating pathways for engagement, maximizing revenue, and casting a wide net of awareness to reach the target audience. Equipping sales teams, orchestrating a comprehensive launch plan, and outlining a customer acquisition strategy elevate the plan from concept to action, empowering entrepreneurs to engage effectively with customers and drive adoption. Establishing feedback mechanisms, assessing scalability considerations, and implementing robust monitoring systems ensure agility and responsiveness, allowing entrepreneurs to evolve and optimize the strategy based on real-time insights. Concurrently, on-going competitive analysis keeps the venture attuned to market dynamics, enabling it to seize opportunities and mitigate threats proactively. Through a harmonious convergence of these components, entrepreneurs can navigate the complex landscape of go-to-market strategies with confidence, maximizing their chances of success in the marketplace. A well-executed go-to-market strategy is not just a launch plan but a dynamic and adaptive approach that evolves with market feedback. By meticulously addressing each component, entrepreneurs can position their ventures for successful market entry, sustainable growth, and long-term success in the competitive entrepreneurial landscape.

5.5.2 Marketing and Distribution Channels

In entrepreneurship, effective marketing and distribution channels are pivotal in connecting innovative solutions with the target audience. The following discussion explores the intricacies of crafting a robust strategy for marketing and distribution, ensuring that the venture reaches its customers efficiently and creates a lasting impact.

Implementing a multi-channel approach (refer discussion 3.4) is crucial in today's dynamic market environment, allowing entrepreneurs to maximize market coverage and engage diverse customer segments across online and offline channels. Leveraging digital marketing strategies, such as SEO and social media marketing, facilitates brand visibility and engagement in the digital landscape, while social media platforms provide opportunities for personalized interactions and community engagement. Content marketing campaigns and influencer partnerships further amplify brand messaging and credibility, fostering meaningful connections with the target audience. Additionally, traditional advertising channels, trade shows, and retail partnerships offer avenues to reach specific demographics and expand the product's physical presence, complementing e-commerce platforms for direct-to-consumer sales. Supply chain optimization ensures efficient distribution processes, while CRM systems enable personalized marketing initiatives and enhanced customer relationships. Analytics-driven decision-making and continuous optimization further refine marketing and distribution strategies, ensuring entrepreneurs remain agile and responsive to market dynamics, driving sustainable growth and success in their ventures. A well-crafted marketing and distribution channel strategy ensures that the entrepreneurial venture reaches its target audience and establishes a strong and sustainable presence in the market. By embracing a mix of digital and traditional channels, entrepreneurs can create a comprehensive approach that resonates with diverse customer preferences and maximizes market reach.

5.5.3 Integrating Feedback for Strategy Optimization

In the dynamic landscape of entrepreneurship, the ability to adapt and refine strategies based on valuable feedback is a cornerstone of success. The following discussion explores into the significance of integrating feedback into the marketing and distribution strategy, emphasizing the iterative nature of optimization for sustained growth and customer satisfaction.

Implementing effective mechanisms to collect feedback is crucial for refining marketing and distribution strategies. Entrepreneurs can utilize various channels, such as surveys, reviews, social media interactions, and customer support, to gather valuable insights. By actively soliciting feedback from customers, stakeholders, and market influencers, entrepreneurs can gain a deeper understanding of their audience's needs and preferences, allowing for continuous optimization of their strategies. Through regular customer surveys and interviews, direct insights into customer experiences and preferences are gained, helping identify areas for improvement and innovation. Structured surveys and in-depth interviews provide entrepreneurs with valuable insights that inform strategic decision-making and enhance customer satisfaction. Social listening tools enable entrepreneurs to monitor online conversations and sentiments across various social media platforms, gaining real-time insights into customer perceptions, market trends, and emerging issues. By analysing customer discussions, mentions, and reviews, entrepreneurs can stay informed about customer sentiment and respond promptly to feedback, ensuring proactive management of brand reputation and customer relationships. Customer reviews on e-commerce websites and social media offer valuable feedback on product performance and customer experiences. Analysing customer reviews helps identify recurring themes, address concerns, and leverage positive feedback to strengthen brand credibility. By actively engaging with customer reviews, entrepreneurs demonstrate a commitment to customer satisfaction and develop trust among prospective buyers.

Website analytics tools offer valuable insights into user behaviour and engagement metrics, allowing entrepreneurs to gauge the effectiveness of their online presence and identify areas for optimization. By tracking metrics such as website visits, page views, bounce rates, and conversion metrics, entrepreneurs can optimize website design, content, and navigation to improve user experience and drive conversion rates. Establishing key performance indicators (KPIs) related to marketing and distribution allows entrepreneurs to track the effectiveness of their strategies. Metrics such as conversion rates, customer acquisition cost, and return on investment provide quantifiable benchmarks for evaluating performance and guiding decision-making. Regular stakeholder communication enables entrepreneurs to identify market trends, anticipate changes, and adapt strategies to market dynamics, strengthening relationships, collaboration, and driving mutual success.

Also, regular competitor analysis is essential for entrepreneurs to benchmark their performance and stay informed about industry trends and emerging strategies. By monitoring competitors, entrepreneurs can identify areas for differentiation and anticipate market shifts. Through comprehensive competitor analyses, entrepreneurs gain valuable insights into competitor strengths and weaknesses, enabling them to refine their marketing and distribution strategies to maintain a competitive edge. Additionally, internal teams involved in marketing and distribution possess valuable insights into customer interactions and market dynamics. By tapping into the perspectives of sales, marketing, and customer support teams, entrepreneurs can gain a holistic understanding of customer needs and preferences. Developing a culture of continuous improvement within the organization is essential for driving innovation and staying ahead in the dynamic marketplace. Entrepreneurs create an environment where innovation thrives by actively encouraging team members to contribute ideas and insights for strategy enhancement. By embracing a culture of continuous improvement, entrepreneurs can adapt to changing market conditions, seize new opportunities, and deliver exceptional value to customers. Collaboration between marketing, sales, product development, and customer support teams is critical for aligning efforts and delivering a seamless customer experience.

Facilitating cross-functional collaboration ensures that feedback loops exist across all functions involved in the customer journey. By breaking down silos and promoting open communication, entrepreneurs can leverage the collective expertise of diverse teams to drive innovation and optimize marketing and distribution strategies. Embracing a rapid iteration and testing culture allows entrepreneurs to respond quickly to feedback and refine their strategies accordingly. By adopting an iterative approach to strategy development, entrepreneurs can accelerate learning, optimize resource allocation, and drive continuous improvement in marketing and distribution efforts. Transparently communicating changes and optimizations resulting from feedback is essential for maintaining stakeholder trust and engagement. By building open communication channels, entrepreneurs can solicit feedback, address concerns, and build stronger relationships with stakeholders, driving long-term success and sustainability. By integrating feedback into marketing and distribution strategies, entrepreneurs position their ventures for resilience and adaptability. This iterative approach enhances customer satisfaction and allows the business to stay responsive to evolving market dynamics and maintain a competitive edge.

5.6. Project Presentation and Evaluation

The culmination of an entrepreneurial venture often involves presenting the project to potential stakeholders, investors, or partners. The following discussion explores the art of effective proposal pitching techniques, providing insights and strategies to ensure a compelling and impactful project presentation.

5.6.1 Effective Proposal Pitching Techniques

Crafting a clear and concise message is paramount in capturing the attention of potential stakeholders. By articulating the core value proposition simply, entrepreneurs ensure that the audience comprehends the problem and the proposed innovative solution. Clarity of message instils confidence in the viability and relevance of the venture, developing trust and engagement among investors and partners. Storytelling adds a compelling narrative to the pitch, making it more engaging and relatable to the audience. Entrepreneurs create an emotional connection that resonates with stakeholders by narrating the journey of identifying the market need, developing the solution, and envisioning the future impact. Effective storytelling captures attention and leaves an impression, compelling investors to envision themselves as part of the venture's success story. Emphasizing the alignment between the identified problem and the proposed solution is critical for demonstrating the venture's relevance and potential impact. By clearly illustrating how the innovative product or service directly addresses the market need, entrepreneurs establish credibility and relevance in the eyes of investors. Aligning the problem with the solution enhances the persuasiveness of the pitch, convincing stakeholders of the venture's value proposition.

Importantly, presenting a compelling case for the market opportunity is essential for attracting investment and support. Entrepreneurs should provide robust data and insights into the size of the target market, potential customer base, and scalability of the venture. By quantifying the market opportunity and highlighting growth prospects, entrepreneurs instil confidence in the venture's potential for success, compelling investors to take notice and participate in its journey. Analysing and presenting the competitive landscape demonstrates an understanding of the market dynamics and positioning of the venture. Entrepreneurs should highlight key differentiators that give the venture a competitive edge, whether unique technology, innovative features, or differentiated value proposition. By highlighting a thorough understanding of the competitive landscape, entrepreneurs mitigate concerns and instil confidence in the venture's ability to capture market share. Clearly outlining the business model and revenue generation strategy is essential for demonstrating the venture's path to profitability and sustainability. Entrepreneurs should address monetization, pricing, and long-term viability questions, clarifying how the venture intends to generate revenue and achieve financial success. A transparent and well-defined business model imparts confidence in investors and partners, developing trust and support for the venture. Providing realistic and well-supported financial projections is crucial for demonstrating the venture's financial viability and potential return on investment. Entrepreneurs should present comprehensive revenue forecasts, expense breakdowns, and profitability analyses backed by thorough research and market data. By demonstrating a deep understanding of the financial aspects and articulating a clear path to profitability, entrepreneurs instil confidence in stakeholders and inspire investment in the venture's growth and success.

Introducing the core team members and their key roles is pivotal for building confidence among stakeholders regarding the venture's ability to execute the project effectively. Entrepreneurs provide insight into the leadership and operational prowess driving the venture forward by highlighting the team's diverse expertise, extensive experience, and collective capabilities. This introduction imparts trust and aligns stakeholders with the project's vision and objectives. Articulating the anticipated impact of the venture is essential for inspiring confidence and garnering stakeholder support. Entrepreneurs must convey the value proposition to customers, investors, and other stakeholders, highlighting how the innovative solution addresses critical needs and delivers tangible benefits. By emphasizing the potential impact and value proposition, entrepreneurs create a compelling narrative that resonates with stakeholders, motivating them to engage with the venture. Additionally, employing visually captivating slides and aids enhances the effectiveness of the presentation by captivating the audience and facilitating comprehension and retention of key information. Incorporating graphics, charts, and images enhances the visual appeal and simplifies the communication of complex ideas and data. Visual aids and presentation design play a crucial role in capturing and retaining the audience's attention, thereby augmenting the overall impact and efficacy of the pitch. Proactively acknowledging potential concerns or objections demonstrates preparedness and foresight, bolstering stakeholders' confidence in the venture's ability to overcome challenges. Entrepreneurs should anticipate questions and apprehensions that stakeholders may have and provide thorough responses that address them comprehensively. By pre-emptively addressing potential concerns, entrepreneurs alleviate doubts and objections, raising credibility and trust with the audience.

Concluding the pitch with a clear call-to-action is imperative for guiding stakeholders on the next steps and encouraging desired outcomes, such as investment, partnership, or further engagement. Entrepreneurs should succinctly articulate their expectations from the audience and provide specific instructions on how stakeholders can support or collaborate with the venture. A compelling call to action motivates stakeholders to act, propelling progress toward the venture's objectives. Conducting thorough rehearsals before the presentation allows entrepreneurs to refine their delivery, timing, and messaging for maximum impact. Seeking feedback from peers, mentors, or advisors offers valuable insights and perspectives that can help entrepreneurs identify areas for improvement and fine-tune their pitch. By dedicating time to rehearsals and soliciting feedback, entrepreneurs elevate the quality and effectiveness of their presentations, thereby enhancing their chances of success. Demonstrating adaptability and flexibility during the pitch is vital for responding adeptly to audience feedback or unforeseen inquiries. Entrepreneurs should be prepared to adapt their presentation on the spot, addressing concerns or providing additional information, as necessary. By displaying agility and responsiveness, entrepreneurs underscore their ability to navigate dynamic situations and adjust to evolving circumstances, reinforcing their credibility and reliability in the eyes of stakeholders.

Mastering effective proposal pitching techniques is crucial for securing support and resources for the entrepreneurial venture. By combining a compelling narrative with data-driven insights, entrepreneurs can captivate their audience and instil confidence in the project's potential for success.

5.6.2 Addressing Questions and Concerns

Effectively addressing questions and concerns is integral to the project presentation and evaluation process. Entrepreneurs should demonstrate respect and attentiveness by actively listening to questions posed by stakeholders, laying the foundation for meaningful dialogue and rapport-building. Seeking clarification when questions are ambiguous or unclear is essential for ensuring mutual understanding between the presenter and the audience. By proactively seeking clarification, presenters can avoid misinterpretations and provide more accurate and relevant responses, fostering a productive exchange of ideas. Structuring responses clearly and organized enhances comprehension and facilitates effective communication. Presenters should break down complex questions into manageable components, addressing each aspect systematically to ensure thorough coverage and coherence in their responses. Additionally, acknowledging the validity of concerns raised by stakeholders demonstrates humility and empathy, building trust and transparency in the presenter-audience relationship. By openly acknowledging concerns, presenters signal their willingness to confront challenges head-on and work collaboratively towards viable solutions. Supporting responses with relevant data and evidence enhances the credibility and persuasiveness of the presenter's arguments. Concrete examples, statistics, or case studies provide tangible proof of concept, reinforcing the validity and feasibility of the proposed project or solution. Moreover, maintaining honesty and transparency in responses is paramount for building stakeholder trust and credibility. Presenters should be forthcoming about limitations, uncertainties, or areas where further research is needed, demonstrating integrity and a commitment to ethical communication practices. By embracing honesty and transparency, presenters develop a culture of accountability and authenticity, strengthening the foundation for successful collaboration and partnership.

In addressing questions and concerns, it is imperative to consistently relate responses to the overarching vision and objectives of the project. By anchoring responses in the project's vision, presenters reinforce the alignment between the proposed solution and the long-term goals and values of the venture. This provides context for the audience and underscores the strategic direction and purpose behind the project, enhancing the coherence and persuasiveness of the presentation. Moreover, presenters can enhance their responses by leveraging the diverse expertise of team members to address specialized questions effectively. By highlighting the collective knowledge and competence of the entire project team, presenters impart confidence in the audience regarding the depth of talent and resources available to support the project's success. This collaborative approach enriches the quality of responses and fosters a sense of unity and cohesion within the team. Handling unexpected or challenging questions with confidence is essential for maintaining credibility and poise during a presentation. Presenters demonstrate professionalism and adaptability by responding gracefully and composedly, even when the answer may not be immediately apparent. This proactive approach instils confidence in the audience and reinforces the presenter's ability to navigate unforeseen circumstances effectively. Skilfully bridging responses back to key messages and value propositions ensures that even detailed answers contribute to the overall narrative of the presentation. By strategically linking responses to core themes and key messages, presenters reinforce the central tenets of their presentation, reinforcing key takeaways and guiding the audience's understanding toward desired conclusions.

Maintaining a respectful and professional tone in all responses is essential for developing a positive and constructive dialogue with stakeholders. Presenters should avoid defensive or confrontational language, even when faced with critical questions, as it may detract from the credibility and effectiveness of their responses. Cultivating an atmosphere of mutual respect and collaboration conducive to productive engagement and discussion, presenters uphold a respectful and professional manner. Additionally, emphasizing the iterative nature of answers underscores the presenter's commitment to continuous improvement and adaptability based on feedback. By acknowledging that responses are subject to refinement and enhancement over time, presenters demonstrate a growth mind-set and openness to learning. This iterative approach encourages on-going dialogue and collaboration, reinforcing the presenter's responsiveness to evolving needs and priorities. Finally, engaging with the audience during the response process facilitates active participation and ensures a comprehensive understanding of the subject matter. Presenters should encourage follow-up questions or additional discussions to effectively address any lingering uncertainties or concerns, creating opportunities for meaningful interaction and exchange and enriching the overall presentation experience for all stakeholders involved.

Effectively addressing questions and concerns instils stakeholder confidence and highlights the entrepreneur's depth of knowledge and preparedness. By employing these strategies, entrepreneurs can navigate Q&A sessions with finesse, enhancing positive interactions and advancing the project evaluation process

5.6.3 Peer and Instructor Evaluation Criteria

During the project presentation and evaluation, both peers and instructors play crucial roles in assessing the merit and viability of the entrepreneurial venture. Figure 5.4 represents the overall Project Presentations Overall Evaluation Criteria. The following discussion outlines the critical criteria against which peers and instructors will evaluate the project, providing insights into the aspects that contribute to a comprehensive and well-received evaluation. The peer evaluation criteria are as follows.

Content Relevance: Assessing the relevance of the project content involves examining how well the proposed solution addresses the identified problem or need within the target market. Peers evaluate whether the project understands the problem statement, identifies relevant market trends and consumer behaviours, and proposes a solution that effectively addresses the identified pain points or challenges. Projects demonstrating a solid alignment between the identified problem and the proposed solution receive higher scores in this criterion.

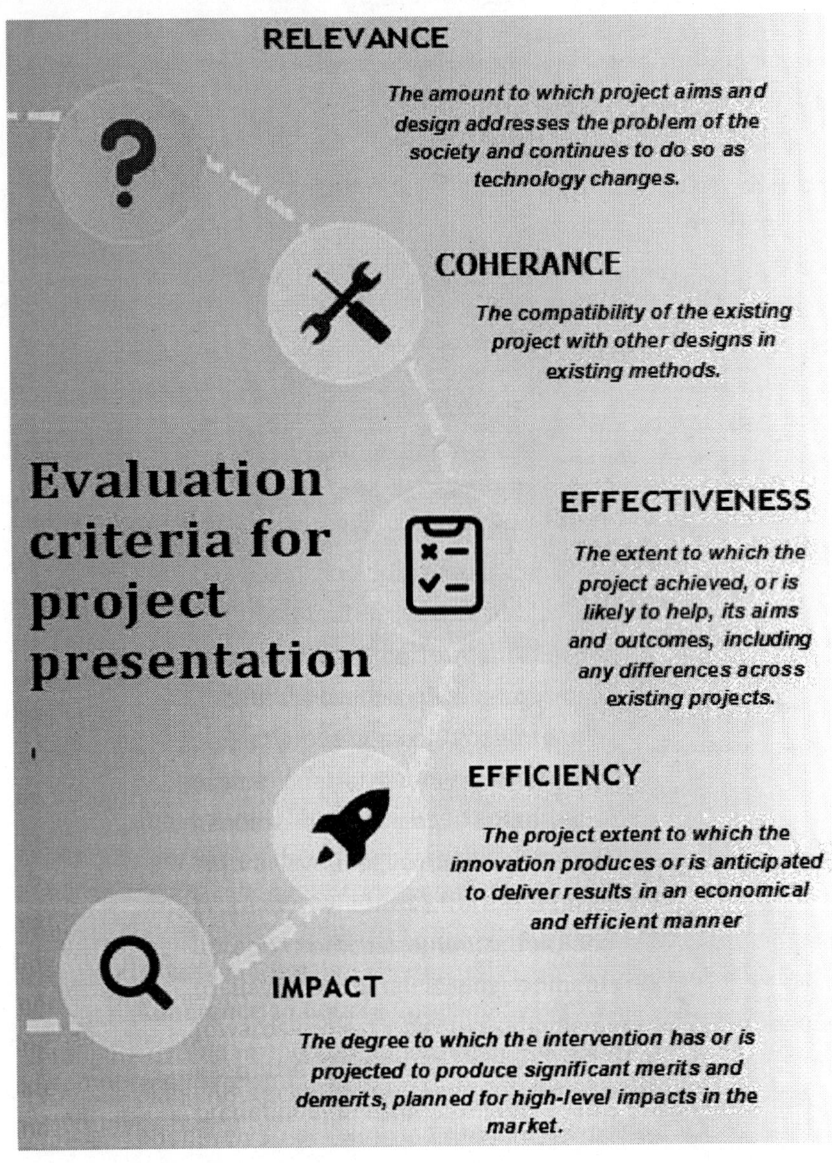

Figure 5.4 Project Presentations Overall Evaluation Criteria

Clarity of Presentation: Peers evaluate the clarity and coherence of the project presentation to determine how effectively the entrepreneur communicates the critical aspects of the venture. This criterion encompasses factors such as the organization of content, the clarity of language and visuals, and the overall flow of the presentation. Projects that present information logically and easy-to-follow, use clear and concise language, and incorporate engaging visuals or multimedia elements tend to receive higher ratings in this category.

Innovations and Creativity: Peers gauge the level of innovation and creativity demonstrated in the proposed solution. They assess whether the project introduces novel ideas, approaches, or technologies that differentiate it from existing solutions in the market. Additionally, peers look for evidence of creative problem-solving, unique value propositions, or innovative business models that set the venture apart from competitors. Projects highlighting originality and creativity in their concepts, designs, or strategies are typically well-regarded by peers.

Feasibility and Viability: Peers analyse the feasibility and viability of the project to determine its potential for success in the market. This criterion involves assessing several factors, such as technical feasibility, market demand, scalability, resource requirements, and potential barriers to entry. Peers evaluate whether the proposed solution is technically feasible, whether there is a market need or demand for the product or service, and whether the venture has a realistic path to profitability and sustainability. Projects that demonstrate a clear understanding of these factors and offer realistic and well-supported plans for execution receive higher scores in this category.

Business Model: Peers evaluate the clarity and effectiveness of the business model presented in the project. They assess whether the revenue generation strategy is clearly defined and aligned with the target market and whether the venture has identified sustainable sources of revenue. Additionally, peers evaluate the scalability of the business model and its potential for long-term growth and profitability. Projects with a well-articulated and financially viable business model supported by evidence and market research receive favourable ratings in this criterion. Figure 5.5 shows an overview of the business Model Canvas, a strategic management tool that helps entrepreneurs visualize and build their company models. This canvas comprises nine major building blocks: customer segments, value proposition, channels, customer relationships, revenue streams, essential resources, key activities, key partnerships, and cost structure. Each block symbolizes an integral part of the firm, and entrepreneurs may utilize the canvas to study and enhance their business model thoroughly. By filling out each block with relevant data, entrepreneurs thoroughly know how their company generates, delivers, and collects value. The Business Model Canvas is also helpful for brainstorming, planning, and successfully articulating business concepts.

Responses to Questions: Peers assess how well the entrepreneur responds to questions and concerns raised during the presentation or Q&A session. They evaluate the depth of understanding demonstrated in responses, the clarity and coherence of explanations, and the ability to address concerns effectively. Peers look for evidence of active listening, thoughtful consideration of questions, and the ability to provide informative and persuasive answers. Projects that demonstrate practical communication skills, confidence, and expertise in responding to questions tend to receive positive evaluations in this category.

Team Collaboration: Peers evaluate the level of collaboration and constructive collaboration within the project team. They assess how effectively team members work together to contribute to the overall presentation and execution of the project. Peers look for evidence of effective communication, mutual respect, and shared responsibility among team members. Projects demonstrating strong teamwork, with each member playing a meaningful role in the project, receive higher scores in this criterion.

The instructor evaluation criteria are as follows.

Project Alignments with Learning Objectives: Instructors evaluate the extent to which the project aligns with the defined learning objectives of the course. They assess whether the project integrates theoretical concepts and principles covered in the course into practical application. Instructors look for evidence that the project reflects an understanding of course materials and applies them effectively to real-world entrepreneurial challenges. Projects that strongly align with course objectives and highlight the application of learned concepts receive higher scores in this criterion.

Depth of Analysis: Instructors analyse the depth of analysis presented in the project, focusing on the thoroughness of market research, problem analysis, and solution development. They evaluate the extent to which the entrepreneur has conducted comprehensive research, gathered relevant data, and critically analysed information to inform decision-making. Instructors look for evidence of a rigorous analytical process, including identifying key insights, evaluating alternative solutions, and justifying chosen strategies. Projects demonstrating a prominent analytical depth and critical thinking level receive favourable evaluations in this category.

Adherence to Course Concepts: Instructors assess how well the project adheres to critical concepts covered in the course, including entrepreneurship principles, innovation frameworks, and business planning techniques. They evaluate whether the entrepreneur has applied course concepts effectively to develop and execute the project. Instructors look for evidence of a solid understanding of course materials, as demonstrated through applying relevant frameworks, methodologies, and strategies. Projects that effectively incorporate course concepts into the entrepreneurial venture receive higher ratings in this criterion.

Professionalism and Communication Skills: Instructors evaluate the professionalism and communication skills of the entrepreneur during the project presentation. They assess factors such as articulation, behaviour, body language, and overall presentation style. Instructors look for evidence of effective communication, including clarity of expression, confidence, and engagement with the audience. Additionally, they evaluate the entrepreneur's ability to convey complex ideas in a clear and accessible manner. Projects demonstrating professionalism and practical communication skills receive positive evaluations in this category.

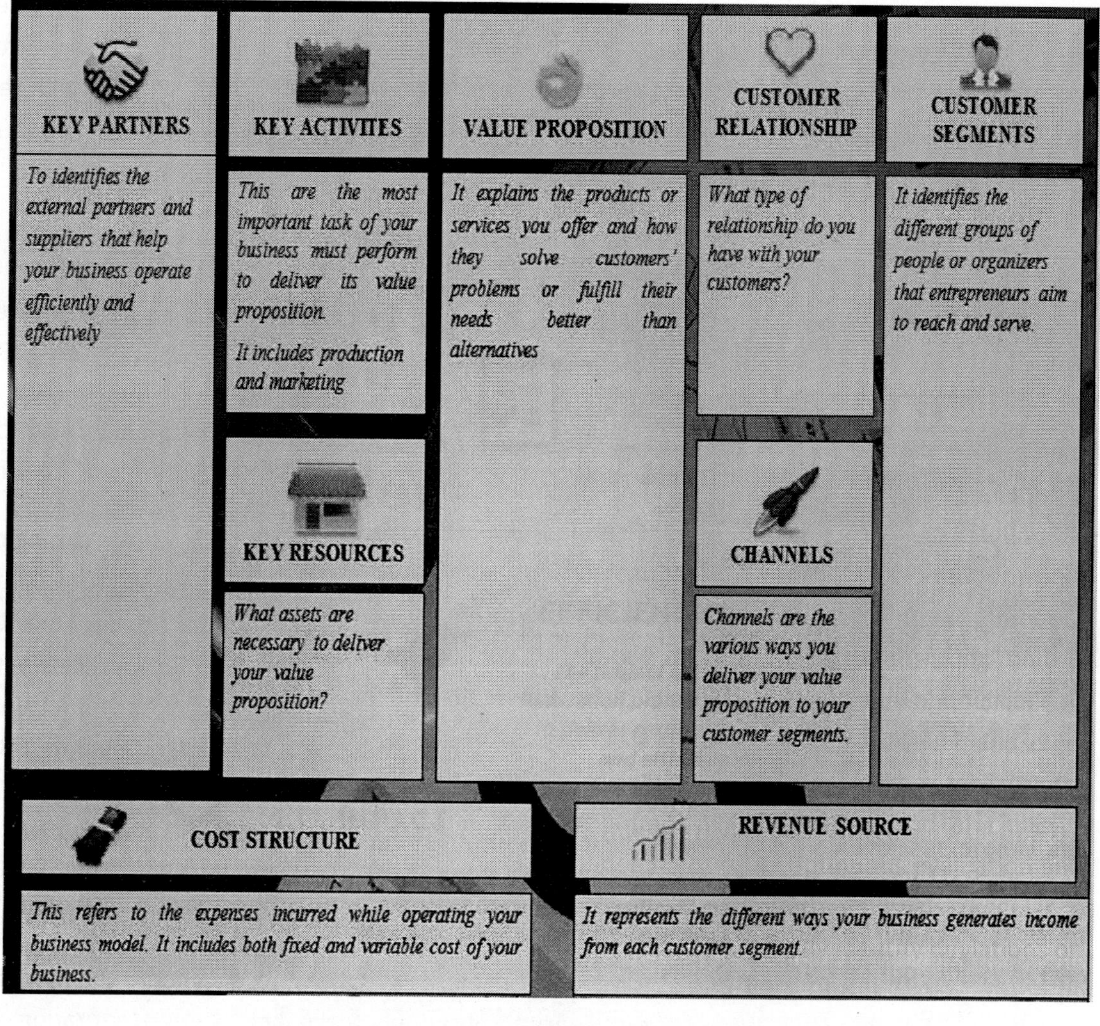

Figure 5.5 Overview of a Business Model Canvas

12. Critical Thinking and Problem-Solving: Instructors assess the demonstration of critical thinking and problem-solving skills throughout the project. They evaluate entrepreneurs' ability to identify challenges, analyse problems, and develop creative and effective solutions. Instructors look for evidence of strategic thinking, adaptability, and resourcefulness in addressing complex issues. Additionally, they evaluate the entrepreneur's ability to anticipate potential obstacles and proactively mitigate risks. Projects highlighting strong critical thinking and problem-solving abilities receive high marks in this criterion.

13. Integration of Feedback: Instructors evaluate how effectively the entrepreneur integrates feedback received throughout the course into the project. They assess the responsiveness to constructive criticism and the ability to iteratively refine the project based on feedback from peers, instructors, or mentors. Instructors look for evidence of reflective practice, willingness to receive input, and proactive efforts to incorporate suggestions for improvement. Projects that demonstrate a willingness to learn from feedback and adapt accordingly receive favourable evaluations in this category.

14. Overall Impact and Contribution: Instructors gauge the project's overall impact and contribution to entrepreneurship. They assess the venture's potential to impact meaningfully through innovation, market disruption, social value creation, or other relevant criteria. Instructors evaluate the entrepreneurial venture's scalability, sustainability, and long-term viability, considering its potential to generate value for stakeholders and contribute positively to the entrepreneurial ecosystem. Projects demonstrating significant potential for impact and contribution receive high scores in this criterion.

By understanding and addressing these evaluation criteria, entrepreneurs can enhance their chances of receiving positive feedback and constructive insights from peers and instructors, contributing to the continuous improvement of their entrepreneurial ventures.

5.7. Project Implementation

Once the entrepreneurial venture successfully navigates the planning and evaluation stages, the focus shifts to project implementation. The following discussion explores the key considerations and steps in translating the conceptualized project into a tangible and operational reality.

5.7.1 Transitioning from Planning to Execution

The transition from the planning to the execution phase marks a pivotal moment in the entrepreneurial journey. The following discussion explores into the critical considerations and steps involved in smoothly transitioning from conceptualization to the active implementation of the project. Ensuring all project teams are aligned with the transition plan is essential for seamless execution. Comprehensive briefing sessions should be conducted to communicate the strategic goals and immediate priorities during the execution phase. By ensuring everyone understands their roles and responsibilities; teams can work cohesively towards common objectives, fostering efficiency and collaboration. Moreover, the execution plan should be reviewed and refined based on insights gained during the planning phase. This includes incorporating any adjustments or optimizations to enhance implementation efficiency. Continuous refinement of the plan enables teams to adapt to changing circumstances and improve their approach to achieving project goals over time. Mobilizing the necessary resources, including human capital, funding, and technology, is crucial for initiating the project. Confirming that all required resources are in place and ready for deployment ensures the project can proceed smoothly without delays or disruptions. Additionally, a robust communication strategy is vital for informing all stakeholders about the transition. Clearly articulating each team member's expectations, roles, and responsibilities as the project moves into the execution stage fosters transparency and ensures everyone is on the same page, facilitating effective collaboration.

Conducting a thorough review of potential risks and challenges that may arise during execution is essential for proactive risk management. Developing a risk mitigation plan enables teams to address unforeseen issues promptly and minimize their impact on project progress. By anticipating and preparing for risks, teams can increase their chances of success. Furthermore, empowering the project team by providing necessary training and resources is crucial for successful execution. Encouraging a sense of ownership and commitment among team members fosters initiative and drives results, enhancing productivity and innovation within the organization. Establishing key performance indicators (KPIs) is crucial for effectively monitoring and evaluating the project's progress throughout the execution phase. By defining clear metrics aligned with the project's overarching goals, teams can track their performance and make informed decisions to ensure goal attainment. These KPIs offer valuable insights into the project's success and areas needing adjustment, facilitating proactive decision-making and progress tracking. Moreover, embracing an agile mindset is essential for adaptability and flexibility during execution. Teams must be ready to adjust strategies based on real-time feedback and emerging insights, enabling quick iteration, process optimization, and seizing opportunities for success. This agility empowers teams to navigate dynamic environments with resilience and efficiency, ensuring continued progress towards project objectives. Implementing a continuous evaluation and assessment system is vital to keep the project on track and aligned with its goals. Regular performance reviews against predefined milestones enable teams to promptly identify deviations or areas for improvement.

By conducting ongoing evaluations, teams can make informed decisions, address issues proactively, and maintain momentum towards achieving project goals. Additionally, establishing a feedback mechanism fosters collaboration and enhances the collective learning experience. An open and constructive feedback culture allows teams to identify strengths, weaknesses, and growth opportunities, cultivating a culture of continuous improvement and innovation. Acknowledging and celebrating key milestones achieved during the execution stages is essential for boosting morale and motivation. Recognizing the efforts and contributions of team members reinforces positive behaviours and strengthens team cohesion. Celebrating milestones serves as a reminder of progress made and inspires teams to strive for excellence. Furthermore, maintaining transparent communication channels ensures stakeholders are informed about the project's progress. Sharing successes, challenges, and lessons learned fosters a collaborative environment, builds trust, enhances stakeholder engagement, and promotes alignment towards shared goals. Regular updates ensure stakeholders remain involved and invested in the project's success. The transition from planning to execution requires meticulous planning, effective communication, and a proactive approach to address potential challenges. By systematically navigating this transition phase, entrepreneurs set the stage for a successful and impactful execution of their entrepreneurial venture.

5.7.2 Overcoming Implementation Challenges

As entrepreneurial ventures move into the implementation phase, they are expected to encounter various challenges that may impede progress. The following discussion explores proactive strategies and considerations for overcoming common implementation challenges, ensuring a smoother project execution. Figure 5.6 presents reflective questions for project evaluation, guiding entrepreneurs in critically assessing their ventures and identifying areas for improvement and growth.

When encountering common implementation challenges like resource constraints, teams must conduct a thorough assessment of resource requirements to effectively address these constraints. By understanding the project's specific needs, teams can better prioritize resource allocation and explore alternative channels, such as partnerships or outsourcing, to supplement existing capabilities and fill gaps where necessary. Prioritizing resources based on critical project needs ensures efficient utilization and minimizes bottlenecks. Another significant challenge is resistance to change, which can be addressed through implementing change management practices. Communicating the project's benefits and how it aligns with overall goals helps stakeholders understand the importance of embracing change. Facilitating open discussions and engaging team members in the decision-making process empowers them to voice concerns and become advocates for the project. By addressing resistance proactively, teams can develop a culture of adaptability and innovation. Implementing a robust change control process is vital for managing scope changes effectively amidst project challenges like scope fluctuations. Regularly revisiting project objectives ensures adjustments align with overarching goals and priorities. Communicating the implications of scope changes on timelines and resources helps stakeholders understand the trade-offs involved. By maintaining clarity and transparency around project scope, teams can minimize disruptions and focus on delivering key outcomes.

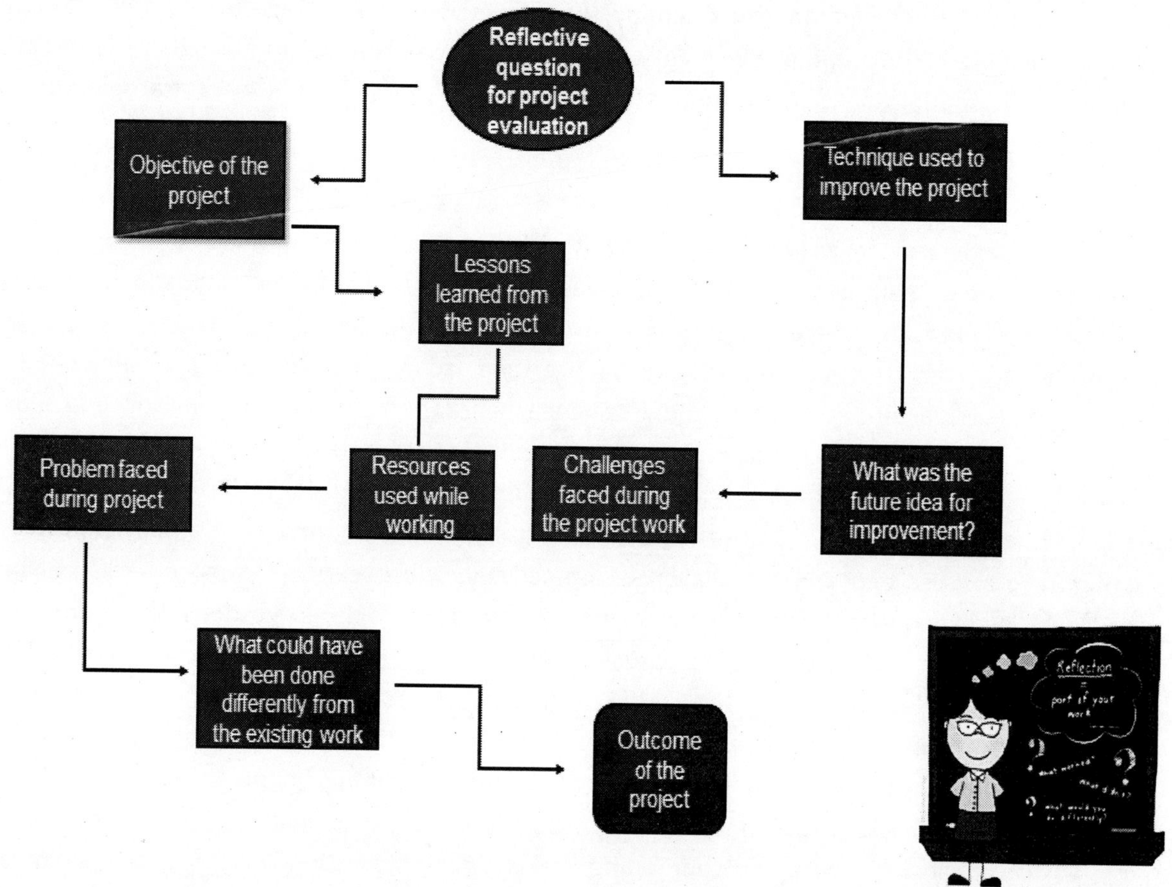

Figure 5.6 Reflective Questions for Project Evaluation

Another significant challenge is inadequate communication, which can be mitigated by developing a transparent and open communication culture. Implementing communication tools and platforms enables real-time updates and collaboration. Scheduled team meetings and stakeholder briefings provide opportunities to address concerns and align priorities. Prioritizing effective communication helps teams develop trust, collaboration, and accountability. Teams must also address unforeseen risks by continuously assessing and updating the risk mitigation plan. Establishing contingency measures enables teams to respond promptly to emerging risks and minimize potential disruptions. Encouraging a proactive approach to risk identification and resolution empowers team members to anticipate challenges and take preventive action. By remaining vigilant and adaptable, teams can navigate uncertainties with resilience and agility. Additionally, building a collaborative team environment is essential for addressing collaboration challenges. Team-building activities promote cohesion and trust among team members, enhancing collaboration. Addressing conflicts promptly through mediation or interventions prevents issues from escalating and disrupting the team's productivity. Open communication channels provide a platform for sharing ideas, concerns, and feedback, developing a culture of transparency and collaboration.

Staying informed about external market dynamics is crucial for navigating uncertainties, especially amidst challenges like proactive monitoring and continuous improvement. Regular market analyses enable teams to anticipate changes in customer behaviour, industry trends, and competitive landscapes. Developing contingency plans allows teams to pivot or adapt strategies in response to market shifts, ensuring resilience and adaptability in dynamic environments. Additionally, implementing proactive monitoring mechanisms enables teams to identify and address challenges early on. Project management tools and dashboards ease real-time tracking of key performance indicators, allowing teams to intervene promptly and make informed decisions for course correction as needed. Cultivating a culture of continuous improvement empowers teams to optimize processes and address challenges proactively, while learning from setbacks enhances resilience and innovation. Encouraging team members to provide suggestions for improvement supports ongoing enhancements to project execution and outcomes. Viewing setbacks as opportunities for learning and growth during retrospective sessions allows teams to analyse root causes, derive valuable lessons, and implement corrective actions for future projects. Moreover, actively engaging with stakeholders facilitates collaboration and alignment. Gathering stakeholder insights and feedback enables teams to incorporate diverse perspectives into decision-making processes, enhancing project outcomes and stakeholder satisfaction. Involving stakeholders in critical discussions and decision-making supports ownership and commitment to project success.

By adopting proactive strategies and maintaining flexibility, entrepreneurial ventures can navigate implementation challenges more effectively, ensuring the successful realization of their projects

5.7.3 Monitoring and Adjusting the Project Plan

As the entrepreneurial venture progresses through the implementation phase, continuous monitoring, and adjustment of the project plan become imperative to ensure alignment with strategic goals and adaptability to dynamic circumstances. The following discussion outlines the fundamental principles and practices for effectively monitoring and adjusting the project plan.

Figure 5.7 illustrates Continuous Learning and Improvement, a conceptual framework that highlights the iterative nature of the entrepreneurial process. In this spiral, entrepreneurs engage in a learning, experimentation, and adaptation cycle to refine their business ideas and strategies over time. The Key Monitoring and Adjustment Practices during the project plan are as follows:

In project management, effective monitoring and adjustment practices are paramount to the success of any entrepreneurial venture. One essential practice is real-time tracking, where mechanisms are implemented to monitor progress against predefined milestones continuously. By implementing project management tools and dashboards, teams can receive instant updates on task completion, timelines, and resource utilization. This allows for quick identification of any deviations from the plan, enabling proactive adjustments to keep the project on track. Another essential aspect is establishing and regularly evaluating key performance indicators (KPIs) relevant to project objectives. These KPIs act as quantifiable metrics to assess the effectiveness and efficiency of ongoing activities. By regularly reviewing KPIs, teams gain actionable insights into areas requiring adjustment or improvement, ensuring that resources are allocated optimally, and goals are met effectively.

Furthermore, milestone reviews conducted at specified intervals are crucial for assessing accomplishments and challenges. These reviews provide an opportunity to identify deviations from the original plan and evaluate their impact on the project timeline and outcomes. By conducting timely milestone reviews, teams can make necessary adjustments to ensure project success, maintain alignment with stakeholder expectations, and address concerns.

Continuous improvement is at the heart of successful project management endeavours. By developing its culture within the project team, organizations can capitalize on team members' collective insights and experiences to drive enhancements and efficiencies in project processes. This involves creating an environment where feedback is welcomed and ideas for improvement are actively sought. Through regular dialogue and feedback sessions, teams can work more efficiently with higher productivity. Transparent and open communication channels are fundamental for effective project management. Maintaining transparent communication within the team ensures that everyone is informed and involved in decision-making processes. By facilitating discussions on potential adjustments to the project plan and encouraging input from all relevant stakeholders, organizations can recognize diverse perspectives to make informed decisions. This transparency builds collaboration and ensures that changes are communicated effectively, mitigating misunderstandings, and promoting alignment across the team.

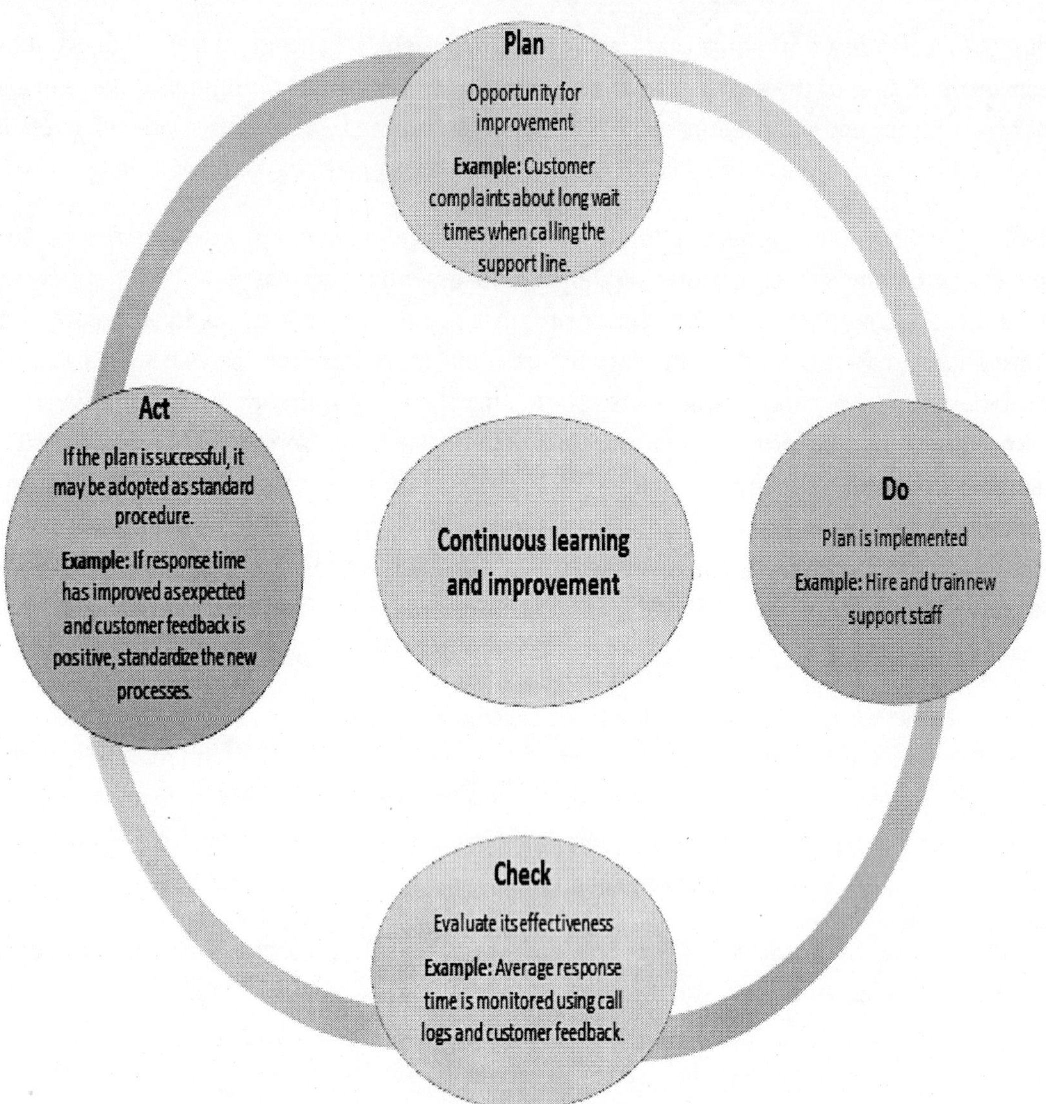

Figure 5.7 Continuous Learning and Improvement

Flexibility and adaptability are essential qualities for navigating the dynamic landscape of project management. In the face of changing circumstances, teams must be prepared to adjust their plans and strategies accordingly. Developing contingency plans for unforeseen challenges enable teams to respond quickly and effectively, minimizing disruptions to project progress. By embracing flexibility and adaptability, organizations can proactively navigate challenges and seize opportunities for innovation and growth. Establishing clear protocols for decision-making is crucial for effective project governance. Defining roles and responsibilities ensures that decisions are made promptly and aligned with project objectives. This clarity streamlines the decision-making process, reducing delays and enabling swift action. By establishing decision-making protocols, organizations can empower team members to take ownership of their roles and contribute meaningfully to project success.

Thorough documentation of all adjustments made to the project plan is essential for accountability and transparency. Regular reporting provides stakeholders insights into the project's progress and facilitates informed decision-making. Documentation also serves as a valuable reference for future projects, enabling organizations to leverage lessons learned and best practices to drive continuous improvement across projects. Regularly assessing the alignment of project activities with strategic goals helps organizations stay focused on their overarching objectives. Organizations can maintain momentum toward project success by adjusting the project plan to ensure alignment with strategic goals. This strategic alignment ensures that project efforts are directed toward achieving meaningful outcomes contributing to the organization's long-term success. Encouraging a proactive approach to problem-solving empowers team members to identify and address challenges promptly. By developing a culture where problems are viewed as opportunities for improvement, organizations can drive continuous improvement and innovation within the project team. Empowering team members to take initiative in problem-solving fosters a sense of ownership and accountability, driving organizational success in the face of adversity.

By incorporating these monitoring and adjustment practices into the project management framework, entrepreneurs can proactively respond to changes, enhance project adaptability, and increase the likelihood of successful project outcomes

5.8. Reflection and Learning

Reflection is a crucial component of the entrepreneurial learning process, allowing individuals and teams to assess their experiences, extract valuable insights, and cultivate a culture of continuous improvement. Herein, the importance of individual and team reflections within the entrepreneurial context is presented.

5.8.1 Individual and Team Reflections

By clarifying personal and team goals through reflection, individuals and teams can enhance their sense of direction and purpose within the entrepreneurial journey. Furthermore, reflection facilitates the evaluation of successes and challenges encountered along the entrepreneurial path. It provides an opportunity to acknowledge and celebrate individual and team achievements, developing a positive and motivating environment. Recognizing successes enhances morale and reinforces commitment to the entrepreneurial endeavour. Conversely, reflection allows individuals and teams to address challenges systematically by identifying root causes and devising practical solutions. This proactive approach to problem-solving promotes continuous learning and improvement, enhancing the overall resilience of individuals and teams. Moreover, reflection plays a crucial role in enhancing self-awareness among participants. Through introspection, individuals can identify their strengths, weaknesses, and areas for development. By understanding their entrepreneurial capabilities more deeply, individuals can leverage their strengths and address areas requiring improvement to maximize their potential for success. Similarly, team reflections offer valuable insights into group dynamics, communication styles, and collaborative processes. By developing a deeper understanding of team dynamics, reflection creates a cohesive and supportive team environment where members can thrive and contribute effectively to collective goals.

Reflection is a powerful tool for iterative learning, enabling individuals and teams to distil valuable lessons from their experiences. Whether reflecting on individual pursuits or team endeavours, participants can leverage insights gained from past successes and setbacks to refine their approaches. It ensures continuous improvement using an iterative nature, where individuals and teams actively contribute to refining strategies based on acquired insights. By embracing a culture of reflection, participants ensure on-going success in their entrepreneurial journey, adapting and evolving in response to emerging challenges and opportunities. Moreover, reflection facilitates open communication at the individual and team levels. Individuals can express their thoughts, experiences, and perspectives openly, creating an environment of trust and collaboration within the team. Similarly, team reflections encourage dialogue among members, enabling a collaborative exchange of ideas. This open communication allows teams to collectively navigate challenges and capitalize on opportunities, leveraging the diverse perspectives and expertise within the group. Furthermore, reflection prompts participants to realign their goals, both at the individual and team levels. Individuals can assess whether their initial aspirations remain relevant and align with their evolving understanding of the entrepreneurial landscape. This process allows for the adjustment of personal goals, ensuring alignment with current objectives. Similarly, team reflections facilitate the evaluation of shared goals, ensuring that the team remains aligned and cohesive in its approach toward entrepreneurial success.

Finally, reflection yields actionable insights that inform individual action plans and team strategies. Individuals can develop actionable personal development and skill enhancement plans, using reflection as a roadmap for achieving their entrepreneurial goals. Similarly, team reflections generate insights that may lead to strategic adjustments, ensuring the adaptability and resilience of the entrepreneurial venture. By translating insights into actionable plans, participants maximize their ability to navigate challenges and succeed in their entrepreneurial endeavours.

Individual and team reflections are pivotal in the entrepreneurial learning journey. By developing self-awareness, celebrating successes, addressing challenges, and facilitating open communication, reflection becomes a powerful tool for continuous improvement and sustained entrepreneurial success.

5.8.2 Learning from Successes and Setbacks

Entrepreneurship is a dynamic journey marked by both successes and setbacks. The following discussion explores the significance of learning from these experiences, providing insights into the entrepreneurial learning process. Celebrating successes, regardless of magnitude, is essential for creating a pleasant and stimulating entrepreneurial atmosphere. By recognizing and acknowledging successes, individuals and teams cultivate a sense of accomplishment and motivation to continue their entrepreneurial journey. Moreover, reflecting on the factors contributing to success is essential for extracting valuable lessons. By analysing success factors such as strategies, decisions, and actions, entrepreneurs gain insights into effective practices that can be replicated and built upon in future endeavours. This process reinforces successful practices, integrating them into the entrepreneurial skill set and decision-making processes for sustained success. Furthermore, setbacks should be embraced as learning opportunities within the entrepreneurial journey. Instead of viewing setbacks negatively, entrepreneurs should analyse the root causes of setbacks to gain valuable insights. Understanding the factors that led to unfavourable outcomes enables individuals and teams to identify areas that may require improvement. Additionally, treating setbacks as opportunities for iterative learning is crucial. By identifying alternative approaches and formulating strategies for similar challenges in the future, entrepreneurs contribute to ongoing improvement and resilience during adversity. Moreover, setbacks test the resilience and adaptability of entrepreneurial individuals and teams. Embracing setbacks as a natural part of the entrepreneurial journey creates a mind-set of resilience and adaptability. Viewing setbacks as opportunities to strengthen resilience and enhance adaptability allows entrepreneurs to navigate challenges confidently and continuously. Ultimately, embracing setbacks as learning opportunities contributes to personal and professional growth, equipping individuals and teams with the resilience and adaptability needed to thrive in the dynamic entrepreneurial landscape.

In team settings, collective learning through team reflections is indispensable for entrepreneurial growth. By sharing experiences, insights, and lessons learned, teams cultivate a culture of shared knowledge and continuous improvement. Conducting regular team reflections allows members to adapt and refine team strategies based on collective learning. This collaborative approach ensures that the team remains cohesive and responsive, ready to navigate the dynamic challenges of entrepreneurship. Moreover, developing open communication within the team creates an environment where members feel empowered to share their experiences openly, enabling the team to benefit from diverse perspectives and insights. Furthermore, integrating learning into future actions is crucial for driving entrepreneurial success. Entrepreneurs must extract actionable insights from both successes and setbacks that inform their future actions and decision-making processes. By applying these lessons, entrepreneurs continuously improve their approaches, ensuring a more informed and strategic trajectory. Embracing a mind-set of continuous improvement is fundamental in entrepreneurship. The journey of learning never ceases, and entrepreneurs must consistently apply their newfound knowledge to refine their strategies. This proactive mind-set equips entrepreneurs to tackle future challenges with enhanced knowledge and adaptability, enhancing the probability of success in ever-evolving businesses.

Additionally, building a resilient mind-set is essential for entrepreneurial resilience. Even in moments of success, entrepreneurs must cultivate resilience by acknowledging that challenges may arise in the future. Understanding that success is not guaranteed prepares entrepreneurs for the uncertainties of the entrepreneurial journey. Similarly, setbacks should be viewed as temporary hurdles rather than insurmountable obstacles. A resilient mind-set empowers entrepreneurs to bounce back from setbacks, learn from adversity, and approach future endeavours with renewed determination. By developing resilience in both success and setbacks, entrepreneurs develop the mental fortitude needed to navigate the trials of entrepreneurship and emerge stronger from adversity.

In conclusion, learning from successes and setbacks is integral to the entrepreneurial journey. Whether celebrating achievements, analysing setbacks, or collective learning in teams, the ability to extract valuable insights contributes to the on-going growth and success of entrepreneurial endeavours.

5.8.3 Extracting Lessons for Future Entrepreneurial Endeavours

Entrepreneurial learning is a continual process that extends beyond individual projects. The following discussion presented the significance of extracting lessons from current experiences to inform and enhance future entrepreneurial endeavours.

Reflecting on Project Dynamics Adapting to Market Trends Leveraging Technology and Innovation Refining Decision-Making Processes:

Reflecting on the dynamics of the current entrepreneurial project is essential for growth and learning. Individuals can gain valuable insights into project outcomes by understanding the project dynamics, including team interactions, decision-making processes, and external influences. Examining how these dynamics shaped the project provides a deeper understanding of its pros and cons, enabling participants to identify areas for improvement in future endeavours. Moreover, identifying patterns of success within the project offers valuable insights for future endeavours. By discerning which approaches, methodologies, or strategies consistently led to positive outcomes, individuals can replicate and build upon these success patterns in subsequent projects, increasing their chances of success. In addition, adapting to market trends is crucial for maintaining relevance and competitiveness in the entrepreneurial landscape. Analysing how the current project responded to market trends and demands provides valuable insights into market dynamics. Understanding the forces influencing the project's trajectory enables individuals to develop strategies for effectively navigating evolving market conditions in future endeavours. Embracing agile market strategies allows entrepreneurs to anticipate and respond swiftly to shifts in customer preferences, industry trends, and competitive landscapes, positioning them for success in dynamic markets.

Furthermore, leveraging technology and innovation is paramount for driving entrepreneurial success in today's digital age. Evaluating the significance of technology in the current project sheds light on technologies that significantly contributed to efficiency, innovation, and overall project success. Integrating these technologies into the toolkit for future entrepreneurial initiatives empowers individuals to leverage technology effectively in their ventures. Similarly, extracting best practices in innovation from the current project enables individuals to develop a culture of innovation in future endeavours. Entrepreneurs can replicate these best practices to drive innovation and differentiation in their ventures by understanding how innovative solutions were conceptualized, developed, and implemented. Moreover, refining decision-making processes is essential for enhancing the quality of future entrepreneurial decisions. Reflecting on the effectiveness of decision-making processes employed during the project allows individuals to evaluate the impact of strategic decisions on project outcomes. By refining decision-making approaches, entrepreneurs can improve their ability to make sound and informed decisions in future ventures. Additionally, analysing risk management strategies employed during the project provides insights into how risks were identified, assessed, and mitigated. Developing more effective risk management strategies and proactive risk mitigation plans prepares entrepreneurs to navigate potential challenges confidently and resiliently in future endeavours.

Fostering Synergy, Skill Growth, Strategic Alliances, Sustainability, and Lifelong Learning:

Assessing team collaboration and dynamics is essential for optimizing project outcomes and fostering a cohesive work environment. By evaluating the effectiveness of team collaboration in achieving project goals, individuals can identify areas of strength and improvement in team dynamics. Implementing strategies to enhance team cohesion, communication, and collaboration sets the stage for tremendous success in future projects. Additionally, reflecting on leadership styles within the team offers valuable insights into their impact on project outcomes. Adapting leadership approaches to align with the specific requirements of future entrepreneurial initiatives ensures effective leadership in diverse contexts. Moreover, enhancing personal and team skillsets is vital for navigating the complexities of the entrepreneurial landscape. By identifying instrumental skill sets in project success, individuals can focus on developing skills that align with the evolving demands of entrepreneurship. Encouraging the development of complementary skill sets within the team fosters a learning environment wherein team members share expertise and continually enhance their collective skill and constructive collaboration, thereby strengthening the team's overall capabilities.

Strategic networking and partnerships play a significant role in entrepreneurial success. Reflecting on the effectiveness of networking efforts during the project offers insights into valuable connections, partnerships, or collaborations that positively impact the venture. Leveraging these insights to build networks in future entrepreneurial endeavours strategically enhances opportunities for growth and collaboration. Similarly, assessing the dynamics of partnerships established during the project enables individuals to identify successful collaboration models and optimize partnership strategies for enhanced effectiveness in future ventures. Furthermore, integrating sustainable business practices and ethical considerations into entrepreneurial endeavours is paramount for long-term success and societal impact. Reflecting on integrating sustainable practices in the current project allows individuals to evaluate their impact on environmental and social dimensions. Developing strategies to incorporate sustainable business practices and prioritize ethical decision-making in future endeavours aligns with the growing emphasis on corporate social responsibility and sustainability.

Lastly, developing a continuous learning culture within the entrepreneurial team is fundamental for staying ahead in a rapidly changing business landscape. Cultivating a mind-set that embraces feedback, values insights gained from experiences, and actively seeks growth opportunities contributes to developing a learning organization culture. Implementing adaptive learning strategies allows the team to respond swiftly to emerging trends, technologies, and market dynamics, ensuring adaptability and resilience in the entrepreneurial journey. In conclusion, extracting lessons for future entrepreneurial endeavours involves a comprehensive reflection on project dynamics, market trends, technology integration, decision-making processes, team collaboration, skill development, strategic networking, sustainable business practices, and cultivating a continuous learning culture. By actively incorporating these insights, entrepreneurs can navigate future challenges with resilience, innovation, and strategic acumen.

Case Study: The Development of Dyson's Revolutionary Cyclone Vacuum Cleaner

In the realm of mechanical engineering and product innovation, few stories are as inspiring as that of James Dyson and his invention of the cyclone vacuum cleaner. This case study provides an in-depth look at Dyson's journey from concept to market, highlighting the mechanical engineering principles, innovation strategies, and entrepreneurial challenges he faced. It serves as an exemplary illustration of how engineering knowledge can be applied to create ground-breaking products and successfully launch them in a competitive market.

Background

James Dyson, a British inventor, and entrepreneur was frustrated with the performance of traditional vacuum cleaners, which often lost suction due to clogged bags. Drawing inspiration from industrial cyclone separators used in sawmills, Dyson envisioned a vacuum cleaner that utilized cyclonic separation to maintain consistent suction power without the need for bags.

Conceptualization and Design

The initial phase of Dyson's project involved thorough problem definition and concept generation. Dyson identified the primary issue with existing vacuum cleaners: the loss of suction due to clogged bags. He then conceptualized a vacuum cleaner that would use centrifugal force to separate dust and debris from the air. Using his mechanical engineering background, Dyson designed a prototype that incorporated cyclonic separation technology. This design featured a series of conical chambers where the air would spiral rapidly, causing dust and particles to be flung outwards and collected in a bin, while clean air was expelled. This concept promised consistent suction power and eliminated the need for replacement bags.

Prototyping and Iterative Development

Dyson embarked on an extensive prototyping phase, building over 5,000 prototypes over five years. Each prototype underwent rigorous testing and iterative refinement to address performance issues and enhance the design. Dyson used tools like CAD (Computer-Aided Design) software and rapid prototyping techniques to speed up the development process.

Key mechanical engineering principles, such as fluid dynamics and materials science, played crucial roles in optimizing the vacuum cleaner's performance. For instance, Dyson experimented with different cyclone chamber designs and materials to maximize efficiency and durability.

Challenges and Problem-Solving

Throughout the development process, Dyson faced numerous challenges. These included technical hurdles, such as optimizing the cyclone's efficiency and managing noise levels, as well as financial constraints and scepticism from traditional vacuum cleaner manufacturers.

Dyson's persistence and problem-solving skills were critical in overcoming these challenges. He sought feedback from users and experts, iteratively improving the design based on real-world performance data. This approach ensured that the final product not only met but exceeded user expectations.

Market Introduction and Entrepreneurship

After perfecting the design, Dyson faced the challenge of bringing his product to market. Traditional manufacturers were hesitant to adopt his bagless technology, fearing it would disrupt their profitable bag sales. Undeterred, Dyson decided to launch his own company, Dyson Ltd., to manufacture and sell the vacuum cleaners directly.

Dyson employed strategic marketing campaigns to highlight the unique features and benefits of his product. By focusing on the superior performance and long-term cost savings offered by the bagless design, Dyson successfully attracted a loyal customer base. His entrepreneurial spirit and innovative approach to problem-solving turned the Dyson cyclone vacuum cleaner into a global success.

Conclusion

James Dyson's journey from frustrated consumer to successful inventor and entrepreneur exemplifies the power of product innovation and mechanical engineering. His development of the cyclone vacuums cleaner showcases how a deep understanding of engineering principles, coupled with relentless iteration and strategic entrepreneurship, can lead to groundbreaking products that redefine industries. For mechanical engineering students, Dyson's story serves as a powerful reminder of the impact that innovative thinking and perseverance can have on solving real-world problems and achieving entrepreneurial success.

Unit summary

This unit focuses on the culmination of student learning through a comprehensive course project. Throughout this unit, students identify market needs, develop innovative solutions, craft a detailed business plan, and formulate a strategic go-to-market strategy. By applying entrepreneurship, innovation, and business strategy principles, students gain practical experience in addressing real-world problems and opportunities. The unit emphasizes critical thinking, creativity, and strategic planning skills essential for success in the entrepreneurial landscape. Through the course project, students demonstrate their ability to conceptualize, plan, and execute a viable business venture from ideation to market launch.

Tutorial questions for practice

Task 1: Brainstorming Session:

Divide students into small groups and conduct a brainstorming session to identify various needs or problems in society or specific industries.

Objective: Encourage students to think creatively and collaboratively to generate potential ideas for their course project.

Task 2: Problem Identification Exercise:

Ask students to individually research and identify a specific need or problem they are passionate about addressing.

Objective: Help students narrow their focus and choose a problem area that aligns with their interests and expertise.

Task 3: Innovative Solution Proposal:

Instruct students to develop innovative solutions to problems identified in the previous task. They should outline their proposed solutions, including the technology, products, or services they plan to implement.

Objective: Encourage students to think critically and creatively to devise original solutions to real-world problems.

Task 4: Business Plan Development:

Guide students through creating a business plan for their proposed solutions. It comprises market analysis, competitive analysis, marketing strategy, operations plan, and financial projections.

Objective: Help students understand the critical elements of a comprehensive business plan and how to communicate their ideas to potential stakeholders effectively.

Task 5: Go-to-Market Strategy Workshop:

Conduct a workshop where students develop go-to-market strategies for their proposed solutions. This should include identifying target markets, positioning strategies, pricing strategies, distribution channels, and promotional tactics.

Objective: Enable students to effectively translate their business plans into actionable strategies for launching their products or services into the market.

Task 6: Peer Review and Feedback Session:

Organize a peer review session where students exchange their project proposals and provide constructive feedback to each other.

The objective is to develop a collaborative learning environment where students can receive valuable insights and suggestions for improving their project ideas.

Task 7: Guest Speaker Session:

Invite guest speakers from entrepreneurship, innovation, or relevant industry experts to share their experience, case studies and real-world insights.

Objective: Provide students real-world perspectives and practical advice to enrich their understanding of the course project topics via a structured written report.

Task 8: Pitch Practice Sessions:

Allocate time for students to practice pitching their project ideas to their peers or instructors.

Objective: Help students refine their presentation skills and gain confidence in articulating their project concepts effectively.

Review questions

1. What are the elements of market analysis for the course project?
2. How can you ensure your proposed solution effectively addresses the identified market needs?
3. Describe the elements of a comprehensive business plan for a course project.
4. What are the essential elements when formulating a go-to-market strategy?
5. How do you conduct market research to validate your business idea for the course project?
6. Explain the importance of innovation in developing a unique value proposition for your course project.
7. Why feasibility analysis needed for business idea evaluation?

8. How do you assess the competitive landscape in your course project planning?
9. Discuss the significance of target market segmentation in tailoring your business plan.
10. How should the communication of the course project be designed to present value to stakeholders efficiently?
11. What are some common challenges entrepreneur's faces when developing a business plan for a course project?
12. Describe the process of identifying potential funding sources for your course project.
13. How do you determine the scalability of your business idea as part of the course project?
14. What are the critical characteristics of a go-to-market strategy document?
15. Why is SWOT analysis essential for course projects?
16. How can you leverage market trends and consumer behaviour insights in shaping your business plan?
17. What should you consider when selecting distribution channels for your course project?
18. Explain the minimum viable product (MVP) and its relevance to your course project.
19. How do you define and measure success criteria for your course project?
20. What role does risk assessment play in mitigating potential challenges in your business plan?
21. Discuss the ethical considerations in developing and executing a business plan for a course project.
22. How do you configure marketing strategy to align with target customers for the course project?
23. Describe the process of conducting a pilot test or prototype for your course project.
24. What strategies can you employ to differentiate your course project from competitors?
25. How do you confirm the financial feasibility of the business plan for the course project?

26. Discuss the significance of continuous iteration and adaptation in refining your business plan.

27. What essential factors should be prioritized when determining pricing strategies for a course project?

28. How do you evaluate your business plan's potential social and environmental impacts?

29. Describe the role of feedback loops in refining and optimizing your course project.

30. What potential exit strategies should you consider for your course project in the long term?

Multiple Choice Questions (MCQs):

1. What is the first step in the Course Project?
   a) Business plan development
   b) Innovative solution brainstorming
   c) Need identification
   d) Go-to-market strategy formulation

   Answer: c) Need identification
2. Which stage of the Course Project involves creating a detailed strategy for entering the market?
   a) Innovative solution
   b) Business plan
   c) Go-to-market strategy
   d) Need identification

   Answer: c) Go-to-market strategy
3. What is the purpose of the Course Project's innovative solution stage?
   a) Identifying market needs
   b) Developing a detailed business plan
   c) Generating new product or service ideas
   d) Evaluating market segmentation techniques

   Answer: c) Generating new product or service ideas
4. Which component is NOT part of the Course Project?
   a) Product development
   b) Business plan
   c) Market segmentation
   d) Financial projections

Answer: c) Market segmentation

5. What is the final stage of the Course Project?
    a) Need identification
    b) Business plan
    c) Go-to-market strategy
    d) Innovative solution

Answer: b) Business plan

Fill in the Blanks:

1. The Course Project begins with the identification of ________ in the market.
   Answer: needs
2. During the innovative solution stage, students brainstorm and develop ________ ideas.
   Answer: innovative
3. The business plan outlines the ________ strategy and financial projections.
   Answer: marketing
4. In the go-to-market strategy stage, students create a detailed plan for ________.
   Answer: entering the market
5. The Course Project involves the development of a comprehensive ________ to guide the venture.
   Answer: business plan

References for Suggested Reading:

1. Schwetje, Gerald, and Sam Vaseghi. *The business plan: how to win your investors' confidence.* Springer Science & Business Media, 2007.
2. Byers, Dorf, and Nelson, Technology Ventures: From Ideas to Enterprise, McGraw Hill, 2010
3. Steve Blank, "The Startup Owner's Manual"
4. T.V. Rao, "Entrepreneurship - A South Asian Perspective"
5. Comes, Stacy, and Lilac Berniker. "Business model innovation." *From strategy to execution: Turning accelerated global change into opportunity.* Berlin, Heidelberg: Springer Berlin Heidelberg, 2008. 65-86.
6. Chelat Bhuvanachandran, Innovision, Khanna Book Publishing, 2022.

Course outcome attainment table

Course outcomes (COs) for this course can be mapped with the programme outcomes (POs) after the completion of the course and a correlation can be made for the attainment of POs to analyse the gap. After proper analysis of the gap in the attainment of POs necessary measures can be taken to overcome the gaps.

Course Outcomes	Expected Mapping with Programme Outcomes *(1- Weak Correlation; 2- Medium correlation; 3- Strong Correlation)*											
	PO -1	PO -2	PO-3	PO -4	PO -5	PO -6	PO- 7	PO -8	PO -9	PO- 10	PO- 11	PO- 12
CO-1												
CO-2												
CO-3												
CO-4												
CO-5												
CO-6												

The data filled in the above table can be used for gap analysis.

Index

Agile and Lean, xxii, 5, 36, 38
Budgeting and Forecasting, 155
business licenses, 228, 235
business model, 145, 174, 184, 186, 187, 188, 189, 190, 191, 219, 220, 237, 240, 249, 251, 252, 287, 293
Business Plan, xviii, xxvii, 254, 276, 277, 281, 311
business proposal, 219, 220, 221, 222, 223
business structure, 231, 232, 233, 234
business vision, 2, 42, 46, 49, 50, 264
Cash Conversion Cycle
  CCC, xiv, 153
Concept & Screening, 43
Copyright, 98, 100
Corporate Social Responsibility
  CSR, xiv, xxvi, 238, 240, 243
Cost Analysis, 88
cost-effective, 29, 71, 72, 73, 76, 78, 89, 152, 273, 275
Course Project Journey, xviii, 258, 260
Customer Feedback, 137, 267
Customer Persona, xxiv, 107, 118, 166
Customer Satisfaction, 90
customer-centric, 8, 16, 23, 36, 122, 187, 196
Design for Assembly
  DFA, xv, 71
design for manufacturability
  DFM, 73
Design Patent, 99
design thinking, vi, 32, 39, 53, 54, 55, 60, 61, 62, 63, 102, 103, 104, 177, 255, 271, 272
digital marketing, 12, 34, 128, 130, 284
distribution channels, 29, 34, 40, 41, 107, 109, 112, 126, 131, 132, 135, 136, 137, 158, 166, 167, 168, 169, 185, 186, 188, 250, 284, 312, 313
economic development, 7
entrepreneurship, **1**
evaluation criteria, 218, 291, 294, 296
external funding, 144, 146, 164, 232
feedback loops, 26, 38, 40, 59, 63, 64, 68, 91, 123, 190, 282, 286, 314
funds, 22
global supply chains, 10
Go-to-Market, xvii, xxi, xxiv, xxvii, 28, 107, 125, 126, 127, 166, 168, 254, 283, 312

Incubator programs, 213, 214, 215, 216, 218
innovative approaches, 10, 176, 182, 187
intellectual property, 41, 42, 54, 96, 97, 99, 100, 101, 102, 103, 105, 139, 146, 185, 188, 197, 211, 215, 229, 236, 263
Intellectual Property, xvi, xvii, xxii, xxiv, 41, 53, 96, 97, 98, 99
iterative design, 27, 36, 38, 39, 64, 68, 271, 272, 273, 274
lawful operations, 235
Leadership Styles, xxii, 43
legal, iii, viii, 90, 96, 97, 98, 99, 101, 115, 137, 139, 141, 148, 151, 155, 172, 173, 177, 197, 199, 205, 206, 208, 225, 226, 227, 228, 229, 230, 231, 233, 234, 235, 236, 237, 240, 243, 247, 249, 250, 270, 275, 279
market Needs, xvii, 26
Market Pull, xxi, 1, 24, 48
Market Research, xxvii, 265
market segmentation, 28, 107, 108, 111, 112, 113, 126, 165, 167, 283, 313, 315
Market surveys, 55
market trends, 8, 21, 56, 79, 82, 114, 115, 116, 117, 136, 149, 166, 201, 207, 237, 261, 262, 266, 267, 277, 285, 286, 291, 307, 308, 313
modern entrepreneurship, 237
Opportunity scanning, 55, 104, 105
patents, 96, 97, 98, 99, 100, 229, 263
problem-solution fit, 38, 39, 40, 255, 262
product innovation, vi, x, 24, 25, 26, 27, 29, 31, 53, 54, 55, 58, 60, 65, 66, 79, 81, 102, 103, 104, 172, 173, 255, 256, 262, 309, 310
product lifecycle management, 35, 183
product quality, 33, 35, 65, 72, 74, 77, 78, 83, 84, 85, 86, 90, 91, 94, 95, 96, 215
proprietorships, 232
prototyping, vi, 5, 32, 37, 38, 39, 49, 51, 59, 65, 66, 67, 68, 82, 83, 102, 103, 104, 106, 190, 263, 272, 273, 274, 309
Quality Assurance Framework, xvii, 93, 94
roadmap, 31, 66, 125, 149, 170, 174, 204, 206, 257, 258, 262, 271, 278, 279, 281, 304
Scaling Strategies, xviii, xxv, 160, 161, 163
SCAMPER technique, 62
Seed Funding, 137, 160
small and medium enterprises, 7
social media, 34, 59, 127, 129, 143, 179, 193, 243, 246, 284, 285
societal challenges, 9, 12
societal development, 15
start-up ecosystem, x, 145, 171, 173, 193, 194, 198, 201, 202, 204, 206, 207, 208, 209, 215, 247, 248
supply chain, 8, 33, 34, 54, 72, 75, 76, 77, 78, 79, 80, 81, 82, 85, 86, 88, 102, 103, 104, 128, 135, 178, 183, 238, 239, 241, 281

surveys, 24, 28, 32, 53, 54, 55, 56, 57, 58, 64, 102, 103, 114, 116, 120, 123, 137, 241, 245, 265, 267, 268, 285
sustainable business models, xvii, 109, 110, 171, 174, 176, 177, 178, 246, 249
Team Composition, xxii, 2, 46, 50
Technology Business Incubators, xv, xxvi, 172, 209, 212
Technology Readiness Levels, xxi, 29, 30, 31, 49, 52
technology-driven entrepreneurship, 8, 12
the New Product Development, 31, 34, 35
Trade Secret, 98
Trademark, 97
Trademarks, xxiv, 96, 97, 99
User-centred Design
UCD, 64
Value Engineering, 86
venture creation, x, 171, 172, 174, 182, 184, 187, 189, 253
Venture Creation, xviii, xxv, xxvi, 171, 182, 246